C0-BVO-829

Reforming
the Regulation of
Electric Utilities

Reforming the Regulation of Electric Utilities

Priorities for the 1980s

[1982]

Richard L. Gordon
The Pennsylvania
State University

LexingtonBooks
D.C. Heath and Company
Lexington, Massachusetts
Toronto

Library of Congress Cataloging in Publication Data

Gordon, Richard L., 1934–
  Reforming the regulation of electric utilities.

  Bibliography: p.
  Includes index.
  1. Electric utilities—Law and legislation—United States. 2. Electric
utilities—Government policy—United States. I. Title.
KF2125.G67   343.73'0929   81–48001
ISBN 0–669–05235–3   347.303929   AACR2

Copyright © 1982 by D.C. Heath and Company

Published simultaneously in Canada

Printed in the United States of America

International Standard Book Number: 0–669–05235–3

Library of Congress Catalog Card Number: 81–48001

To Nancy

Contents

Contents

List of Figures

List of Tables

Preface and Acknowledgments

The idea for this book arose from my continued research on fuel choice in the electric-power sector. Exposure to the subject disclosed widespread feelings of ill ease concerning the state of the electric-power industry. However, the general impression was that the difficulties lay in the regulations directed primarily at controlling power-plant construction. When I began examining the problem more closely, I quickly discovered that something more critical was at work: The long-lived but much criticized system of public-utility regulation was proving unable to adapt to changing electric-utility market conditions. Problems resulted from the industry's inability to respond to basic changes in market conditions because public-utility commissions and other regulators limited the industry's flexibility. It was also apparent that the industry and both academic and consulting-firm specialists in the subject were virtually unanimous in concluding that the regulation was malfunctioning and in need of reform. However, discussions of the subject were generally fragmentary. Moreover, the basic economics of electric power proved not to have been reviewed in any single place. The need for a fuller discussion about reform and the underlying economics inspired my efforts.

As usual, many debts were accumulated in the process of preparing this book. I had the assistance of both my own university—The Pennsylvania State University—and the Massachusetts Institute of Technology. Penn State granted me a sabbatical for the 1980–1981 academic year and, prior to that, Arnulf Muan, associate dean for research of the College of Earth and Mineral Sciences, made funds available for preliminary research. The sabbatical was spent at the Center for Energy Policy Research of the Energy Laboratory at MIT, which provided further support.

Henry D. Jacoby, who directed the center until the fall of 1980, arranged for my visit and was an invaluable continual source of assistance. Loren Cox, who succeeded Jacoby, administered my stay and also was a source of unfailing aid. The staff of the Energy Laboratory continually rendered vital assistance. Peter Heron, the editor, worked with me through numerous revisions of the chapters completed at MIT (all but chapters 5 and 6); Alice Sanderson and Deborah Harrington handled the typing on a word processor. Betty Bolivar and Joan Bubluski, the center's secretaries, provided numerous services, including ably handling my correspondence, mailing numerous drafts of study, and assisting in proofreading the transcript. Information Specialist Shelly Rosenstein kindly responded to my incessant demands to receive new material yesterday.

Many people at MIT assisted me. Particular gratitude goes to those who took the time to comment on the drafts—including M.A. Adelman, Roger Bohn, Ben Golub, Paul Joskow, James Paddock, Richard D. Tabors, Horst Siebert, and Arthur Wright. Others who aided me included Drew J. Bottaro, Alan Cox, Neil Goldman, James Gruhl, Raymond Hartman, Fred C. Schweppe, R.M. Solow, Martin Weitzman, and David O. Wood.

At Penn State, my secretary, Theonas Fleming, handled innumerable tasks associated with the research, ranging from handling the initial correspondence to typing the final parts of the manuscript.

Numerous people outside of the two schools provided aid of various sorts. Leonard Hyman of Merrill Lynch, Pierce, Fenner & Smith and Jerome Delson of the Electric Power Research Institute (EPRI) both provided material and thoughtful comments on portions of the manuscript. Further comment was provided by James Plummer, also of EPRI. Herman Roseman and Lewis Perl of National Economic Research Associates generously made available numerous NERA reports. William Hughes of Charles River Associates discussed the work with me on several occasions, made work his firm had done on related areas available to me, and arranged for me to present an overview at a CRA seminar. (Our prior joint work on the Fuel Use Act was helpful to me in formulating the present chapter 6). Daniel Klein and Robert Spann of ICF made several of that firm's reports available to me. Walter Baer gave me an opportunity to discuss my work at the RAND Corporation and enabled me to meet the people there who were working on related issues. Larry Hudson of New York State's Energy Research and Development Administration arranged with me to visit regulators in Albany.

I was able to visit thirty-four different electric utilities, including twenty-two of the twenty-five largest. Several other companies provided substantial amounts of material, and all were willing to make available basic reports.

My family, as usual, had to endure my preoccupation with the work and to undergo the extra burden of remaining in temporary quarters for nine months. My wife, Nancy, also prepared the figures.

The reader should note that an elaborate bibliography on the subjects treated here appears at the end of the book. All the works cited are listed, as are a number of books and articles consulted as background material. These may not all be of interest to the reader, and some are cited only to show my awareness of them. The references can be located by checking under the authors' names in the bibliography.

As the editing of the manuscript progressed, 1980 data became available, but only the most critical were incorporated. Similarly, interesting additions to the literature have continued to be made as the book moved toward publication, but most of this work has not been cited, because it would only have added more details to support the arguments already made.

**Reforming
the Regulation of
Electric Utilities**

1 Introduction

During the 1970s, the U.S. electric-power industry entered a period of radical transformation. The industry previously had enjoyed a high, fairly steady growth in demand, presenting an image of solidity and stolidity. Yet, by the end of the 1970s, the industry considered itself beleaguered and possibly headed for disaster. Construction plans were being altered radically. Proposals for extensive capacity additions, made in the first half of the decade, were canceled or deferred. The industry had completed a substantial shift to oil use, then the rise in world oil prices motivated efforts to reverse the transformation. There arose serious uncertainties about how regulatory forces would affect nuclear power and coal. More basically, sharp cost increases caused concern about the optimum level of output.

The ensuing debate was marked by emotional statements both from the industry and groups critical of the industry's performance. The industry expressed its concern that financial problems and environmental regulations would imperil the efficient provision of power. The industry claimed that it was being victimized by myopic politicians who were more concerned with avoiding short-run problems than with encouraging efficient long-run development; the industry also feared that it was being made the target of groups that want to restructure society in a way that places less emphasis on industrialization.

The critics counterargued that industry's unimaginative management was mindlessly devoted to growth and inadequately devoted to efficient ways of generating energy through conventional methods, the adoption of new technologies, and conservation.

While neither side behaved faultlessly, their contentions tended to overemphasize human frailty and neglect inherent difficulties that even the wisest of decision makers found difficult to resolve.

If the specific arguments are questionable, the malaise they reflect is not. The growing consensus is that the electric-power industry in the United States is facing severe difficulties. This book attempts to identify the problems, to explain how they arose, to explore their implications, and to provoke efforts at correcting the problems.

The nature of the difficulties is reasonably well understood by those familiar with the problem. Basically, the conditions facing the industry have

1

changed radically, but the institutions that control the industry have not adapted to the new circumstances. First, electric power, like the rest of the economy, was affected by the unexpected acceleration in inflation. Second, numerous new regulations, particularly those related to the environment, tended to raise the cost of producing electricity. Third, the massive rise in world oil prices combined with rising real costs of construction made electricity more expensive in real terms and discouraged growth in consumption.

The impact of these changes was profoundly different for electric-utility companies than for others facing similar problems. Utilities have long been subject to the regulation of rates, profits, and related aspects of their business. They must secure permission from regulators to raise rates—a vital step if the companies are to survive the impact of cost increases. Many industry observers contend that regulators have failed to provide adequate rate relief. They argue that traditional regulatory processes were not designed to insure the automatic adjustment of prices to anticipated inflation and, furthermore, that the needed discretionary regulatory steps were not taken when inflation became rapid. Also, it appears that traditional regulatory practices produce less response to rising real costs and inflation than is economically efficient.

Economists observing the situation have identified a key problem: the companies are concerned mainly with achieving rates high enough to ensure survival, yet, from the point of view of economic efficiency, such rates may be too low. Rates high enough to permit the industry to recover costs may be too low to reduce consumption to an economically efficient level. In more technical language, marginal costs exceed average costs. The extent to which prices are, in fact, below marginal cost is difficult to determine, but it is known that the systems whose average costs are heavily influenced by the availability of low-cost water power (such as those in the Pacific Northwest) are likely to have the greatest problems. Other systems may have been locked into ownership of uneconomic capacity, with too much of that capacity being oil-fired. Such companies could conceivably be facing the problem of earning too little to recover past investment but charging more than is efficient. In fact, as the estimates made in chapter 7 suggest, under-pricing clearly prevails for all but possibly one or two companies in the United States.

The cause and implications of overinvestment need more careful discussion than usually is given. The error is in forecasting, and the key issue is how such mistakes should be treated when an industry's profits are regulated. Regulation has always involved a compromise between holding down profits and maintaining solvency of the regulated companies. The literature on regulation has long emphasized the need not to stress one goal over the other. The *capture theory* of regulation holds that some regulatory agencies become primarily concerned with protecting the industry while others neglect solvency in favor of lower profits. Both views are legitimate because regulators, depending on the time, place, or industry involved, have been guilty of overstressing either the stimulation or the limiting of profits. However, adequate profits cannot be neglected indefinitely if any industry is to survive.

What is not clear is how regulators should handle the issue of investments that retrospectively prove to have been unwise. One basic principle of a private-market economy is that firms should be responsible for their errors. However, the regulators can and probably do greatly influence behavior. Thus, even the most relentless adherent of private responsibility would have problems in sorting company error from regulatory-commission error and then apportioning costs accordingly.

To sort through the various aspects of the issue and to determine feasible solutions requires explaining the critical forces at work, suggesting their consequences, and reviewing possible solutions. The emphasis here is on the public-utility regulation aspect. World-energy issues, the impacts of environmental regulations, and the problem of inflation have been discussed widely elsewhere, so in this book these influences are treated as background. A complete separation is not appropriate. Different types of regulation have become so intertwined that they greatly complicate decision making and regulatory reform. Specifically, the distinction between environmental policy and public-utility regulatory policy breaks down in practice. Environmental reasons can be used as excuses for actions actually taken on the basis of traditional public-utility concerns regarding customer needs. Conversely, the argument that customer needs dictated an action can be used to disguise something that was environmentally based. The problem, in short, is a proliferation of actors, all of whom have imprecise roles. For example, there are separate public-utility and environmental agencies. The environmental agencies may be split into individual areas, such as air, water, land use, and nuclear power. Similarly, regulation can be simultaneously imposed by federal, state, and local governments. A utility's decision may affect several different cities or states, and every concerned agency at every governmental level can become involved. It is popular to propose the creation of superagencies to resolve these crises. Unfortunately, as this book shows, the experience with superagencies has been discouraging.

This book attempts to suggest the magnitude of the difficulties facing the electric power industry—from the cost/investment issue to the number of actors involved—and to stimulate efforts to resolve the problems. However, anyone expecting a neat solution must turn elsewhere. Many commentators are quite definite about what should be done but disagree violently with each other's proposed solutions. Reliance on coal, nuclear power, unconventional power sources such as the sun and the wind, and conservation are all alternatively described as solutions. Facts can be found to support any of these proposals.

The bias of this book is toward accepting uncertainties and adapting to them rather than attempting to determine a complete solution for problems whose true dimensions will not become clear for many years. This outlook produces a discouraging view of the electric-power situation. More adaptivity requires simpler, more flexible institutions. Following the tradition of economic analysis, this principle usually is used to advocate greater reliance on private industry. Economists specializing in the study of regulated industries suggest that too much control is exerted.

However, it may be exceedingly difficult to produce greater freedom for private firms. Current movements to lessen regulation appear to be quite timid. Resistance to reform is considerable. To complicate matters further, there is much strong justification for regulation, particularly in the environmental realm. Thus, there are severe limits to freeing the electric-power industry from regulation.

A principal conclusion of this book is that reforms must be very comprehensive to guarantee an efficient electric-power industry. To enact such reforms, policymakers must be encouraged to delineate and debate measures that range as broadly as possible. A comprehensive program of deregulation should be considered. At a minimum, such a program would include: (1) total removal of public-utility regulation of the electric-power industry, (2) more vigorous and sensible application of antitrust laws, (3) replacing the existing system of air and water pollution rules by pollution taxes, and (4) eliminating the Nuclear Regulatory Commission and removing the Price-Anderson Act's limits on private-utility liability for nuclear accidents. These proposals are not presented for their political attractiveness or even out of a conviction that they are the best possible way to proceed. Rather, they are meant to suggest that radical approaches may be needed to untangle the mass of extant regulatory barriers.

Chapter 2 begins the discussion with an extensive examination of the conceptual issues associated with electric power. The chapter provides an integrated analysis of the economics of the industry and the implications for public policy. The discussion includes further reflections on the problems of policymaking. Attention is given to the empirical implications of the theoretical analysis. The discussion makes explicit what should be known, so the importance of data gaps becomes better understood.

Chapter 3 treats some institutional characteristics of electric-power production and delivery. This discussion analyzes the importance of the geographic location of production and consumption of electricity, the fuels used, the nature of the organizations—private, public, and cooperative—that constitute the industry, and the cooperation that occurs among these organizations.

Chapter 4 outlines the nature of the public-utility regulation process, provides indicators of the impacts of regulation on the health of the industry, and examines some developments of the 1970s and early 1980s. These include the efforts of California and New York to coordinate electric-power planning and the decision of the U.S. Congress, made in 1980, to establish a Pacific Northwest group to plan power development.

The next two chapters provide background on other policies. Chapter 5 deals with environmental regulations, including those affecting nuclear power; chapter 6 discusses the issue of forcing electric utilities to curtail oil and gas use.

Chapter 7 estimates the impacts of prevailing pressures. The chapter discusses the formidable estimation problems involved and attempts to indicate, given the data problems, the impact of prevailing forces on the price of electricity and its availability in the 1980s and beyond. Chapter 8 reviews the range of possible policy reforms and provides a summary and conclusions.

2

The Economics of Electric Power and Its Regulation

This chapter presents analytic material critical to the evaluation of the electric-power industry and its regulation. The objective is to explain the theoretical elements of an economically efficient allocation of industry resources. The discussion has two basic goals: to suggest theoretical arguments that support reform of electric-utility regulation, and to warn of the formidable problems of accurate quantification in electric-power economics. A third goal is to provide a more general discussion of electric-power economics than is found in other literature.

The discussion begins with a description of the key characteristics of the electric-power industry. This presentation is intended to suggest the critical analytic questions that must be answered before guidelines for the industry can be set.

The treatment of the analytic material starts with a review of the economics of capital budgeting, which, it is argued, is the best method for treatment of electric-power issues. The review serves both as the foundation of subsequent analyses and as a reminder of important theoretical problems that complicate quantification of electric-power costs.

The next issue examined is whether the industry truly enjoys economies of scale and, thus, whether the traditional concept of a natural monopoly is really applicable to electric-power companies. Then, the discussion turns to the alleged effects of high capital costs on profits in the absence of natural monopoly.

Issues related to optimal variation of electricity prices also are examined. First, the essence of the *peak-load-pricing argument*—that is, that prices should vary with demand fluctuations—is reviewed. Second, the desirability of cutting off power deliveries when it is not possible to change prices in response to changes in demand is examined. Attention then turns to the wisdom of the 1978 Powerplant and Industrial Fuel Use Act and the extent to which electric utilities should be subject to governmental control.

Appendixes to the chapter deal with the literature on the topics discussed in the chapter, with the role of equity considerations in public policy toward individual firms, and with pricing schemes either to transfer economic rents from producers to consumers or to shift consumer surplus from consumer to producer. Technical appendixes deal with capital-budgeting questions and the optimization of prices and sales.

The Characteristics of Electric-Power Markets

Work and living habits and seasonal conditions greatly affect the level of electricity demand. Lighting occurs mostly at night, air-conditioning use increases with hot weather, and industrial and commercial demand for electricity are highest during those hours when businesses are open. Electricity per se, moreover, cannot be stored cheaply, although postponing some demand and storing the output of some end uses of electricity are possible. For example, hot water can be stored to encourage use during low-demand periods. Some appliances, such as air conditioners, turn themselves on and off to maintain desired temperature level.

Total demand tends to grow over time, and until 1973 the rate of growth was sufficiently steady that simple trend extrapolation provided reasonably accurate forecasts. However, since 1973 large and difficult-to-predict cost increases have slowed demand growth. Forecasting has become much more difficult because it is now necessary to anticipate price changes and estimate how customers will respond to them.

Demand variation can be graphed in two ways. The first way, shown in figure 2-1, simply plots output rates (loads) as a function of time. However, for many purposes, the critical concern is not when but how often a given level of demand prevails. Load-duration curves, illustrated in figure 2-2, have been developed to provide an illustration of how often demand levels occur. In principle, the first point on the load-duration curve is the highest load level shown in figure 2-1. The next point in figure 2-2 is the second highest point in figure 2-1, and so on. Thus, the curve rearrays the loads in order of magnitude instead of occurrence.

Because making operating decisions requires a knowledge of timing, the approach in figure 2-1 is better for operational decision making. However, when undertaking capacity expansion, it is critical to have a clear picture of how long given demand levels will prevail. Figure 2-2 better indicates this. The convention usually is to consider hourly levels (see appendix 3A for a discussion of the units in which load and output are measured).

The industry and its analysts conventionally divide the load-duration curve into three or more portions. The lowest level that demand reaches during the year (represented in figure 2-2 by Q_B) is called the *base load*. The highest level (Q_P in figure 2-2) is called the *peak load*. Between these two levels are intermediate loads. Finer subdivisions are sometimes made. For example, in the ICF work discussed in chapter 7, a daily peak level that occurs 5 to 10 percent of the time is distinguished from a seasonal peak that may last for 15 percent of the year.

Industry activity is conventionally divided into three phases: generation, transmission, and distribution. The first element refers to the production process. Transmission involves long-distance movement at voltages

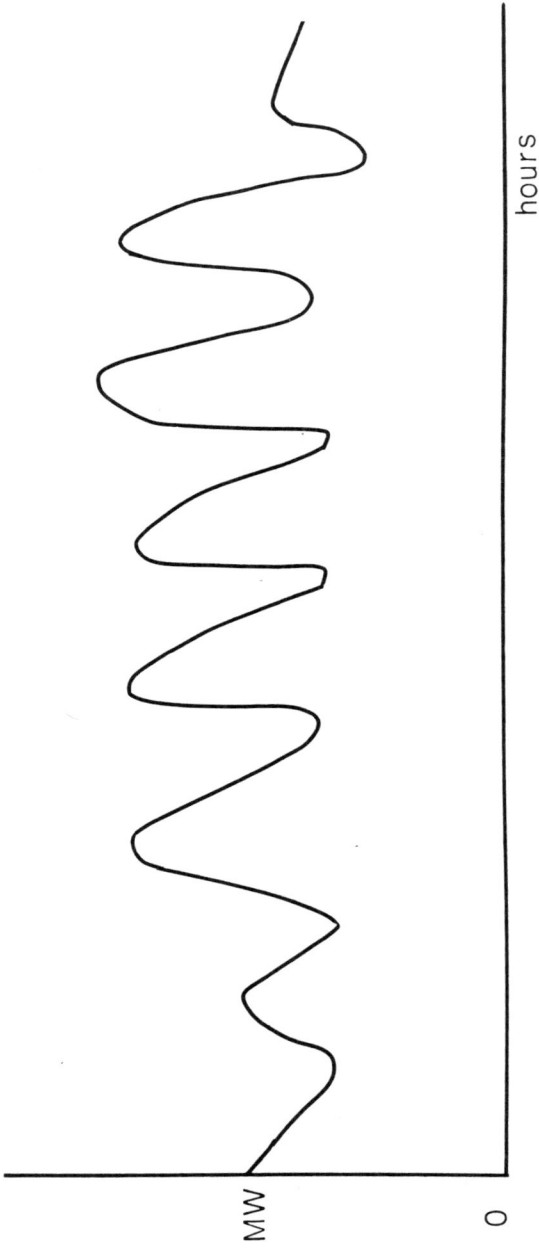

Figure 2–1. Weekly Load Curve (Smoothed)

load
(kW)

Q_p

peak load
generation

intermediate
load generation

Q_b

base load
generation

hours

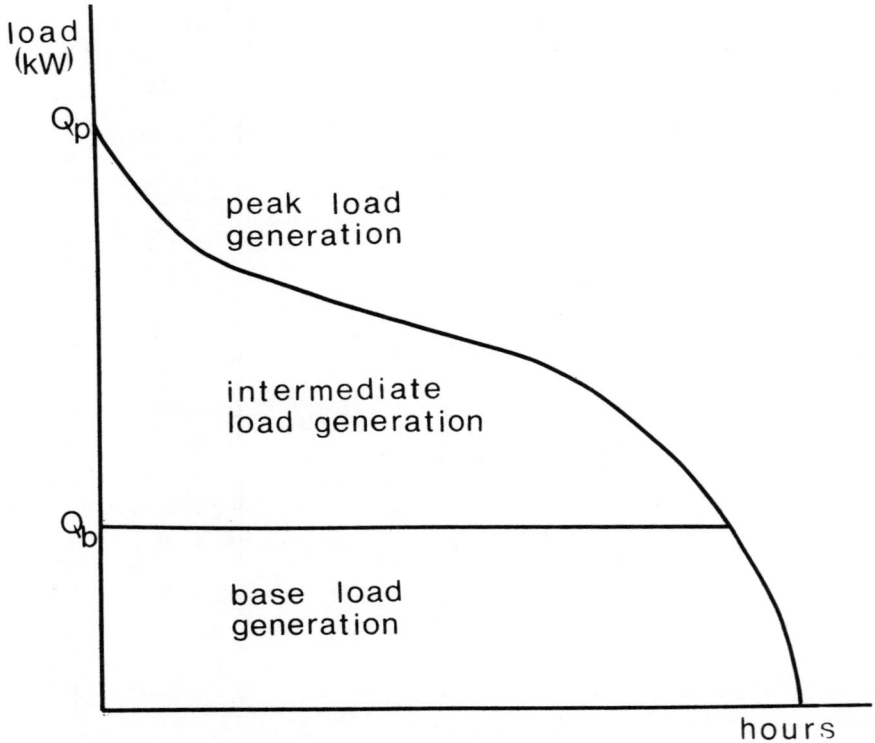

Figure 2-2. Idealized Electric-Utility Load-Duration Curve

higher than most customers use. The distribution network then takes electricity from the transmission network, transforms it into lower-voltage electricity, and delivers it to consumers. Few special analytic problems arise with distribution. The nature of distribution networks is largely determined by the location of customers and whether the lines are underground or aboveground. Underground lines are more expensive, as is a wider geographic separation of customers.

Transmission greatly broadens the generation-supply options available to a firm. There are three basic reasons transmission is used. First, a company may choose to build plants more distant from its markets than existing plants. This would be justified if the reductions in generation costs exceeded or equaled the costs of transmission. Second, choosing a distant location may facilitate a cost-reducing joint venture with other utilities (such as the Keystone and Conemaugh plants in central Pennsylvania, which are jointly owned by Pennsylvania, New Jersey, Maryland, Delaware, and District of

Columbia utilities). Finally, the existence of transmission capabilities permits a utility to seize profitable opportunities to buy power from others.

There are various institutional approaches for effecting optimal exchanges of power. In the Northeast (see chapter 3), centralized power pools arrange for the transfer of power among members. Some of the larger companies approach these pools in size. With or without these pools, direct communication between companies permits transfers of power. Arrangements are made regularly for deliveries over periods of many years.

Various forces can encourage shifting patterns of transmission. The Department of Energy's *National Power Grid Study* explains the distinction the industry makes among economy, diversity, and emergency interchanges.

In a general sense, because they reduce costs, all interchanges promote economy. However, the electric-power industry uses the term *economy* to refer to savings that persist for extended periods. If one company has built capacity that will exceed its customer needs for the next several years, the idea of making a long-term contract with another utility that wishes to buy excess capacity would be attractive to that company. *Economy exchange* is the term used to describe such continuing arrangements. Historically, a major reason for availability of extra energy was the practice of building plants larger than needed to meet the immediate growth of the company. Extra power could be sold while the company grew into the capacity. The massive oil-price rises of the 1970s raised the cost of operating oil-fired plants, and these and other cost increases have slowed electricity growth to the extent that nuclear and coal-fired capacity built in anticipation of faster growth is available to displace oil-fired capacity.

Diversity interchange involves taking advantage of differences in the temporal variation in demands. A northern company that has heavier demands in the winter might exchange with a southern firm that has greater demands in the summer—although this possibility has become less important as the spread of air conditioning has made summer peaking more common nationally. Companies also have differing intraday or intraweek variations due largely to differing customer needs. Companies with numerous users with twenty-four hour operations will have the steadiest loads. Power companies heavily reliant on commercial customers would have much higher loads in the day than at night. Time-zone differences promote intraday variations and dictate east-west or west-east flows.

A variety of unexpected events may lead to altered power flows, and these situations are known as emergency interchanges. The most visible emergencies arise when a surge of demand necessitates out-of-state purchases. Variations in supply are influenced by water-power availability, coal-mine strikes, and nuclear-power-plant shutdowns.

A wide range of choices is available for electricity generation. Power is needed to rotate generators. Every known source of power can be and probably has been used to generate electricity. The main approaches are steam and direct drive. Steam drive usually involves boiling water, then using the steam to rotate the generator. Naturally occurring steam can also be used. Direct drive involves using a basic power source to rotate a generator. This is how water power, internal-combustion engines, and combustion turbines (stationary versions of jet engines) operate.

These technologies have considerably different characteristics. Obviously, those using water or natural steam must be located at the power source. Other technologies can be used near fuel, near markets, or at some intermediate location. The availability of land and some economic method of waste disposal influence the choice of technology.

A power plant requires substantial amounts of land for fuel storage in the case of fossil-fuel-fired operations (especially coal) or as an exclusion zone in the case of nuclear power. (Fossil-fuel-fired plants also require convenient access to facilities for transporting fuels.) Techniques for dispersing waste heat all require access to water. Cooling traditionally involves drawing in water to absorb waste heat, then discharging it back into the water source.

The effects of heating on bodies of water led to requirements that various alternative waste-disposal methods be used. These methods avoid the heating of natural waterways by dispersing steam into the atmosphere, most notably with cooling towers. Another alternative—creating an artificial body of water to disperse heat—involves problems of losses due to leakage and evaporation.

At the very least, power plants will compete with other users for access to land. In addition, environmental dangers may be associated with power plants, and location shifts are one way to lessen environmental impact.

Available fuel-using technologies differ considerably in their basic characteristics, their capital costs, their fuel needs, and other operating costs. The costs of fuels, moreover, can differ considerably at any given time. Among the basic general characteristics of power plants are their reliability and size. Reliability relates to the length of time a plant can operate without breaking down. Performance, moreover, is affected by both the amount of output and its variability. Starting and stopping operations strain the facilities. Thus, given two otherwise equal units, the one subject to more interruptions in operation is more likely to break down sooner.

A basic question about a facility is its ability to shift from one to another power source. At one extreme, there are hydroelectric and nuclear-power plants, which are deliberately designed to use only one power source. (Strictly speaking, alternative nuclear fuels could be employed, but this is not relevant here.) Boilers represent the opposite extreme; ideally a boiler can be designed to burn anything combustible. However, in reality, most boilers are able to burn only a limited variety of fuels. Internal-combustion engines and combustion turbines can burn only oil or gas.

Whatever fuel is used, differences arise in the fuel input required to produce a kilowatt hour (kWh) of electricity. The usual measure used to determine the required fuel input is the heat rate—the number of British thermal units (Btu) needed to produce a kilowatt hour. The number of kilowatt hours that can be produced by one million Btu is a critical factor in calculating the costs per kilowatt hour of electricity, and this number is determined by dividing one million by the heat rate.

Fuel costs are frequently presented as prices per million Btu. The fuel cost per kilowatt hour, then, is the price per million Btu of fuel divided by the number of kilowatt hours producible by one million Btu. Output per million Btu has the further advantage of serving as a measure of productivity. In particular, a rising number of kWh/Btu means that a Btu produces more power.

What is critical here is not the measurement method but the forces that affect the fuel requirements. There are various ways to increase the kWh/Btu ratio. For example, the combined-cycle approach of attaching a conventional boiler to a combustion turbine increases the output per million Btu because the heat that would otherwise be wasted is used in the boiler to produce additional electricity. Techniques, such as operating at higher pressures, can be used to increase the thermal efficiency of boilers. These gains can be secured only by additional investment. The resulting increase in the complexity of facilities may reduce reliability, thus requiring greater maintenance expenses and greater investment in spare capacity.

More generally, capital and nonfuel-operating costs differ substantially depending on plant design (see appendix 7C for additional data). The lowest capital investment costs are associated with combustion turbines; combined cycles are the next cheapest; and boilers are the most expensive, with costs rising as the boiler's ability to burn different fuels increases.

In the absence of pollution-control requirements, the lowest capital costs are associated with gas-fired plants and the next lowest with oil-fired plants. Coal plants are the next most expensive and nuclear-power plants are the most expensive, requiring more capital than coal-fired plants. The difference between oil and gas is smaller than that between coal and oil. The step up from gas to oil requires somewhat larger boiler and storage facilities. Using coal requires an even larger boiler and considerably more elaborate facilities for receiving, storing, and transporting the coal to the boiler and for injecting the coal into the boiler. Commonly, the coal is pulverized into a fine powder by equipment built into the boiler.

Environmental regulations tend to cause modest increases in oil-plant capital costs, mainly for controlling particulates—various solid wastes—in the oil. The imposition of environmental regulations on coal burning causes much greater increases in capital costs. Controlling particulates from coal burning is much more difficult than limiting that from oil burning because coal contains so much more particle matter. In addition, in the United States, considerable stress is placed (see chapter 5) on reducing sulfur-oxide pollution by using stack *gas scrubbers* (devices that remove sulfur oxides after combustion and before discharge to the atmosphere). These requirements can significantly narrow the difference between coal and nuclear-power capital costs.

The U.S. Energy Information Administration's (EIA's) *Annual Report to Congress* for 1980, which was issued in 1981, provides estimates of the capital costs of new coal-fired plants (vol. 3, pp. 273–274). These are set at one thousand dollars per kilowatt (1979 prices) for a plant burning high-sulphur coal using scrubbers. Nuclear costs might be equal to those of the coal plant or as much as 50 percent greater.

Differences in the cost of different fuels to specific utilities arise from many factors. The cost includes transportation charges, which differ with the mode used and the distance traveled. The delivered cost of fuel can be affected in varying degrees by its two components—the price f.o.b. the fuel producer and transportation charges. At one extreme, there are power plants (such as Keystone in Pennsylvania and Four Corners in New Mexico) that are built next to mines, so transportation represents only a small percent of the total cost to the utility. Conversely, Wyoming coal delivered to Texas can cost $27 a ton, of which $18–$20 is for transportation.

Further price variations arise because of different levels of such contaminants as sulfur, ash, and various metals. Cleaned fuels are more expensive. Utilities frequently arrange for long-term contracts for fuel (see Gordon 1974 and 1975); these contracts often use price-adjustment formulas that inadequately insure that charges reflect any changes in market prices that may occur during the life of the contract. On the one hand, natural-gas contracts signed in the 1960s or earlier generally failed to include provisions allowing prices to rise in line with later increases in natural-gas prices. Conversely, coal contracts signed in the middle 1970s may have been designed on the assumption that the price-increasing market forces then prevailing would persist. Thus, prices set under such contracts may have failed to reflect the weakening of prices in the late 1970s.

Finally, the economics of interfuel competition are such that the price per million Btu of different fuels in a given market may differ from each other greatly. Even if prices reflected those economic forces that made it attractive for suppliers of different fuels to compete for electric-power demands in that area, the prices would have to differ to compensate for the differences in other costs. Coal to be competitive in any location must be cheaper than oil. Moreover, it may not be economically attractive for the suppliers of one fuel to compete with suppliers of another fuel in electric-utility markets. Oil may cost much more than coal. Coal producers, however, normally cannot take advantage of the abdication of the market to raise coal prices to levels that would be barely competitive with such high oil prices. Competition among coal producers usually insures that actual coal prices are much lower.

In the 1960s, in some markets, oil sold for much less than was barely necessary to undersell coal. Specifically, the price of fuel oil delivered on the U.S. east coast dropped to levels below the price of coal in the same region because of growing competition within the oil industry. A fuel that could have earned premium did not do so. However, the price was not low enough to undercut the advantage of inland coal producers. Inland oil had to be transferred by expensive alternative shipping methods, and buyers closer to coal fields paid less for coal transportation than did customers on the coast. Thus, for coastal buyers, both fuel and capital costs were lower for oil than for coal. Inland oil buyers, however, had higher fuel and lower capital costs. The subsequent rises in world oil prices have made oil-fuel costs far higher than coal-fuel costs everywhere in the United States and perhaps the world. Nuclear-fuel costs are below coal-fuel costs.

Gas economics are more complex. Near the wellhead, the tendency is for prices per million Btu to be well below oil prices, because it pays to compete with oil in more distant markets and gas is more expensive to transport than oil. Whether this produces costs below those of coal differs over time (see Gordon 1979a and 1981 for more complete discussions of why these patterns emerge).

Some examples of these relationships (as of 1981) can be found in U.S. government reports on the prices of fossil fuels delivered to major electric-power plants. In June 1981, Gulf States Utilities had plants supplied with natural gas under the terms of very old contracts, which set delivered prices at about $0.25/million Btu. The plants had heat rates of approximately 10,500 Btu, so one million Btu produced about 95 kWh. Thus, fuel costs were about $0.0023 per kWh. The most thermally efficient coal plants have heat rates of approximately 9,000 Btu, thereby producing 111 kWh per million Btu. The June 1981 price for bituminous coal delivered to a coal plant east of the Mississippi River ranged from $1.00 to $2.00 with the majority of prices grouping around the middle range. With a Btu heat rate of 9,000 and a $1.50 price the cost was approximately $0.0135 per kWh. Oil prices differ considerably according to sulfur levels; in 1981 most prices fell in the $3.50–$6.50/million Btu range. At a $6 price and a high heat rate of about 11,000 Btu, the oil-fuel cost was $0.066 per kWh (see U.S. Department of Energy, *Cost and Quality of Fuels for Electric Utility Plants*).

Pollution control involves special outlays, for example, the expense of the limestone used to trap sulfur oxides from flue gases. Another cost is the power used to run pollution-control equipment; this appears in the data as an increase in the heat rate for net output.

A satisfactory model of electric-utility economics must deal with optimizing the prices charged; the quantities provided; the facilities installed to generate, transport, and distribute; and the use of these facilities at each moment.

The optimization process is complicated by the high cost of effecting price changes and the problems associated with limiting consumption. The familiar approach was to place a meter on the user's premises to record electricity use. This meter was read periodically, usually monthly or bimonthly. Most meters were able to record only the total use of electricity; they could not determine when the use occurred. Price rigidity was increased when institutional forces prevented establishment of different rates for different meter-reading periods.

Only limited possibilities existed to curtail deliveries selectively, mainly in the form of cut-off switches on water heaters and agreements by large industry customers to endure load interruption. When system capacity was strained, only a few actions (such as reducing voltage and selectively blocking out part of the service area) could be taken to limit the possibility of total system breakdown.

Important economic and technological developments promise to change this pattern radically. The costs of failing to raise prices with demand surges or to have a substantial ability to curtail consumption have increased. Simultaneously, the technology to facilitate price variation and supply curtailment has been greatly improved. Thus, it has become more attractive to install meters that record time of use, to vary prices on a preannounced schedule, and to cut off supplies. Various analysts, such as the Homeostatic Control Study Group at MIT, believe that emerging technologies may permit even more radical changes in the price and supply arrangements established with customers, particularly larger users.

The MIT group suggests exploring three practices: spot pricing (comparable to the pricing process of a stock market), microshedding, and dynamic control. Assuming that these options are efficient for some customers to adopt, any optimization process must incorporate such methods.

All options are extensions of existing practices, but the first is the most radical. Spot pricing would involve introducing, for customers who find it attractive, an option for regularly reallocating supplies. Spot pricing would include large customers in the pricing process that power pools use to govern energy exchanges among electric companies. Prices could be set as often as every five minutes, a timing based on the prevailing frequency of adjustment among utilities.

Microshredding is based on the interruptible-supply concept. Customers could be offered options regarding how much load could be interrupted and the duration of both individual cutoffs and the total cumulative cutoff. Patterns could then emerge in which firms had some portion of assured supply, with the rest subject to various amounts of interruption. The buyers would be compensated with a lower price for a higher willingness to be interrupted.

Similarly, dynamic control would involve using techniques that interrupt power flows to selected users or selected appliances in the user's facility in order to reduce the strain on load.

Investment Analysis and Electricity-Utility Economics

Substantial investments occur in the electric-power sector, and, therefore, this analysis must treat investment problems. As Irving Fisher (1930) established, the long-run versus short-run distinction in price theory is an analytic shortcut for dealing with investment analysis. The concept of fixed costs deals only implicitly with the problem of recovering adequate rate-of-return investments (see Gordon 1981).

In Fisher's analysis, investments are outlays that later produce one or more inflows. Investment analysis is concerned with the adequacy of the inflows relative to the outlays. Numerous texts discuss how the financial concept of present value is used to appraise investments. Thus, the standard compound-interest formula indicates that an initial outlay invested for t years at r percent interest yields the future amount, $A_t = I_0(1 + r)^t$. Multiplying both sides of the equation by $(1 + r)^{-t}$ gives $A_t(1 + r)^{-t} = I_0$. I_0 is what must be invested now to yield A_t in the future. This is the present value of A_t.

The present value of inflows is a measure of how much profitably can be invested in securing these inflows. The worth calculation determines whether any arbitrary investment of a given quality is better than the most obvious alternative—placing the money in the capital market and earning the prevailing rate of interest for ventures of equal riskiness. The analysis involves comparing lending to using income within the firm. As long as the marginal payoff of using the funds internally is greater than investment in the capital market, such internal investment should continue. This excess payoff is known as *net present value.*

In its entirety, Fisher's analysis shows how opportunities to invest money in different firms, the desire of some consumers to borrow to finance consumption, and the desires of others to lend interact to determine the market rate of interest. J.R. Hicks (1946) takes this a step further by stressing that investment is a shorthand for all the possible substitutions of current inputs or outputs for future inputs or outputs.

Both Hicks and Fisher emphasize that the relevant conditions are marginal. The marginal present worths of the costs and benefits should be equated. Efficiency requires that, for whatever input considered, the marginal cost of expanding output should be equal to the marginal cost of ex-

panding output by using any other input. Hicks's formulation of investment theory further indicates that here, too, an equality prevails. The key
equality is that the discounted marginal cost of any action taken to increase
output at any moment must equal the discounted marginal benefit of any
other action or response. Such trade-offs influence every investment decision the electric-power industry must make, whether deciding which power
sources should be used and to what extent, or choosing the operating heat
rate for the plants.

As explained more fully later, conventional cost-curve analysis conceals
the Fisher-Hicks explanation of investment and can be misleading unless the
analysis is conducted carefully. The Fisher-Hicks rules say that any flow
of future incomes that provides a sufficient present value will justify the
investment. Many different patterns of repayment cumulatively could provide sufficient income. There could be a stable flow, a steadily rising flow,
a steadily falling flow, or some more erratic pattern. As long as the total
income is high enough, the investment could still be justified.

A falling flow of income is less profitable than a constant flow of equal
duration, providing the beginning amounts were the same. Therefore, if
that constant flow were barely enough to justify the investment, the cumulatively lower income from a falling flow starting at the same level would
be insufficient. However, if the flow fell from a high enough initial level,
the total income could be raised enough to justify the investment. By analogous reasoning, if annual incomes rise over time the minimum initial level
of repayment sufficient to justify investment is less than the equivalent
required constant income level. Finally, fluctuations around any trend must
cancel out in present-value terms to permit repayment (see appendix 2C
for a mathematical analysis of these cases). The defect of the cost-curve
approach to the theory of the firm is that it provides no way to deal precisely with anything but stable repayment processes.

Explicit consideration of income variation is critical in electric-utility
economics since the flows of income from a plant may be uneven from year
to year and, as noted earlier, certainly within the year. Technical problems
in perfecting the plant and decisions to build in anticipation of demand can
produce rising operating rates in the first few years a power plant operates.
Building in anticipation alternatively primarily may reduce the operating
rates of older, more expensive to run plants. The available capacity in either
new plants or older ones in one system may economically serve another
company. Conversely, numerous factors, especially physical deterioration
in older facilities and technological improvement in newer plants, tend to
make aging facilities less attractive to operate. Thus, there is a tendency
toward declining operations as power plants age.

In conducting any type of economic analysis, it is essential to adjust for
inflation. Economic analysis stresses that no real gain accrues to price and

income increases attributable to inflation. If money incomes and assets double while prices double, people are no better off. Thus, an appropriate analysis must distinguish real changes from the impacts of the changing purchasing power of money.

Discussions of electric power often ignore this proposition. For example, misstatements of the implications of inflation on nuclear power are made frequently. Critics of nuclear power claim that it is less desirable because nominal costs are more severely inflated than those of fossil-fuel plants because construction lasts so much longer and is so much more expensive in real terms. Thus, more investment is subjected to the effects of inflation over a longer period of time. Nuclear advocates reverse the argument, contending that acceleration of nuclear projects is desirable to lessen the impacts of inflation. At best, a half truth exists. The rise in nominal cost by definition is offset by the devaluation of money. The only problem is if regulation hinders adjustment to inflation. One way to lessen the impact of such imperfect regulation is to adopt options less subject to inflation.

Numerous problems arise in making the separation of inflationary effects precise. It is essential that a satisfactory index of purchasing power be used to measure the overall changes affecting all the useful goods. The index should include not only direct consumer purchases but also government services and all *investment expenditures,* which are expenditures that facilitate future output. The measure should indicate the total social impact. Thus, the implicit deflator for the gross national product (GNP) is, in principle, the best price index to use since it is the Department of Commerce's estimate of the rate of price change for total social output. The deflator has been criticized for defects in the way it measures some of its components. For example, government services have no observable market price and so are valued at cost. This approach fails to adjust for improvements in the quality of the service and thus overstates the price.

No matter how good the index, inflation occurs simultaneously with adjustments in real prices. As these real prices change, consumers adjust by shifting patterns of consumption—usually increasing use of goods with falling real prices and decreasing consumption of those with rising real prices. It is well-established that there is no measure of the effects of inflation that can accurately account for these responses to real price changes (see, for example, Samuelson 1947, ch. 6).

A particularly vexing question is the extent to which inflation has real effects. Institutional arrangements can be established to insure that inflation·has no real effects. What is required is that all long-term arrangements, such as loans, long-term contracts, and tax structures, include provisions that assure that neither side gains from inflation. Thus, interest payments would rise to cover inflation, and tax rates would be adjusted to prevent taxation of inflation-based rises in money income. Where inflation is anticipated adequately, specific adjustments can be negotiated in advance; where the possibility of inflation is recognized, contracts can provide that adjustments are made for compensation. Society is far from having completely implemented procedures for making such adjustments; however, only rigid preexisting contracts, laws, regulations, and similar legal barriers to adjustment preclude response to inflation. Thus, the analytic problem is to determine what barriers exist and what their impacts might be. This task is central to any analysis of economic behavior in inflationary periods. As discussed in appendix 2C, it makes no difference whether calculations are in constant or inflated dollar terms, so long as they are done correctly. What does matter is identifying the real impacts of inflation. Unanticipated inflation long has been described as a device to transfer money from creditors to debtors by reducing the real value of the monies repaid. However, the essence of adjustment mechanisms is to prevent such transfers by compensating creditors for inflation. A prime concern about the electric-power industry is that regulation acts as a barrier to inflation adjustment. Tax laws aggravate the problem.

Economics of Scale, Capacity Limitation, and Natural Monopoly in the Electric-Power Industry

The concern over regulation of electric power has inspired considerable discussion about whether the traditional natural monopoly argument for regulation justifies continued control. The most frequently encountered proposition begins with the observation that the generation portion of the industry is served by numerous individual units. It is suggested that each unit could be owned and operated by an independent firm, thus creating a competitive generating industry that could be allowed to operate without regulation. It would still be necessary to control transmission and distribution. A variant approach would also deregulate transmission, and control only distribution.

This argument is not wholly satisfactory. Many of the rationales for deregulation of generation clearly apply to transmission and also may be applicable to distribution so total deregulation might be defensible. Moreover, the existence of important economies of centralized management of numerous generating plants and vertically integrating generation with transmission and distribution may imply that segmenting the industry is undesirable. Therefore, it might be unwise to adopt the strategy of making each power plant an independent unregulated company because the benefits of integration would be lost. This might mean that deregulation is not desirable or that total deregulation would be preferable to decontrolling only generation. The importance of resolving this issue is critical because partial deregulation may be more difficult to implement than full deregulation (see chapter 4). If distribution remained regulated, the regulators might impose restrictions on what can be paid for generation and transmission services; this could have the same effect as explicit regulation.

This section examines the nature of facility and system economies and diseconomies of scale for generation, transmission, and distribution. Also, two familiar propositions in the literature on natural monopoly are challenged. It is shown that even if it is most efficient to have one firm conduct a specific activity in any one area, this does not necessarily imply that large monopoly profits will arise in the absence of government controls. It is further demonstrated that the single firm still might be able to break even without setting prices in excess of marginal cost. The argument that short-run marginal costs will persistently lie below long-run average costs long has been refuted in economic theory. A further result of the analysis is that regulation leads to underpricing of electricity.

In the electric-power industry, the critical questions relate to the limits to optimal size. It is recognized widely that up to a point substantial savings accrue with larger sized plants and that efficient sizing involves facilities far larger than other fuel users could build profitably. Moreover, the economies of large size mostly come from conventional sources. A substantial and growing fixed cost is associated with the design, attainment of permits, and construction of large facilities, and some parts of the unit (such as the control room) may have costs largely independent of size.

Components of the plant tend to have characteristics known to produce economies of scale: namely, costs dependent on the surface area of the facility and capacity dependent on volume. For example, the basic structure of a boiler is a rectangular solid. Costs are proportional to the surface area of that rectangular solid, but capacity is a function of volume. A given percent increase in surface area will produce a proportional increase in volume greater than that of area. Thus, total capacity rises faster than total cost, and average cost falls. (If doubling the area produced a tripling of capacity, and costs varied exactly with area, a $100 total cost at ten unit output becomes a $200 cost at thirty unit output. Average costs fall from $10 to $6.67).

The ability to increase facility size is subject to several limits. First, there are various technological strains produced by larger sizes. A variety of construction problems can arise, and reliability may decrease. Second, the facilities require land with special characteristics, and this may restrict the size of a facility at any one location. Third, there are limits on the size of the plant that can be accommodated by the system.

The construction problem is simply that at any given time, there are barriers to the size of the components that manufacturers can produce and that transportation networks can deliver. Serious difficulties may be involved in developing the technologies to permit construction of larger plants. However, there are fears that reliability decreases when size is increased sharply.

Companies disagree about the magnitude of the reliability problem. Several major companies (for example, the Tennessee Valley Authority (TVA), American Electric Power (AEP), Duke Power, and Commonwealth Edison) pushed fossil-fueled unit sizes above 1000 megawatts (Mw) for units put in service in the early 1970s. AEP has continued to build coal-burning units of 1300 Mw, but the others have shifted to nuclear units of comparable size. Commonwealth's tentative plans for new fossil plants call for 550 Mw (albeit for more irregular use than the larger units, with the concomitant strains such operations place on the unit). Other utilities building fossil-fired plants for regular operation have chosen not to scale up to the 1300 Mw level, partly due to the uncertainty about reliability.

There are two different types of construction economies of scale at the plant level. First are those usually stressed involving benefits and costs relating to an individual unit—the steam system and the generator set. Second, benefits and costs accrue to locating several units at one site.

Another critical consideration is the need for land for power plants, transmission lines, and distribution facilities. It is a classic proposition of economists, intimately associated with the early nineteenth-century work of David Ricardo, that land acquisition is an increasing-cost industry. The influence of land requirements similarly may make electric power an increasing-cost activity. This is most clearly true for generation and transmission.

Given that there are limits to the optimal size of a facility and that the industry requires a large number of optimally sized facilities, even if the construction and operating costs of each facility were the same, rising land costs would lead to an overall rise in costs with output. Also, the cost of producing at a given location will depend on such factors as land cost, environmental restrictions, the cost of construction, the delivery cost of fuel, and the cost of transmission to customers. Changes in any of these costs could increase the cost of expanding capacity at a given site.

Cost increases are likely. Efforts to expand would place upward pressure on land values. Environmental pollution control costs might rise faster than output, particularly if the expansion caused the firm to pass over a regulatory threshhold (for example, rules that require controls only when pollution exceeds some level). Output expansion might exert upward pressures on fuel costs. If the rise is sufficiently large, it may be preferable to locate new units at a new site. It is conceivable but unlikely that a firm could have an unlimited number of fresh locations at which costs were identical, given sufficient limitation of the number of units at each location. It is more probable that costs would rise because the differences among sites will not cancel out.

Even if it were economically feasible to concentrate plant expansion in large energy parks, this might reduce rather than offset the pressures increasing costs. Expansion may still produce pressures on land values, environmental controls, and fuel supply. The advantage of the parks would be that the increase would be less than if expansion were more dispersed.

The idea of energy parks met with considerable opposition when they were proposed for central Pennsylvania. It was apparently feared that the cost increase might be greater than with dispersed sites. Concentrating the pressures on land, the environment, and fuel supplies, might magnify them. Additionally, the site would probably serve several different markets and involve more transmission than if scattered sites were located closer to the particular market. Another problem is that transmission also uses land and thus is subject to similar pressures.

Congestion, rather than rising land costs, is probably the major pressure on distribution costs. As more and more electric lines are crowded into a given area, costs may rise because construction and maintenance become more difficult.

Another set of size limitations arises from the need to maintain system reliability. Generation units and transmission lines can and do fail unexpectedly, and the system should be designed to limit the effects of such failures. Efforts are made to insure that most of the time enough spare capacity is available so output can be maintained even if a large generating unit or transmission line goes out of service. Reliability is secured by both increasing interactions among companies to develop a larger system and limiting the size of facilities. It is undesirable to build either power plants or power lines so large that their loss will interrupt supply. One virtue of having large systems is that the extra capacity to replace a facility of any given absolute size is a smaller percentage of total capacity. One thousand Mw of reserves is 100 percent of the peak output of a 1000 Mw system but only 1 percent of a 100,000 Mw system. Moreover, larger systems can take advantage of the law of large numbers to reduce reserve requirements. However, any system will have multiple transmission lines as well as multiple plants because of the limits to optimal size.

These reliability arguments simultaneously reinforce the argument that there are limits to plant-level economies and demonstrate the existence of system-level economies. The critical policy question about the latter is whether large integrated firms are needed or whether cooperative arrangements for interchange are sufficient to provide the economies.

A further question about electric power and other industries is whether economies of scale exists in multiplant management as well as in the individual plant. The planning, design, and construction of facilities clearly requires considerable skill that can be better supplied by an experienced organization. What is less clear is the optimal way to integrate these activities into utility operations. In principle, each activity could be conducted by outside firms, an individual utility, or by consortiums of companies. The intraindustry cooperation discussed in chapter 3 involves coordination of planning and joint financing ventures. Larger companies maintain design engineering departments, but smaller companies hire outsiders. At least one major company, Duke Power, has its own construction department.

Even if it were optimal to have only one electric utility for each region, it is not necessarily true that monopoly power will exist and justify regulation. Significant monopoly power can arise only when there are no close substitutes for the local utility's services. To the extent that customers have options to change locations, self-generate, or easily shift to alternative energy sources, monopoly power might be small. To what extent this is valid is an important empirical question that cannot be resolved here.

There are possibilities for using energy sources other than a specific utility. The issue is how great these possibilities are for different customers; the degree of flexibility varies among customers depending upon their ability to relocate, use other fuels, or engage in selfgeneration. Several situations prevail. At one extreme, substitution possibilities might be so great that no regulation is needed. This would not require the perfect ability to substitute. Regulation is an expensive process, and deregulation would be justified if there were competition sufficient that the monopoly gains were less than the cost of regulation. In this case, regulation would cost more than its benefits (eliminating monopoly profits) and be uneconomic. Of course, the traditional fears might prove correct.

A second concern is over the ability of electric utilities to earn income sufficient to justify investments without exercising monopolistic power or the assistance to regulated prices. Reiteration of a standard argument adequately disposes of the issue in the electric-power case (that is, the problem is not one in which it is essential to use explicitly the Fisher-Hicks approach).

Break-even means that total revenues equal total costs, or that unit revenues (that is, prices) P, equal average costs, AC. Economic theory shows that efficiency prevails when marginal costs, MC, equal prices. Price is a measure of what people will pay for consumption, and cost is a measure of the value of the resources sacrificed to permit production. The marginal principle is that each change in output should be evaluated in terms of its contribution to social welfare. A change should be made only if welfare is increased; this occurs when the value to society, the price, is at least as great as the marginal cost to society. Society loses when marginal costs exceed the benefits produced. The insure efficieny and break-even, marginal costs must equal or exceed average costs ($P = MC \geq AC$).

Marginal costs can exceed average costs only if average costs are rising. This is explained in every basic economics text and is rigorously proved by noting that total costs are by definition average costs times output, Q, and marginal costs are the derivative of total costs, TC. Thus, $TC = ACQ$; $MC = dTC/dQ = AC + Q\, dAC/dQ = 0$. This last term must be zero or positive to insure that $MC = AC$. The basic principle is that averages rise only when additions are above the average. For example, a student going into finals with a C average may need a high A to raise his average to a B.

The usual explanation of why a firm is a natural monopoly is that it is subject to falling average costs over so large an output range that it is much cheaper for it to operate without competition. This will remain true even if the firm is actually operating in the range of increasing average costs, so long as the excess of actual output Q over that output at which average costs are minimized is sufficiently small. The surrender of that additional output to a second firm would be uneconomic if the second firm had to operate at a low scale and at the high costs such low scale implies.

For example, consider an industry in which increasing average costs of any firm began when output reached 1 million units and that marginal costs were equal to price at an output of 1.1 million units. Thus, one firm could operate at an output of 1.1 million units and would have increasing average costs. However, if the output were split between two firms producing 550,000 units each, each would be operating in the range of decreasing average costs.

Thus, so long as a firm reaches the range of increasing average costs, prices equal to marginal costs will permit recovery of average costs. As noted, there are reasons to believe that all sectors of the electric-power industry are operating in the range of increasing average costs and thus can break even when equating marginal cost to price.

Another issue is the relationship between long- and short-run marginal costs. This relationship was explained by Jacob Viner (1931), who indicated that long- and short-run marginal costs in equilibrium both would be equal to each other and, with increasing costs, would be equal to or in excess of the amount needed to recover all costs. The Viner analysis indicates why many concerns about the distinction between long- and short-run marginal costs are excessive. A well-defined relationship between long- and short-run costs will emerge, as will a relationship among the costs of every possible way to alter costs. The Hicks analysis, moreover, implies that Viner's analysis is fully applicable to a Fisher-Hicks approach to economic analysis.

The argument can be expressed in Fisher-Hicks terms by noting that as a result of any arbitrary past investment program, an industry will have accumulated a specific stock of facilities with different operating costs. These existing facilities then determine the short-run marginal-cost schedule. The available supply will be determined by those investments that have been undertaken. Clearly, the greater the past investment, the greater the supply.

Efficient operation of the plant then involves equating marginal costs

dollars

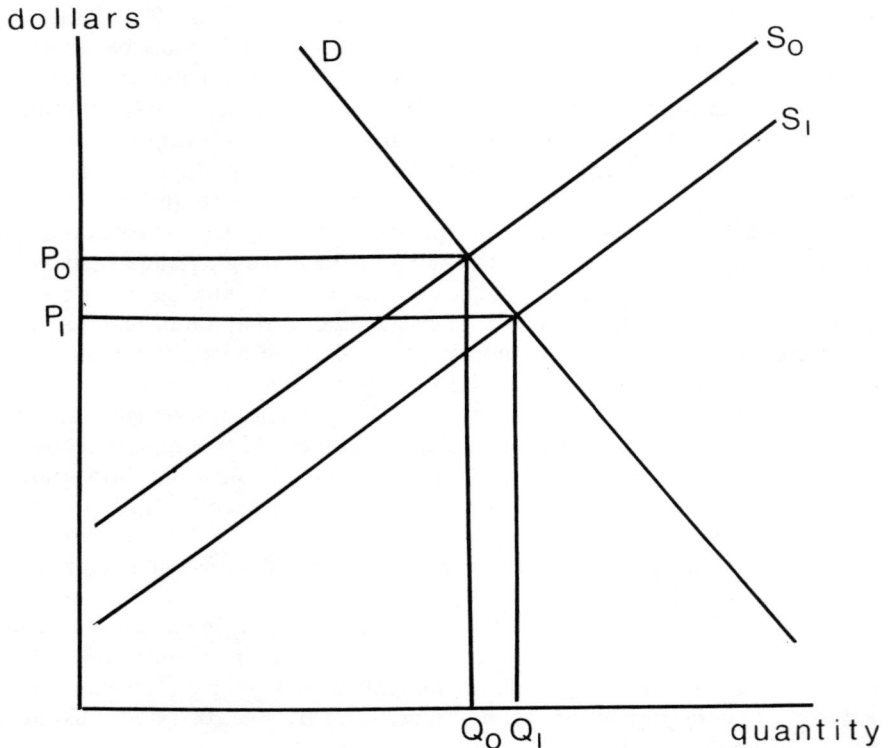

Figure 2–3. Alternative Short-Run Industry Equilibriums

to price at every moment in time. The optimal price for any given demand level will be higher if supply is lower. Thus, in figure 2–3, demand is set at D and there are two supply schedules, S_1 and S_0, with the former being greater than the latter. The respective outputs at which $MC = P$ are greater with S_1 than with S_0, and the price with S_1 is P_1, which is lower than P_0, the price with S_0. Thus, lower supplies involve higher prices and in the increasing cost cases show greater excesses of prices over operating costs (since the formula presented above indicate prices will exceed average costs). In the short run, this will apply to marginal and average operating costs.

To insure recovery of capital costs, investment must be limited to levels that allow the firm to operate on a short-run marginal-cost curve low enough for high prices to occur. *Sufficiency* is defined as insuring that no facility is added unless the additional revenue generated by additional investments is high enough to repay the present value of building and operating the plant. Therefore, increasing average costs imply that some contri-

dollars

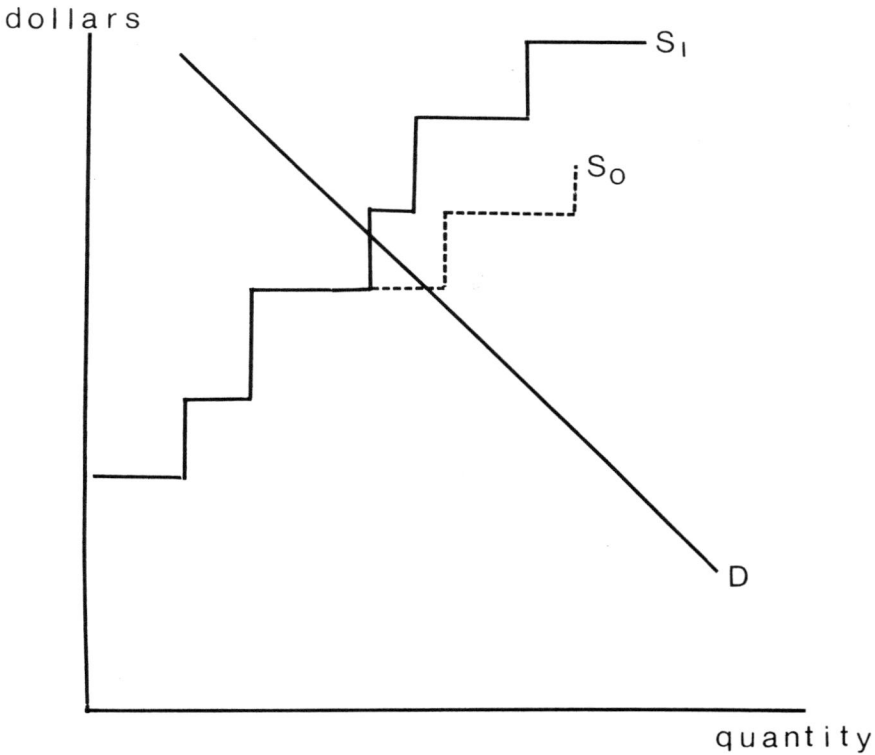

S_1 = efficient
S_0 = inefficient
Figure 2-4. Profitable versus Excess Supply: The Step-Function Case

bution is made to the recovery of initial investment and the interest on it; limiting investment to insure high enough prices will raise the cumulative contributions to a sufficiently profitable level.

Much of the fear of inadequate income expressed by electric-utility specialists arises from failure to recognize that system operating or running costs (the cash costs of the most expensive unit used) may not always be the correct measure of marginal costs. Assume that the industry uses several technologies with different operating costs, but every unit of output produced by each technology has the same operating costs. This produces a step-function-supply curve, such as that shown in figure 2-4. Costs jump as one switches to the next most expensive technology.

The supply/price relationship is as follows: So long as excess capacity for a given supply type is available, prices will equal the operating costs of that type. If demand is heavy enough to absorb all the capacity of one type but not sufficient to raise prices enough to induce use of the next most expensive technology, prices will lie between the costs of the two technologies. A price high enough above running cost must be charged to equate the quantity demanded to the quantity supplied. In particular, the price should equal that at which the quantity demanded equals the output possible without resort to higher-cost facilities. The horizontal portions of the supply curve relate to the range of output at which a given capacity type is not fully utilized; the vertical portions indicate the situation when that capacity is strained, but the next most expensive type is not competitive.

Those concerned with profit adequacy fear that even at peak periods, the demand curve will intersect the supply curve at a point on the horizontal portion of the supply curve. In this case, the price will cover only the operating expenses of the highest-cost technology in use. Thus, the capital costs of that technology cannot be recovered from operating that plant.

However, there is not an inherent inability to earn profits but only the problem that excessive investment has been undertaken in the case just described. With lesser investment, the horizontal portion of the last step will terminate at a lower output, and the demand curve will intersect the supply curve on one of its vertical portions at a price sufficiently above operating costs to help repay the investment (see figure 2-4). Thus in figure 2-4, efficient supply is S_1 rather than S_0. (Note that this argument holds for all possible patterns of repayment since no restriction was imposed on the size of each contribution.) Therefore, as long as I am correct that electric power is an increasing-cost industry, it is possible to secure adequate returns on investment when prices are equal to marginal costs. (Even if decreasing costs prevail, questions still can be raised about whether regulation is needed to resolve the problem; see appendix 2B.)

The traditional view that the electric-power industry possesses significant monopoly power and the new view that the optimal policy is to regulate only generation are not the only possible outlooks. The argument used for generation may also apply to transmission. Given sufficient competitive pressures from intercompany and interfuel competition, the monopoly power of distribution companies would be too small to be worth regulating or further controlling by antitrust policy.

A further critical consideration is that to the extent that economies exist to having a single company be vertically integrated and own numerous plants, the attractiveness of separating individual plants or otherwise divorcing generation from transmission and distribution will lessen. Many different regulatory strategies might be preferable to those already proposed, and an effort should be made to determine which is the best.

A final consideration is that the analysis just presented also implies that regulation that limits revenues to equality with costs will produce inefficiently low prices. As noted, efficient prices should equal marginal costs, and marginal costs of a single-product firm should exceed average costs. Therefore, prices should also exceed average costs and yield total revenues in excess of total costs. Generally, revenues of a multiproduct firm should exceed costs.

The Application of the Theory to Optimal Production, Pricing, and Investment

To complete the analysis of electric-power economics, examples are provided of how an electric utility will produce, price, and invest to attain long-run efficiency. A major complication relates to the costs of effecting either price changes or cutoffs of deliveries. The obvious conclusion is that such costs imply less price flexibility and curtailments than would occur if price changes and quantity curtailment were costless. The equally obvious conclusion that inflexibility is a cost tends to be neglected.

The essence of short-term operation already has been outlined. At any moment, a short-run marginal-cost curve such as that in figures 2–3 or 2–4 will exist, regardless of the shape of the long-run cost functions. In the short run, units will differ markedly in operating costs, which will produce cost curves of the type postulated. The curves reflect the obvious proposition that cheaper-to-operate units will be used first. This ranking by costs is termed the *merit order* by the electric-power industry.

The prior arguments about demand fluctuations and variations in unit availability indicate that both supply and demand curves will fluctuate markedly over the year. The fluctuations have expected implications. The higher the demand and the lower the supply, the higher the price will be. At any moment, there will be a marginal unit, and prices will be at or perhaps above the operating cost of that unit. A price in excess of operating cost arises in the step-function case. By definition, lower-cost units will then have a greater excess of prices above operating costs than higher-cost units. The payoff to any unit operating at any moment, then, is the difference between its operating cost and the prevailing price. Again by definition, the annual payment is the sum of these individual payoffs.

Given any arbitrary system, we cannot be sure that a unit receives sufficient income to insure that it can recover capital charges. The annual income will be a function of the time pattern of prices, the extent to which the unit operates at a given price, and the operating costs. The merit-order principle implies that operation will occur only if the unit is at a lower cost than the most expensive unit needed to meet a given desired output level. Outages due to unexpected failures or preventive maintenance will limit utilization. There will be some period in which the unit would have been operated but is not because of an outage. However, when operation is desirable and possible, the unit will earn income in excess of operating costs equal to the difference between revenues and operating costs.

The annual contribution of operations to the recovery of capital charges depends on hours of operation, when they occur (and thus the prevailing price), and the operating cost (which may also vary with time if, for example, there are seasonal price variations for fuel). A key point of the vast literature about peak-load pricing is that the failure to vary prices with changes in demand and supply, while still supplying the quantity demanded at prevailing rates, implies that high-cost units will lose money when operating. The prevailing rate will be some weighted average of costs. Under traditional rate-of-return regulation, that rate would bring in revenues sufficient to recover operating costs and cover capital charges on the total plant. By the definition of averaging, the rate will be below the costs (including capital recovery) of the most expensive units operating in times of high demand and will probably also fall short of the operating costs of such plants, for reasons discussed later. Thus, a flat rate undercharges for peak energy and overcharges for offpeak energy, and capital recovery is produced by sufficient overcharges in the offpeak periods to cover the losses in peak periods.

However, the efficient pattern of prices and the way prices should be set must be examined. The literature on peak-load pricing shows how one would price if demand were perfectly predictable and price changing were costless in the sense that no extra investment or operating cost were needed to implement a flexible pricing system. The cost usually stressed is that of special meters, which can determine when electricity is consumed and thus permit charging the price prevailing at that time. Other costs are incurred in communicating the prices to consumers.

Textbook discussions of pricing in industries that are fully responsive to demand or supply fluctuations typically presume that reaction is made through institutions such as stock and commodity exchanges, which are designed to respond immediately to changing market conditions. Frequent negotiations with a power company would be cost effective only for very large consumers. Even such customers might not be able to react rapidly enough to sudden changes in the market conditions, such as a demand surge or a forced (unexpected) outage. The spot pricing proposed by the MIT Homeostatics Group provides a better, although not a perfect response to prices by allowing prices to be based on the latest available information about probable conditions in the next pricing period. However, if demand and supply were perfectly predictable, the difficulties would vanish.

The literature on peak-load pricing has concentrated on defining the optimum price, given that prices can vary with market conditions. The literature shows that in this case the appropriate price in each time period is the short-run marginal cost of the most expensive unit to operate.

What tends to be neglected are the short- and long-run patterns of capital-cost recovery under such systems. The outcome emerges from straightforward application of standard economic principles of optimum behavior. However, the logical possibilities are considerable. For present purposes, the critical result to note is that while peak periods will make a major contribution to recovery of investment costs, additional income may have to be earned offpeak to justify investment. Further discussion in appendix 2D shows that even with simplifying assumptions, many outcomes are possible.

Moreover, truly optimum decisions must be determined in a model that explicitly considers the costs of price changes. This analysis must include treatment of load reduction by policies to prevent the supply of all that would be demanded at a given rate. Such curtailment could involve the *rolling-blackout concept:* shutting off whole areas of the system for short periods to distribute cutoffs equally among customers.

Alternatively, more systematic approaches could be adopted. As is presently the case, industrial customers could agree to have at least part of their loads interrupted during peak periods. It is similarly possible to interrupt service to other customers. In practice, emphasis is placed on cutting off electricity to particular appliances, such as water heaters, but it is conceivable that systems could be developed by which the customer could choose what would be shut off. (Appliances that responded to a utility signal of impending curtailment or rate increase by turning off whatever the customer wanted eventually might be widely employed.)

As technology develops, a wide spectrum of pricing strategies could be adopted. At one extreme is the still widespread practice of keeping rates level for long periods. This intuitively seems more rigid than is justifiable. Meters must be read reasonably frequently—at least six times a year—and it should not be very costly to change rates every time the meter is read.

A more interesting question is the optimal frequency of meter reading. Given sufficient shifts in demand-supply relationships within a given month and the resulting disparities between marginal production costs and rates, it might be beneficial to increase the frequency of reading and perhaps to adopt alternative metering technologies. Methods for electronically indicating usage to the company could obviate on-site inspection and lower monitoring costs. The next step would be to install meters capable of recording time of consumption. Prices then could be varied between metering periods. This could involve either a price schedule set well in advance, spot prices as advocated by the MIT group, or even prices set after the fact. Since there are economies of scale in the administration of flexible prices, it is likely that the attractiveness of such pricing methods will be greater to larger-volume consumers. Given that not all consumers will be charged spot prices, it becomes necessary to consider simultaneously the introduction of optimal reductions of supplies to given customers.

The solution to this problem would emerge from an exercise that maximized the efficiency of electricity supply given all the costs involved. An optimal pricing system could involve different arrangements with various customers. Some might remain under the conventional arrangement where prices were constant, at least between meter readings, and supply would be subject to disruption only through an arbitrary blackout procedure when demand exceeded capacity. A second group might be subject to rates that varied with time periods under rules set well in advance. A third group could be subject to spot prices of the type advocated by the Homeostatics Group.

Any one of these groups could additionally be subject to installation of devices that allow utilities to cut off (load shed) specific power flows. However, use of such devices is an alternative to price variation and would be expected to be most valuable to customers subject to fixed prices and least valuable to customers charged spot prices. A further distinction is between the spot price that would have been charged if price variation were costless and the actual appropriate spot prices in a mixed system.

The basic principle guiding the choice of which combination is appropriate for a given customer is that the benefits must at least equal the costs. The costs are those of more complex methods of setting prices, recording consumption, and varying supplies systematically. The benefits are eliminating the inefficiencies of prices that do not adjust to marginal-cost variation. The key analytic problem is to characterize these costs.

A general analysis qualitatively treats the critical comparison between what would emerge if flexible prices could be employed costlessly and any system of less flexible prices. The analysis draws on the standard results of economic theory concerning the efficiency effects of the presence or absence of flexible prices. The critical point to reiterate is that efficiency in *production* is maximized when marginal costs equal price. Therefore, a failure continually to equate marginal costs to price produces efficiency losses. Thus, an industry without flexible prices can be considered a less productive or more costly one than the same industry with flexible prices. Unfortunately, more costly or less productive does not necessarily mean higher production costs or lower total output. Part of the inefficiency arises from providing improper signals to consumers and encouraging overconsumption in high-demand periods.

Figures 2–5 and 2–6 sketch the factors involved. Figure 2–5a shows a situation in which prices are above marginal costs. In this situation, the consumer demands less than the producers are willing to supply; consumption falls to the quantity Q_1 demanded at the inefficiently high price P_1; the firm reduces output to Q_1 and costs to MC_1. The social cost then is that of the net of the loss (ABDC) to lower consumption and the production-cost savings (ABFC). Since values exceed cost, the lost benefits exceed the lower costs.

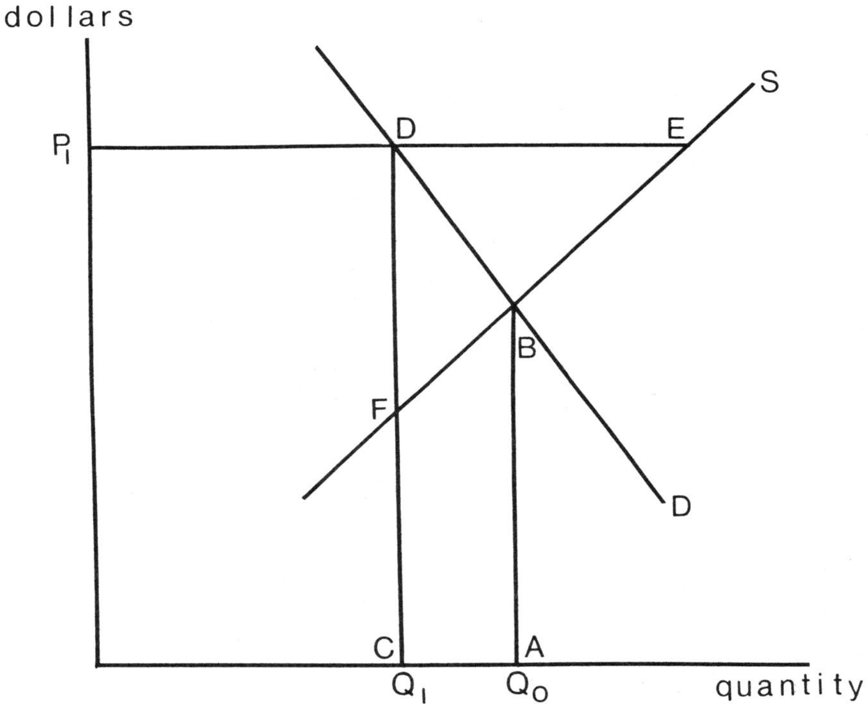

dollars

Figure 2-5a. Production Inefficiency with Rigid Prices and Excess Supply

Figure 2-5b shows the case of actual price below the proper flexible price. Here consumers wish to consume Q_1 at the inappropriate price P_1. This situation is more complex than the case of a price above the appropriate flexible price. Prices set too low imply that it is inefficient to supply all that is demanded. A variety of actual supply reponses could occur. The firm could choose to satisfy all or a part of the excess demand. To complicate matters further, the investments and marginal costs under flexible prices could differ from those under more rigid ones. Thus, the industry could have a lesser or greater ability to supply if prices were rigid instead of flexible. Figure 2-6 illustrates this outcome for the case of increased investment. The short-run supply increases from S to S' and the quantity that firms are able to produce at any marginal cost rises. Thus, if actual supply is limited to that producible at the marginal cost equal to price, the supply is higher with S' than with S. However, the net social cost of meeting demands fully falls from *FHG* to *FDB*.

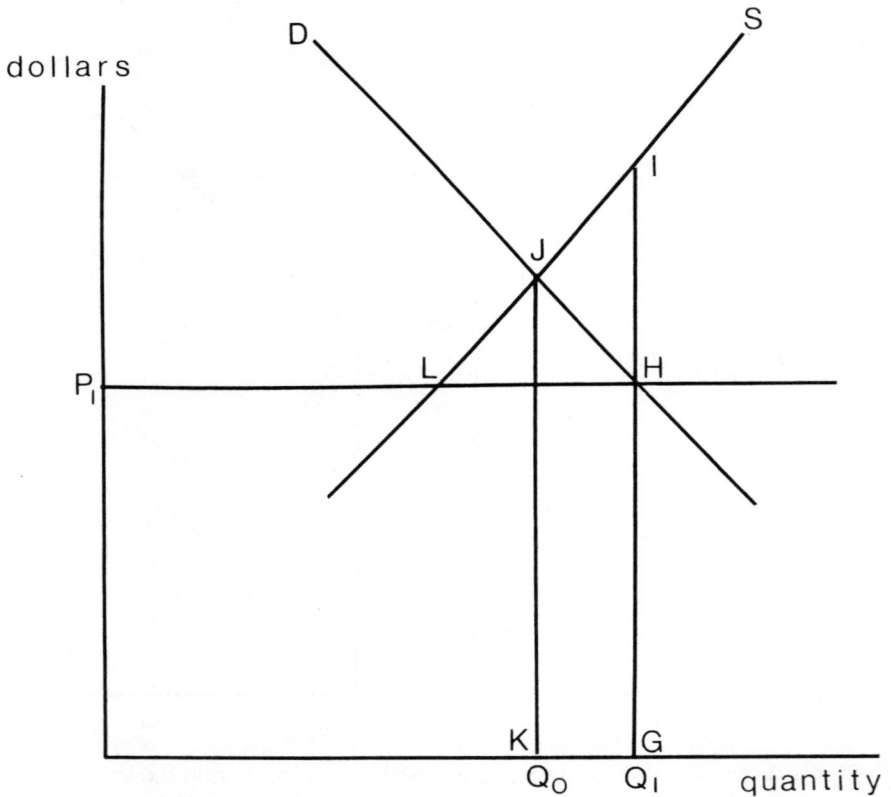

Figure 2–5b. Production Inefficiency with Rigid Prices and Excess Demand

Thus, when fixed prices are too low, consumers can get more or less than if prices were flexible. If they do get more, the situation is one of a net loss consisting of the difference between higher production costs and the value of additional consumption. If consumers end up with less, the losses are the same as in the case of overly high prices—a loss of consumption less than the cost savings.

The simplest issue to resolve is when is it efficient to increase price variation. This occurs when the cost of administering a scheme of more flexible prices is less than the social losses. Much more complicated questions arise with the proper way of selecting the correct combination of more rigid pricing schemes with a supply-curtailment method (as in figure 2–5b) and in determining the impact of that system of prices and quantities. The selection of the optimum pattern emerges from maximizing efficiency, given all the benefits and costs of the system.

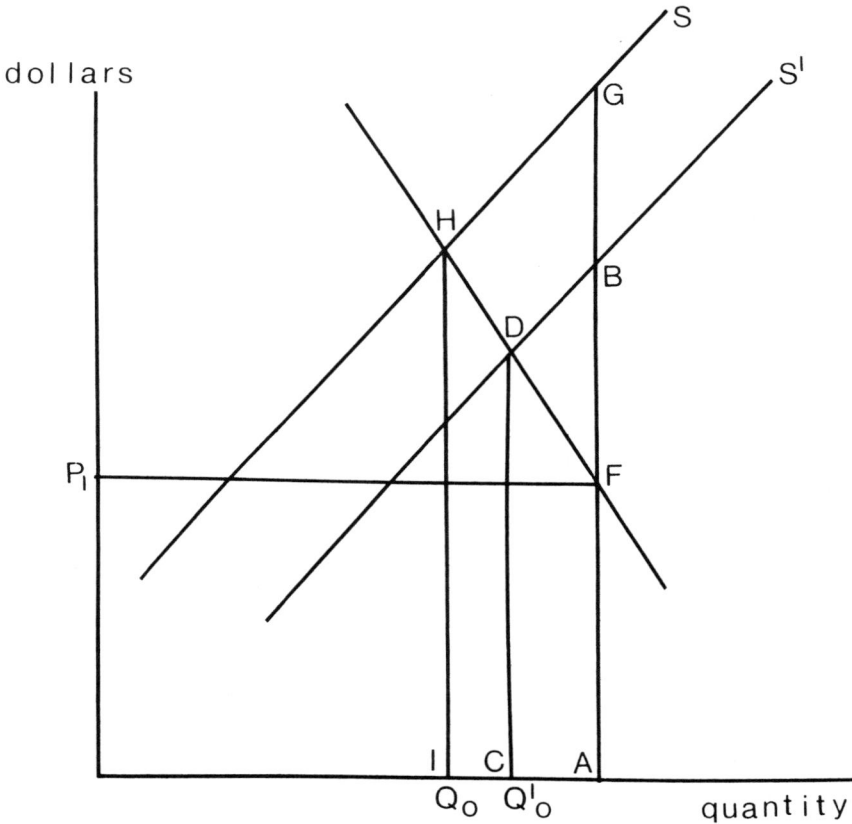

Figure 2–6. Supply Increase and Production Inefficiency with Rigid Prices: The Excess-Demand Case

Consideration of polar cases suggests the range of possible effects of different pricing systems. At one extreme, the key effect of flexible prices as opposed to rigid prices without complete rationing could be to encourage the electric-power industry to supply peak power although self-generation would have been cheaper. In this case, the power industry produces more cumulatively and incurs higher costs than under flexible prices. The other extreme is when the only loss is the failure to stimulate consumption that would have occurred at lower prices. Here output is lower than it would have been if flexible prices existed. Downward pressures on production costs are exerted by the reduction of output and the disincentive this creates to further investment. Thus, costs to the electric-power industry and outputs are lower. The costs to society of the lost production exceed the industry's cost savings. The cost of inflexible prices may or may not raise the costs to the electric-power industry. What is critical is that a cost increase to society does occur.

Much more remains to be determined about the design of an efficient system of rigid prices. Among issues deserving attention are those about whether any a priori restrictions can be placed on the outcomes. (Appendix 2E sketches some of the simpler results and analyzes the key issues.)

The prior analysis only treats the differences between inflexible prices and flexible ones. What we actually observe are prices, capacity, and output mix as determined by interactions between regulators and companies. Output and capacity may be higher than is efficient, and possibly even higher than under flexible pricing.

However, the analysis also suggests that there may be a more satisfactory explanation for overinvestment than is usually provided. The explanation would help reconcile the conflicting observations on electric-utility behavior that center around the work of Averch and Johnson (1962). The Averch-Johnson model alleges that regulators allow a rate of return in excess of the cost of capital. Their analysis shows that a firm regulated only by this limit would invest more than was efficient. Some econometric studies (for example, those of Spann 1974) found that excessive investment had occurred.

However, Baumol and Klevorick (1970) present the counterargument that regulation covers more than the rate of return; they suggest that these additional controls would prevent overinvestment. Regulators reviewed the rates themselves and in some cases may have even examined investments (see chapter 4). Such challenges of investment decisions became common in the 1970s, as illustrated by the disputes over who would pay the cost of the Three Mile Island and other nuclear accidents. But at least one critic of the Averch-Johnson model suggests that such challenges arose in earlier years (Ostergren, 1975).

However, other observers (for example, Telson 1975) argue that utilities overinvest in reliability. My analysis suggests that any such overinvestment in reliability may be a regulatory response to the consequences of rigid pricing. Lesser investment may increase the chance of system outages, and regulators may fear the consequences so much that they exert pressures to maintain high reliability. This tendency was particularly great during the period between the November 1965 power failure in the Northeast and the period of rising costs and falling growth that began in the middle 1970s.

More generally, so many forces are affecting electric-utility rates that the true situation may be difficult to determine. As chapter 4 demonstrates, many indicators suggest that rates are too low to provide an adequate real return on existing investment. However, the relationship between rates and long-run marginal costs is more ambiguous. Rising real costs in terms of movement along upward-sloping marginal-cost curves and upward shifts of the marginal-cost curves put the marginal costs of an optimal capacity level above its average costs, in current dollars. Inadequate inflation adjustment puts rates below average costs, in current dollars.

However, rate-increasing pressures are created by allowing returns on economically obsolete capacity and whatever regulatory barriers exist to economically justified conversions from oil to coal or nuclear. As discussed in later chapters, the situation differs considerably from region to region. The Pacific Northwest has little obsolete capacity and so much low-cost waterpower that its marginal costs are well above rates. The Northeast, with high capacity and heavy dependence on oil, might have rates above long-run marginal costs, but most and probably all rates actually are too low (see chapter 7).

Thus, the discussion of the theoretical complexity of an optimum set of rates suggest that verification of such conjectures will require large amounts of highly reliable data. Later chapters indicate that even the historical data are inadequate. The discussion thus far also should have made it clear that to evaluate the efficiency of the industry, both current and forecast prospects of existing plants must be evaluated. No one remotely familiar with the perils of energy forecasting would argue that accurate predictions are likely to emerge.

The Problem of Selecting a Mix of Power Plant

The argument thus far has focused on how an existing system would respond to different pricing and delivery systems, indicating that the long-term investment would be adjusted so every plant built would produce income sufficient to justify the investment. In particular, minimizing costs by applying the merit-order principle would be the short-run approach. Capital recovery could occur in many fashions.

The last issue that needs appraisal is what influences the choice of options. Here a simple levelized-cost analysis conveys the essence of the argument. The basic proposition is that whatever the actual price pattern, the shorter the time period during which some returns to capital are earned, the more must be earned per period. One way to reduce required income per period for a given operating rate is to adopt a technology that involves lower annual capital charges. Since the levelized charge is the annual charge divided by output and given two ways to produce the same output Q, a lower annual cost—say, K_1 versus K_2—produces a lower levelized cost K_1/Q as compared to K_2/Q. The optimal investment is always the one with the lower present value or equivalent levelized cost. An increase in operating rates invariably lessens and, if sufficient, eliminates the cost disadvantage of an option involving higher capital costs. For example, if Q is the initial rate and the rate is increased by a factor $\alpha > 1$, the costs become $K_1/\alpha Q$ and $K_2/\alpha Q$ and fall in the proportion $1/\alpha$. The fall is greater if the absolute amount is higher. This can be seen by making annual capital costs of option one β times those of option two with $\beta > 1$, so $K_1 = \beta K_2 > K_2$. The levelized costs become $L_1 = \beta K_2/Q$ and $L_2 = K_2/Q$. The cost difference $L_1 - L_2$ is then:

$$\frac{\beta K_2}{Q} - \frac{K_2}{Q} = \frac{(\beta - 1)K_2}{Q} \qquad (2.1)$$

This difference decreases as Q rises. This can be proved by differentiation as follows:

$$\frac{\partial(L_1 - L_2)}{\partial Q} = \frac{-(\beta - 1)K_2}{Q^2} \qquad (2.2)$$

$(\beta - 1) > 0$, $K_2 > 0$, $Q^2 > 0$ combine to imply the derivative is negative. For example, if we have options with annual costs of \$200 and \$100, respectively, and each produces only one unit, the per unit costs are \$200 and \$100, leaving a \$100 difference. If we double output, we have unit costs of \$100 and \$50, or a difference of only \$50.

In any case, the argument that lower annual cost investments are preferable at lower annual operating rates is conventionally but imprecisely described as meaning that options with lower investment per kilowatt of capacity should be chosen. In fact, the annual charge both increases with the initial investment and decreases with the life of the investment. It is conceivable, but probably not true in practice, that the initial cost advantage of a technology could be offset by its shorter operating life. The options also can differ markedly in levelized operating costs. Lower capital-cost options are attractive only when the savings is not offset by a difference in levelized operating costs.

As a further complication, there are two major possibilities, which can be pursued simultaneously, for building in response to intrayear load variation. There are responses both to the effects of the type of technical progress that often occurs in the electric-power industry and to the impact of system growth. Technical progress in electric power often takes the form of *embodied progress:* progress that can only be implemented by installing new equipment. A further distinction is made between *retrofitting*—the addition of equipment to existing plants—and incorporating the change into new plants. Retrofitting usually is more expensive than incorporating. Moreover, an important type of innovation is developing more economic ways to build larger plants. Such innovations cannot be retrofitted.

An additional influence is that the growth of the system reduces the threat to reliability of a larger generating unit or transmission line, allowing construction of cheaper-to-operate, larger plants. If the conditions described prevail, new plants will be cheaper to operate than older ones. Thus, the position of plants progressively deteriorates in the merit order. A facility begins operating as fully as physically possible but may ultimately be used only in peaking service. However, a U.S. policy of requiring more stringent environmental controls on new plants could eliminate the cost advantage of new plants.

The second option is deliberately to build plants for continually low rates of utilization. Construction of such plants would be justified if there were limits to the economic ability to reduce operating rates. Among the reasons that shifts in merit order might not be the optimal approach are slow technical progress and a tendency for increased demand fluctuations, which make it necessary to operate an increasing proportion of the plant at lower rates. The limits on how much utilization may be reduced economically relate to the nature of start-ups and shutdowns of conventional boilers. The strains of frequent starts and stops lead to increased maintenance costs. (Gas turbines have a greater ability to start and stop rapidly.)

Where plants are deliberately built for use at less than base-load levels, differences in fuel prices over time and the variation in prices among regions can greatly affect the optimal mix. Generally, the wider the gap among fuel prices, the greater the capital-cost savings needed to compensate for it. With coal at, say, $0.002/kWh and oil at $0.003, a levelized capital-cost savings of a bit more than $0.001 suffices to justify oil use. When the respective fuel costs rise to $0.015 and $0.060, the required offsetting capital-cost savings is $0.045. This widening of fuel-price differences has profoundly affected the economics.

For base-load plants, the central question since the middle 1970s has been the comparative attractiveness of coal and nuclear power. The question is whether, with the socially efficient level of environmental and safety rules applied to both technologies, nuclear power would have a cost advantage. The usual presumption is that it would involve higher capital costs but lower operating costs than a coal plant. In earlier times, oil and gas were low enough in cost in parts of the country to be competitive in the base-load period.

At intermediate loads, nuclear power is considered less attractive because of the impacts of higher, levelized capital costs. Oil and gas standings have changed rapidly, and there are distinct possibilities that in the 1980s oil-fired plants will produce cost savings only in serving temporary surges of load. Combustion turbines, which can only use oil and gas, have a superior ability to start quickly when load surges. Conventional boilers must be kept idling because rapid start-up can produce severe strains.

Externalities: The Actual and the Induced

Economic theory, particularly Samuelson's theory of public goods, indicates that a primary justification for government intervention arises when it is impossible or prohibitively expensive to charge all beneficiaries for their consumption of the service. Samuelson (1966, vol. 2, pp. 1223–1239 and 1969) stresses the concept of *nonexlusivity:* the good is available to everyone or no one. For example, everyone in an area is affected by air quality, and all benefit from improving it. At the very least, it would be very expensive to develop institutions to charge society for clean air. Moreover, individuals might have incentives to mislead policymakers about their preferences. When people are subject to charges, they may understate their willingness to pay in the hope that they can shift the burden to others or in the jargon of the theory, become "free riders."

Ronald Coase (1960) used an argument similar to Samuelson's to clarify the economic analysis of such side effects (externalities) of economic activities as pollution. He showed that when the number of victims was small, they could privately secure efficient levels of relief. Nuisance law allowed them to sue for compensation. If redress were not secured, the victims could pay those causing the damages to undertake abatement. When the victims became numerous and scattered, private negotiations broke down. Only the government could efficiently insure control. Thus, it is widespread effects, that is, publicness as defined by Samuelson, that are critical in justifying government intervention when externalities arise.

An extensive literature exists indicating that government policies can cause inefficiency. Examples include energy price controls and restrictions, such as building codes and lending limits, that are imposed on private decision making. Care has to be taken to distinguish between inherent market defects and those created by public policy. Inherent defects can only be cured by some kind of government action, but when a public policy is the problem an available alternative is to change the original policy. This is often preferable.

The Role of Governmental Conservation and Fuel-Shifting Policies

As discussed more fully in chapter 6, the U.S. government has enacted numerous laws attempting to encourage reduced use of energy and a shift from presumedly more scarce fuels, such as oil and gas, to allegedly more plentiful fuels, such as coal, solar energy, wind, and even foot power applied to bicycles (the National Energy Conservation Policy Act of 1978). The proponents of such policies assert that the reduction of oil imports is desirable and consumption controls are the best way to produce lower imports. These assertions lack supporting economic analysis. Unless the danger of oil imports is precisely measured, the optimal level of import limitation cannot be determined. It is even less clear that conservation and fuel-shifting policies are the best way to proceed. In fact, the theory of the optimum way to deal with market imperfections suggests that the best policy is one aimed directly at the source of the problem (for example, see Corden's 1974 survey of how the analysis applies to international trade). In the case of insecure oil supplies, the appropriate approach would be a tariff that incorporates any externalities associated with supply uncertainty.

Properly choosing the level and composition of personal consumption is generally considered best left to free-market mechanisms. The most obvious explanation for imposing such policies to override the market is, as argued already, that such intervention is the inevitable consequence of government decisions to intervene in other ways with the market.

In particular, price controls on oil and gas have tended to promote underpricing of these fuels, encouraging more use of fuel in general and oil and gas in particular than would be true in a free market. The actual policies implicitly taxed refiner savings from buying price-controlled domestic oil instead of foreign oil to subsidize increased imports of oil, among other things (see Gordon 1981). One way to offset this stimulus is to attempt to determine administratively what would have occurred in the absence of price control, then force that pattern to emerge by regulation.

An irrefutable criticism of regulation is that it increases the cost of the price-control system. The design and implementation of regulations necessarily involves expenditures. Moreover, even the most enthusiastic advocate of government regulation should have considerable doubt about the ability to estimate the response of millions of American fuel consumers to higher prices.

Skeptics about intervention might suspect that preconceptions of the regulators might lead to advocating actions of questionable merit. The clearest example of this is that within a year of the 1978 imposition of requirements that electric utilities cease burning gas between 1990 and 2000 (see chapter 6), serious doubts arose about the wisdom of the action. Concerns developed that the presumption might be wrong that gas use in electric power deprived someone else of gas and forced oil use. The gradual, partial deregulation of gas that was set in motion, for example, might produce enough additional gas so that some would be available for electricity generation.

The battle over mandatory speed limits and the skepticism about alternative energy sources illustrates other administrative directives that are disputed, if not invalid.

Another rationale centers around alleged market failures. It is suggested that consumers are so ignorant or require so high a payoff on investments that they inadequately invest in saving energy. Like all market-failure arguments, the assertion that ignorance is the critical problem can never be disproved totally. It is very difficult to explain conclusively why people fail to act. Nevertheless, there is good reason to suspect that the argument is not applicable to energy users in general and to large users in particular. If the problem is mere ignorance, the best solution would be education. Arguments could be made that educating the household sector and home builders, bankers, retailers, and manufacturers who affect the available energy consumption options would be less expensive than direct controls. This would depend on the differences in direct costs and how high a value society places on preserving the rights of individuals to choose for themselves.

In any case, the argument is particularly weak for the large energy consumers that were singled out for forced conversion. These users have the largest stake in reducing fuel costs and are thus the most likely to become knowledgeable about choices. As large companies, they are also more likely to have the best possible access to funds. Fossil-fuel use by industry in 1980 was 4.5 percent below the use in 1973, although industrial production was 13 percent higher, suggesting that reaction to higher prices already had occurred.

In practice, the problems of electric utilities in securing rate relief and specifically rate relief directed at reducing oil and gas use may prevent action. Regulators may insist that all the savings be passed on to consumers, thus making the investment unprofitable. Fuel-conversion legislation is one means of exerting pressure on regulators, but this is inferior to full regulatory reform. Whether this is the best and most politically feasible policy remains to be proved. (Chapter 6 provides evidence that fuel-conversion policies proved quite ineffective through 1981).

Another set of arguments in favor of intervention concerns the problems associated with reliance on imports. The arguments for intervention include the impact of imports on oil price, the security premium due to direct impacts of supply disruption, the issue of macroeconomic stabilization, and the balance-of-payments problem. Only the first involves a clear externality, which would be best handled by a tariff. The oil-import argument is a special application of the concept of an *optimum tariff*, often discussed in international-trade economics. This optimal-tariff argument involves the principle that the exercise of monopoly power benefits the monopolist at the expense of everyone else. The optimum-monopoly tariff involves actions by a nation that take into account the combined control over price exercised by a nation. This is a different tariff from one instituted to cover the costs of supply disruption.

This optimum-monopoly-tariff argument has been brought into the fuel choice alteration decision process by Nordhaus (1980), Stobaugh and

Yergin (1979), and by the Economic Regulatory Administration of the Department of Energy (DOE) (1979). Their arguments are straightforward applications of part of the optimum-tariff argument to world oil markets. Unfortunately, by only implicitly using the optimal-monopoly argument, the advocates have overlooked critical elements of the theory that undermine the case for controls on consumption. In particular, the theory states that if any gain is available, it can be secured with certainty only through imposing a tariff. Fuel shifting is more akin to a quota on imports, and the theory holds that it is unclear just who will benefit from a quota (for example, see Meade 1955). It is precisely these principles that have caused M.A. Adelman (1979) to suggest that forced restrictions on consumption are undesirable but oil import tariffs might be appropriate.

The minimum problem with using the monopoly-buying-price argument to justify consumption controls is that it presumes a high sensitivity on the part of the members of the Organization of Petroleum Exporting Countries (OPEC) to market fluctuations. It is suggested that even the small demand changes that would be produced by proposed fuel shifts would produce price reductions. In reality, OPEC may not be able to react to such modest changes.

A strong counterargument has been presented by M.A. Adelman (1979). He suggests that the model inappropriately applies principles to a cartelized market that are relevant only to a competitive industry. Prior to the 1979–1980 oil price rises, he argued that OPEC prices were below their monopoly profit-maximizing level. Prices, therefore, would continue rising even if demand were restricted (Whether this is still true remains to be seen.) He argues further that we should recall the basic proposition in monopoly theory that decreasing demand does not inevitably produce lower prices. The theory points out that the marginal revenues of monopolists are affected by the elasticity of demand. An elasticity decline tends to produce higher prices. Thus, a demand increase accompanied by an elasticity decline can actually produce higher prices. Elasticity reduction, moreover, is likely to occur if the U.S. reduces oil imports by quotas or fuel-use regulations. U.S. import demand is generally more elastic than that of the rest of the world, and fuel-shifting policies concentrate on the most elastic demands. Thus, Adelman suggests that once OPEC has attained its profit-maximizing price level, reduced U.S. imports would lead to higher rather than lower oil prices.

The remaining arguments involve various degrees of belief in the desirability of alternatives to market decisions in handling the impacts of price changes of oil. The argument is most clear-cut in dealing with the real costs of an oil-supply disruption. An unfettered market seems capable of dealing with the problem. Profits can be made by making oil available during the disruption, so there are obvious incentives to stockpiling. It is debatable whether those who undertake such investments will do so efficiently. The key barrier is not lack of foresight, but that the fear of excess profits leads to expropriation of profits on stockholdings. A government-created market failure necessitates intervention to offset it.

Whether this same argument applies to problems of stabilizing the domestic economy and international monetary relations depends on the correct model of how these macroeconomic systems work. Those who believe successful stabilization only requires will power would consider energy policies to cushion macroeconomic shocks to be inferior substitutes to the exercise of will power. Less sanguinity about the ability to stabilize the economy implies more sympathy toward the argument that there is an intrinsic need to control energy developments.

These arguments establish that some intervention is needed to counteract other intervention or truly treat externalities. What the proper intervention should be is not generally evident but presumably would involve taxes on use of imported oil, with the proceeds subsidizing measures to cushion the impact of crises. Thus, fuel-shifting policies may not be an optimal response to whatever threat imports may pose. Moreover, the alleged dangers that are avoided are difficult to value accurately, and a distinct risk is that arbitrarily high values will be adopted to force maximum conversion (see chapter 6).

A Note on the Principles and Practices of Environmental Policy

The basic case for environmental regulation has already been made: the benefits are too widely dispersed for anyone but the government to effect adequate controls. All that needs to be noted here is that there is considerable doubt about whether the implementation of these regulations has been satisfactory.

The best established criticism of existing air-pollution policies is that they rely too heavily on detailed regulation of what each polluter should do. Numerous economists have argued that this approach is defective (for example, see Kneese and Schultze 1975; Mills 1978; and Gordon 1981). The primary criticism is that regulators become more deeply involved than is economically efficient in the choice of pollution-control options. Regulators make decisions about both the extent and method of pollution control. For this to work, regulators must have good information about the costs of different abatement strategies to individual polluters. Since such information does not exist, regulation will be inefficient. Another decisive objection is that the rule-making process has been designed to make fighting the rules an attractive alternative to vigorous compliance.

The alternative is to impose taxes on pollution. Adopting control technologies to reduce emissions then will occur when the tax exceeds the cost of control. An invariable further result is that taxes discourage activities such as electricity generation of which pollution is a by-product. This allows the firm to decide what is the cheapest way to lower emissions and how much emission reduction it can undertake. Raising the tax sufficiently will insure that the desired amount of overall pollution reduction occurs. Taxes, moreover, are harder to evade and easier to administer than regulations.

Efforts by the U.S. government to quantify the impacts of air pollution have involved greater reliance than is desirable on statistical analysis of mortality data. The best of those studies suffer from defects that substantially overstate pollution damages. The most fundamental defect involves an incorrect vision of the problem. Current deaths are related to current pollution. This neglects the problem of cumulative effects and resultant acceleration of mortality. Other defects include failure to control for the effects of such other influences as smoking rates and such social and economic characteristics as income and education, which affect the ability to secure health services. A growing literature has suggested that existing studies have handled these questions poorly.

In short, the nature of air-pollution damages is subject to at least as much uncertainty as most policy issues. In all cases, this uncertainty should be explicitly recognized and systematically incorporated into decision making. Thus, policies should be more flexible than is presently the case.

Economic theories of decision making under uncertainty greatly assist the development of the case for greater flexibility. All these theories share the basic proposition that under uncertainty many outcomes are possible and decision makers should somehow weight these outcomes. The weighting may or may not be made by using the statistical concept of a mean. It is further argued that risk is undesirable and a risky investment with the same average expected payoff as an unrisky one will be less valuable. Actual policy seems to have been based on overestimating the average payoff and grossly underestimating the uncertainty. Thus, overly stringent regulations have been imposed.

There are two other significant policy problems. First, the dangers are poorly defined, so we do not know precisely what should be controlled. Second, because one pollutant may transmit another and be easier to control, policy might best concentrate on control of the transporter. Various observers have suggested that U.S. policy may overemphasize sulfur-oxide control at the expense of particulate control. Particles, especially small ones, may be the true culprit, the critical transmission mode, or both. In any case, it appears that the case for a pollution tax must be supplemented by efforts to determine exactly what to tax. A particulate rather than a sulfur tax might be best.

Conceptual Aspects of Regulatory Reform: The Theory and Its Status

Three basic questions can be raised about government control of rates and profits of electric power companies. Consider first the issue of the rationale for controls. Second, remember the questions raised about the applicability of these principles to electric utilities. Third, there are questions about how to best improve the situation.

Before proceeding, further comments should be made about the present status of the debate on regulation in general and regulation of electric utilities in particular. There is ample evidence that regulation, particularly of electric utilities, needs reform. The Brookings Institution and the American Enterprise Institute are often contrasted as bastions of liberalism and conservatism. Yet both organizations have sponsored numerous studies criticizing the practice of regulation. Similarly, the study group assembled by the Ford Foundation and coordinated by Resources for the Future leaned toward liberalism yet was highly critical of energy policies, including electric-utility regulation (see Landsberg 1979). This concern with electric utilities is shared by a spectrum of economists as diverse as Richard Schmalensee, Paul Joskow, George Stigler, and Charles Cicchetti.

The standard justifications for regulation are based on equity, efficiency, or both. Appendix 2F presents the argument that the efficiency criterion is preferable. Difficult questions remain about how strong the evidence must be before action should be taken to control inefficiency. I noted above that the best rationale would be the existence of a natural monopoly that imposed large enough costs on society that increased economic efficiency would repay whatever regulatory administrative costs arose.

It is conceivable that some market imperfection other than natural monopoly justifies public-utility regulation. However, no important imperfection of this type has been established. It would be excessive to claim that the absence of such clear evidence justified inaction. Some observers, such as John Blair (1972), seem to advocate intervention on the basis of fears they cannot document. Others argue that regulation is an expensive venture that should not be undertaken unless there is compelling evidence of danger.

Thus, three different cases for regulating electric utilities could be made: an equity case, a natural-monopoly case, and an unknown efficiency case. Only the natural-monopoly case requires further attention. The basic question is whether the industry is really a natural monopoly, and if so, what is the optimal response.

The easiest situation to consider is that in which there is no justification for regulation; the optimal policy is to remove or avoid controls. The longstanding existence of regulation may have created barriers to immediate full decontrol, in which case gradual decontrol might be better. Conversely, it might be that rapid decontrol might be more efficient.

Where a natural monopoly exists, questions arise about its extent and about specific ends and means of regulation. The evaluation should set criteria that can be used to judge whether or not the existing system should be altered. As noted, such an appraisal should recognize that change is not costless.

The most sweeping conclusion possible is that no regulation is needed. The next possibility is that the scope of regulation should be reduced, for instance to control only transmission and distribution. A third possibility is that regulation is justified but the basic approach should be changed.

Unfortunately, what we know about the alternatives is not very encouraging. It can be argued that if well conducted, any alternative will work, but the prospects of implementing it well are questionable. Two problems exist. First, nothing can work well without well-defined objectives, and a high correlation exists between the need for regulation and the difficulties of reaching an accord about goals. Intervention means imposing major changes that are generally designed to impose costs on someone such as the beneficiary of monopoly power. Thus, at least the victim of such cost increases will try to resist the change. Second, extensive review suggests that serious flaws exist in the ability to implement any of the available alternative ways of imposing controls.

As long as reform simply shifts the arena in which conflict occurs, very little change will result. The European Economic Community and its forerunner, the European Coal and Steel Community, were not granted powers to resolve the competing claims of domestic coal producers seeking protection and consumers wishing freedom to secure cheaper energy. Thus, Western Europe spent the 1960s futilely seeking to establish an energy policy; it subsequently became content to conduct only perfunctory exercises in energy policymaking (see Gordon 1970).

The United States plunged into its energy-policy debates unaware of the European record, then proceeded to imitate it. We thus confirmed Santayana's overquoted warning about the perils of ignoring history and also the warnings of O.C. Herfindahl (1974) of the pitfalls of U.S. energy policymaking. If the difficulty is really conflict resolution, in principle it will be possible to resolve the problem using existing institutions so long as we are willing to force decisions about the contested points. More realistically, the conflicts are so deep and extend to so many areas that accord may remain elusive. It may be necessary to settle all issues simultaneously. As chapter 4 suggests, public utility and environmental regulations have become so intertwined at the state level that they will be difficult to unravel.

The two most widely used approaches to control industry are government ownership and creation of regulatory agencies. Both options, and the third possibility of selling franchises, have been subject to considerable criticism, well summarized by Schmalensee (1979).

Government ownership is the older and more well established alternative (see chapter 3). The classic concern among economists viewing the general question of government ownership is whether or not government-owned companies could be made to behave more like competitive firms than a privately owned company with the same market power. Lange's celebrated program for efficient socialism involves creating an independent planning body to insure that prices are equal to marginal costs (Lange 1936–1937). Numerous critics have contended that Lange's scheme could not be implemented effectively. Moreover, since the planning board rather than government ownership is the source of efficiency, Lange's socialism is more public-utility regulation than classic socialism.

Observers of existing conditions in the electric-utility industry wonder if ownership roles might force governments to be more accountable for the consequences of regulations. The standard criticism of prevailing regulatory-commission attitudes is that these commissions make the major decisions determining the state of the industry but the private companies are blamed for the outcome. Government ownership removes the distinction between nominal and actual decision makers.

The basic criticism of regulation is that it is poorly implemented; it is unlikely that this defect can be eliminated. Numerous outside observers suspect that the process of regulation by commission as practiced in the United States encourages short-sighted behavior that may approach, if not attain, demagoguery. Serving as a commissioner or as a staff member on a regulatory commission is not regarded as a high calling to which people fruitfully may devote their lives. The position often is considered a base from which to attain a better position elsewhere. The problem seems to be that regulation is fundamentally a boring occupation; the cases tend to be quite repetitive. Little opportunity exists to develop useful new principles. The literature on regulators documents a tendency toward restlessness.

For commissioners one possible route is to attain visibility that will allow them to move on to higher office. This may encourage commissioners to exploit or even generate distrust of utilities. Short-term political advantages can be obtained by attacking the utilities and more critically by failing to insure their financial strength.

These points do not affect the conclusion that a willingness to resolve conflicts is the key. The defects noted do not appear inherent in the regulatory process. If there were sufficient determination, there would be different incentives to regulators, or regulation could be moved to more appropriate institutions.

However, the drawbacks to regulation may be such that the United

States would find it easier to cut loose from regulation rather than to develop high-quality regulation. There is ample evidence that we are not willing to devote enough resources to insure effective regulation.

Franchise bidding involves competitive bidding for the right to service an area. For example, franchise bidding is widely used in establishing cable-television systems in various cities. Well-established economic principles governing competitive bidding indicate that if bidding takes the standard form of awards to the firm offering the highest price, it will transfer excess profits to the government agency offering the franchise. The critical part of the definition of competition is that there be a large enough group of well-informed bidders. Well informed does not mean perfect foresight or perfect risk pooling. Given the costs of risk pooling, it is optimal to limit risk sharing to the point where marginal gains equal marginal transaction costs.

The critical drawback to simply selling a franchise is that it transfers rather than eliminates excess profits. To the extent that these windfall profits are attributable to the exercise of monopoly power, the franchise-bidding process leaves monopoly intact. The strongest case for franchise bidding is when excess profits are due only to rents on low-cost facilities. The existence of such rents is explained by the prior argument that when average costs are increasing, marginal costs exceed average costs and thus prices equal to marginal costs exceed average costs. If the only barrier to marginal cost-based prices were the resulting rents, franchise bidding would be workable and possibly very attractive (see appendix 2B).

More complex schemes might be devised so that granting a franchise might involve contractual arrangements that exerted pressures to be more efficient. For example, the annual payment might be reduced in return for producing higher outputs at lower rates. The objective would be for the public agency to structure payments so a return of the monopoly gain portion of the income could in some way be used to subsidize production. Such a technique is easy to define in principle and is nothing other than an adaptation of the principles of optimum subsidy of pollution abatement. The franchise bid could be used as the baseline for payments, and the output expected under monopolistic restriction of output could be used as a baseline for production incentives. The franchise holder would be given a subsidy to raise output, financed from the franchise payment. The effect could be produced most simply by reducing the payment when outcome rose, instead of making the largest possible payment, then having the effect reduced by a subsidy.

Given what we know about the difficulties of running government programs, grave doubts exist about the practicality of franchise bidding. A further problem is that there is no guarantee that the optimum franchise bid is sufficient to finance optimum output. The fact that decreasing average costs imply marginal costs below average costs also means that a price may exceed marginal costs and just equal or even fall short of average costs. Thus, the monopoly profit can be zero or negative. In markets where the demand-average cost relationships are in or close to that position, the franchise payment is insufficient to subsidize the efficient output.

Appendix 2A:
Notes on the Literature

The literature on electric utilities has at least four major components, two of which are stressed here. The first key element is the effort of various observers, notably Turvey (1968), to reformulate parts of basic economic theory to make them applicable to electric utilities. A second and much more extensive literature deals with the theory and practice of regulating utilities. Particularly important works here are Kahn's 1970 text on regulation and Schmalensee's 1979 review of the drawbacks and advantages of different approaches to controlling natural monopoly.

The other main areas of the literature are branches of the first two. Many writers propose pricing systems that properly respond to variations over time in the demand for electricity. This is generally described as the peak-load-pricing problem. The 1980 MIT work already noted involves applying the theory to the proposed innovations in pricing and load management (Schweppe 1980). Also, an enormous literature was inspired by Averch and Johnson's 1962 suggestion that the regulatory practice of allowing rates of return in excess of the cost of capital leads to an excessive use of capital. These works involve extensive review of the validity of the theory, efforts to test empirically whether the predicted results actually occurred, and examination of whether the assumptions of the theory correctly described regulation.

Appendix 2B:
Windfalls and Their
Expropriation—The
Theory and Its Extensions

A substantial amount of economic theory and political practice has been devoted to the existence and proper allocation of windfalls. The debate over windfall profits in minerals has been particularly well publicized. A less well known principle is that windfalls can be used to finance the deficits that arise when decreasing-cost industries equate marginal cost to price. This argument has been well presented by Paul Joskow (1975) and long was used implicitly by specialists in public-utility economics.

This appendix develops the case and extends an analysis I developed to deal with price controls on oil and gas, discussing the problems of effecting programs of windfall transfers (Gordon 1981). This analysis was developed because such legislation as the 1978 Natural Gas Act and the 1980 Pacific Northwest Electric Power Planning and Conservation Act appeared to require windfall reallocation schemes that may be particularly difficult to implement.

Windfalls are conventionally divided between producer surplus (also known as windfall profits or economic rents) and consumer surplus. *Producer surplus* is the gain from selling a unit of a commodity at a price greater than the maximum price at which the producer would be willing to sell. *Consumer surplus* is the gain from buying at a price less than the price one is willing to pay. Producer surplus, on a given increment of output, is simply measured as the difference between price and marginal cost. Similarly, the consumer's surplus initially is represented as the difference between the price a buyer will pay for a commodity and the price actually paid. (The two concepts are shown graphically in figures 2B–1 and 2B–2.) However, the technical problems described here make this an imperfect measure in the case of households. The two graphs deal with surpluses due to increasing costs of production and decreasing value of consumption. Additional surpluses can rise from exercise of monopoly power in buying and selling, but these are best handled by separate analyses of monopoly and monopsony.

The theory is designed to deal with the most profitable ways to engage in *price discrimination*—paying or charging different prices on different transactions. The consumer-surplus idea shows that sellers would like to segment markets so each item sold bears a different price equal to the the willingness to pay, which the theory indicates decreases as sales rise. Lower

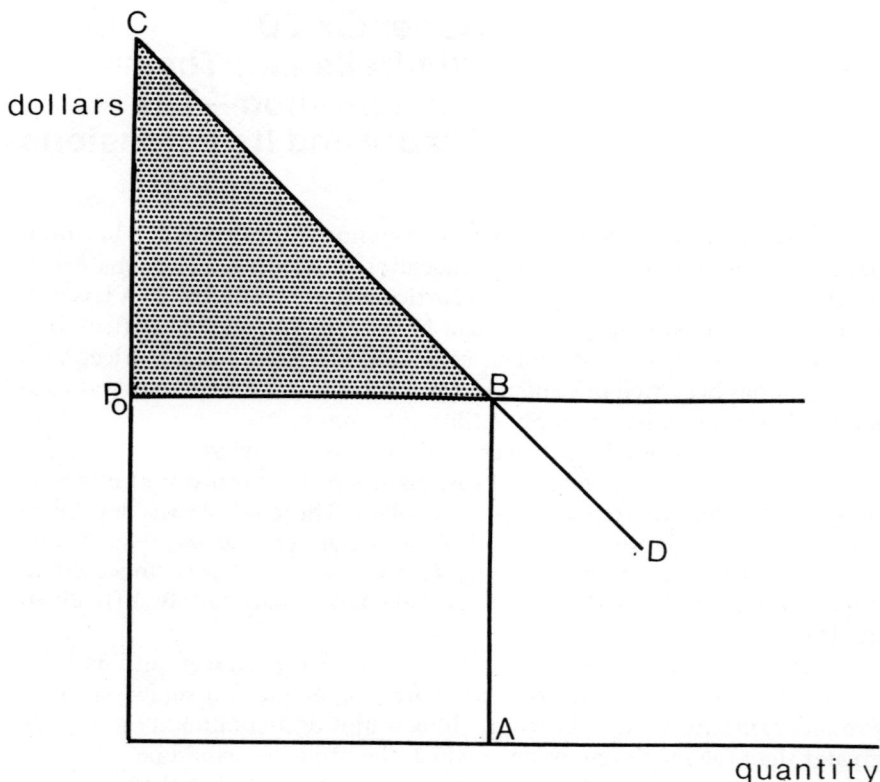

Figure 2B–1. Consumer Surplus, Indicated by Triangle BP_0C

prices are needed both to secure new customers and encourage existing customers to purchase more. Clearly, the price cutting is more attractive if it can be limited to the increased sales and not shared with old customers. Consumer surplus is the measure of the difference between what would be paid on an increment and what is actually paid. The objective of discrimination is a set of prices that transfer all this surplus to sellers. Similarly, buyer discrimination seeks to purchase each item at a producer's marginal cost and transfer producer surpluses to buyers. Of course, competition precludes segmentation and establishes a single price on all transactions. Actual monopolists, moreover, are able to engage in much coarser price discrimination. Only broad differences, such as customer location, can be recognized in pricing.

An equivalent and simpler-to-implement approach to taxing the surplus on a given increment of production or consumption is to impose a tax on

dollars

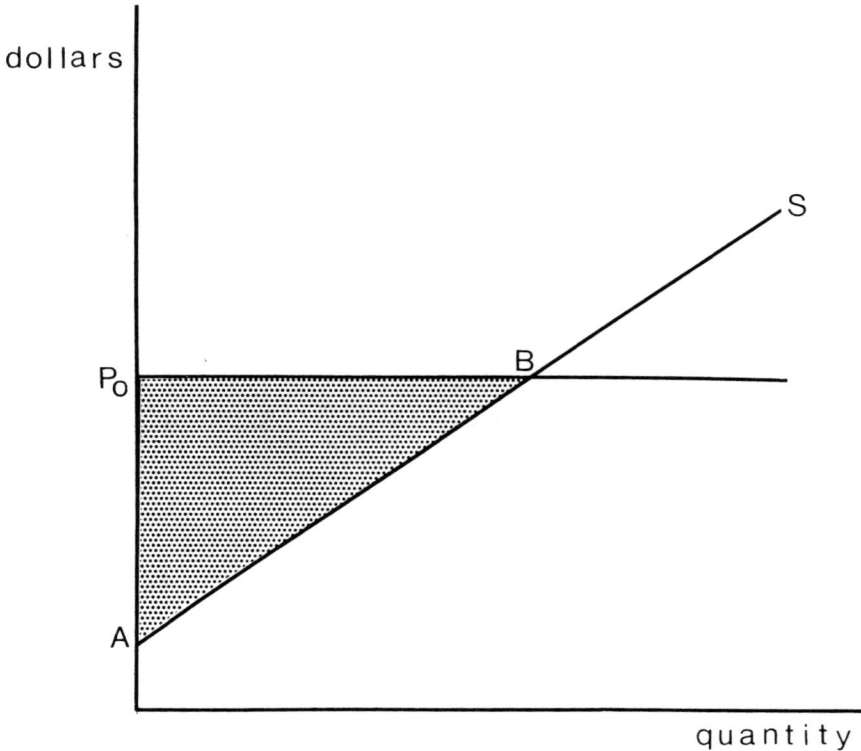

Figure 2B-2. Producer's Surplus, Indicated by ABP_0

the total gain. The total is the sum of the gains from each increment of production and output.

The consumer-producer distinction obscures the argument and hides the sources of ambiguity. More general economic models indicate that structuring an analysis in a fashion such that participants are divided between buyers and sellers is a convenient but basically arbitrary expedient. The underlying process is the exchange of one participant's goods and services for another participant's goods and services. The buyer of any one good can also be treated as the seller of whatever is sacrificed to get that good.

The theory of the firm was developed explicitly to treat optimization, using two concepts of the buyer and the seller. The theory of product markets treats the firm as selling a product to customers, who buy with money. However, the theory of input purchase treats the firm as buying such inputs with the income from their product sales. These approaches are perfectly equivalent ways of reaching the same conclusion. The product-sale approach will lead to treating any excess income as a producer surplus; the input-purchase approach would lead classification of the excess as consumer surplus. However, it is actually the same surplus, and the choice of names is arbitrary.

In the case of the competitive firm, output price is equal to marginal cost, and input price is equal to marginal value product: output price times marginal physical product. However, marginal cost is equal to input price divided by marginal physical product, so the conditions are restatements of the same principle. If Q is output, P the output price, L input, and W input price, then $MPP = \partial Q/\partial L$ is the marginal productivity of the input and $MC = \partial C/\partial Q$. The optimality conditions for all inputs are $P = MC$, $W = P(MPP)$, and $MC = W/MPP$. If we rearrange the middle condition to $P = W/MPP$, the third condition implies $P = MC$, the first condition.

Whether a consumer- or producer-surplus approach is taken mainly depends on convenience of analysis. Most applications to firms are best handled by the producer-surplus approach. An important exception is when the input supplier is a natural monopoly. Then the consumer-surplus alternative is the best way to discuss how surpluses can be used to overcome the problem of covering the losses if marginal costs are equated to price. Transferring the surplus from consumer to producer can subsidize increasing output to the level at which marginal cost equals price.

There is a long tradition of using the consumer-producer distinction to treat the differences between households and firms. Firms are merely organizations for buying inputs, transforming them into products, and selling these products. As such, firms are interested in maximizing money income in its present value terms. Households are interested in maximizing satisfaction, and money is an imperfect measure of such satisfaction. The basic problem is caused by what are technically called *income effects*. One of the effects of changing any one price is that it alters purchasing power; the rise in the price of any one good for a given money income means that consumption of that good can be kept constant only if consumption of something else is reduced; similarly, the consumption of other things can be maintained only if consumption of the good that has risen in price is reduced. Thus, it is necessary to reduce the consumption of something, and this is a reduction in real income. The measurement of household surplus is complicated by the problems of incorporating this income effect.

The problems of using transfers of surplus as a policy tool can be illustrated by defining a baseline case in which the shortcuts taken to implement rent-collection schemes do not distort resource allocation. The assumptions made in this case are unlikely to be realized in practice, and the next step is to consider what distortions are produced if realism is reintroduced.

The policymaking expedient analyzed involves subdividing consumers

dollars

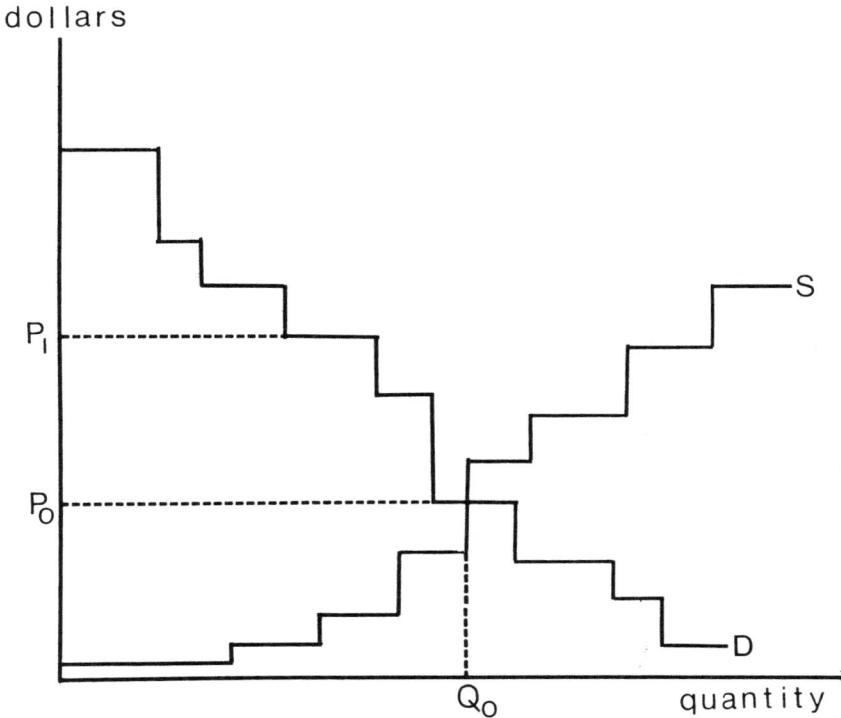

Figure 2B-3. Surpluses with Step-Function Supply and Demand

and producers into a limited number of categories, then assigning a different buying or selling price to each category. This approach could be efficient if we lived in a world of step-function demand-and-supply curves and if regulators could correctly determine the step to which a given activity of a given producer or consumer should be assigned.

The step-function concept on the demand side is that demand consists of a series of horizontal segments, each below the other by an observable amount (see figure 2B-3). Similarly, step-function supply involves horizontal segments lying at discrete intervals from each other. Since the more readily rationalized and more relevant case is where increasing costs prevail, the step-function supply curve in figure 2B-3 shows increasing costs. The optimum price equates the quantity demanded to the quantity supplied.

The step-function supply curve would be empirically valid if cost variation arose only from the need to shift to greatly more expensive technologies. Specifically, we would array the technical options in their merit order. However, we would make a very special assumption about the supply of each option. Marginal costs would be the same at all outputs between zero and the maximum physically possible. Once that physical limit was reached, we would adopt the lowest cost unexploited option. Obviously, this could be an incorrect qualitative description of the available options. A rising rather than flat supply curve might apply to each option. Even if a step-function supply curve did prevail, the regulatory desire for simplification might lead to compressing some steps.

Step-function demand functions are more difficult to rationalize. An example suggested in unpublished work by R.L. Bishop is a commodity for which household consumption is zero above some price, rises to one unit at some critical lower price, and does not increase with further price decreases. Then, when consumers actually are charged the highest price they are willing to pay, the income effect problem disappears. The demand curve records the value of consumption, given the real income associated with that price. (This is because the usual definition of an individual's demand curve states that it is defined for the real income associated with the price prevailing at each point on the curve.) Alternatively, the input demands for a facility having a step-function supply curve and competitive market prices not affected by the output could also take a step-function form. The long-run marginal productivity of each input could be constant at every output up to capacity.

As long as these assumptions are met, it is possible to finance efficiently the extra production from a decreasing-cost industry. Transferring surplus from buyers to sellers of the commodity with decreasing costs provides this financing. Rate schedules that set prices so those customers on each step paid the price associated with the step would then transfer the surplus. Everyone would pay the price at which they valued service, and the efficiency rule that marginal cost equals prices would be satisfied by charging only the last block of customers a price equal to marginal cost.

Here and in the case of transfer to customers, it is convenient to illustrate the process by comparison between customers with some arbitrary critical price P_1, greater than P_0, such that at any higher price consumption ceases and customers whose critical price is P_0. Whatever the critical price, the essential point to recall is that, by construction, consumption will persist so long as the actual price is at or below the critical level. The P_1 customer can be charged any price at or below P_1, and full surplus extraction involves a price of P_1. The customer for whom P_0 is the maximum has no surplus since a price higher than P_0 will cause consumption to cease.

With step-function demand-and-supply curves, there are an infinite number of ways to transfer economic rents from sellers to buyers without distorting economic efficiency. All we need to do is charge each customer who should be served, because the value of consumption exceeds the price at which demand is equated to supply, a price less than or equal to the maximum the customer is willing to pay. So long as each customer who is willing to pay P_1 actually pays P_1 or less, all demand at that price is satisfied. Producers would be willing to produce so long as they receive at least the minimum price they require, that is, prices that range downward from P_0.

Unfortunately, this produces an embarrassment of riches. Any producer can serve any consumer at the producer's minimum required price. By construction, that price will never exceed what any consumer is willing to pay. The last are all at or above P_0, while what the producers need are at or below P_0. Thus for an arbitrary supply price below P_0, this combines to give $P_1 > P_0 > P_2$. Obviously, every consumer would prefer to buy from the cheapest seller at that seller's minimum required price. If producers are forced to charge no more than the minimum, regulators must step in and arbitrarily decide how to allocate the resources. This is administratively inferior to a tax on the producer surplus.

This problem does not arise with programs to collect consumer surplus, because there is a critical difference in the goals of the two types of policies. The consumer-surplus-collection program is tied to the specific objective of stimulating production of a commodity produced under conditions of decreasing costs. This defines precisely how the surplus should be used. The producer-surplus-collection goal is justified by a belief that some transfer to consumers should exist. Thus, no concrete rules can be given about how best to use the money. Inverting the consumer-surplus-collection model to relate to producer surplus creates allocation problems that do not exist in the consumer-surplus case.

Enthusiasts of the lifeline-rate approach to pricing electricity believe that a feasible solution can be reached. Lifeline rates give households a very low rate on the first block of kilowatt hours used each month, then charge higher prices on successively higher increments. Implicit in this approach is the idea that direct transfer to households as a group is the most equitable use of the surplus.

As suggested, the defect of my model is that it can grossly misspecify the demand-supply situation. Customers may be assigned to demand categories that misrepresent their actual situation. This is true whether the consumer is assigned to a single demand category paying a single price or whether some segmentation is employed so, for example, the first 100 kWh bear one price, the next 100 kWh another price, and so on down the consumer's demand curve.

Figure 2B-4 deals with an arbitrary multistep rate function. These rates become the supply curve for the customer. The consumer selects the consumption level at which his demand curve intersects the supply curve. As the distinction between P_0 and P_1 shows, in cases where the demand curve intersects a horizontal portion of S, the price is the maximum the buyer is willing to pay for that total consumption. However, an intersection with a vertical

dollars

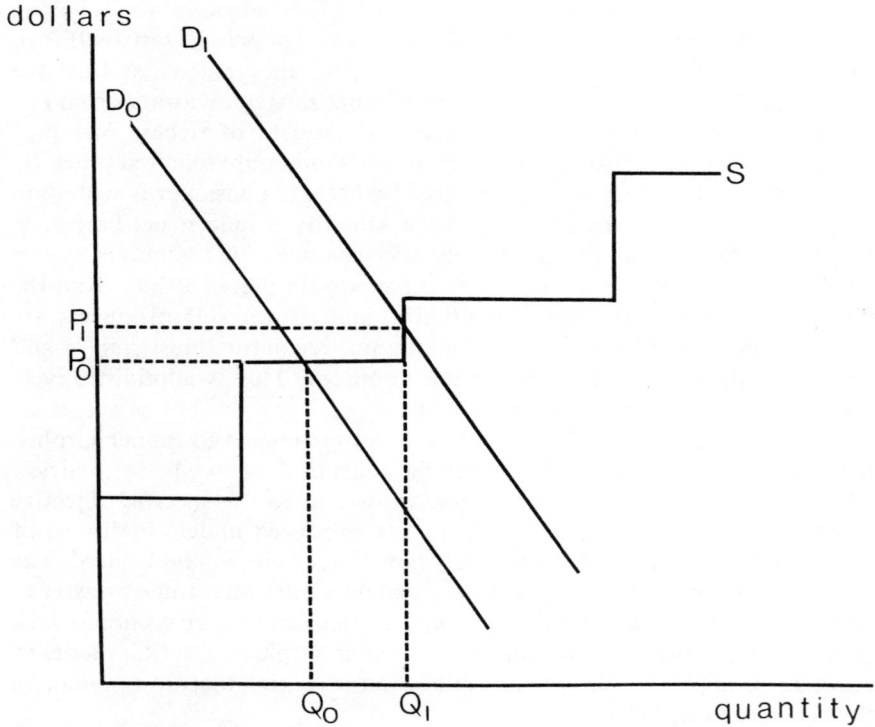

Figure 2B–4. Consumer Response to a Step-Function Rate Schedule

portion of the schedule leaves a residual consumer surplus P_1 less P_0 because Q_1 is available at a marginal price of P_0. Unless the marginal rate paid is the market clearing price, it will produce an inefficiently low or inefficiently high consumption level. As usual, too low a price means too high a consumption level, and too high a price means too low a consumption level. The multiple-rate approach means there are several different prices that might turn out to be the one paid for marginal consumption. Intersection with the rate schedule determines what is actually paid; again, it can turn out to be too high or too low.

The argument need not be repeated for production. What is involved ideally is demand curves set by regulation and the usual supply curves. Unfortunately, regulators cannot identify precisely what output will be produced first. Rents may accrue because some output is assigned to a higher price category than is warranted by its economic attractiveness, while other output is lost because its costs are underestimated and too low an allowable price is set (see Gordon 1981 for a further discussion of this case). The source of kilowatt hour 121 may be priced as if it were the millionth.

All this suggests that the public-utility tradition about how to stimulate output of natural monopolies is justifiable. So long as rates are set with the surplus collection concentrated around low levels of consumption and with a long last step for all customers equal to marginal costs of optimal output, this will be a good way to finance optimal output.

Inverting the principle, however, creates difficulties that make it less attractive. These include the problems of devising an adequate formula for allocating the surplus and the greater difficulties in insuring efficient production levels. It was observed that the allocation problem made rent taxation preferable to price control; the production problem is another reason to prefer rent taxes.

Appendix 2C:
Annuitization,
Levelization,
Inflation, and Taxes

The main text suggested that present-value analysis can handle all possible investment issues. This is true in the presence or absence of inflation, taxes on investment income, or both. However, the mathematical analysis is cumbersome, and calculations have become simple only because of the widespread availability of specialized pocket calculators. To aggravate matters, present values are not easily related to anything with which most people are familiar. Therefore, various expedients are often adopted in presenting the results in forms that intuitively are more appealing.

Understanding the nature of these expedients and how to use the data they produce is critical to this analysis. The basic simplification concepts are annuitization and levelization. *Annuities* in finance are payments of the same amount every year over some fixed period; the term comes from the insurance industry, which traditionally has offered annuities in return for an initial cash payment.

Annuitization refers to determining a constant annual payment, called the *annual annuity* for short, that is equivalent in present value to some variable income stream. A standard example is a calculation of the constant annual payment that repays an initial investment and the required interest on it. One could go a step further and calculate the present value of operating costs and determine the constant annual income that would have the same present value. Adding this figure to the constant amount sufficient to recover investment gives a measure of the constant annual income that recovers all the costs of the firm, with interest. A third step would be to compute the present value of revenues and convert that to a constant annual value, which would represent the constant revenue stream equal in present value to the actual one. The difference between this annual revenue stream and the constant annual income stream sufficient to repay costs with interest would then be an indicator of the average annual economic profit level. (These would be profits above the income needed to repay investors and are termed pure or *excess profits*.)

Levelization takes the process a step further and makes calculations per unit of output. Here several methods could be proposed for averaging actual or required income per unit of output. The technique invariably used in electric-utility analysis is to determine the constant price that must be maintained to recover investment with a constant annual output. It is also possible to calculate the constant price that must be maintained to recover an investment given a steady growing or declining output level. The first type of levelization has a drawback, in that the choice of output is arbitrary. The relevant computation will only determine the total annual revenue requirement, and the analyst must subjectively select the output level by which to divide required revenues to derive the required unit income. A simple unweighted average of cumulative output or even initial year output might be used. This introduction of an arbitrary output value makes the constant output assumption less satisfactory than considering the actual output trend.

Correctly conducted annuitization and levelization merely transform the data in a fashion that does not alter the underlying profitability analysis. The present value of receipts and the present value of revenues are simply multiplied by the same constant: the annuitization or levelization factor. Whether the critical *profitability criterion* (the present value of cost equals the present value of receipts at the margin) is satisfied can be determined using any presentation. If $NPV_C = NPV_R$, then multiplication by any constant α gives $\alpha NPV_C = \alpha NPV_R$. The transformations, particularly levelization, convert the numbers to a more understandable form. The result is greater but not full comparability. We obtain a measure of the average difference between what actually prevails and what must prevail to justify the investment, then compute the average in a fashion that is in accord with the present value principle. However, this procedure may have suppressed important details about the actual path followed to secure those revenues.

A problem is that most published uses of levelization fail to indicate clearly whether the principles outlined here have been followed. The usual purpose of such analyses is to compare the economic attractiveness of different alternative base-load plants, such as coal versus nuclear.

The most problematic shortcut in these analyses is the assumption of constant annual operating rates throughout the life of the plant. It is never clear whether or not the operating-rate assumptions implicitly incorporate the techniques sketched later for employing adjustment factors to account for variations in output. If such considerations are neglected, outside observers cannot easily determine the direction and magnitude of the error.

These impacts interact with errors in estimating actual initial investment and the rise of operating costs. These errors could either reinforce or offset the errors attributable to incorrect levelization.

What is more critical for present purposes is that, even if the calculations accurately indicate which is the cheaper technology, levelization may not adequately handle the question of whether a plant should be built in the first place, particularly for a system that employs prices that vary over the course of the year. Levelization analyses may handle inadequately these revenue variations. Given variable prices and constant unit-operating costs, the contribution per unit of output to recovery of the initial investment will differ at different points during the year. The actual receipts, therefore, will be quite different from the required levelized receipts.

Thus, discrepancies between required levelized incomes and actual incomes are likely to be substantial at any moment and may or may not average out over the course of each year so that the total annual repayments of capital are constant over time. What matters, however, is whether the incremental lifetime income due to the facility is large enough in present value to justify the investment. To determine this, the actual monetary flows must be examined.

Public-utility regulation can introduce problems by failing to set the payments equal to those necessary to recover the investment. The regulators can provide the correct amount of total income but provide inefficient timing. Assuming that the total payment is correct, that the efficient way to recover capital is in equal real installments, and that inflation occurs at an even and correctly anticipated rate incorporated into the allowable rate of return, a regulatory formula with constant nominal dollar repayments involves overpayment in earlier years offset by underpayment in later years. Since the critical assumptions are not likely to be satisfied, the actual inefficiency may be quite different.

The problems with the fixed-cost concept of simple cost-curve analysis are essentially failures to consider explicitly the annuitization and levelization process. Presumably the capital recovery requirements that are the key component of what are called *total fixed costs* are, in fact, the constant per period payments that will repay investments. This implicit annuitization works reasonably well in conventional cost analysis but is unsatisfactory for appraising the electric-power industry. Most simple textbook theories are formulated to assume away the price fluctuations that can arise in electric power. Analysis of that industry requires explicit consideration of present value.

Having seen the general nature of annuitization, levelization, and their relationship to fixed costs, it is desirable to turn to other points in investment theory, particularly the implications of real-cost changes and inflation.

Technical progress can lead to falling real (or even nominal) costs while real-cost increases can occur if the real payments to the inputs rise more sharply than input productivity. The basic conclusion is simple. Rising costs create an incentive to decrease the use of the input, and falling costs create an incentive to increase it. Of course, this is a generalization of the standard proposition in economics that cost increases reduce supply and cost decreases increase it and that when the price movements of two competing commodities change unevenly, a substitution will be made in favor of the one with the lesser rise or greater fall.

The simplest influences to treat are changes in operating costs. If costs rise, supply will immediately decrease, inspiring a reduction in investment in capacity expansion. The opposite response would naturally be produced by cost decreases. To the extent that the changes favor a given fuel, this will cause efforts to shift the fuel mix. Such shifts will take into account the tendency of rising comparative operating costs of a fuel to cause reduced use by the plants using it. In any case, capital investment and operating decisions will involve greater reliance than in the case of stable prices on fuels whose operating costs rise less rapidly or fall more rapidly than those of other fuels.

The same considerations apply to changing capital costs. Again, rises retard and declines stimulate consumption and investment, and developments more favorable to one method than another cause shifts to that method. A further consideration is whether it pays to stockpile supplies to beat the cost increases. This appears to be a problem similar to the optimal production of exhaustible resources. (This similarity originally was suggested in 1957 by Samuelson, who noted the analogy between exhaustible resource theory and the theory of stockpiling crops between harvests. (Samuelson 1966, vol. 2, pp. 946–984).

The theory of exhaustion was initially suggested by Gray (1914). In 1931 Hotelling formulated the basis of a general theory whose full implications only became recognized in the 1970s (see Gordon 1981 and Dasgupta and Heal 1979). The theory shows how efficient markets act to optimize the spacing of activity over time in such situations as mineral exploitation and storing crops between harvests.

An analogy to the general rule for optimum provision for the future seems to exist. Specifically, there are at least three benefits to earlier construction: larger scale, future operating-cost savings, and capital-cost savings. If only the last benefit is secured, we are governed by a counterpart to the simple Hotelling rule that a rise in payoff at least equal to the interest rate is required to induce hoarding of minerals. So long as investment expenses rise faster than the market rate of interest, it pays to stockpile. The process of expanding construction will be self-limiting by causing current prices to rise enough to eliminate faster rises over time. Where other benefits exist, a slower rise in plant costs will justify earlier construction.

Advocates of locating power plants near fuel sources and transmitting power rather than locating nearer customers and transporting fuel raise the argument that the combined effect of escalation in real capital and operation costs causes transmission to be more attractive. The cost of the initial investment is a higher portion of the present value of transmission than of transportation. By definition, cost escalation only affects cash outlays. Thus, only operating and deferred investment costs are influenced, but initial investment is not. A higher role of initial investment in costs means that less cost will be subject to escalation. A similar benefit would be produced if a construction speedup allowed taking advantage of economies of scale.

More generally, changes in the same direction of capital and operating costs reinforce the separate effects on output and investment. Mix effects will depend on which fuels are most heavily affected. Similarly, where movements are in the opposite direction, the only prediction is that the relative role of the inputs with falling costs will improve. The effects on output, investment, and fuel mix will depend on the circumstances.

Given the characteristics of the available technologies, the actual investments that have been made to adopt a mix of these technologies, and the numerous types of changes that affect costs, electric-utility cost functions are likely to shift frequently and in complex ways.

A final concern is deriving a specific technique to treat inflation. It is widely argued that the same results will be produced in both real and nominal analyses. Nominal analysis involves adjusting both the real-income expenditure stream and the present-worth factors applied to it by inflation adjustment factors that cancel each other out. We multiply each component of the real-income stream by $(1 + s)^t$, where s is the rate of inflation per year and t is the number of years, but also multiply the discounting factor by $(1 + s)^t$.

Conversely, we would use a real-discount factor and insure comparability of income flows expressed in nominal terms by converting them to real terms by dividing by $(1 + s)^t$.

While this principle is valid, existing tax laws are such that attaining the required real income involves complexities that require special examination. A major analytic issue is the problem of year-to-year variations in the inflation rate. This issue and the related one of year-to-year variations in real required rates of return are simpler to resolve than tax problems. Any method of adjusting inflation or rate variation based on a weighted average will lead to undercharging in years of above-average levels of the combined real-rate and inflation-adjustment factor and overcharging in below-average years.

The tax problem arises because the tax laws artificially divide the repayments to capital into several components, each of which is treated differently. Specifically, one portion of the payment cumulatively limited under existing laws to the nominal initial cost of the investment is called *depreciation;* it is free from taxation. The remainder can be called an expense and escape taxation on the funds from bonds or other fixed-value loans. However, if the income is a return on common or preferred stock or the individual investor's own money, a tax is imposed. Therefore, to adjust fully for inflation, earnings must be high enough to compensate for the taxation on part of the flows.

An alternative approach would be to change the method of depreciation so annual depreciation charges equaled the inflation-adjusted amount of repayment received. Again assuming that capital recovery occurred in equal annual real installments, the depreciation factor would rise over time since equal annual real payments mean rising real repayments, and inflation produces an additional rise in nominal amounts. The greater the extent to which the tax laws fail to insure the untaxed recovery of the initial real investment, the more before-tax income must be raised to compensate for a given inflation rate.

In further examination of investment analysis, a critical point is that analyzing a specific case has become much simpler than treating the general problem. The formulas used in financial analysis involve nonlinearities that complicate the analytical derivation of the critical properties. However, numerical results are easily calculated (see Appendix 7C for examples). The process is eased if, as is done here, a continuous time approach is employed. This simply means that exponential functions of the form e^{xt} are used instead of the usual $(1 + y)^t$ type of discrete time formula. (See Allen 1938 or Gordon 1981 for a discussion of the relationship between continuous and discrete time analysis.) Cumulative present worth then becomes an integral rather than a sum, and the properties of such integrals can be used to provide analytic solutions for special cases; most simply for those in which all changes are exponential. In contrast, the rise of electronic calculators means that actual computations can be made more quickly using the discrete-time approach.

The basic annuity formula interrelates the initial payment, the annual repayments, time, and the prevailing interest rate. Given any three elements, the fourth can be calculated. Annuitization determines the annuity equivalent in present worth to an uneven income stream.

The basic consideration is that by the nature of such transactions, the present value of the annual net cash inflow $F(t)$ will cumulate to equal what was initially paid, $I(0)$. At an interest rate r and years of repayment T, this would be represented as:

$$I(0) = \int_0^T Fe^{-rt}dt = F\frac{(1 - e^{-rT})}{r} \tag{2C.1}$$

The term by which F is multiplied may be denoted as A_{rt} and represents the present value of a \$1 per year repayment at interest rate r and repayment duration T. The reciprocal of A_{rt} then gives the amount per year required to repay a \$1 loan, given r and T.

Although the basic properties of this equation are well known to financial analysts, it is desirable to recall them here in detail to ease the subsequent discussion.

e^{-rT} decreases with increases in T, so $1 - e^{-rT}$ increases with T. Thus, a given F implies that I will be larger if T is longer; continuation of income makes it more valuable, as expected. Conversely, for a given I, a lower F is acceptable if T is longer; the annual repayments are less if the repayment period is longer. It is more directly apparent that raising either I or F raises the value of the other. The effect of interest-rate changes is not as apparent since r appears in both the numerator and denominator of A. The basic principle is that the interest rate is the gain to lenders. Given this principle, a higher interest rate equivalently implies that given initial payment produces higher repayments or that less needs to be paid initially to produce a given repayment. Thus, A falls with r. This can be proved by calculating the derivative of A with respect to r; the differentiation is tedious but straight-forward.

These properties can be used to explain the impact of exponential growth or decline in various elements of cash flow. The analysis can be applied to gross revenues, costs, or their difference. In any case, the total can be decomposed into the quantity and the per-unit value; changes in the total can be in either direction, as can the unit value of the output.

To be more concrete, this discussion relates to revenues decomposed into the product of price and quantity. Price is assumed to grow, quantity is assumed to decline, but the product can either rise or fall. The orientation on revenue has more profound implications than the assumptions about the direction of price and output. Examining the algebra shows that these sign conventions about rates do not matter. However, care must be taken to recall that the implications of rises or falls in gross or net cash inflows are different from changes in the same direction in costs. A higher cost makes the investment less valuable to lenders; a higher revenue or net makes the investment more valuable.

We might describe a revenue stream as the product of a growth in price $P(t) = P(0)e^{st}$ and a falling output $Q(t) = Q(0)e^{-vt}$. Then the present worth of the flow at any time would be $P(0)Q(0)e^{st}e^{-vt}e^{-rt} = P(0)Q(0)e^{(s-v-r)t} = P(0)Q(0)e^{-wt}$, where $w = -(s-v-r)$. Then this case involves an integral in which a single factor w shows the combined effect of price increases, output declines, and present value factors on the cumulative present value.

This shows that price and output decline have mathematical effects equivalent to interest-rate increases, and the prior conclusions about interest-rate differences can be extended to show the implications of price growth and output decline. Three ranges of possibilities should be noted. The first is when $s < v$ and $w > r$: an output decline faster than a price rise is equivalent to a higher interest rate. The effect of $s < v$ is declining revenue over time. This implies that with everything else being equal, a declining revenue stream is less valuable than a constant one. The second case is when $s > v$, which generally means that $w < r$ and thus is equivalent in effect on present worth to the effects of lower interest rates; rising revenue is more valuable than constant revenue.

While these two cases fully explain the critical points, an important subdivision of the second case should be recognized. If s is sufficiently large (or more generally if v actually rises while s also rises to sufficient degree), $-w$ may be a positive number. Formula A still produces the correct calculation, but normally when $-w$ is positive, $-w = (-1)(w)$ would be shown in the formula. Formula A then becomes $e^{w'T} - 1/w'$, where $-w$ is simply rewritten as w' to make explicit that positive numbers now appear in A. This shift is a continuation of the process by which faster revenue growth makes an investment more attractive to the range in which present worths rise over time. The only special problem associated with this case is that if T were infinite, present worth would also be infinite.

Given these manipulations, it is possible to derive numerous conclusions about levelizations. The most basic point is that correctly conducted annuitization or levelization is a transformation of present values that does not affect the basic results. Correctness was defined as multiplying everything by the same constant. The prior discussion suggested that many different constants could be adopted. Annuitization always has only one meaning: the present worth of any stream is calculated and divided by the A that corresponds to receiving that present worth in equal annual installments. Levelization can be conducted using factors that make various assumptions about w. Replacing r with w thus can represent a family of levelization factors applied to arbitrary present worths. Alternatively, the formula can be interpreted as illustrating the effect of alternative actual patterns on present worth and showing the implications for present worth of errors in predicting the actual pattern. Incorrect levelization always means incorrect calculation of the actual present worth. The generalized version of A using a value of w such that $v = 0$ can be used to obtain the correct levelizing factor for any arbitrary Q (or more critically in practice, the correct Q for a given A).

Now we examine inflation. By definition, inflation represents a deterioration of the purchasing power of money. This has critical effects on income streams. To maintain a constant real income, actual income must grow with the rate of inflation. By the same line of reasoning, an earnings stream that is constant in nominal terms will decline steadily in real value as inflation proceeds. However, the principles already outlined can be used to show that there is a constant nominal stream equal in present value to any constant real stream. The principle, stated earlier, that a larger interest rate implies a larger required repayment applies to inflation that naturally requires a constant nominal repayment that exceeds the constant real repayment. Thus, the constant real repayment starts at a lower initial value and grows at a constant rate in nominal terms. An equivalent constant nominal income starts at a higher level and steadily declines in real value.

Critics of regulatory practices (for example, see Myers 1979) have argued that, as a result, constant nominal annuity formulas for recovery of capital lead to overpayment in early years and underpayment in later years. The assertion involves the implicit assumptions that a constant real annuity is the proper way to recover investment and that regulators select a nominal annuity equivalent in present value to the proper real annuity. Where the facility generates a declining real inflow of the proper magnitude (namely, equal to the inflation rate), a nominal annuity would be the appropriate formula. This would be an unreasonable coincidence to expect, but it does suggest that the closer the revenue decline rate corresponds to the inflation rate, the less error the formula produces; that real revenue declines faster than the inflation rate causes the error to be one of undercollection in the early years. Reality is complicated by the effects of belated or inadequate compensation for inflation.

Even leaving aside the broader issues associated with the overall effects of taxation, its introduction as practiced is a major complication in the analysis. The effect of taxes is generally to create a difference (namely, the amount of tax collected) between the payments made by consumers and the receipts by producers. Were taxes levied on gross income to capital or on some constant fraction of gross income, the inflation of capital costs to account for taxes would require only a simple multiplication.

Thus, if L is total taxes, y required gross receipts, $x(t)$ required net, γ the tax rate, and α the portion of y to which γ applies, then $y = x + L = x + \gamma\alpha y$; $(1 - \gamma\alpha)y = x$; $y = x/1 - \alpha\gamma$. If $\alpha = 1$, $y = x/1 - \gamma$.

Actual rules for accounting taxes destroy this simplicity by failing to decompose the taxes in the required fashion. The only case where the rules clearly are partially satisfied is if $x(t)$ is constant in nominal terms and the depreciation allowance $D(t)$ is constant in nominal terms and is applied over the actual useful life.

$$x(t) = \bar{x} \tag{2C.2}$$

$$D(t) = \bar{D} = \beta\bar{x} \tag{2C.3}$$

$$y = \bar{x} + t(y - \beta\bar{x}) \tag{2C.4}$$

$$y = \bar{x} - t\beta\bar{x} + ty \tag{2C.5}$$

$$y - ty = (1 - t\beta)\bar{x} \tag{2C.6}$$

$$y = \frac{(1 - t\beta)\bar{x}}{(1 - t)} \tag{2C.7}$$

An important difference arises between the first formula that sets the untaxed proportion as a constant fraction of the total required income, and the second formula that relates the untaxed portion to a depreciation schedule. With higher interest rates, interest is higher and capital recovery is a lower portion of the required flows. Thus, β in the second formula will be lower with higher interest rates, while in the first formula α can be set independently of the interest rate.

If the rules do not insure a smooth relationship between before-tax and after-tax income, the analysis becomes cumbersome. A smoothly growing before-tax yield will grow unevenly after tax, or uneven before-tax growth is needed to secure an even after-tax flow. For example, if the untaxed portion of income is a constant amount, it becomes a rising fraction of a falling required income stream and a falling fraction of a rising required income stream. The gross flow then must decline less rapidly or rise more rapidly than the net. Comparable statements could be made about other types of shifts in the relationship between the required income and the portion not subject to tax. Proper pricing formulas thus must somehow factor in the adjustment required because of these effects of the tax laws.

Inflation interacts with tax procedures principally by creating the need for nominal receipts to be greater, the larger the rate of inflation. Tax rules, however, prevent the untaxed portion from rising with inflation, thus forcing the gross to grow more rapidly than the rate of inflation to offset the implicit tax increase.

Therefore, in conducting financial analysis in inflationary periods, the basic difficulty of determining the required rate of return is complicated by difficulties in calculating the appropriate before-tax returns that will yield the required net. The relevant amount will be a function of the required rate of return, capital structure, pattern with which the investments produce yields, tax treatment of depreciation, regulatory treatment of depreciation, other tax provisions, and the rate of inflation.

Appendix 2D:
The Required-Selling-
Price Problem—
Analysis and Examples

The main text noted that levelized prices differ from selling prices when prices change with demand fluctuations. Prices above levelized costs occur when prices rise; thus, lower prices are required during lower-demand, lower-price periods. The analytic procedure used here is to move backward to the required off-peak prices from a peak price that is calculated by assuming a constant return-to-scale peaking technology. Separate technologies are assumed to exist off-peak, subject to constant returns to scale.

The analysis is further simplified by assuming a limited number of prevailing demand levels that occur with fixed, predictable frequencies. Four levels are considered. Instead of the utilization rates used in conventional levelization models, I use reserve factors, which can be set at different levels for different plant types. In the absence of forced outages, these reserve rates are the reciprocals of the average operability factor of the plant as a proportion of *needed operability* (that is, the number of hours that plants of a given type must operate). The ratio would be set higher to cover forced outages.

Higher loads are met by the continued operation of plants designed to meet a persistent level of demand, plus plants designed specifically to meet a higher level of demand. In each of the four periods, we can look at either the demand or the difference in demand over the next lower level. In determining the needed amount of capacity of a given type, it is the increments that count. Base-load plants are presumed to operate year-round to meet the demand level Q_B (in kilowatts) that prevails year-round. If the next higher period is called low-intermediate demand and is at a level Q_L, the units designed for low-intermediate use, then, only are needed to meet the *increase* in demand from the low-demand period. These low-intermediate units operate when demand is at or above the low-intermediate level. Similar arguments prevail for the other two categories: high-intermediate and peak demand.

Thus, there is a distinction between hours of operation and hours at which a given demand level persists and between the demand level Q_i and its difference between that of a lower period. For costing, it is the incremental demand that counts, since each capacity type is built to serve the demand increment. Similarly, to obtain the actual required off-peak prices, it is the duration of each of the four demand levels that matters. The total operation level is only relevant in calculating conventional levelized costs.

The other point to note is that levelization usually involves dividing annual costs by the utilization factor times 8,760 (the number of hours in a non–leap year). The equivalent idea is used that, to generate base load with plants that operate at, say, .60 percent factors, capacity 1.67 times base-load levels are required. Similarly, a nonbase period of, for example, 500 hours duration served by plants that can only operate 400 hours a year requires 500/400 = 1.25 times the incremental load in capacity.

This is not necessarily a fully correct description of how a system would operate even without forced outages and demand uncertainties. Some base or intermediate load might be met by using plants designed only for lower duration operation. However, this really means that base-load periods are those when only base-loaded plants operate. Low supply as well as low demand could lead to use of higher-cost units. If the calculations relate to the weighted average of output levels during the relevant time periods, any need to substitute higher-cost equipment will automatically be treated correctly.

Analysis of the peak gives its contribution to recovery of all capital types. Capacity installed to cover the high-intermediate-demand level can recover any remaining costs only in the period where demand is at the high-intermediate level. Low-intermediate-demand-serving equipment can recover income in peak, high-intermediate, and low-intermediate periods. The base-load plants can recover income in all periods. However, only 100 percent recovery is needed, and a price high enough to insure repayment of the more expensive unit's capital costs in a higher demand period can lead to rents for lower-cost units. Once these incomes accumulate to at least the required annual payments, no further charges are needed.

The analysis involves basic assumptions that collectively imply that the price of peak power equals levelized costs of owning and operating peaking units. This allows determination of what each nonpeaking unit earns during the peak. Subtracting the income for high-intermediate-demand plants from total costs of such plants gives the required capital charge and price at the high-intermediate output level, and this price in turn allows calculation of the contribution to recovering the capital costs of units that serve base or low-intermediate demand. From the combined incomes of peak and high-intermediate demands, the required income at the low-intermediate-demand level can be calculated. This gives the income for base plants in the low-intermediate-demand period, and this plus the income in the peak and high-intermediate-demand periods are subtracted to determine the remaining amount required.

The notation used to treat this is as follows.
Subscripts:

B base

L low intermediate

H high intermediate

T peak

i index of plant type

j index of time period

α_i duration in hours of each demand level

β_i number of hours per year a plant type operates (for example, $\beta_B = \alpha_B + \alpha_L + \alpha_H + \alpha_T$)

Q_j demand in kilowatts in period j

P_i levelized price of capacity type i

K_i unit cost for plant type i

μ_i capacity multiplication factor for plant type i

C_i running cost of plant type i

r annual charge rate assumed identical for all plant types (that is, they are equally long lived).

Now let:

$$\Delta Q_B = Q_B \tag{2D.1}$$

$$\Delta Q_L = Q_L - Q_B \tag{2D.2}$$

$$\Delta Q_H = Q_H - Q_L \tag{2D.3}$$

$$\Delta Q_T = Q_T - Q_H \tag{2D.4}$$

These increments are critical, since, as noted, nonbase capacity is used to cover increments over base levels. The respective capacity requirements and total annual costs are then:

$$\mu_i \Delta Q_i \tag{2D.5}$$

(Capacity is the demand level times the excess capacity factor, as explained previously.)

$$r\mu_i \Delta Q_i K_i \tag{2D.6}$$

The cost per kilowatt of load is $r\mu_i K_i$. The usual levelized cost is:

$$P_i = C_i + \frac{r_i \mu_i K_i}{\beta_i} \tag{2D.7}$$

for peaking units $\beta_T = \alpha_T$ and $P_T = P_T'$.

The total contribution of the peak to recovery of capital costs of other plant types is then:

$$\alpha_T \Delta Q_i (P_T - C_i). \tag{2D.8}$$

The required price at the high-intermediate level is C_H only when $\alpha_T \Delta Q_H (P_T - C_H) \geq r\mu_H \Delta Q_H K_H$. The same argument applies to the prices at lower Q_i levels. Otherwise:

$$C_H + \frac{r\mu_H \Delta Q_H K_H - \alpha_T \Delta Q_H (P_T - C_H)}{\alpha_H \Delta Q_H} = C_H + \frac{[r\mu_H K_H - \alpha_T (P_T - C_H)]}{\alpha_H} \tag{2D.9}$$

Analogously, at the low-intermediate level:

$$P'_L = C_H + \frac{1}{\alpha_L} [\mu_L r K_L - \alpha_T (P_T - C_L) - \alpha_H (P'_H - C_L)] \tag{2D.10}$$

and at the base:

$$P'_B = C_B + \frac{1}{\alpha_B} [\mu_B r K_B - \alpha_T (P_T - C_B) - \alpha_H (P'_H - C_B) -$$

$$\alpha_L (P'_L - C_B)] \tag{2D.11}$$

It should be noted that since constant returns to scale prevail, the unit costs are independent of Q_i, which cancels out of the equations.

The equations show that the extent to which a higher-demand period contributes to recovery of investment of plants also operating in lower-demand periods will depend on the duration of α_i, the difference in operating costs among technologies, and the difference in capital costs.

The longer the duration of a high-demand period and the bigger the gap between prices in that period and the operating cost of an option, the more will be the absolute amount of capital recovery. However, the higher the required capital recovery, the less a given yield in a higher-demand period will suffice to repay the investment.

The data presented in appendix 7C suggests that the economics of electric power in the 1980s could differ greatly. At one extreme, the optimum mix could be coal-fired plants serving all loads except short-lived surges, which occur 10 percent or less of the time. Alternatively, nuclear power might be the base-load unit; coal, the low-intermediate unit; combined cycle, the high-intermediate unit; and gas turbines, the peaking unit.

One possible pattern is that the peak and high-intermediate periods would contribute most, if not all, of the required income. The difference in annual capital costs and unit operating costs among base, low-intermediate, and high-intermediate plants would be small if they were all coal fired. Thus, prices in the peak and high-intermediate periods sufficient to recover the cost of high-intermediate load plants would also largely recover the similar capital costs of base or low-intermediate load plants. Prices at lower-demand periods would be close to operating costs. It can be shown that the costs are very sensitive to the assumptions adopted. In short, the analysis here identifies further problems in estimating the optimum pattern in electric power.

Appendix 2E:
On the Optimal
Selection and Use
of Inflexible Prices

Many prices do not fluctuate with variations in short-run supply, and the existence of such rigidities has long been recognized in a literature too vast to cite here. Concern extends to price rigidities throughout the economy. The literature on peak-load pricing contains many admissions that totally flexible prices may be too expensive to impose, given the metering and other administrative costs. Unfortunately, analysis of the problem seems to stop at this point. No literature exists on determining the optimal system. Neither how rigid prices should be set nor to whom they should apply seems to have been analyzed.

The application argument is far simpler to resolve. The discussion of the main text indicated the costs and benefits of any system of prices that fails to adjust fully to changing demand-and-supply conditions and indicated that a more flexible pricing system is efficient if its administration costs less than the inefficiencies eliminated.

Numerous issues must be resolved in handling the optimization process. First, while the inefficiency problems introduced by any method of presetting prices are the same, the causes of inefficiency and probably the cures are quite different. A price that is unchanged between meter readings (a rigid price) guarantees inefficiency in production no matter how well demand can be forecast. The inefficiencies arise because no response is taken to demand fluctuations. However, inefficiency arises with preset time-of-use rates only because of forecasting errors. Perfect foresight means that the right time of use rate could be preset. Another consideration is the basic difference between excess demand and excess supply. Consumers cannot be forced to buy more than they desire at existing prices but can be prevented from securing all that is demanded. Systematic or random load shedding can be used to prevent the satisfaction of all or some demand. A final concern is that efficiency appraisals must include the use of an existing system and the choice of an efficient investment pattern for the system.

The first case to 'analyze is that of the inefficiencies of rigid prices employing the policy of supplying all demands. (This has been standard electric-utility practice.) Then the role of load shedding can be considered, and discussion can turn to inefficiency with preset spot prices.

Instinct suggests that with preset prices and without load shedding, the price should be somewhere between the highest and the lowest price that would have been charged by the industry were prices flexible (and the supply curve was the one that actually prevailed). Examination of the effect of an inefficient price confirms intuition. The inefficiency at any moment is an increasing function of the deviation of the preset price from the price that equates marginal production cost to price.

This relationship is graphed in figures 2E–1 and 2E–2. The first figure treats the excess of marginal cost over price when the price charged falls below the efficient price P_E and the quantity demanded is provided. As output rises from its efficient level Q_E, and excess cost occurs and rises steadily as costs rise and the price falls. Thus, at a price P_F, the marginal excess of cost over price is CE (CD less DE) and the total loss is BCE. Lowering the price raises the marginal loss to FH and the total to BFH. Similarly, a price above market clearing levels produces a loss that grows as the price is raised. Inefficiency grows as prices are moved above or below the optimal flexible price. (In figure 2E–2, the rise is from CE to FH for the marginal loss and from DCE to DFH for the total.)

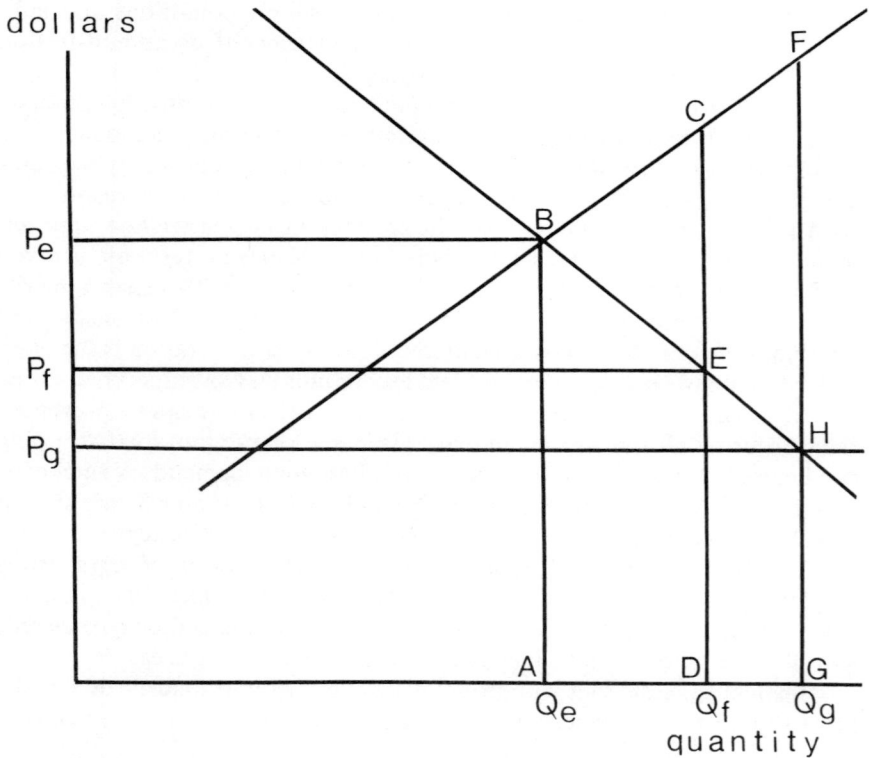

Figure 2E–1. Production Inefficiency with Too Low a Rigid Price

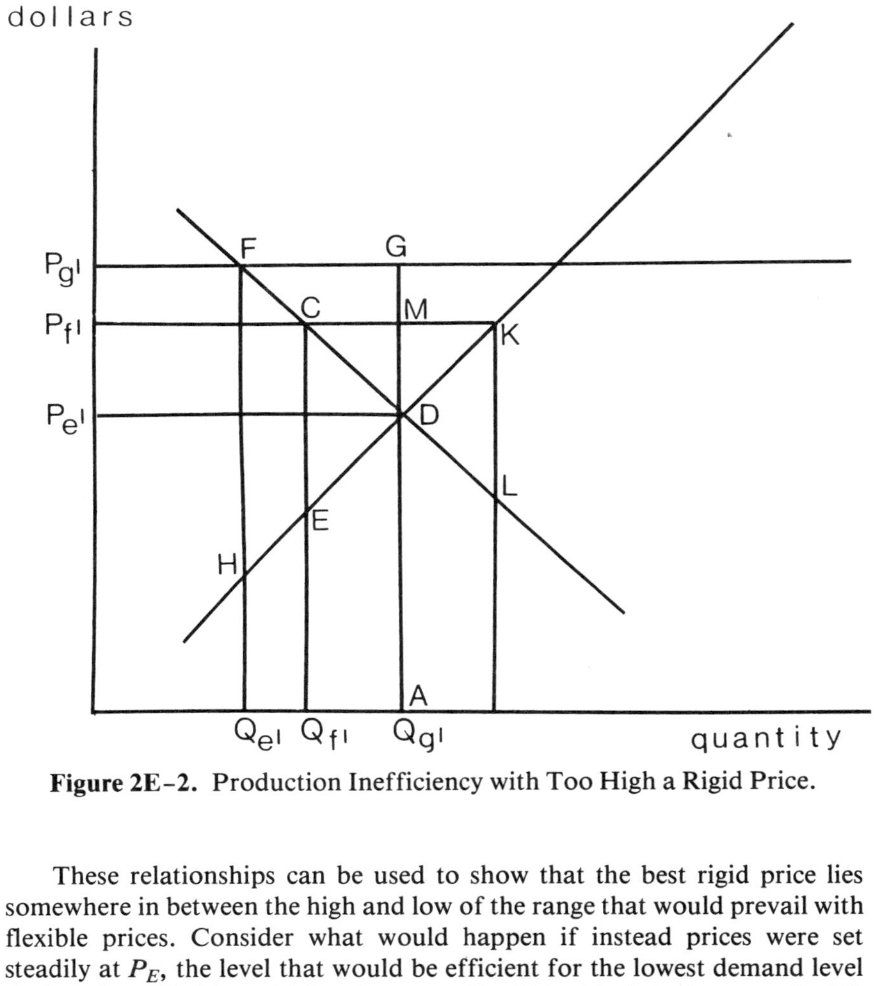

Figure 2E-2. Production Inefficiency with Too High a Rigid Price.

These relationships can be used to show that the best rigid price lies somewhere in between the high and low of the range that would prevail with flexible prices. Consider what would happen if instead prices were set steadily at P_E, the level that would be efficient for the lowest demand level during the period for which prices were fixed. In this situation, zero inefficiency would occur only in the subperiod of low demand. In every other subperiod, costs would exceed price. A still lower price would aggravate the inefficiency by increasing it in subperiods of higher demand and creating inefficiency in the low-demand period.

However, raising prices reduces inefficiency. There is zero inefficiency in the low-demand period and successively higher inefficiency for each higher-demand level. Thus, in figure 2E-2, if prices are set at $P_{E'}$, zero loss occurs with the demand shown. If demand rose to a level (not explicitly shown) that intersected with supply at K but prices remained constant, a loss of KL would occur. Raising the price would lower the loss given the new demand but create losses when the lower demand occurred. $P_{F'}$, would produce zero loss with the higher demand but raise the loss given the lower demand to CE.

Established principles of economic theory suggest that readjustment should proceed until marginal costs equal marginal benefits. Raising the fixed price lowers inefficiency in every period in which the old and new fixed prices are too low and raises inefficiency in periods in which the old and new prices are too high. The process of raising prices, moreover, shifts some periods from being ones of too-low prices to being ones of too-high prices. As prices rise from the lowest level considered (or fall from the highest level that is efficient for the highest demand in any subperiod), the nature of the inefficiency changes. There will be some intermediate demand level at which the inefficiency is smallest, but inefficiency will be greater for demands that are both higher and lower than the critical intermediate level.

In any case, the benefits of raising the fixed price are all the reductions in inefficiency in periods of underpricing. The costs are all the rises in inefficiency in periods of overpricing. An increase is justified if the benefits exceed the costs. Raising prices from the lowest possible levels is desirable for the reasons already given. The further discussion of the effects of rises leads to concluding the familiar diminishing-payoff principle limits the optimum extent of price increases. Each price increase lowers benefits and raises costs. The exact intermediate price selected will depend on demand-and-supply elasticities and the duration of different demands. The taxonomy of possible outcomes does not seem worth pursuing. What is interesting is just what else the optimal inefficiency rule implies, particularly for investment.

The rule suggests two other economic models involving departures from equality of prices and marginal production costs. The first is the theory of optimal intervention as developed by Corden (1974). The other is the user cost of the pure theory of exhaustion. This cost is the excess of price over marginal production costs to account for exhaustion. The inefficiency cost of rigid prices has a critical difference from the costs in other models. The other cases involve changes that can affect only two variables, and very simple equalities prevail. In the simple pure theory of exhaustion, the present value of the price-marginal cost gap is equated among periods. With efficient rigid prices, the gap between price and marginal cost cannot be equal in every period.

The sum of the gap reductions is equated with the sum of gap increases. Thus, the cost is more complex than an exhaustion cost. However, the cost is measurable and should be internalized by the firms if efficiency is to be attained.

Specifically, we want our market mechanism to insure, first, that given any arbitrary short-run supply, the efficient rigid price is selected; and second, that an efficient level of investment, that is, one that gives the optimal short-run supply, is chosen. It can be further asked what can be said about the relationship of the short-run supply curve to that selected under flexible pricing.

The critical problem is to show how the combined producer-consumer losses can be expressed properly by the separate actions of buyers and sellers. To examine whether efficient markets exist, it is essential to specify the explicit market processes that must emerge. The institutional constraint that demands must be satisfied implies that all adaptations to inefficient prices come from supply adjustments that the suppliers would prefer not to make. Specifically, suppliers must be dissuaded from producing more than is demanded when the fixed price is inefficiently high and persuaded to produce more than they desire when the fixed price is inefficiently low.

A standard method for discouraging production is to impose charges, such as taxes, and a standard method for encouraging production is a subsidy. These approaches are not only relevant here, but the required tax and subsidy levels are precisely the ones that we desire them to be. The tax that will reduce output to the quantity demanded when prices are too high is the excess of price over marginal cost. The required subsidy is the excess of marginal cost over price. The income from production limitation taxes could finance the subsidy on extra output. Thus, the balancing actually is guided by the social costs and benefits of mispricing. Moreover, imbalances between tax income and subsidy needs have the desired effects. Consider what happens when the fixed price is lower than the optimal fixed price. The subsidy needs will be higher than can be financed by the tax, and this will put an upward pressure on prices. Conversely, with too high a fixed price too much is available for subsidy, and prices are pushed downward. The charge-subsidy system alternatively could be operated by middlemen who take advantage of the desires of producers to sell more than can be marketed and of the desires of consumers to buy more than can be produced or occur through integrated firms that tax and subsidize themselves.

The final concern in analyzing this case is the effect of price rigidity on investment. Economic inefficiency usually implies higher costs and less output and investment. However, rigid prices involve the peculiarity that a commitment is made to cover demands that would have been discouraged by flexible prices. Analysis must determine whether this investment-stimulating effect predominates.

The complexities can be traced by starting with a simple case with assumptions designed to make the need to meet peak demands a particularly important influence on the investment decision. Let us assume there are only two available technologies and both are subject to constant returns to scale but involve fixed input coefficients. One technology involves higher capital output ratios than the other. It may be assumed further that the industry is in some sense so flexible that the optimal amount of investment is always maintained. Finally, let us deal with a case in which the demand fluctuations consist only of an occasional rise of a fixed duration above the base level. The duration must be such that the lower capital using technology is cheaper for meeting peak-demand increments and the more capital using technology is better for the base. This model is a simplified version of the model in appendix 2D where we now only have two demand periods.

The analysis in appendix 2D combined with this analysis shows that the result of maintaining a rigid price is simply more investment in peaking capacity than in the flexible-price case. The argument is that the rigid-price strategy involves necessarily meeting demand that would not be met with flexible prices. Moreover, the only critical special assumption is that of fixed input coefficients.

Before examining the effect of the ability to vary input coefficients, the effect of rigid prices on profits must be examined. When the rigid price charged consumers is above the efficient price, the necessity to impose charges to restrict output places the realization after the charge below the optimal price. However, subsidy of output in high-demand periods raises profits since a higher price is paid on a higher output. More critically, the subsidy is financed from charges on both consumption and production in low-demand periods. If enough of the income comes from consumption, the profit gain in high-demand periods could exceed the loss in low-demand periods. What is involved here is that the output restriction required during low-demand periods can and normally will raise the income to the production coordinators. The key consideration is that maintenance requires the same action and, therefore, produces the same effect as attempting monopolization; output is restricted below the efficient level and profits rise if the restriction is not too great.

In any case, the direction of profit change in the rigid-price case is not clear. Where profits rise, this reenforces the effects of meeting higher demands in stimulating investment. Where profits fall, this discourages investment. Thus, it is not determinant a priori whether limiting output raises or lowers investment. However, investment is more likely to rise since a profit decline and a high degree of substitutability of inputs would be required to produce a net decline in investment.

Removing the assumption that all demand will be met does not greatly complicate the argument. Load shedding, when excess demand prevails, potentially reduces the cost of rigid prices. The cost when demands are actually served has already been noted. The loss to load shedding is the consumer's surplus lost.

Weitzman's 1974 application of the duality principle to show that there are quantity limitations equivalent to price signals applies to ideal systems of load shedding. We could use a system of perfect load shedding to reduce consumption to the level that can be served efficiently with existing facilities. In this case, no short-run efficiency losses occur during periods of high demand; however, costs may be incurred in imposing load shedding.

In the absence of costs of load shedding, the optimal short-run price would be one in which excess supply never occurred. By assumption, enduring excess demand is costless to the utility while providing excess supply is costly. Thus, it pays to eliminate all excess supplies. A long-run financing problem would arise but since the case is unrealistic, its analysis is unnecessary.

The interesting case is where there are costs of load shedding. Such costs include the administrative costs and losses because no actual load-shedding system can confine cutoffs to low-valued consumption. Where the costs are higher than simply meeting demands, the prior model will apply. The application of load shedding occurs when it costs less than meeting all demands. The optimum level of load shedding, moreover, can range between zero and the entire excess demand at the present price. Again, the system works by lessening the use of a higher rigid price as a device for limiting consumption and thus leads to a lower fixed price than would prevail if all demands were met.

The argument can be extended directly to analysis of more general systems in which rigid prices coexist with preset time-variable prices, and spot prices. In such a system, as many as six demand types would exist: one for each combination of pricing method and the presence or absence of load-shedding possibilities.

The coexistence of these systems means that different sources and effects of inefficiency can be at work simultaneously. Rigid pricing creates inefficiency because of a deliberate decision to ignore demand fluctuations even if they can be foreseen perfectly. The inefficiency of preset time-variable or spot prices comes only from any errors in price forecasting. These inefficiencies would be expected to be smaller than those with rigid prices, and spot prices should be more efficient than preset ones. Unless prices are totally unpredictable (which is an inappropriate assumption), presetting will get prices nearer their optimal level than rigid prices. Spot prices are based on even better information and surely will further reduce mispricing.

A further consideration is that, in general, while the magnitude of the error from different pricing systems can be compared, the direction of error in any time period is not necessarily the same. Every possible combination could occur. A fixed price clearly would be too low when demand is high. However, the preset flexible price and even the spot price could be too high. Demand might be higher but not by as much as predicted. A customer could unexpectedly drop its spot demand. Thus, pricing errors under one system might either compensate for or reenforce errors produced by another system.

Appendix 2F:
Efficiency, Equity,
and Public Policy

Economic theory recognizes that public policy should be concerned with equity and efficiency. *Equity* refers to the socially desirable sharing of income. *Efficiency* means attaining the occurrence of every transaction that is profitable to society because the marginal benefit exceeds the marginal cost. Economic theory has a great deal more to say about efficiency than about equity. This reflects basic differences in the analytic nature of the two issues and does not necessarily imply any view about their practical importance. Equity involves resolving subjective issues about who is deserving, but more concrete rules can be provided about efficiency.

Identification of equity effects and their correction can be left to those more competent to treat them. However, efforts to regulate markets to improve equity have been unsuccessful and often harmful. Economists are as divided as the rest of society about the extent to which income should be redistributed. Considerably more agreement exists about the best methods for effecting the redistributions that society deems desirable.

Many economists feel that redistribution of income should be conducted separately from the regulation of individual industries. To be sure, the equity effects of the intervention cannot be ignored, but the proper response is to alter the amount of direct aid provided. Some observers would add that where consumers or producers receive windfalls from a policy change, taxes on these windfalls would be appropriate (see appendix 2B).

Observers of efforts to improve equity by regulating individual markets conclude that the drawbacks are so great that they frequently offset benefits. By definition, equity-based intervention starts with a deliberate decision to reduce efficiency in the hope of improving equity. Unfortunately, the initial sacrifice of efficiency in the regulated industry is only the first loss. Further costs arise in administering the controls, which can become quite expensive. Additional costs often arise in administering policies designed to lessen the inefficiencies caused by the initial policies (such as the fuel-shifting efforts discussed later). There are dangers that the supplemental policies will be so defective that they actually increase inefficiency. Further costs arise from inappropriate transfers. Efforts to keep prices down in the interest of equity indiscriminately aid all consumers of the good. If the good is widely used, all of society shares in the transfer of income, not just those segments deemed most deserving.

The problem is aggravated by the tendency, particularly in energy policy, to divert substantial amounts of aid to persons many observers would consider undeserving. In particular, a "small" business bias has long existed. Policymakers generally define *small* as smaller than the giant companies. Quite often the beneficiary is a multimillion-dollar corporation closely owned by a millionaire far less deserving than the average stockholder of an even larger oil company and thus probably even less deserving than an electric-utility stockholder. Moreover, as Bork (1978, p. 54) notes, consumers who lose from the protection are generally smaller than small businesses.

Further problems arise when examining who shares in the redistribution and efficiency losses. The presumption often made by those who impose controls in the name of equity is that the losers are the owners of resources that have appreciated in value and that these resources owners are undeserving. Such reasoning has several defects. A primary concern is who will suffer most from the inefficiencies created. To the extent that the status quo is protected, it will be the struggling poor that lose most because they must endure the effects of lower efficiency.

Moreover, the desirability of transferring windfall profits by regulation is questionable. At the very least, there are easier-to-administer redistribution policies that have less deleterious effects on efficiency. In particular, the major role of federal and state governments as the owners of natural resources and the tendency to tax heavily private incomes from such resources and other sources of windfalls insure that transfers can be effected without regulation of markets.

Further complications arise because the identity of the losers from these transfers is as difficult to determine as the identity of the beneficiaries. In any given industry, the number of customers usually exceeds the number of potential beneficiaries from windfall profits. Thus, equity-based policies for a given industry would transfer money from a narrower to a broader group. However, it would be difficult to determine whether the narrow group was richer or poorer on average than the broad group.

Moreover, everyone is both a consumer and producer of something. If equity-based controls on markets become widespread, everyone will suffer a loss somewhere. The net result is lower total output and a collection of gains and losses to each individual that rarely, if ever, would constitute a net gain to anyone.

As Schumpeter (1950) suggests, equity-based intervention arises because of the asymmetry just noted between concentrated effects on the producers in an industry and dispersed effects on consumers. The concentrated effects are more likely to be recognized and lead to policy developments than the dispersed ones. From this follows the principle that interest groups generally will promote more vigorously prevention of their losses in a given situation than others will be willing to fight being sacrificed. However, an interest group can make itself sufficiently unpopular that it becomes politically attractive to inflict an equity loss to that interest group even at the expense of efficiency. In either case, efficiency interests are overwhelmed, and if this neglect becomes too widespread, the losses can be devastating. Thus, any one equity-based policy is likely to produce undesirable results, and a proliferation of such policies unquestionably will.

The case for equity-based intervention lies in a belief that benefits exceed costs and that better alternatives are not feasible. Whatever the correct presumption, little further fruitfully can be said here regarding income distribution. The required appraisal would involve first determining the distributional effects of the policies that increase efficiency and deciding whether the results are truly undesirable. Then it would have to be decided how best to react to any undesirable effects. This would involve altering income transfers, altering or rejecting reform proposals, or some mixture of both. The measurement of distributional impacts is too formidable a task to attempt here. Others should explore the validity of my conclusions about efficiency to determine what equity problems, if any, will arise, and design cures for these inequities.

3 The Structure of the Electric-Utility Industry

The electric power industry generates and delivers electricity to users. The delivery process is conventionally divided between transmission and distribution. Transmission involves longer distance, higher voltage movements while distribution is shorter, lower voltage movements to end users.

Reliability has always been a major concern to electric utilities. No electricity-generating facility can operate continuously. There must be periodic shutdowns for preventive maintenance, and nuclear plants must be periodically taken offline for refueling. These shutdowns are called *planned outages*.

There are also unexpected or forced outages. Because demand fluctuates over the year, days of the week, or hours of the day, so does the load on the generating system. Historically, the regular or base load was borne by the newest, cheapest plants; then as load increased above the steady base level, successively older plants were brought into service. The rare surges in demand, such as during a summer heat wave, were met by the very oldest plants.

The decreases, if not reversal (due to more stringent environmental control regulations), in the advantages of building new plants and the availability of new technologies have led to considerable additions of plants designed for less than full-time use. Surges in demand can be met by using gas turbines, which are stationary adaptations of jet engines, or by peak hydro. The latter can be obtained either by building a dam to store natural flow for release at peak hours or by creating special pumped storage facilities. In these facilities, water is pumped from below using power generated by other plants during low-demand periods, then released to the turbines when needed. Another development is a tendency to build fossil and hydro plants for intermediate-term use (roughly in the 25 to 50 percent utilization-rate-range).

When the emphasis was on using old plants to meet peaks, it could be assumed that if enough capacity existed to meet peak demands given greater-than-expected surges, outages would be rare. Now that extensive efforts have been made to build units specifically for peak use, it is possible that a company can have adequate peak capacity but lack the ability to meet load requirements on a sustained basis. A demand surge might last longer than a peaking unit could be operated, particularly a water-powered one. For example, the Los Angeles Department of Water and Power has a 1247

Mw pumped storage plant. This represents 31 percent of the 1979 peak load of 4000 Mw and would be 21 percent of the 6000 Mw load predicted for 2000.

Cooperation among utilities in dealing with this problem has several potential advantages. Differences in the timing of demand can make it possible to conserve generating capacity by exchanging power. Unused capacity in one area could be used to serve another area where demand was rising. Similarly, cooperation can conserve the amount of reserves needed. One of the simplest standard illustrations of the rules for insuring that demand is met is that no unit should be so large that its loss would preclude covering the load. The larger the group that is sharing capacity, the smaller is the relative burden for compensating for the loss of a large facility. A 20,000 Mw system would only need 5 percent reserves to guard against the loss of a 1000 Mw power plant or transmission line. However, a 2000 Mw system would need a 50 percent reserve. Thus, smaller utility systems must carry higher reserves, build smaller plants, or both. Cost penalties are attached to both higher reserves and smaller plants. Generally, the law of large numbers should lessen the danger of failures in a large system.

The electric-utility system in the United States involves many different types of organizations that own the facilities and coordinate activities. Among the critical considerations are the legal form of ownership, the activities of individual entities, the cooperative arrangements, geographic patterns, and fuel-use situations.

Ownership Forms

There are three basic ownership forms of electric utilities: private, public, and cooperative (see table 3–1). Many distinctions exist within and among the sectors. These include variations in the involvement of the industry in different phases of generating and delivering electricity and differences in the legal basis of organization.

The private sector is the dominant source of generation, providing over 78 percent in 1979. Less than 20 percent is provided by government, the majority of which comes from federal projects. Looking at long-term trends, the private share decreased for many years until around 1960, when it fell to about 77 percent, then moved upward slightly. Through 1960, the largest gain in share was by federal power. Since 1970, the federal share has fallen somewhat, and the state share has risen. Municipals have lessened in importance since 1946. The federal share was about 12 percent in 1946, 15 percent in 1970, and 10.5 percent in 1979. The respective state shares were 1.61, 2.73, and 5.07; for municipals, 5, 5, and 4. Cooperatives rose from

Table 3-1
Data on the Role of Alternative Ownership Patterns in U.S. Electricity Generation in 1979

	Thousand kWh	Percent of Total
Private	1,756,180,368	78.14
Cooperative	54,407,751	2.42
Federal	235,570,628	10.48
Municipal	87,269,421	3.88
State and power authorities	113,943,693	5.07
Total government	436,783,742	19.44
U.S. total	2,247,371,861	100.00

	Thousand kWh	Percent of U.S. Total	Percent of State Total
Federal Power in Major States			
Tennessee	57,650,454	24.47	98.19
Alabama	40,422,419	17.16	52.71
Kentucky	21,706,518	9.21	39.64
Total above	119,779,391	50.85	n.r.
Washington	46,449,430	19.72	51.14
Oregon	22,591,281	9.59	63.95
Total Washington-Oregon	69,040,711	29.31	n.c.
Total shown	188,820,102	80.15	n.c.
Municipal Power in Major States			
California	23,954,050	27.45	15.76
Florida	13,872,986	15.90	14.76
Texas	13,428,019	15.39	7.16
Washington	7,157,670	8.20	7.88
Michigan	3,982,947	4.56	5.09
Kansas	3,186,650	3.65	13.50
Louisiana	3,091,341	3.54	6.63
Total shown	68,673,663	78.69	n.c.
State and Power Authority in Major States			
New York	32,573,046	28.59	30.93
Washington	25,782,948	22.63	28.38
Arizona	18,729,572	16.44	53.67
Nebraska	15,649,429	13.73	89.85
California	8,121,300	7.13	5.34
South Carolina	6,238,628	5.48	14.99
Texas	5,653,029	4.96	3.01
Total shown	112,747,952	98.95	n.c.

Table 3-1 continued

	Thousand kWh	Percent of U.S. Total	Percent of State Total
Cooperatives in Major States			
North Dakota	10,580,608	19.45	76.23
Kentucky	9,863,280	18.13	18.01
Missouri	9,090,253	16.71	19.30
Colorado	3,955,820	7.27	17.57
Wisconsin	3,498,093	6.43	9.19
Oklahoma	2,538,817	4.67	6.10
Arizona	1,901,176	3.49	5.45
Alaska	1,889,261	3.47	62.40
Total shown	43,317,308	79.62	n.c.

Comparison of DOE and REA Figures on Comparative Generated Electricity in 1979
(million kWh)

	REA	DOE
Alabama	1,076	1,083
Alaska	1,913	1,889
Arizona	1,987	1,901
Arkansas	2,070	712
Colorado	2,280	3,956
Georgia	4,894	0
Illinois	1,460	1,459
Indiana	1,572	1,552
Iowa	2,089	404
Kansas	788	742
Kentucky	7,718	9,863
Louisiana	1,117	1,118
Michigan	427	429
Minnesota	2,163	73
Mississippi	1,290	1,291
Missouri	6,359	9,096
New Mexico	331	332
North Dakota	8,542	10,581
Ohio	3,621	0
Oklahoma	2,536	2,539
Texas	1,790	1,783
Wisconsin	3,501	3,498
TOTAL	59,776	54,408

Sources: U.S., Department of Energy (DOE), Energy Information Administration (EIA), *Power Production, Fuel Consumption and Installed Capacity Data from 1979 (Final)* (Washington, D.C.: 1980), p. 36; U.S., Rural Electrification Administration (REA), *1979 Annual Statistical Report, Rural Electrification Borrowers* (Washington, D.C.: U.S. Government Printing Office, 1980), p. xxx.

Notes: n.c.: not calculated.

The REA tabulation omits small amounts in Florida, Idaho, Maine, Nebraska, North Carolina, Utah, Virginia, Washington, and Wyoming reported by source.

less than 0.2 percent in 1947 —the first year of separate reporting) to 2.42 percent in 1979.

Ownership characteristics have been influenced by nearly forgotten ideological debates of the first half of the twentieth century. The electric-utility industry initially consisted of numerous, largely privately owned companies. Early in the development of the industry, efforts were made to create larger, presumably more efficient systems. Extensive private efforts to rationalize the system further and pressures to develop alternatives to private ownership ensued. Both government ownership and cooperatives developed. All levels of government have been involved: federal, state, county, other intermediate-level entities, and municipalities.

Reorganization of private ownership extended beyond the consolidation of contiguous operations into a single company. Holding companies that owned a variety of utilities arose. In some cases, these holdings were adjacent and provided the basis for a larger, physically integrated system. However, many of the holdings were scattered and not necessarily all in the electric-utility industry. The Public Utility Holding Company Act of 1935 was passed in reaction to the spectacular failure of Samuel Insull's holding-company empire, Middle West Utilities, in the 1929 stock market crash. The act required that holding companies be reduced to physically integrated systems, dealing solely with gas or electricity. The Securities and Exchange Commission (SEC) was required to supervise the reorganization and activities of holding companies.

Neither the merger nor the holding-company movement managed to divide service territories into discrete units. Quite frequently, parts of one company's territory are separated by the territory of another company. One example is a small island of territory of the Allegheny Power System's West Penn Power surrounded by territory of General Public Utilities' Pennsylvania Electric. There are many similar examples, such as the intertwining of Niagara Mohawk and New York State Electric and Gas's territories.

When SEC reorganized the holding-companies, some were restructured into the large, geographically integrated holding companies that survive to the present day. Others, such as Electric Bond and Share (Ebasco) and Stone and Webster, which lacked close connections to particular operating utilities, became engineering-consulting firms.

The impact of the Holding Company Act on the industry is uneven. The severe barriers to creating larger companies are discouraging to those who wish there were more mergers. Conversely, the limits on the extent to which existing large companies can be fragmented are unsatisfactory to those who would like to see smaller companies. In fact, the overall structure involves a combination of many different regional structures, so it is possible to believe simultaneously that some companies ought to merge while others should be fragmented.

Most existing holding companies were preserved from portions of old, parent companies. Many smaller units of the holding companies were made independent and remained so largely because they could not be easily merged. For that matter, there are several cases of contiguous companies that were once in the same holding company and are now still separate. These include Illinois Power and Central Illinois Light (both part of Commonwealth and Southern) and Central Maine Power and Public Service of New Hampshire in Insull's Middle West Utilities. There are even more examples of merger candidates that were parts of different holding-company systems.

The result was a structure in which companies with different sizes have coexisted and, had the desire for larger companies been stronger, many of the smaller companies would have had natural merger partners. The net effect of the creation and substantial breakup of holding companies was to create a very diverse structure. A side effect of the restructuring was that some municipals acquired private companies (for example, Los Angeles and San Antonio).

A major development in the public and cooperative sectors was the creation of joint ventures to own and, in most cases, operate power plants. These organizations have become particularly important in the cooperative sector, where they account for the vast majority (95 percent in 1979) of cooperative generated power. Of all the states for which data are shown in table 3–1, only Alaska lacks such generating and transmission cooperatives, and only New Mexico has more generation from distributing groups than from generating and transmission organizations.

Most of the consortiums involving public power have projects still under construction in 1981. The most ambitious and complex is the Washington Public Power Supply System. Other bodies have arisen in California, Georgia, Massachusetts, North Carolina, and Texas. (In some cases, the body is a coordinating group, and members own plants directly.)

These public and cooperative groups use various combinations of owning and operating their own plants; owning portions of plants operated by other, usually private utilities; and operating plants that are also partially owned by other organizations, including private ones. On balance, cooperatives own more capacity than they operate. The biggest excess ownership and use come in Georgia and Ohio, where all cooperatively owned power is generated by plants operated by private companies. Other important participation occurs in Arkansas, Iowa, and Minnesota. However, cooperatives in Colorado, Kentucky, Missouri, and North Dakota operate more capacity than they own.

The historical legacy is mixed. As discussed later, cooperation among sectors is increasing. Industry critics complain that the leading government-owned power companies are the same as other utilities. My interviews with staff in a few such public companies suggested that, at least in terms of being oriented to power-supply expansion, government-owned companies do have attitudes similar to those of investor-owned companies (but this does not indicate that the similarity is bad, only that it exists). Because their borrowing power is stronger than that of many private utilities, the publics may be more growth oriented. Nevertheless, residual animosities remain. A recurrent theme is battles of municipal utilities dependent on private companies for authority to secure more power at more favorable rates (see chapter 4).

The Private Sector

The private sector collectively generates about as much electricity as it sells (see U.S., Department of Energy, *Statistics of Privately Owned Utilities,* 1980, p. 491.) Several basic organizational forms prevail among private companies. The most prevalent in terms of sheer numbers is the single corporation.

There are three other forms of electric-power corporations. The most common is for a main operating company to have one or more subsidiaries. Second, a parent holding company can be established to own the operating companies. Eleven such companies operate in the United States, and they account for a major portion of output; a bit less than 20 percent of the U.S. total for all types of ownership in 1979. These holding companies range in size from American Electric Power (AEP) and the Southern Company, which rank second and third behind the U.S. government-owned Tennessee Valley Authority (TVA), to Eastern Utilities Associates, which supplies about 0.1 percent of national output. (See table 3–2 for data on the largest companies.)

A third and less important form is a company owned by several other utilities. Two such companies (one of which, in turn, has a subsidiary) were founded to provide power to U.S. government nuclear-energy activities: Electric Energy, Inc. and Ohio Valley Electric Company. The other big group consists of the Yankee companies, each established to own a nuclear plant in New England. Most companies generate, transmit, and distribute electricity, and such companies conduct most of all three activities in the United States.

The nonelectric activities of the companies differ widely. In principle, holding companies are prohibited by the Public Utility Holding Company Act of 1935 from engaging in both gas and electricity distribution. In practice, some exceptions prevail. One is a company created in the 1960s (Northeast Utilities); another, New England Gas and Electric Association, has been exempted from the act, but others are AEP and Middle South Utilities,

Table 3-2
The Largest Electric Utilities in 1979

	Role in Generation		
Utility	*Million kWh*	*Percent of U.S. Total*	*Cumulative Percent of Total*
1. Tennessee Valley Authority[a]	119,474,529	5.32	5.32
2. American Electric Power[b]	109,413,016	4.87	10.18
3. The Southern Company	91,533,997	4.07	14.26
4. Bonneville Power Authority[a,c]	76,039,056	3.38	17.64
5. Commonwealth Edison	62,133,010	2.76	20.41
6. Southern California Edison	59,398,679	2.64	23.05
7. Texas Utilities	58,051,429	2.58	25.63
8. Houston Lighting and Power	54,678,407	2.43	28.06
9. Duke Power	54,603,861	2.43	30.49
10. Pacific Gas and Electric	53,403,420	2.38	32.87
11. Central and Southwest Corp.	45,292,453	2.02	34.89
12. Florida Power and Light	44,749,986	1.99	36.88
13. Middle South Utilities, Inc.	43,439,109	1.93	38.81
14. Detroit Edison	35,347,429	1.57	40.38
15. Allegheny Power System	34,347,358	1.53	41.91
16. Pennsylvania Power and Light	33,009,502	1.47	43.38
17. Virginia Electric and Power	32,834,489	1.46	44.84
18. Power Authority of the State of New York	32,543,042	1.45	46.29
19. Carolina Power and Light	30,302,562	1.35	47.64
20. Union Electric	26,909,564	1.20	48.84
21. General Public Utilities Corp.	26,744,326	1.19	50.03
22. Northern States Power	25,304,775	1.13	51.15
23. Public Service Electric and Gas	24,746,562	1.10	52.25
24. Gulf States Utilities	24,348,852	1.08	53.34
25. Public Service Co. of Indiana	23,689,759	1.05	54.39
26. Consolidated Edison	22,942,441	1.02	55.41
27. Ohio Edison	22,208,342	0.99	56.40
28. Consumers Power	21,857,545	0.97	57.37
29. Niagara Mohawk Power	21,798,075	0.97	58.34
30. Oklahoma Gas and Electric	21,185,846	0.94	59.28
31. Philadelphia Electric	20,415,008	0.91	60.19
32. Pacific Power and Light	19,487,235	0.87	61.06
33. Baltimore Gas and Electric	19,119,244	0.85	61.91
34. Potomac Electric Power	18,505,600	0.82	62.74
35. Los Angeles Department of Water and Power[d]	18,225,574	0.81	63.55
36. Cleveland Electric Illuminating	17,069,914	0.76	64.31
37. Florida Power Corp.	17,001,980	0.76	65.06
38. Illinois Power	16,895,455	0.75	65.81
39. Northeast Utilities	16,543,436	0.74	66.55
40. Wisconsin Electric Power	16,506,481	0.73	67.28
41. Ohio Valley Electric	15,928,504	0.71	67.99
42. Utah Power and Light	14,895,049	0.66	68.66
43. Cincinnati Gas and Electric	14,878,716	0.66	69.32
44. Public Service Co. of Colorado	14,357,553	0.64	69.96
45. Duquesne Light	13,884,806	0.62	70.57

Table 3–2 continued

	Role in Generation		
Utility	Million kWh	Percent of U.S. Total	Cumulative Percent of Total
46. New England Electric System	13,491,579	0.60	71.18
47. Boston Edison	12,758,756	0.57	71.74
48. Missouri River Basin Authority[a,c]	12,331,235	0.55	72.29
49. Southwestern Public Service	12,284,377	0.55	72.84
50. South Carolina Electric and Gas	11,832,986	0.53	73.36
51. Arizona Public Service	11,593,301	0.52	73.88
52. Long Island Lighting	11,085,348	0.49	74.37
53. Tampa Electric	10,998,057	0.49	74.86
54. Public Utility District No. 2 Grant County[e]	10,971,000	0.49	75.35
55. Idaho Power	10,785,282	0.48	75.83
56. Indianapolis Power and Light	10,507,437	0.47	76.30
57. New York State Electric and Gas Corp.	10,430,061	0.46	76.76
58. Dayton Power and Light	10,361,995	0.46	77.22
59. Central Illinois Public Service	10,185,767	0.45	77.68

Sources: Total: U.S., Department of Energy, *Power Production, Fuel Consumption, and Installed Capacity Data for 1979 (Final)* (Washington, D.C.: 1980).

Private Companies: U.S., Department of Energy, *Statistics of Privately Owned Electric Utilities in the United States—1979 Classes A and B Companies* (Washington, D.C.: U.S. Government Printing Office, 1980). (Source reports subsidiaries and units of holding companies as separate entities; data were consolidated on the basis of company reports on ownership and similar data in FPC earlier editions of this source.)

Public companies: U.S., Department of Energy, *Statistics of Publicly Owned Electric Utilities in the United States—1979,* (Washington, D.C.: U.S. Government Printing Office, 1980).

[a]Fiscal year ending 30 September 1979.
[b]Includes Columbus and Southern Ohio Electric, acquired in early 1980.
[c]Consists of output of projects marketed by the Authority.
[d]Fiscal year ending 30 June 1979.
[e]Not reported by DOE; figure is for 1978; other districts in Washington had 1979 output similar to 1978.

long extant and regulated holding companies (albeit with small gas businesses). The financial reports, especially 10Ks, of Northeast and Middle South Utilities indicate that two quite different forces were at work. Middle South's New Orleans Public Service Company was considered to have so fully integrated a gas and electric system that divestiture was undesirable. The two Connecticut companies that are the major components of Northeast Utilities both were engaged in gas distribution. SEC efforts to produce sale of these properties are still in adjudication, and Northeast has not been able to find a buyer.

Otherwise, a rough examination of the data suggests that noninvolvement in gas is somewhat more common than participation. Gas operations, if they exist, tend to produce much lower revenues than electricity. Two major exceptions are Pacific Gas and Electric in California, which earned $2.5 billion in electric revenues and $2.3 billion in gas in 1979, and Public Service Electric and Gas (of New Jersey) which earned $1.7 and $0.7 billion.

Less prevalent businesses include steam supply in large cities, water companies, and bus service (such as Middle South's bus named Desire) left over from the streetcar era. There is a growing tendency to enter fuel production. The most visible effort is in coal production, where three of the top ten producers in 1979 were subsidiaries of Texas Utilities, Pacific Power and Light, and AEP. Montana Power's coal-mining subsidiary was the thirteenth largest producer (see Keystone 1980). Texas and AEP produce solely for their own use; Pacific Power and Light and Montana produce for themselves, partners in jointly owned plants, and third parties.

Involvement exists in other fuels. For example, Commonwealth Edison owns its own uranium mines and mills; Southern California Edison is a partner with Rocky Mountain Energy, a division of Union Pacific, in a mine and mill. There is also involvement in oil and gas ventures.

Government Power

Several different institutional arrangements prevail in the public-power sector. Federal power, which involves only generation and transmission, accounts for the majority of the kilowatt hours generated by public power. TVA, the largest electric utility in the United States, accounted for 52 percent of federal power in fiscal 1979. The next largest share (about a third of the total) is associated with the Bonneville Power Authority, which markets power primarily produced by dams run by other U.S. government agencies, but supplemented since the 1970s, by access to portions of power produced in plants built by various private companies. (The control is through long-term contracts for power rather than outright ownership.)

All federal power is wholesaled to distribution companies or large direct users. TVA is the only federal entity that can be considered an integrated generation and transmission organization. The Bonneville pattern of a marketing agency for a collection of waterpower projects has four counterparts: a Southeastern, a Southwestern, a Missouri River Basin, and an Alaskan Power Administration. A few projects operate as independent units.

The next component of public power consists of operations of state, county, and other nonmunicipal organizations. The largest is the Power Authority of the State of New York (PASNY). As was often the case for major projects in New York state during the middle twentieth century, PASNY was developed by Robert Moses. PASNY started with hydroelectric plants near Niagara Falls, built its own nuclear plant, bought a nuclear unit and an oil-fired unit from Consolidated Edison in 1974, and tried in vain through 1981 to build additional plants.

The next largest concentration of such operations is in Washington, where there are a number of county power districts. These districts joined in a complex, controversial, and expensive procedure to build five nuclear units through the Washington Public Power Supply System. On close examination, this process proves to be far more than a joint effort by the county districts and municipals in Washington who own the system. The participants in the plants also include private companies, other public-power organizations, and cooperatives from Washington, Oregon, Idaho, and Montana. Bonneville is guaranteeing three of the units by earmarking revenues from power sales to finance the construction, under a concept called net billing (see chapter 4).

Other important entities include the various authorities that produce most Nebraska power (where the rest is federal or municipal) and large authorities in South Carolina, Texas, and Arizona. The major Arizona venture—the Salt River Project—effectively is a cooperative to which governmental powers have been delegated. About half the municipal generation is in California, Texas, and Florida. Such large cities as Los Angeles, Sacramento, San Antonio, and Jacksonville are involved. (Table 3–1 provides summary data on the 1979 breakdown of generation by type of ownership.)

More broadly, the entities in the industry differ widely in size, with the majority of generation provided by a group of very large organizations. (These can be clustered in several ways. Table 3–2 presents data on all organizations producing more than 10 billion kWh in 1979, a cutoff chosen to keep the tabulation more manageable.) About twenty-five organizations account for half the generation.

The leading entities after TVA are two holding companies, American Electric Power and the Southern Company. The first operates mainly in Ohio, Indiana, and West Virginia with other operations in Kentucky, Virginia, and Michigan. Bonneville ranks fourth. PASNY, ranked eighteenth in generation, is the only other nonprivate entity in the top twenty-five companies.

Federal operations grew universally from involvement in water-power projects. During the 1950s, TVA ran out of sites for large hydroelectric-generating stations. Strong political pressures encouraged TVA's entry into the construction of steam-powered plants. This was brought to a head early in the Eisenhower administration when an effort to reintroduce private power into the region was turned into a cause célèbre. Much was made of the employment of a White House consultant by an investment banking firm with close ties to the private companies involved. Whatever the merits of the charge, considerable turmoil resulted. The immediate resolution was that the city of Memphis, which would have been served by the private plant, announced it would build a plant itself. (However, the Eisenhower plan was actually more complex. Nominally, the private plant would have sold to the U.S. government. The actual implementation involved shifting TVA power to these government facilities and using the new private plant to provide replacement energy to Memphis.) Subsequently, TVA was allowed to build fossil plants and acquired management of the plant built by Memphis.

As noted, Bonneville is backing steam plants. Otherwise federal involvement is limited to waterpower. The decision to establish power districts and municipals seems to have developed on an ad hoc basis.

Cooperatives were fostered by the Rural Electrification Administration, which provided low-interest loans to promote cooperatives and by laws giving preferred access of cooperations (and public power) to federal power. Initially, cooperatives stressed distribution. However, the exhaustion of federal power and a desire to secure independence from private companies encouraged cooperatives to become involved in generation. Attitudes reversed in the 1970s. Initially, the cooperatives and municipals fought for the right to buy into nuclear plants under provisions of the Atomic Energy Act that required the Justice Department prevent behavior inconsistent with the antitrust laws. As financing of such plants became more difficult, the private utilities appeared to be vigorously encouraging cooperatives and municipals to participate.

Cooperation among Utilities

For the reasons cited, not even the largest entities operate independently. The most universal form of cooperation is the grouping of most of the industry into nine reliability councils. These councils exchange information about demand growth and plans for expansion. This exchange leads to efforts to coordinate plans for more efficient operations of the industry.

The geographic extent of each council region is determined by grouping together companies with reasonably close relationships (see figure 3-1) These relationships affect power exchanges, as explained in chapter 2. Some of the day-to-day power interchanges are effected by a central dispatching center that chooses a cost-minimizing pattern of generation and flows. Additionally, companies undertake significant exchanges through frequent telephone communications. Considerable controversy exists about whether it would be efficient to increase coordination through creation of more dispatch centers or through some intermediate organization, such as a joint communications center.

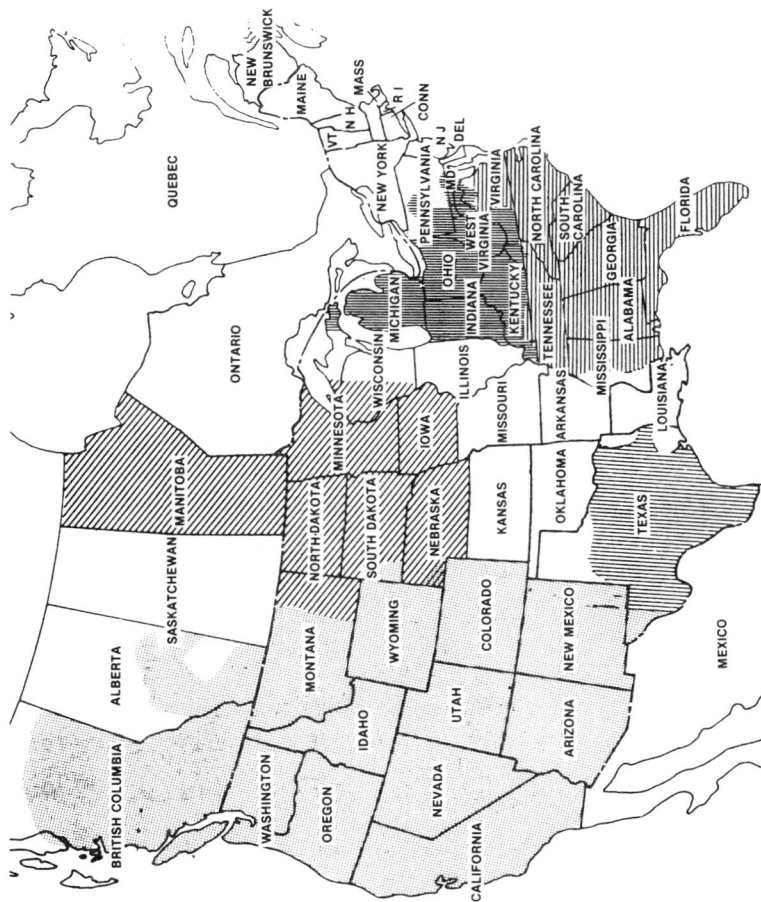

Figure 3-1. Electric Reliability Councils

ECAR	East Central Area Reliability Coordination Agreement	
ERCOT	Electric Reliability Council of Texas	
MAAC	Mid-Atlantic Area Council	
MAIN	Mid-America Interpool Network	
MARCA	Mid-Continent Area Reliability Coordination Agreement	
NPCC	Northeast Power Coordination Council	
SERC	Southeastern Electric Reliability Council	
SPP	Southwest Power Pool	
WSCC	Western Systems Coordinating Council	

Natural geographic relationships are important influences on the size and composition of councils, but these connections are imcompletely governed by political boundaries. Thus, the council regions have a limited relationship to the standard census regions or any other grouping of states. In fact, there is cooperation with Canadian utilities. The nature and attitudes of companies also influence the makeup of the nine councils.

1. The Northeast Power Coordinating Council (NPCC). This council is the only one whose borders coincide with political boundaries. It encompasses New York and New England and includes Canadian members in Ontario and New Brunswick. New York and New England each constitute unusually close-knit regions. Each maintains one of the few regionwide operation centers for dispatching power among all its members. The New England utilities maintain a unified expansion plan and frequently engage in joint ventures to build plants. The Yankee company pattern has been replaced by the practice used in other regions of jointly owning plants. Another unusual feature is that several holding companies in the area—New England Electric, New England Gas and Electric Association, and Eastern Utilities—are organized with one subsidiary undertaking most or all of the generation that is wholesaled largely to other companies in the system. This places the basic rates under control of the Federal Energy Regulatory Administration (FERC) of the Department of Energy (DOE).

Joint planning has been fostered and pushed by New York state oversight of utility plans into directions the utilities would not have preferred. Since 1973, the companies have been required to file a joint annual report on their plans. These were originally submitted to the Public Service Commission but now are received by a state Energy Planning Board. The board issued its own long-term plan in 1980 (see chapter 4). Joint ventures are common, including one with a Pennsylvania company. However, efforts to create a new company owned by the others to build plants did not secure Public Service Commission approval.

2. The Mid-Atlantic Area Council (MAAC). This council encompasses all of New Jersey, Delaware, the District of Columbia, most of Maryland and Pennsylvania, and a bit of Virginia. Splitting Pennsylvania and Maryland involves distinguishing between companies oriented to the East and those oriented to the West. The westward-looking excluded Maryland company is the Potomac Edison subsidiary of Allegheny Power. The Pennsylvania exclusions also involve Allegheny, a subsidiary of Ohio Edison (Pennsylvania Power), and Duquesne Light. The Virginia inclusions are portions of the territory of the principal company in Delaware and the Washington, D.C. area utility. Joint dispatch of the entire region is maintained by the Pennsylvania-New Jersey-Maryland (PJM) pool. Joint ventures are common.

3. The East Central Area Reliability Coordination Agreement (ECAR). This consists of Indiana, Ohio, West Virginia, all of Michigan except the western upper peninsula, most of Kentucky, the remaining parts of Pennsylvania and Maryland, and a bit of Virginia and Tennessee. The leading company is AEP, and it and Allegheny account for the inclusions in Virginia. AEP sells, but does not generate, in a small part of Tennessee. The Kentucky exclusion is the territory of TVA; that in Michigan of operations served by a Wisconsin company.

While AEP and Allegheny each jointly dispatch among all their companies, only one other centralized dispatch operation prevails. Several important joint facility planning arrangements exist. First, the two prinicipal Michigan utilities cooperate (Detroit Edison and Consumers Power), and a group of western Pennsylvania and northern Ohio companies constitute the Central Area Power Coordination Group (CAPCO). The members are Duquesne, Ohio Edison, Cleveland Electric Illuminating, and Toledo Edison. The Michigan companies dispatch jointly but build plants separately (except for one pumped storage plant); the CAPCO companies have engaged in numerous joint ventures.

Two other groups have fragmented. One consisted of three Ohio companies: Columbus and Southern Ohio Electric, Dayton Power and Light, and Cincinnati Gas and Electric. The first was acquired in 1980 by AEP. Previously, the three had planned and engaged in joint ventures. An Indiana-Kentucky group planned together but did not engage in joint ventures. Its members included Public Service of Indiana, Indianapolis Power and Light, Kentucky Utilities, and the Eastern Kentucky Cooperative. Discord between Public Service of Indiana and the others—particularly over the Public Service's commitment to nuclear power—caused Public Service to terminate the agreement. The commitments under the accord would not be completed until 1990.

4. The Southeastern Electric Reliability Council (SERC). This region includes all of Alabama, Georgia, North and South Carolina, Florida, most of Tennessee, the part of Virginia not in MAAC or ECAR, the part of Kentucky not in ECAR, and eastern Mississippi. The biggest entities are TVA and the Southern Company. The part of Mississippi included in the region is mainly the territory of Southern Company's Mississippi Power; the included part of Kentucky is TVA's operation in that state, and TVA also serves most of Tennessee. There are no pools beyond the integrated dispatch for TVA and Southern and the large operations of Duke Power and Florida Power and Light. Important regional subgroups arise between Virginia and the Carolinas and in Florida. The Southern Company and TVA cover most of the remaining area.

5. The Mid American Interpool Network (MAIN) consists of Illinois,

most of Wisconsin, the portion of Michigan noted, and the eastern half of Missouri. No intercompany dispatching pools operate; the largest company is Commonwealth Edison, which serves the Chicago area. The principal Missouri participant, St. Louis-based Union Electric, coordinates with Illinois Power and Central Illinois Public Service. The four main Wisconsin members cooperate and jointly own plants.

6. The Electric Reliability Council of Texas (ERCOT). This council encompasses an area deliberately confined to less than the whole state of Texas. The limitation reflects the strong desires of the leading companies, mainly Texas Utilities and Houston Lighting and Power, to avoid federal regulation. This difference between Texas and New England appears related to regulatory climates. New England utilities and the financial analysts who rate regulators consider FERC to be more favorable to companies than are the New England regulators (see chapter 4). The reverse view prevails about Texas. The Texas Public Utility Commission was not established until 1976 and is rated as one of the most sympathetic to utilities. Previously Texas had municipal-level regulation (which still coexists with state regulation). These trends have prevailed for many years. At least one of the New England arrangements predates federal regulation but has been preserved and expanded.

The scope of ERCOT was, therefore, designed to exclude the single corporation, interstate companies operating in Texas (such as Gulf States Utilities, El Paso Electric, and Southwestern Public Service). This left Central and Southwest in an anomalous position. It has two subsidiaries in ERCOT Texas, one in non-ERCOT Texas and other states, and one outside Texas. It faced pressures from the ERCOT companies to keep its ERCOT operations separate; customers outside ERCOT complained that the separation was not consistent with the Holding Company Act. A 1978 effort by Central and Southwest unilaterally to connect the system produced severe reactions by the other leading ERCOT participants, but an accord was worked out to permit the interconnection to occur while meeting the concerns of the other companies. Pooling does not exist, and Texas Utilities separately dispatches its divisions. There are joint ventures with nuclear plants.

7. The Southwest Power Pool (SWPP). This consists of Oklahoma, Louisiana, Arkansas, Kansas, the portion of Mississippi not in SERC, the portion of Missouri not in MAIN, and parts of Texas and New Mexico. The included portions of Texas consist largely of the territories of Gulf States, Southwestern Public Service, and non-ERCOT Central and Southwest. Southwestern Public Service operations are the included part of New Mexico. The biggest entity entirely in SWPP is Middle South Utilities with operations in Louisiana, Mississippi, Arkansas, and a bit in Missouri. The most

important joint ventures involve cooperation among utilities in Kansas and Western Missouri.

8. The Mid-Continent Reliability Coordination Agreement (MARCA). This includes Iowa, Minnesota, North Dakota, Nebraska, the portion of Wisconsin not in MAIN, most of South Dakota, the eastern fourth of Montana, and Manitoba. The included part of Wisconsin is served by Minneapolis-based Northern States Power; the critical included company in Montana is Montana-Dakota Utilities, and the South Dakota exclusion is Black Hills Power and Light.

9. The Western Systems Coordinating Council (WSCC) covers the remaining forty-eight states. This includes California, Washington, Oregon, Idaho, Nevada, Utah, Arizona, Wyoming, and Colorado. British Columbia and part of Alberta are also part of the Council. Black Hills Power and Light in South Dakota is included, as is the Texas service area of El Paso Electric. Most of Montana and New Mexico, except as noted, are in WSCC. Despite the size of the region, it is becoming increasingly interrelated. The West Coast has tended to dominate generation and consumption. A complex system of generation has arisen in the Northwest. The large single grouping in the region was the power marketed by the Bonneville Power Authority, and Bonneville has served as the planning coordinator for the region. A mixture of private companies, municipals, and the Washington power districts constitute the rest of the system. A significant portion of surplus power goes to California. As noted, the non-Bonneville companies have been involved in nuclear joint ventures, partially supported by Bonneville. There have been joint ventures for coal-fired plants, largely involving the private companies.

Historically, the California companies tended to operate as individual entities, although Pacific Gas and Electric in the northern part of the state did coordinate with a variety of nearby municipals and state agencies. The remaining major operations—Southern California Edison, San Diego Gas and Electric, and the Los Angeles Department of Water and Power—tended to be independent. Edison wholesaled to several municipals in the area.

During the 1960s, difficulties in power-plant siting led these last three companies to cooperate with each other and with a group of southwestern companies that included Nevada Power, Arizona Public Service, the Salt River District, New Mexico Public Service, Tucson Gas and Electric, and El Paso Electric. A series of coal-fired plants were jointly built in Nevada, Arizona, and New Mexico, and jointly owned nuclear plants are being built in Arizona.

More recently, Pacific Gas and Electric joined Nevada Power and Southern California Edison in planning a joint venture (from which the

California companies withdrew in 1981), and Los Angeles has joined other California municipals, Utah Power and Light, and Utah municipals in another joint venture.

Electricity Generation and Its Growth

We now turn to an examination of where consumption and generation occur. To simplify, historical figures are provided only on generation, with a qualitative review of the difference between consumption and production. Table 3-3 presents state-by-state data on generation in 1946 and 1979, and table 3-4 provides growth-rate calculations.

The levels and trends generally are consistent with the expectation that economic activity, the local attractiveness of electricity use, and fuel availability all influence the level and growth of generation. Generally, growth has been faster in areas noted as fast-growing regions.

Such anomalies that exist tend to be related to shifts to out-of-state power as a source of generation. West Virginia appears to be the most sustained user of the ability to act as a power exporter. The rise of mine-mouth plants in Pennsylvania and various mountain states created export develop-

Table 3-3
Electricity Generation by States in the United States, 1946 and 1979

	1979 Patterns				
	Million kWh	*Percent of United States*	*Cumulative Percent of United States*	*Percent of State Privately Generated*	*1946 Million kWh*
Texas	187,547	8.35	8.35	88.58	7,339
California	151,978	6.76	15.11	76.03	17,314
Pennsylvania	127,764	5.69	20.79	99.99	16,881
Ohio	116,797	5.20	25.99	99.14	13,976
New York	105,318	4.69	30.68	68.84	22,892
Illinois	104,646	4.66	35.33	96.65	13,878
Florida	93,995	4.18	39.51	84.86	3,042
Washington	90,835	4.04	43.56	12.60	9,039
Michigan	78,230	3.48	47.04	93.87	10,058
Alabama	76,691	3.41	50.45	45.88	7,300
North Carolina	68,158	3.03	53.48	97.33	5,677
West Virginia	67,758	3.01	56.50	100.00	5,244
Indiana	67,035	2.98	59.48	96.63	7,273
Tennessee	58,711	2.61	62.09	1.81	6,580
Georgia	56,192	2.50	64.59	95.88	2,669

Table 3-3 continued

| | 1979 Patterns | | | | |
	Million kWh	Percent of United States	Cumulative Percent of United States	Percent of State Privately Generated	1946 Million kWh
Kentucky	54,764	2.44	67.03	38.42	2,381
Missouri	47,126	2.10	69.13	74.36	2,729
Louisiana	46,655	2.08	71.20	90.98	2,884
South Carolina	41,622	1.85	73.06	82.80	2,584
Oklahoma	41,618	1.85	74.91	87.54	2,009
Wisconsin	38,045	1.69	76.60	89.71	4,885
Massachusetts	35,768	1.59	78.19	98.51	4,888
Oregon	35,326	1.57	79.76	34.41	4,149
Virginia	34,990	1.56	81.32	97.08	3,386
Arizona	34,897	1.55	82.81	21.73	2,842
Maryland	34,056	1.52	84.39	99.69	3,965
Minnesota	30,970	1.38	85.77	95.12	2,941
New Jersey	26,553	1.18	86.95	99.02	7,576
Connecticut	23,877	1.06	88.01	99.76	3,215
Kansas	23,610	1.05	89.06	83.36	2,344
Colorado	22,516	1.00	90.06	65.73	1,168
Wyoming	22,055	0.98	91.04	95.21	316
New Mexico	20,500	0.91	91.96	96.61	605
Iowa	20,280	0.90	92.86	91.76	3,111
Nebraska	17,417	0.77	93.63	0.00	1,393
Arkansas	16,794	0.75	94.38	77.06	837
Mississippi	16,640	0.74	95.12	89.95	225
Montana	15,756	0.70	95.82	67.08	2,466
Nevada	14,730	0.66	96.48	88.66	2,488
North Dakota	13,879	0.62	97.10	4.05	350
Utah	10,788	0.48	97.58	93.78	457
Idaho	9,206	0.41	97.99	66.73	1,335
South Dakota	9,203	0.41	98.39	31.25	321
Maine	7,468	0.33	98.93	99.80	1,371
Delaware	6,978	0.31	99.04	93.14	43
Hawaii	6,424	0.29	99.32	100.00	n.a.
New Hampshire	6,147	0.27	99.60	100.00	1,014
Vermont	4,403	0.20	99.79	96.97	759
Alaska	3,028	0.13	99.93	3.01	n.a.
District of Columbia	1,035	0.05	99.97	100.00	1,942
Rhode Island	595	0.03	100.00	99.44	1,060
U.S. total	2,247,372	100.00	100.00	78.14	223,179

Source: For 1979: U.S., Department of Energy, 1980, *Power Production, Fuel Consumption, and Installed Capacity Data for 1979, (Final)*, p. 36.

For 1946: Edison Electric Institute, *Historical Statistics of the Electric Utility Industry Through 1970*.

Note: n.a.: not available.

Table 3-4
Average Annual Percent Growth in Electricity Generation by States,
Selected Periods 1946-1979

	1946–1960	1960–1970	1970–1979	1946–1979
Connecticut	6.54	9.62	2.24	6.26
Maine	5.67	4.32	5.72	5.27
Massachusetts	7.42	8.20	2.26	6.22
New Hampshire	5.65	8.82	2.11	5.61
Rhode Island	3.43	(0.70)	(10.30)	(1.74)
Vermont	0.74	0.79	19.13	5.74
New England	6.26	7.78	2.82	5.77
New Jersey	6.26	7.72	(3.70)	3.87
New York	6.02	6.27	1.11	4.73
Pennsylvania	6.93	6.36	5.35	6.33
Middle Atlantic	6.39	6.55	2.25	5.29
Illinois	8.43	5.60	3.88	6.31
Indiana	10.90	5.48	2.69	6.96
Michigan	7.50	7.36	3.73	6.41
Ohio	9.45	4.84	4.38	6.65
Wisconsin	7.75	7.02	3.73	6.42
East North Central	8.90	5.80	3.77	6.54
Iowa	6.91	6.23	3.79	5.85
Kansas	8.98	7.27	4.59	7.25
Minnesota	8.83	6.13	6.59	7.39
Missouri	10.14	10.61	5.57	9.02
Nebraska	8.48	6.24	9.07	7.96
North Dakota	12.32	14.11	8.49	11.80
South Dakota	12.64	15.70	2.60	10.70
West North Central	8.94	8.47	5.71	7.91
Delaware	32.72	9.50	2.47	16.67
District of Columbia	(4.80)	12.11	(11.34)	(1.89)
Florida	13.53	11.93	6.04	10.96
Georgia	10.39	9.54	8.71	9.67
Maryland	6.23	9.76	4.24	6.73
North Carolina	9.41	9.94	3.15	7.82
South Carolina	10.33	4.97	10.73	8.79
Virginia	12.80	4.53	2.30	7.33
West Virginia	7.27	9.79	7.40	8.06
South Atlantic	9.65	9.05	5.67	8.37
Alabama	9.06	6.73	5.55	7.39
Kentucky	16.38	8.53	2.18	9.97
Mississippi	20.68	13.04	5.08	13.93
Tennessee	13.77	0.83	3.38	6.86
East South Central	12.68	5.26	3.91	7.97
Arkansas	14.01	9.55	2.84	9.51
Louisiana	10.63	11.00	3.68	8.80
Oklahoma	10.66	10.92	6.61	9.62
Texas	12.71	10.38	6.63	10.32
West South Central	12.09	10.50	5.85	9.88

Table 3–4 continued

	1946–1960	1960–1970	1970–1979	1946–1979
Arizona	8.25	4.28	11.58	7.92
Colorado	11.81	7.80	7.44	9.38
Idaho	11.55	1.39	2.97	6.03
Montana	6.55	5.28	5.15	5.78
Nevada	0.47	7.72	11.38	5.54
New Mexico	12.23	17.31	3.53	11.27
Utah	14.49	(0.29)	15.48	10.05
Wyoming	12.22	15.11	14.57	13.73
Mountain	8.50	6.99	8.54	8.05
California	9.77	6.70	2.46	6.80
Oregon	8.15	9.17	1.88	6.71
Washington	9.96	7.74	2.62	7.24
Pacific	9.62	7.33	2.44	6.93
Contiguous forty-eight states	9.08	7.32	4.34	7.24

Sources: For 1946, 1960 and 1970: Edison Electric Institute, *Historical Statistics of the Electric Utility Industry Through 1970* (New York, 1974).
For 1979: U.S., Department of Energy, *Power Production, Fuel Consumption and Installed Capacity Data from 1979 (Final)* (Washington, D.C.: 1980), p. 36.

ments in the 1960s and 1970s. The trades had the expected depressive effects on generation in such importing states as California, New Jersey, and Virginia. (See table 3–5 for comparisons between generation and consumption in 1979.)

Not all the trade shifts are due to plants near or nearer fuel sources. New England patterns have been altered by construction of Maine and Vermont Yankee, which can export substantial amounts of power to other states. Supply of Rhode Island has shifted to a plant (Brayton Point) in Massachusetts near the state line. Similarly, power plants to serve Washington, D.C. have been built in Maryland and Virginia.

An Examination of Methods of Generation: 1946–1979

The interaction of different regional positions of energy sources for electricity generation, changes in these positions, and growth differences have produced major changes in the role of different power sources in electricity generation. The most persistent trend has been a relative decline in the role of hydroelectric power (see tables 3–6 and 3–7). This decline reflects a general absence of sites to meet demand growth economically. Nuclear power has been increasing its share. The role of natural gas trended upward until 1970, then tended to decrease.

Table 3–5
Comparison of 1979 Electricity Generation and Consumption

		Consumption	
	Generation in Million kWh	in Million kWh	As Percent of Total
Maine	7,468	7,909	0.38
New Hampshire	6,147	6,060	0.29
Vermont	4,403	3,558	0.17
Massachusetts	35,768	32,950	2.58
Rhode Island	595	5,056	0.24
Connecticut	23,877	21,215	1.02
New England	78,258	76,448	3.69
New York	105,318	107,031	5.15
New Jersey	26,553	48,783	2.35
Pennsylvania	127,764	100,917	4.85
Middle Atlantic	259,635	256,731	12.35
Ohio	116,797	122,682	5.90
Indiana	67,035	56,788	2.73
Illinois	104,646	98,794	4.75
Michigan	78,230	71,649	3.45
Wisconsin	38,045	36,982	1.78
East North Central	404,754	386,895	18.61
Minnesota	30,970	33,583	1.62
Iowa	20,280	24,618	1.18
Missouri	47,126	38,694	1.68
North Dakota	13,879	5,178	0.25
South Dakota	9,202	4,791	0.23
Nebraska	17,417	13,691	0.66
Kansas	23,610	21,684	1.04
West North Central	162,483	142,239	6.84
Delaware	6,978	5,794	0.28
Maryland	34,056	40,258	1.94
District of Columbia	1,036	a	
Virginia	34,990	46,777	2.25
West Virginia	67,758	20,924	1.01
North Carolina	68,158	60,606	2.91
South Carolina	41,622	36,531	1.76
Georgia	56,192	49,917	2.40
Florida	93,995	85,941	4.13
South Atlantic	404,785	346,748	6.68
Kentucky	54,764	52,284	2.51
Tennessee	58,711	71,735	3.45
Alabama	76,691	52,006	2.50
Mississippi	16,640	22,889	1.10
East South Central	206,806	198,884	9.57
Arkansas	16,794	21,772	1.05
Louisiana	46,655	57,449	2.76
Oklahoma	41,618	29,374	6.41
Texas	187,547	167,334	8.05
West South Central	292,613	275,929	13.27

Table 3–5 continued

	Generation in Million kWh	Consumption in Million kWh	Consumption As Percent of Total
Montana	15,756	11,066	0.53
Idaho	9,206	15,676	0.75
Wyoming	22,055	6,420	0.31
Colorado	22,517	20,706	1.00
New Mexico	20,500	9,024	0.43
Arizona	34,897	25,402	1.22
Utah	10,788	10,573	0.51
Nevada	14,370	9,589	0.46
Mountain	150,488	408,456	5.22
Washington	90,835	73,177	3.52
Oregon	35,326	37,687	1.81
California	151,978	166,773	8.02
Pacific	278,138	277,637	13.35
Alaska	3,028	2,774	0.13
Hawaii	6,424	6,170	0.30
U.S. total	2,247,372	2,079,221	100.0

Sources: For generation: U.S., Department of Energy, 1980, *Power Production, Fuel Consumption, and Installed Capacity Data for 1979, (Final)*, p. 36.

For consumption: Edison Electric Institute, *Statistical Yearbook of the Electric Utility Industry 1979* (Washington, D.C.), p. 31.

[a]Included in Maryland.

Table 3–6
The Role of Alternative Sources of Electricity Generation
(generation in million kWh)

Year	Total	Hydro-electric	Coal	Petroleum	Gas	Nuclear	Other
1946	223,178	78,406	111,654	14,082	18,820		216
1947	255,739	78,426	136,985	16,925	23,072		331
1948	282,698	82,470	152,910	16,762	30,123		433
1949	291,100	89,748	135,451	28,547	36,967		386
1950	329,141	95,938	154,520	33,734	44,559		390
1951	370,673	99,750	185,204	28,712	56,616		391
1952	399,224	105,103	195,437	29,750	68,453		482
1953	442,665	105,233	218,846	38,404	79,791		389
1954	471,686	107,069	239,146	31,520	93,688		263
1955	547,038	112,975	301,363	37,138	95,285		277
1956	600,668	122,029	338,503	35,947	104,037		152
1957	631,507	130,232	346,386	40,500	114,212	10	167
1958	645,098	140,262	344,366	40,372	119,759	165	175
1959	710,006	137,782	378,424	46,840	146,619	188	153
1960	753,350	145,516	403,067	46,104	157,970	518	174

Table 3-6 continued

Year	Total	Hydro-electric	Coal	Petroleum	Gas	Nuclear	Other
1961	792,039	151,850	421,871	47,120	169,286	1,692	220
1962	852,314	168,283	450,249	46,983	184,301	2,270	228
1963	916,793	165,755	493,927	52,001	201,602	3,212	296
1964	983,990	177,073	526,230	56,954	220,038	3,343	352
1965	1,055,252	193,851	570,926	64,801	221,559	3,657	458
1966	1,144,350	194,756	613,475	78,926	251,151	5,520	522
1967	1,214,365	221,518	630,483	89,271	264,806	7,655	632
1968	1,329,443	222,491	684,905	104,276	304,433	12,528	810
1969	1,442,182	250,193	706,001	137,847	333,279	13,928	934
1970	1,531,609	247,456	706,102	182,488	372,884	21,797	882
1971	1,612,589	266,314	714,676	218,608	374,026	38,106	859
1972	1,749,637	272,626	772,871	272,530	375,735	54,092	1,783
1973	1,860,710	272,083	847,651	314,343	340,858	83,479	2,294
1974	1,867,140	301,032	828,433	300,931	320,065	113,976	2,703
1975	1,917,649	300,047	852,786	289,095	299,778	172,505	3,437
1976	2,037,696	283,707	944,391	319,988	294,624	191,104	3,883
1977	2,124,323	220,475	985,219	358,179	305,505	250,883	4,063
1978	2,206,330	280,419	976,627	364,175	305,391	276,403	3,315
1979	2,247,372	279,783	1,075,601	302,962	329,485	255,155	4,387
1980	2,286,034	276,021	1,161,562	245,589	346,240	251,116	5,506

Sources: Total for 1948–1970, by fuel 1951–1970: Edison Electric Intitute, *Historical Statistics of the Electric Utility Industry Through 1970* (New York: Edison Electric Institute, 1974).

For 1946–1958: National Coal Association, *Trends in Electric Utility Industry Experience, 1946–1958* (Washington, D.C. National Coal Association, 1960).

For 1970–1972: Edison Electric Institute, *Statistical Yearbook of the Electric Utility Industry* (New York: Edison Electric Institute).

For 1973–1978: U.S., Department of Energy, *Monthly Energy Review* (March 1980), p. 60.

For 1979: U.S. Department of Energy, *Power Production, Fuel Consumption and Installed Capacity Data for 1979 (Final),* Energy Data Report, 12 June, 1980.

Table 3-7
The Role of Alternative Sources of Electric Generation
(percent of total)

Year	Hydro-electric	Coal	Petroleum	Gas	Nuclear	Other
1946	35.13	50.03	6.31	8.43	0.00	0.10
1947	30.67	53.56	6.62	9.02	0.00	0.13
1948	29.17	54.09	5.93	10.66	0.00	0.15
1949	30.83	46.53	9.81	12.70	0.00	0.13
1950	29.15	46.95	10.25	13.54	0.00	0.12

Table 3-7 continued

Year	Hydro-electric	Coal	Petroleum	Gas	Nuclear	Other
1951	26.91	49.96	7.75	15.27	0.00	0.11
1952	26.33	48.95	7.45	17.15	0.00	0.12
1953	23.77	49.44	8.68	18.03	0.00	0.09
1954	22.70	50.70	6.68	19.86	0.00	0.06
1955	20.65	55.09	6.79	17.42	0.00	0.05
1956	20.32	56.35	5.98	17.32	0.00	0.03
1957	20.62	54.85	6.41	18.09	0.00	0.03
1958	21.74	53.38	6.26	18.56	0.03	0.03
1959	19.41	53.30	6.60	20.65	0.03	0.02
1960	19.32	53.50	6.12	20.97	0.07	0.02
1961	19.17	53.26	5.95	21.37	0.21	0.03
1962	19.74	52.83	5.51	21.62	0.27	0.03
1963	18.08	53.88	5.67	21.99	0.35	0.03
1964	18.00	53.48	5.79	22.36	0.34	0.04
1965	18.37	54.10	6.14	21.00	0.35	0.04
1966	17.02	53.61	6.90	21.95	0.48	0.05
1967	18.24	51.92	7.35	21.81	0.63	0.05
1968	16.74	51.52	7.84	22.90	0.94	0.06
1969	17.35	48.95	9.56	23.11	0.97	0.06
1970	16.16	46.10	11.91	24.35	1.42	0.06
1971	16.51	44.32	13.56	23.19	2.36	0.05
1972	15.58	44.17	15.58	21.48	3.09	0.10
1973	14.62	45.56	16.89	18.32	4.49	0.12
1974	16.12	44.37	16.12	17.14	6.10	0.14
1975	15.65	44.47	15.08	15.63	9.00	0.18
1976	13.92	46.35	15.70	14.46	9.38	0.19
1977	10.38	46.38	16.86	14.38	11.81	0.19
1978	12.71	44.26	16.51	13.84	12.53	0.15
1979	12.45	47.86	13.48	14.66	11.35	0.20
1980	12.07	50.81	10.74	15.15	10.98	0.24

Source: Calculated from table 3-6.

The coal and oil shares have been more variable. The reversals of shares in generation up to 1956 are too numerous to permit simple description. From 1957 to 1975 the coal share trended downward but until 1968 was still above the levels prevailing in most years before 1955. Since 1977, the coal share has risen but remained below prior peaks up to 1980. Irregular movement of the oil share persisted through the early 1960s, then came a rise that peaked in 1973. Since then the share has fallen.

Other important differences among states occurred in the role of specific energy resources. These interstate discrepancies are important, among other things, for creating a legacy of regional differences in the ability to burn coal. These differences, in turn, have caused considerable resistance at the state level to federal pressures to increase coal use.

To ease data analysis, the developments are treated in three stages. First, the declining role of waterpower is examined. Then the small but regionally concentrated role of nuclear power is noted. Finally, the role of fossil fuels is examined.

Electric utilities usually burn what is known as heavy or residual fuel oil, which is quite tarry. Transportation is most economical by water and, therefore, the prime markets are those near water. Since the principal source of supply is the Caribbean, plants near East Coast seaports were the first to begin important oil use.

The reduced role of waterpower is almost universal. A substantial rise in the importance of hydropower occurred in the Dakotas after World War II as the Missouri River Basin project developed. In North Dakota, hydro-generation was nonexistent in 1946, provided the majority of the power in 1960, but its share fell below 10 percent by 1979. The rise lasted longer in South Dakota, and the decline was less pronounced. The share went from 5 percent in 1946 to almost 90 percent in 1970; it was still 67 percent in 1979. For states east of the Mississippi that received the majority of their power from water in 1946, the 1979 share was universally much lower, with the highest 1979 share being 24 percent in Maine. The western picture is more varied. Sharp drops occurred in Wyoming, Arizona, Utah, Nevada, and California; more modest drops occurred in Montana, Washington, and Oregon (see table 3-8).

Nuclear generation has become more significant in several states, mostly those east of the Mississippi.

A variety of forces have influenced the share of fossil fuels in generation. The fundamental developments include an initial rise of gas use followed by a shift to coal as relative economics changed, and the rise and decline of oil competition with price movements and changing environmental policies. The variations from year to year and from state to state are too considerable to be treated adequately in a simple table. Therefore, no tabulations are attempted for years prior to 1979, but a verbal summary is provided (see appendix 3A).

In a substantial part of the United States, electric utilities have predominantly used coal through most of the 1946–1980 period. This region includes all of the East North Central states, Pennsylvania outside the Philadelphia area, West Virginia, North Carolina, Kentucky, Tennessee, North Dakota, and Wyoming. The significant rise in oil use came in the 1970s. Given growing pressures to reduce pollution, low and falling oil prices in the late 1960s, and a consensus among oil companies, consumers, and outside observers that these price trends would continue, utilities decided to convert existing plants to oil and build new ones that were not coal

Table 3-8
The Role of Water Power and Nuclear Energy in Electricity Generation in 1946, 1970, and 1979

	Hydroelectric as Percent of Total Generation			*Nuclear as Percent of Generation From Fuel*
	1946	*1970*	*1979*	*1979*
Maine	89.03	42.26	23.77	79.00
New Hampshire	78.23	20.71	17.08	0.00
Vermont	98.37	79.47	19.46	98.15
Massachusetts	12.93	2.33	1.04	7.17
Rhode Island	0.40	0.19	0.56	0.00
Connecticut	8.28	1.67	1.91	54.25
New England	29.79	7.72	5.77	36.26
New York	32.98	25.98	24.92	23.42
New Jersey	0.00	0.00	0.00	24.63
Pennsylvania	10.69	1.57	0.96	14.85
Middle Atlantic	19.81	12.05	10.47	18.90
Ohio	0.10	0.01	0.00	2.71
Illinois	0.30	0.20	0.11	26.27
Michigan	13.87	2.81	1.51	19.65
Wisconsin	28.89	5.83	5.32	28.90
East North Central	6.18	1.32	0.93	14.01
Minnesota	26.43	4.16	2.47	38.09
Iowa	30.63	0.44	4.42	14.91
Missouri	21.33	3.21	2.33	0.00
North Dakota	0.00	42.24	19.71	0.00
South Dakota	5.34	89.56	68.75	0.00
Nebraska	36.18	17.19	7.15	53.54
West North Central	21.67	13.52	8.05	15.43
Maryland	32.00	8.14	6.43	30.36
Virginia	19.11	2.28	4.33	21.08
West Virginia	7.20	1.23	0.76	0.00
North Carolina	50.41	8.46	11.61	11.30
South Carolina	90.12	13.56	9.39	48.31
Georgia	48.31	9.28	7.78	9.83
Florida	1.00	0.53	0.26	16.42
South Atlantic	31.56	5.02	5.10	16.20
Kentucky	63.71	7.03	7.20	0.00
Tennessee	93.59	18.54	20.96	0.00
Alabama	82.79	16.13	15.44	34.06
East South Central	83.21	12.87	13.58	12.36
Arkansas	47.34	16.55	20.10	28.86
Oklahoma	12.78	6.01	5.58	0.00
Texas	10.83	0.96	0.64	0.00
West South Central	83.21	2.61	2.36	1.36

Table 3–8 continued

	Hydroelectric as Percent of Total Generation			Nuclear as Percent of Generation From Fuel
	1946	1970	1979	1979
Montana	98.62	87.22	65.65	0.00
Idaho	99.83	100.00	99.56	0.00
Wyoming	84.58	15.51	4.78	0.00
Colorado	27.25	10.45	7.15	1.02
New Mexico	16.79	0.44	0.33	0.00
Arizona	86.33	47.17	20.75	0.00
Utah	77.43	25.01	7.43	0.00
Nevada	99.76	29.46	11.65	0.00
Mountain	83.41	37.04	21.27	0.18
Washington	98.05	96.37	87.38	31.54
Oregon	96.28	99.87	84.46	85.15
California	73.06	31.07	22.32	7.68
Pacific	83.62	61.24	51.46	12.89
Contiguous forty-eight states	35.13	16.19	12.48	13.06

Sources: For 1946: National Coal Association, *Trends in Electric Utility Experience, 1946–1958* (Washington, D.C. National Coal Association, 1960).

For 1970: Edison Electric Institute, *Historical Statistics of the Electric Utility Industry Through 1970* (New York: Edison Electric Institute, 1974).

For 1979: U.S. Department of Energy, *Power Production, Fuel Consumption and Installed Capacity Data for 1979 (Final),* Energy Data Report 12 June, 1980.

capable. Major new plants were constructed in Illinois, Michigan, Pennsylvania, and New York state, outside the New York City area. Alabama began the post–World War II period with about a 60 percent-40 percent coal-natural gas split of the market and by 1956 moved to nearly total coal dependence. A similar development occurred in Georgia.

The West North Central and Mountain states predominantly use coal in electricity generation, with natural gas playing a much reduced role. This summary conceals considerable differences. Collectively, the electric utilities in the West North Central states secured the majority of their fossil fuel for electricity in 1946 from coal, and the coal proportion shows a downward trend until the late 1950s. The 1946 gas share in the Mountain states was a bit over a third, dropped in the late 1940s, and stayed fairly flat at about 20 percent of steam-plant generation until the late 1950s.

In the West North Central states, the 1979 pattern showed coal heavily dominating among the fossil fuels in every state but Kansas, where gas accounted for over 40 percent of generation and coal slightly above 50 percent. Kansas was moving away from coal through 1970, then radically reversed the trend. Missouri, Minnesota, and Iowa were already obtaining the majority of their electric-power fuel from coal in 1946. In the first two states, the role of coal grew steadily; in Iowa, the share contributed by coal first declined through the middle 1960s, then rose.

Interstate variations are even greater in the Mountain region. The situation there is further complicated by the construction of large coal-fired plants to serve several units of the Western Council. In 1946, coal was the dominant fuel in Colorado, Utah, and Wyoming. In Colorado, gas gained at the expense of coal until the late 1950s, when coal began to absorb most of the market. From 1952 to 1972, Utah Power and Light obtained sufficient oil in the form of pitch produced in a local refinery to generate about as much electricity as was produced using coal. When this supply was withdrawn, coal assumed over 90 percent of the market. As noted, coal dominance persisted in Wyoming throughout the period.

Arizona Public Service was responsible for introducing coal use to Arizona and New Mexico. Until 1962, coal use was absent in Arizona. An Arizona Public Service plant that started operating in 1962 accounted for about 10 percent of steam-plant fuel use over the next several years. In New Mexico, coal accounted for a small part of fuel use (3 to 7 percent) until 1963, when Arizona Public Service started the first of three wholly owned units at the Four Corners plant. By 1964, coal comprised about 44 percent of steam-plant fuel.

The jointly owned Navajo plant in Arizona with units completed in 1974, 1975, and 1976; the jointly owned units at Four Corners; and the nearby San Juan joint venture raised the coal shares in both Arizona and New Mexico above 66 percent. A similar pattern arose in Nevada, where a coal unit started in 1965 accounted for 24 percent of fuel use by electric utilities. Expansion of that plant and the Mohave joint venture raised the coal share above 66 percent.

Several other states initiated or reinitiated coal use at various times since 1946. The earliest such development occurred in Florida in the early 1950s. Coal use was confined to the Florida west coast, where transportation economics were much more favorable to coal. Fuel oil for coastal plants was largely imported, and longer hauls and higher oil costs were involved on the west coast than the east. Conversely, the west coast was more favorably located for water shipments from the Illinois basin. Coal use edged up to about 25 percent by the late 1960s, retreated with the oil and environmental developments, then recovered. However, in the interim, Florida Power built oil units.

Mississippi began significant coal use only in the late 1960s, reaching a 32 percent share of total generation in 1979. A peak share of around 28 percent was reached in the middle 1970s; then a decline arose that reversed sharply in 1979. Again the coal-using utility added an oil unit during this period. Coal use reentered the West South Central region in the 1970s. It appeared first in Texas in 1971; the first Oklahoma plant started in 1976; the first in Arkansas, in 1978. The effect was to make coal the source of about 20 percent of regional generation and a quarter of that in Texas. The first large coal-burning plant ever built in Washington started operating in 1973. Thus, the fossil-fuel-use pattern radically shifted from small use of a few oil-fired units to predominant reliance on coal. Georgia displayed a pattern similar to some western states of reducing gas dependence from 60 percent in 1946 to a few percent by the early 1970s.

As noted, California has never directly burned coal for electricity generation but has relied heavily on power from joint ventures discussed above. The prospects for future coal plants are discussed in chapters 4 and 7. Tentative plans have been made for such plants, but there are questions about their feasibility.

Another group, consisting of Delaware, the District of Columbia, Maryland, South Carolina, and Virginia, is a belated convert to oil. From 1946 through the late 1960s, oil use in these areas rarely accounted for more than 1 to 3 percent of generation. The oil share jumped in 1968 in Delaware and the District of Columbia and in 1969 in Maryland, Virginia, and South Carolina. The degree of shift and the ability to reverse it differed considerably among these areas. Generation in the District of Columbia through 1980 remained entirely oil fired; however, output was curtailed and greater reliance was placed on plants, many of which were coal fired and operated outside the District. In Delaware, oil share rose to over 66 percent in 1978 and dropped below 53 percent in 1980. Maryland's highest relative use of oil—about 60 percent—came in 1975. By 1980, the oil share in fossil generation was 28 percent. The South Carolina oil share peaked around 20 percent in 1974 and fell below 7 percent in 1980. The oil share in Virginia similarly went over 30 percent in 1973 and 1974, accounted for the majority of fossil generation in 1978 and 1979, and dropped to 41 percent in 1980. However, plans are underway to reduce oil use by converting more Virginia plants back to coal. The moves to oil were accompanied in Delaware, Maryland, South Carolina, and Virginia by construction of plants with only oil capability.

A final main group, consisting of Connecticut, Massachusetts, New York, New Jersey, and the Philadelphia area, began as sites of intense coal-oil competition, then turned to oil dominance by the late 1960s. Massachusetts was the most intense battleground, with large but widely fluctuating market shares for both coal and oil. In New Jersey and the New York City area, the oil share was somewhat lower, in the 20 to 40 percent range. A 10 to 15 percent share for oil prevailed in Connecticut and Philadelphia.

The oil-price and environmental-policy developments already noted produced the end of coal use in Massachusetts, Connecticut, and the New York City area. Two utilities on the Hudson River, Central Hudson Gas and Electric and Orange and Rockland Utilities, also converted to oil. A Niagara Mohawk plant in upstate New York converted to oil, too. New Jersey and the Philadelphia area reduced but did not eliminate coal use. The oil share in New Jersey reached a high above 80 percent in 1972, remained in the 65 to 75 percent range, but declined in 1979 and 1980 as the ability arose to reduce generation by purchasing power and to increase gas use. The oil share of fossil-steam-plant fuel purchases was around 38 percent in 1980. Through the 1970s and into 1980, Philadelphia-area oil use ranged from 65 to 75 percent of the steam-plant total. In all these New England and Middle Atlantic areas, the move to oil again was accompanied by construction of plants incapable of coal use.

The only other New England states with significant fossil generation are Maine and New Hampshire. After 1953, coal use in Maine occurred only in 1960; New Hampshire, however, started a major coal-fired unit in 1956, and the share of coal jumped from 6 to 40 percent. Numerous subsequent fluctuations left the 1980 coal share at 55 percent.

Table 3–9 illustrates the impact through 1979 of all these hydroelectric, nuclear, and fossil fuel developments. The table shows the role of different power sources nationally, by census region, and, for those components of a census region with patterns markedly different from the regional norms, by state.

As can be seen, dependence on fuels differs widely among regions. Coal use occurs mainly in the North Central, South Atlantic, and East South Central regions, and the majority of the electricity is generated by coal-fired stations, as is true for the Mountain states. Gas is the predominant power source in the West South Central states which, together with California, dominate electric-utility gas use. Oil use occurs primarily on the East Coast and in California. The East Coast and East Central states are also higher-than-average users of nuclear power. The only significant other energy source is the geothermal energy used by Pacific Gas and Electric (whose reported geothermal output amounts for all but 40 out of 4 million Mw hours of power production from other sources in California).

These regional differences have major implications for several policy issues, particularly the efforts to discourage use of oil and gas and the desires to eliminate nuclear power. Given the uneven distribution of fuel use and the tendency of many plants to be unable to burn coal, fuel shifting would concentrate in a few regions.

Table 3-9
Regional Importance of Power Sources in 1979 Electricity Generation
(percent)

	Hydro	Coal	Oil	Gas	Nuclear	Other	Total
Share of Source in Regional Generation							
United States	12.45	47.86	13.48	14.66	11.35	0.20	100.00
New England	5.77	3.69	55.41	0.94	34.16	0.04	100.00
Middle Atlantic	10.47	44.34	24.63	3.62	16.91	0.03	100.00
East North Central	0.93	78.70	4.81	1.67	13.88	0.01	100.00
West North Central	8.05	67.44	2.07	8.25	14.19	0.00	100.00
South Atlantic	5.10	56.39	18.90	4.24	15.38	0.00	100.00
East South Central	13.58	69.65	3.26	2.84	10.68	0.00	100.00
West South Central	2.36	18.28	5.29	72.72	1.32	0.03	100.00
Mountain	21.27	63.77	3.16	11.63	0.14	0.03	100.00
Pacific	49.94	2.70	24.11	15.96	5.87	1.43	100.00
Share of Region in U.S. Generation by Source							
New England	1.61	0.27	14.31	0.22	10.48	0.74	3.48
Middle Atlantic	9.71	10.70	21.11	2.85	17.21	1.62	11.55
East North Central	1.35	29.62	6.43	2.05	22.01	0.82	18.01
West North Central	4.67	10.19	1.11	4.07	9.03	0.00	7.23
South Atlantic	7.38	21.22	25.25	5.20	24.40	0.00	18.01
East South Central	10.04	13.39	2.22	1.78	8.66	0.00	9.20
West South Central	2.47	4.97	5.11	64.58	1.52	1.95	13.02
Mountain	11.44	8.92	1.57	5.31	0.08	1.18	6.69
Pacific	51.33	0.72	22.89	13.93	6.61	93.64	12.80
U.S. Total	100.00	100.00	100.00	100.00	100.00	100.00	100.00
Share of Source in Generation in Selected States							
New York	24.92	13.26	38.04	6.15	17.57	0.07	100.00
Pennsylvania	0.96	74.79	9.45	0.10	14.71	0.00	100.00
Maryland	6.43	39.52	23.79	1.85	28.41	0.00	100.00
Virginia	4.33	35.31	39.48	0.72	20.16	0.00	100.00
Florida	0.26	19.39	47.94	16.03	16.37	0.00	100.00
California	22.32	0.00	40.59	28.76	5.77	2.56	100.00
Share of Selected States in U.S. Generation by Source							
New York	9.38	1.30	13.22	1.96	7.25	1.62	4.69
Pennsylvania	0.44	8.88	3.98	0.04	7.37	0.00	5.69
Maryland	0.78	1.25	2.67	0.19	3.79	0.00	1.52
Virginia	0.54	1.15	4.56	0.08	2.77	0.00	1.56
Florida	0.09	1.69	14.87	4.57	6.03	0.00	4.18
California	12.12	0.00	20.36	13.27	3.43	88.86	6.76

Source: U.S. Energy Information Administration, *Power Production, Fuel Consumption and Installed Capacity Data for 1979 (Final).* Energy Data Report 12 June 1980

Examination of 1980 data indicates coal contributed over half the generation for the first time since 1968, and nuclear surpassed oil for the first time ever because oil generation fell much more than did nuclear (table 3-10). The rise in coal shares occurred in every census region and involved

Table 3-10
Regional Importance of Power Sources in 1980 Electricity Generation
(percent)

	Hydro	Coal	Oil	Gas	Nuclear	Other	Total
Share of Source in Regional Generation							
United States	12.07	50.81	10.74	15.15	10.98	0.24	100.00
New England	4.35	5.80	60.34	0.74	28.71	0.06	100.00
Middle Atlantic	10.25	45.90	22.01	6.86	14.97	0.01	100.00
East North Central	0.89	80.29	3.65	1.13	14.02	0.02	100.00
West North Central	7.01	74.44	0.68	6.92	10.93	0.02	100.00
South Atlantic	3.74	59.75	15.53	4.04	16.95	0.00	100.00
East South Central	9.85	73.19	1.74	4.00	11.22	0.00	100.00
West South Central	1.27	23.86	2.47	69.86	2.50	0.03	100.00
Mountain	22.30	65.84	1.79	9.65	0.42	0.01	100.00
Pacific	57.18	2.92	14.64	18.71	4.59	1.95	100.00
Hawaii and Alaska	5.82	3.09	71.82	19.27	0.00	0.00	100.00
Share of Region in U.S. Generation by Source							
New England	1.23	0.39	19.21	0.17	8.94	0.89	3.42
Middle Atlantic	9.67	10.29	23.34	5.16	15.53	0.24	11.39
East North Central	1.28	27.44	5.89	1.30	22.17	1.15	17.37
West North Central	4.27	10.78	20.47	3.36	7.32	0.57	7.35
South Atlantic	5.65	21.48	26.40	4.87	28.18	0.00	18.26
East South Central	7.64	13.49	1.52	2.48	9.56	0.00	9.37
West South Central	1.44	6.43	3.15	63.17	3.12	1.43	13.69
Mountain	12.83	9.00	1.16	4.42	0.27	0.32	6.95
Pacific	55.78	0.68	16.06	14.55	4.92	95.41	11.78
Hawaii and Alaska	0.20	0.03	2.81	0.53	0.00	0.00	0.42
U.S. total	100.00	100.00	100.00	100.00	100.00	100.00	100.00

Source: Calculated from U.S., Department of Energy, Energy Information Administration, 1981, *Power Production, Fuel Consumption and Installed Capacity Data, 1980 Annual,* p. 51.

larger absolute levels. The largest increase by far was in Texas. Similarly, only New England departed from the national trend of falling generations amounts and shares from oil. Here the biggest decline was in California where the drop accompanied reduced generation, the largest increase in gas generation of any state, and more hydrogeneration. The overall small rise in gas share and amount involved increases in the Pacific, South Central, and Middle Atlantic regions offset by falls elsewhere.

Appendix 3A:
Notes on
Electricity-Utility Data
and Terminology

Electricity has the technological peculiarity of involving a unit of power intensity (the *watt*) and a measure of work accomplished (such as the *watt second* or *joule* and *watt hour*), which involves maintenance of power for a specified period. Since watts and watt hours are small units, data are expressed in kilowatts and kilowatt hours. Terms such as *power, load,* or *demand* are used to describe the number of kilowatts being supplied; terms such as *energy* or *production* are used to describe the kilowatt hours produced. Laymen are likely to use terms imprecisely and, where no ambiguity was involved, I have followed the more popular use of terminology.

Neither of the two traditional sources of energy and electricity data—the Federal Power Commission (FPC) and the U.S. Bureau of Mines—prepared summary data volumes giving a long-term overview of industry developments. Trade associations have undertaken to provide such compilations, largely consisting of tabulations of government-compiled data. The critical document for electric utilities is the Edison Electric Institute's *Statistical Yearbook of the Electric Utility Industry.* It is a mixture of government-compiled data and special material reported directly to the institute. Longer-term data periodically are assembled into a larger compendium.

The creation of the Energy Information Administration (EIA) of DOE simultaneously helped fill the gap in data and consolidated energy and electricity data in one agency. One major element in the program—the *Monthly Energy Report,* a compilation of basic energy data for the most recent years—was originated by the Federal Energy Administration (FEA). EIA added a compilation of longer-term information as a volume in its *Annual Report to Congress.* EIA, moreover, has taken over and modified the energy statistics programs of the Bureau of Mines, FPC, and FEA.

One basic set of materials is the series of Energy Data Reports that provide material on fuel use and generating capacity. These currently include reports on generation, fuel use, sales, and rates in the electric utility sector. In 1980 consolidated reporting on generation was instituted. Another important element is the continuation of long-standing FPC reports with detailed information on companies and plants. Two books are published on companies, one for the publics and one for the private, and both contain large amounts of data about individual companies. The presentation has major deficiencies, particularly on the public-entity side. The publicly owned entities are allowed to report using whatever fiscal year they choose, and they apparently are allowed to omit reports, since the coverage differs from year to year. Cooperatives remain the subject of a separate, less detailed report by the Rural Electrification Administration.

Individual units are the subject of the "cost books" (a shorthand for their long full titles). The oldest cost book relates to steam plants, but ones now appear on hydro and on gas-turbine units. A much newer FPC program provides material on fuel deliveries to both state and individual electric-utility plants. The reports are based on a survey of deliveries. Both a monthly and an annual report are available. Several private organizations obtain and report the full data supplied to FERC. Earlier data on fossil-fuel use could be found easily only in one report, *Steam Electric Plant Factors,* compiled by the National Coal Association. DOE has also continued FEA initiatives to compile data on extant and planned generating units. An annual directory of such units is issued, as are maps of their location and a guide to the maps.

A major source of discrepancies is the distinction between operation and ownership of joint ventures. Many statistical reports assign a joint venture to the company that operates it. Company reports and their presentation in EIA company-statistic reports prorate the plants among their owners. The assignment to operators is clearly followed with fuel-use data and apparently applies to generation data. The key discrepancies between EIA and REA data on cooperatives (shown in table 3–1) are explicable by EIA assignment of cooperative shares in joint ventures to the private company operating the plants. (A similar problem exists with Arizona; the high share of power authority power apparently includes total output in joint ventures that Salt River operates.)

Perhaps the biggest gap in all these data is material that traces the flow of power among companies. Excellent data are available on generation and sales, but complete, consistent data on transfers are unavailable. The DOE book on companies does provide data on the total amount of transfers by companies individually and collectively.

The material in chapter 3 was derived from DOE reports and supplemented by information obtained directly from the utilities. Particular use was made of the form 10K report that is required of private companies by the SEC, the securities prospectuses of the largest public companies, and the Uniform Statistical Report designed by the Edison Electric Institute (EEI) for reporting individual firm data. The 10K presents supplemental information, and the SEC has exerted considerable effort to broaden the content and to encourage wider circulation. EEI receives uniform statistical reports only from private companies and relies generally on other data to report on the rest of the industry. The material on pooling was taken from the caption to a map in the DOE *National Power Grid Study.* Information on company history was obtained by examining various issues of *Moody's Public Utilities.*

The reports containing data on individual firms provide a considerable amount of financial and physical data. These include summaries of the three basic firm financial statements (the balance sheet, income statement, and sources and uses of funds statement); details on the breakdown of cash expenditures and on the value of different types of assets; breakdown of the physical quantities and dollar amounts of electricity sales by broad customer type; and some physical data on generating, transmission, and distribution facilities.

EIA now systematically aggregates all these data. Some important problems arise with the aggregation. Electricity is double-counted to an unknown extent. For each company, sales include resale to others; resales within either the public or private sector are not netted out when the sums are calculated. The public-sector data are reported for whatever fiscal year the bodies maintain, and in some years organizations fail to report data altogether. The double-counting of resales inflates both sales revenues and costs, so data involving either are inaccurate. However, the role of resales is sufficiently stable so the exaggeration is similar from year to year.

The reports have other peculiarities and omissions. For example, only undepreciated cost details are provided for assets; only more aggregated figures are reported on accumulated depreciation. The uniform statistical reports are supposed to provide these details, but a few companies omit them. Similarly, EIA reports do not provide data on current outlays for new plants and equipment. The EEI yearbook does provide industry figures broken down only into the broad categories of generation, transmission, distribution, and other. Again, the uniform statistical reports provide fuller details.

Therefore, much data exist but suffer from the usual defects of accounting data, particularly failure to adjust for inflation, and some special problems such as inappropriate methods of aggregation.

The fuel-use discussion here deliberately links data calculated on slightly different basis. It was simpler to recognize the differences among the reporting methods and adjust the analysis appropriately than to reconstruct consistent series.

Generation can be subdivided in several different ways, and available reports use many of the different possibilities. One distinction involves removing various parts of the industry from the reporting. The largest possible figure is total generation. When the self-generation of large users is subtracted, the remainder is generation by the electric-utility industry. Deducting waterpower gives generation by fuels. Removing nuclear then gives generation by fossil fuels. Eliminating generation in turbines and

and internal combustion engines gives generation by steam plant. Deducting small plants (less than 25 Mw), leaves larger plant generation.

Most available detailed reports relate only to the electric-utility sector. The Edison Electric Institute's *Statistical Yearbook* reports data by state that separates first among hydro, conventional steam, nuclear, and internal combustion, then allocates total generation by fuels among coal, oil, gas, and nuclear. The National Coal Association's *Steam Electric Plant Factors* reports on total fossil-steam-plant generation from 1950 to 1974. From 1975 on, new FPC data covering only larger plants were aggregated for the summary table. Particularly when dealing with fossil fuels, it is possible to report either heat input or electricity output. The pre–1975 Coal Association data are on a Btu input basis; subsequently, generation is stressed. Because the National Coal Association reports provide calculations of the share of fossil fuels in fossil-steam-plant heat input, these data were used to obviate over 4000 fresh calculations.

Even more detailed data on individual companies appear in the "Form 1" report that companies file annually with FERC. The name refers to the designation the FPC gave to the standardized form on which extensive data must be entered. Among the data presented but not readily available elsewhere are reports on construction-in-progress amount on individual projects and detailed reports of the purchases and sales of power with other specified utilities. Thus, FERC has available but has not extensively reported on many details about which I raise questions in chapter 7. The data details also show that a distinction is made among types of exchanges that cause the peculiarities appearing in table 7A–3 in which companies record negative purchases plus positive sales. This arises from a FERC definition that subdivides the interchanges into different categories. Some are classed as definite resales and show up in the sale accounts; others are treated as part of the process of power swaps and reported purchases are, in fact, the net of purchases and the portion of sales classified as part of power swaps. This explains the negative purchase figures.

Appendix 3B:
Further Notes on
Leading Entities

An extensive effort was made to examine the nature of the 205 private companies distinguished by DOE. The tabulation for 1979 on private companies lists those 205 companies producing a total of 1,743 billion kWh out of a separately reported private total of 1,756, or 98.6 percent of the total. The number of independent entities is considerably less. About 105 companies are apparently separate from other power companies (including two owned by manufacturing companies). Another 47 are units of the 11 holding companies. Another 43 are units of 16 parent companies and various subsidiaries, including 5 companies owned by the Aluminum Company of America. Eight companies are jointly owned by other utilities. Finally, Cleveland Cliffs Iron owns a small utility and 88 percent of another; its partner is Upper Peninsula Power. Depending on how restrictive the definition, the number of independent entities ranges from 130 to 135. The high range includes the Cleveland Cliffs-Upper Peninsula companies as three separate companies and includes other companies owned by manufacturing firms. A possible source of overestimation is that the data examined—earlier EIA reports and large company uniform statistical reports—may have omitted some holdings.

The holding companies include the two largest private companies, AEP, and the Southern Company. The first operates primarily in Ohio, Indiana, West Virginia, and Virginia with other sales in Michigan, Kentucky, and Tennessee. It was the survivor of a largely autonomous component of Ebasco. Southern was the successor to Commonwealth and Southern, whose other holdings were several North Central states utilities. The next cluster of companies—Texas Utilities, Central and Southwest, and Middle South (ranking seventh, eleventh, and thirteenth, respectively)—are in the South Central states. Texas and Middle South were largely parts of Ebasco, and Central and Southwest was assembled from Insull companies. Texas operates entirely in Texas. The majority of Central and Southwest's business is also in Texas, with another 31 percent in Oklahoma, and the rest in Louisiana and Arkansas. About 47 percent of Middle South's sales are in Louisiana, 31 percent in Arkansas, 19 percent in Mississippi, and the rest in Missouri. The next companies are number 15 company, Allegheny Power System, with 48 percent of sales in Pennsylvania, 28 percent in West Virginia, 18 percent in Maryland, and small portions in Virginia and Ohio; and the number 21 company, General Public Utilities (GPU), which operates in

Pennsylvania and New Jersey. Allegheny consists of the electric utilities once held by American Waterworks which, as the name suggests, owned (and still owns) numerous water companies. GPU belonged to a smaller holding company group, Associated. The four remaining and much smaller companies are all in New England: Northeast Utilities, which operates in Connecticut and Massachusetts; New England Electric, in Massachusetts, Rhode Island, and to a minor extent New Hampshire and Vermont; the New England Gas and Electric Association, only in Massachusetts; and Eastern Utilities Associates, in Massachusetts and Rhode Island.

The main text of chapter 3 provides the most critical information on public power. The largest cooperative, Associated Electric Cooperative of Missouri, in 1979 generated about 60 percent of my cutoff for inclusion in the listing of companies. The states with more than one major generating cooperative are Iowa, Kentucky, Texas, and the Dakotas. Alaska is unusual in having all its cooperative generation by companies that also distribute.

4

The Practice of Electric-Power Regulation in the United States

Background: The Diversity of Control

The similarities in public-utility regulation to other aspects of government regulatory policy are more critical than the differences. Many of the same analytic questions arise in electric power as in other realms of regulation, and regulatory agencies often have responsibilities broader than just control of natural monopoly. Many activities of various industries all may be regulated by the same agency.

The literature distinguishes a special public-utility regulatory process, which imposes limits on the prices, profits, and outputs of firms. Economists argue that this form of regulation is most appropriate for natural monopolies (recall chapter 2). Several difficulties arise with this distinction. As has been well publicized, controls often are extended to industries that are not natural monopolies, such as trucking. Sometimes the only justification for control is an equity argument. In other cases, regulation is more akin to efforts to control quality, such as in the fair-business-practice portion of the Federal Trade Commission's activities or in product-standards-setting efforts by numerous other federal agencies.

More critically, the distinction between public utility and other electric-power-industry forms of regulation is not sharply drawn in practice. Public-utility regulators have been required to consider other issues, notably environmental ones, while other agencies have been required to examine questions such as "need" that were part of the public-utility regulatory process. This overlapping of responsibilities makes deregulation particularly complex and burdensome.

This chapter critically reviews electric-power regulation in context with the basic pattern of regulation in the United States. The discussion begins with an effort to characterize this control, drawing on an extensive survey conducted by the National Association of Regulatory Utility Commissioners (NARUC). Special attention is paid to efforts to alter the procedures for siting power plants. More specifically, the elaborate formal planning attempts by California and New York are closely reviewed as case studies in the pitfalls of institutional reform. The discussion also examines the 1980 Northwest Power Act and 1978 federal legislation that attempts to alter regulation of electric utilities.

131

Electric Power and the Regulatory Process

In discussing regulation, a basic issue involves which industries should be regulated. Another issue involves which activities of that industry should be controlled. A closely related set of concerns regards the requirements that should be imposed on the industry in support of regulation. Finally, there are issues concerning how regulatory agencies should be organized.

Regulation of electric power and other industries is split among federal, state, and local authorities. A basic consideration is that control occurs through regulation, ownership, and their interaction. There is a varied approach to regulating public power. For example, the Federal Energy Regulatory Commission (FERC) has power over Bonneville, but this power is not exercised (compare NARUC, p. 397 to p. 391). The Tennessee Valley Authority (TVA) and most other federal-power administrations are exempt from FERC control. Federal power plants are thus effectively regulated by the operating agencies themselves. Most states either do not regulate municipally owned utilities or confine regulation to activities outside the owning municipality (see table 4–1), but some states do regulate fully (NARUC 1980, pp. 393–401, 410) State regulation of electric utilities is nonexistent in Nebraska and minimal in Tennessee, where private activities are minor due to the presence of the TVA. In addition to whatever self-regulation cities owning electric power organizations may impose, some municipalities exercise regulatory control of private utilities, notably in Texas and Louisiana (New Orleans alone) (NARUC 1980, p. 410).

The pattern in the federal government is toward creating numerous large, specialized regulatory agencies. On the other hand, the states tend to assign many responsibilities to a few small agencies; most states have only one agency to handle all public-utility regulation problems.

Federal regulation of the electric-utility industry is divided between the FERC and the Securities and Exchange Commission (SEC). FERC exercises conventional rate-regulation power over interstate wholesale transactions, while also trying to encourage nationwide efforts to improve the bulk power system.

The various patterns of company structure, the principles of the Holding Company Act, and the federal-state split in regulation generally produce complicated regulatory relations. Basically, interstate sales among utilities are covered by FERC; all other sales are covered by state agencies. Corporate structure can be a major influence. One major distinction is the form of a joint venture. Separately incorporated firms running a venture (such as the Yankee companies) are considered to be wholesalers, and FERC regulates transfer of power to the owners. However, when companies directly own a portion of the plant, the state in which the sale occurs regulates rates on electricity from any owner's portion that is sold directly to customers of

Table 4-1
Selected Data on U.S. Public-Utility Regulation

	Staff	Number of Commissioners	Appointed or Elected	Percent Income from General Revenues	Rate Regulation Municipal	Rate Regulation Cooperative
1. California	979	5	A	58.9		
2. New York	640(706)	7	A		S	
3. Pennsylvania	538	5	A		S	
4. Virginia	456	3	A	11		X
5. Florida	354	5	A		S	S
6. Oregon	351	1	A			
7. Ohio	332	3	A			
8. Michigan	315(344)	3	A			X
9. Illinois	269	5	A			
10. Missouri	254	5	A	3		
11. New Jersey	227	3	A			
12. Oklahoma	223	3	E			X
13. Washington	203	3	A			
14. Arizona	194	3	E			X
15. Kansas	192.5	3	A		S	X
16. North Carolina	168	7	A	70		
17. West Virginia	151	3	A		X	X
18. Wisconsin	146(199)	3	A		X	
19. South Carolina	145	7	A			
20. Tennessee	142	3	E			
21. Minnesota	133	5	A	94		S
22. Iowa	129(142)	3	A			X
23. Massachusetts	122	3	A		S	
24. Texas	110(848)	3	A		S	X
25. Georgia	108	5	E	97		
26. Maryland	107	5	A		X	X
27. Connecticut	107	5	A	100		X
28. Indiana	103	3	A		X	X
29. Louisiana	99	5	E			
30. Colorado	95	3	A		S	X
31. Mississippi	89	3	E			
32. Alabama	81	3	E			
33. Maine	76	3	A		X	X
34. Kentucky	73(445)	3	A			X
35. Nevada	72	3	A			X
36. Nebraska	56	5	E	100		
37. Idaho	56	3	A	8		
38. Arkansas	53(85)	3	A		S	X
39. North Dakota	50	3	E			
40. New Hampshire	45	3	A	19	S	X
41. Montana	44	5	E		X	
42. Wyoming	37	3	A		S	X
43. Alaska	37(75)	5	A	100	S	X
44. South Dakota	35	3	E	62		
45. Rhode Island	35	3	A	30	X	X

Table 4-1 continued

	Staff	Number of Commissioners	Appointed or Elected	Percent Income from General Revenues	Rate Regulation	
					Municipal	Cooperative
46. District of Columbia	31	3	A	47.2		
47. New Mexico	29(126)	3	A	100	S	X
48. Utah	26	3	A	7		X
49. Vermont	26	3	A		X	X
50. Delaware	18	5	A			X
51. Hawaii	17	3	A	100		

Sources: All data from National Association of Regulatory Utility Commissioners, *1979 Annual Report on Utility and Carrier Regulation.*

Staff numbers: pp. 748–763. Where a second number appears in parenthesis in staff column, it represents the total for all reported agencies; the first number relates to the commission covering utilities. Some states do not report all agencies.

Number of commissioners and how selected: pp. 732–734. A is appointed; E is elected.

Revenues source: p. 768.

Rate Regulation: pp. 393–401. X indicates full control; S indicates limited control as follows: only service outside owning municipality in Pennsylvania, New Jersey, Colorado, Arkansas, New Hampshire, and Wyoming; only service three miles outside owning municipality in Kansas; only service five miles outside owning municipality in New Mexico; New York exempts the Power Authority and its municipal customers from control; Florida controls only rate structures of municipals and cooperatives; Massachusetts only limits earnings; Texas acts as appellate jurisdiction over municipal regulators; Alaska only regulates competitors of private utilities; Minnesota cooperatives regulated only if they want it.

that owner. Thus, New Jersey would regulate rates on Atlantic City Electric's sale to its customers of Atlantic City's share in the Keystone Plant in Pennsylvania. More generally, the state of sale rather than the state of generation regulates power produced and sold in one state to final customers of the plant owner in other states.

Further, each unit of a holding company is regulated as if it were a separate company. Interdivision sales, therefore, are regulated by FERC. As noted in chapter 3, most holding companies are organized so their principal units each generate, transmit, and distribute electricity. Therefore, FERC control is limited. Exceptions occur in New England, where three of the four holding companies are organized so one component does most of the generating and sells to the other units. These transfers are FERC regulated.

The SEC has authority over industry reorganization, as mandated by the Public Utility Holding Company Act of 1935. The relevant provision of the act requires SEC approval of mergers. The acquisition of Columbus and Southern Ohio Electric by American Electric Power (AEP) was announced in 1968 but not approved until 1980. Other proposed mergers of closely co-operating companies such as the Capco group and several New England companies (Boston Edison, New England Electric, and Eastern Utilities) were withdrawn in the face of such delays by the SEC.

The SEC role seems to have originated from the belief that the main problem was of unsound financial practices rather than monopoly, which the FPC or an antitrust agency would treat. The concern with financial manipulation was a major legacy of the 1929 stock market crash. A good example comes from the often-cited Berle and Means book on corporate concentration. Berle and Means' primary concern about separation of ownership from control was over the potential for securities fraud. This concern has persisted. The critics of conglomerates during the 1960s were worried about financial manipulation as well as monopoly.

In addition to the basic question of whether reorganization of the electric-utility industry is socially beneficial, concern can be raised about whether regulatory responsibility rests with the proper agency. However, some observers might fear that FERC would be unduly lenient toward mergers or that antitrust agencies would be as inappropriately stringent, as some critics feel has been the case with the SEC.

FERC's other responsibilities are with natural gas and oil pipelines and a few oil issues assigned to it when it was made a part of the Department of Energy (DOE). The SEC is concerned dominantly with the securities businesses.

Numerous other agencies affect other aspects of the electric-power industry. The most important include the Nuclear Regulatory Commission (NRC), the Environmental Protection Agency (EPA), and the Economic Regulatory Administration (ERA) of DOE. NRC regulates nuclear-power plants; EPA sets basic national air-pollution rules and monitors state compliance; ERA enforces the Fuel Use Act and other DOE regulations. When a utility requires access to federal land, the Department of the Interior may become involved in the regulatory process.

The states typically regulate electric, gas, telephone, and water utilities and various forms of transportation (NARUC 1980, pp. 725-730). Some states also regulate a few other areas, such as warehouses and docks, sale of securities, toll roads, and grain dealers (in Iowa). Thirty-eight states and the District of Columbia entrust all regulation to a single agency. Another seven states—Arkansas, Delaware, Iowa, New Jersey, New York, Vermont, and Wisconsin—divide regulation between a utility and a transportation commission. In Minnesota, the Public Service Commission regulates utilities but shares control over transportation with the Department of Transportation. In New Mexico, one commission regulates electricity, gas, and water, and another controls telephones, telegraph, radio, and transportation. Alaska has a regulatory commission for utilities, another for most forms of transportation, and a third for oil and gas pipelines.

Texas has an unusual regulatory structure, widely discussed in the literature on petroleum economics. The Railroad Commission is charged with a wide range of responsibilities, including regulation of oil and gas production and most transportation operations. However, a separate Aeronautics Commission created in 1945 supervises aviation. In 1976, a public-utilities commission was established to regulate electric, water, and telephone utilities; control previously was exercised municipally.

Kentucky had four commissions. Utility regulation was split between an Energy Regulatory Commission for gas and electricity and a Utility Regulatory Commission for other areas. The commissions shared staff. (This division was abolished in 1981, and the single commission form was restored). Another pair of commissions include one for rail and water and another for road transportation (see NARUC 1980, pp. 679, 721–730).

As table 4–1 shows, state regulatory commissions are typically quite small. The vast majority of states employ fewer than 200 people in regulation; 20 states employ fewer than 100. In comparison, FERC employs 1,621 people; SEC, 1,953; NRC, 3,067 (NARUC 1980, p. 764–765). In 32 states and the District of Columbia, the commission regulating public utilities has only 3 commissioners; 14 states have 5-member commissions; 3 have 7; and Oregon has 1. Eleven states elect commissioners; the rest appoint them (NARUC 1980, pp. 732–767). Most commissions secure the bulk of their financing from charges on the utilities (NARUC 1980, p. 768 and table 4–1 here).

As surveyed by NARUC, regulatory techniques extend far beyond the setting of limits on rates of return stressed by Averch and Johnson (1962). The selection of allowable yields is only one among many of the elaborate methods used to determine the actual charges for electric power. Control also extends to many other areas. A wide variety of actions (such as mergers, purchase and sale of properties, issuance of securities, and construction of facilities) almost universally require commission approval. Other areas into which some commissions have entered include setting rules about when competitive bids are required, promulgating company performance standards, divising methods for allocating power during shortages, establishing billing rules, preventing damage to underground facilities of utilities, and promoting conservation (see NARUC 1980, pp. 482–486, 487–491, 496–520, 529–541, 636–642). Most states provide commissions with the authority to regulate billing practices and require the use of competitive bidding when selecting securities underwriters, designers, and contractors. This latter requirement is not widely exercised. Emergency allocation, facility damage prevention, and conservation efforts also are practiced less widely.

Generally, the states have not been major influences over mergers. The principal exception was a decision in 1979 by the New York Public Service

Commission to prevent the formation of a joint venture by all the privately owned utilities in the state to build power plants. The denial could be justified simply because the arrangement did not make sense in the climate of reduced-growth prospects. However, a point more critical to the prospects for reform is that the commission also seemed concerned about the transfer of control to FERC that would take place if the new organization were created.

Another aspect of regulation can be described as providing for supporting activities such as conventional financial audits, management audits (reviews of business practice usually conducted by management consultants), submission of forecasts, and other reporting requirements (NARUC 1980, pp. 463–480, 631).

The complexities of ratemaking, moreover, are considerable. The commissions have considerable discretion over how to define income, costs, and invested capital. Therefore, a given outcome can be produced in many different ways. A higher rate of return, for example, can be granted directly or by defining cost or investment liberally. Profits can be disguised as costs or disallowance of costs may overstate profits. Raising the value of investment allows earning more profits given the permissible rate of return. A major consequence of this flexibility is that what in theory are undesirable practices may actually be second-best ways to secure indirectly relief otherwise unattainable. The mechanics of alternative rate-setting formulas can be explained through straightforward but tedious accounting exercises. Such discussions are available in the specialized literature. Here it is sufficient to know that such options exist.

A primary consideration is the extent to which present rates can be based on projections of future conditions—an approach technically known as the future test-year method. This method is used explicitly by only a minority of states (see table 4–2, and NARUC 1980, pp. 405–407). However, as elsewhere in public-utility regulation, the lack of explicit policies does not necessarily mean that relief is not provided. The rates granted may include a deliberate adjustment for the absence of explicit forecasting or of other means of rapid relief. Thus, several people familiar with a Massachusetts rate decision indicated to me that it simultaneously rejected the use of forecasts, yet still set rates high enough to insure that income covered forecasted costs. The practice of implicit adjustment is sufficiently widespread that a term, *attrition,* has been devised to describe it. However, explicit or implicit use of forecasts is no panacea. The forecasts could inadvertently or even deliberately underestimate cost escalation.

Implementing rate making to provide an adequate return of investment requires establishing numerous rules. The proper rate of return itself must be estimated. NARUC indicates that states set allowable rates of return on both total investment and common equity (1980, pp. 443–448). Then rules

Table 4-2
Selected Characteristics of State Regulation of Electric Utilities

	Bans on Automatic Fuel Clause	Use of Forecast Test Year	Construction In Progress in Rate Base	When Given Power	Time Limit on Decisions	Average Decision Time Reported
Alabama			X	1919	6M	6M
Alaska			X	1960	6M[a]	6M
Arizona			X	1912		9M
Arkansas			X	1935	6M	8-10M
California		F	C	1912	365D[a]	12M
Colorado			X	1913	120D	7M
Connecticut	X			1911	150D	n.a.
Delaware		P	X	1949		6M
District of Columbia				1913		18M
Florida			D	1951	30D	9M
Georgia	X	P	X	1906		4M
Hawaii		F	X	1913	9M[a]	1Y
Idaho				1913		7M
Illinois		P	D	1913	120D	10M
Indiana			D	1963		22M
Kansas			C	1911		7M
Kentucky			X	1935		6M
Louisiana			X	1921	1Y	9M
Maine				1914		9M
Maryland		P	X	1910	n.a.	200D
Massachusetts	X			1885	6M	6M
Michigan		F	X	1909		1Y
Minnesota		F	D	1975	90D	9M
Mississippi			X	1956	180D	5M
Missouri	X			1913	120D	7M
Montana	X			1913	9M	9M
Nevada				1920	n.a.	6M
New Hampshire				1911	1Y	1Y
New Jersey		P	D	1911	8M[a]	8M
New Mexico			X	1941	10M	6M
New York		C	X	1905	60-90D	11M
North Carolina	X		X	1913	270D	1Y
North Dakota		F		1919	12M	6M
Ohio			CD	1913	175D	9M
Oklahoma			D	1913		3M
Oregon				1911	6M	7M
Pennsylvania		P		1913	9M	9M
Rhode Island				1969		9M
South Carolina			X	1912	12M	10M
South Dakota				1975	15M	9M

Table 4-2 continued

	Bans on Automatic Fuel Clause	Use of Forecast Test Year	Construction In Progress in Rate Base	When Given Power	Time Limit on Decisions	Average Decision Time Reported
Texas			X	1976	180D	5M
Utah	X	F	D	1917	140D	6M
Vermont			C	1923		1Y
Virginia			X	1914	60–90D	9M
Washington			D	1909	10M	7.5M
West Virginia	X			1915	270D	2Y
Wisconsin		P		1907		9M
Wyoming				1915	10M	4M

Source: All data from National Association of Regulatory Utility Commissioners, *1979 Annual Report on Utility and Carrier Regulation.*

Notes: Bans on fuel clause exist if X entered, pp. 403–404. Ban may be offset by rapid hearings.

Test year: F is full forecast used; P is partial forecast used; some mixed cases are treated as full forecasts if forecasts were dominant method, pp. 405–407.

Construction in progress, pp. 416–417; X is full allowance; C or V for almost complete facilities; D is discretionary grants.

Year power granted, p. 408.

Allowed time for decision and actual times, pp. 737–741.

a after allowed time indicates that the request does not automatically go in force after the deadline is missed.

n.a. indicates that a limit exists after which the rate goes into effect but the exact time is not reported.

must be established to determine how to measure the numerator (revenues less allowable costs) and the denominator (investment levels) of the actual-return ratio to check whether the rate of return is being maintained.

The investments eligible to earn profits constitute the rate base. The critical questions are what is included and when, and how the investment is valued. The predominant method of valuation is the original cost. Some states allow valuation to be based on "fair value;" this can be an estimate of the replacement cost, but there is no guarantee that this interpretation will be adopted. Leonard Hyman, the chief electric-utility analyst of Merrill Lynch, Pierce, Fenner & Smith, argues that fair value rarely adequately reflects cost inflation (Hyman 1979, p. 17).

Since investment levels vary over time, various expedients must be adopted to determine the time at which the rate base is measured. Approaches either use a year-end figure or an average of the levels at the start and end of the year or of the average of the monthly levels (NARUC 1980, pp. 424–425).

A particularly controversial question is when investments should enter the rate base. This is critical since facilities remain under construction from five to ten years, tying up sizable portions of company assets. These facilities produce benefits only on completion. Efficient pricing requires that the plants not be constructed unless consumers are willing to pay enough to yield an adequate rate of return. Utility rates should be high enough so the willingness to pay the required price is translated into realization of that price.

Critics opposing earlier placement of the outlays in the rate base stress the appropriateness of having the investment repaid through actual operation. This neglects the apparent unwillingness of regulatory commissions to allow the appropriate rates, not only on a new facility when it is completed, but also on most existing facilities. One means of lessening the problem of inadequate returns is to incorporate the cost of construction work in progress into the rate base.

A further problem was suggested by the 1979 accident at General Public Utilities' (GPU) Three Mile Island (TMI) unit 2. Concerns were raised that GPU had rushed completion of the unit because of a desire to speed its entry into the rate base. Whether the exertion to start the plant caused deficiencies in training and thus in the response to the malfunction will long be debated. What is important is that the TMI experience created concern, if not evidence, that a rush to get a facility included in the rate base could lead to carelessness.

The primary culprits, however, are an unfavorable regulatory climate and a year-end basis for the rate base. A fully responsive regulatory system would eventually raise rates to compensate for delays in plant completion. This could be accomplished through rapid rate decisions or by providing sufficient attrition adjustments to compensate for regulatory lags. A valuation method for plant in service based on monthly averages rather than the year-end level used in Pennsylvania greatly reduces the advantage of completion at year end.

Commissions also are concerned with what constitutes a legitimate cost and how it should be measured. Perhaps the most widely discussed element of cost appraisal is the treatment of such devices as the investment tax credit, the right to use accelerated depreciation techniques, and depreciable lives shorter than the useful economic lives of facilities. Commissions either normalize profits so the benefits of these tax provisions are retained by the stockholders or require flow-through accounting, which causes the benefits to reduce rates to customers.

Resolution of the issue of where the benefits ideally should go is not possible. Tax favors are an effort to offset perceived distortions in the allocation of resources caused by the tax system. However, economists have not been able to determine conclusively whether the problem is one of reducing profits to stockholders, raising costs to consumers, or some combination of the two. Again, a major difference exists between regulated and unregulated industries. Since any tax credit is effectively a tax reduction, the same market forces that produced the initial impacts of the tax will inspire reversals of these effects.[1] Regulators once again face the problem of trying to determine and duplicate the behavior of markets. The problem of rate inadequacy, however, implies that normalization might provide some relief.

Two other key elements of rate regulation are the extent to which elements of costs can be passed on to customers automatically and pressures on the commission to make decisions (see table 4-2). Automatic adjustment has been allowed for rapidly changing items, principally fuel costs. This inspired frequent complaints that decision making is distorted because fuel use is favored over employing other inputs whose costs must be specifically approved.

This is a problem, but removing fuel adjustment would make a bad situation worse. The adjustment insures that some actions can be taken to avoid bankrupting the company in the presence of steadily rising costs. The critics are right that where cheaper methods exist for responding to fuel-price increases, the utilities should be encouraged to take them. This requires a willingness on the part of commissions to authorize these cost-saving actions. No guarantee exists, as is implicitly assumed by critics of fuel adjustment, that its removal would create pressures for adopting more efficient responses.

Actually, the inability to secure approval for new investments and the ability to secure rate increases for fuel costs reflects an inherent defect of rate-making principles. Rate regulators are unwilling to let rates reflect current costs (see later discussion). Rates to consumers are lower than true costs and an investment that lowers fuel cost can at least temporarily raise rates.

Further, the fuel-adjustment clause may decrease willingness to bargain aggressively for fuel. This argument implicitly assumes that some market imperfection exists so utilities can lower costs by more aggressive buying. However, this is not valid currently for either oil or gas. In the cases of coal and uranium, it is also true that market power in the conventional sense does not exist for the electric utilities. However, a different type of buying problem can arise. A wide variety of institutional arrangements can be employed to secure coal and uranium, ranging from spot transactions to entry into mining and fuel processing. Intermediate steps include contract purchases of various durations, lending to suppliers, and financing mines that are operated by other firms.

Every method can be challenged. FERC generated a report suggesting that American Electric Power's self-owned and operated mines were too expensive. Here a possible counterargument is that AEP is being unfairly compared to mines selling under old contracts based on past conditions or, more critically, that AEP is being faulted for not adequately anticipating that environmental regulations would depress the market for the type of coal it produced. These counterarguments may or may not be valid.

Electric-utility-coal ventures west of the Mississippi are highly success-ful. However, a draft Department of Energy report on captive coal mining east of the Mississippi argues that in that part of the country captive mines have lower productivity and higher prices than comparable noncaptive mines. Eastern captive mining is quite different from western captive min-ing. One of these differences is a source of high costs and low productivity. Specifically, many eastern utilities ended up owning mines because the inde-pendent owner either was held in default of a contract or, in one extreme case, declared bankruptcy.

One company was accused of contracting for fuel at the wrong time, and another was attacked for buying too much spot coal at about the same time the second company was contracting. This all adds up to a few possible cases of error by an industry that buys over 30 percent of the fuel consumed in the United States—hardly a record suggesting widespread ineptitude. Nevertheless, some states have chosen to limit the grant of price relief. A ban apparently does not mean no pass-through so much as requiring more complex ways to secure approval.

For example, Massachusetts and North Carolina have banned fuel adjustment, but both have alternative procedures that provide relief. North Carolina has a periodic review process similar to one instituted in Virginia; it is also being implemented in West Virginia, South Carolina, and Florida. In each case, rates are periodically set on the basis of forecasted energy prices with an adjustment for past over- or undercharges. Reviews occur semiannually in West Virginia, South Carolina, and Florida, and every four months in North Carolina. Virginia started with annual reviews and shifted in 1980 to a system of semiannual review but with no relief provided in the midyear review unless specified limits to rises or falls are exceeded.

The time limit concerns the extent to which states force commissions to act to offset the erosion of profits that delay will cause in periods of rising nominal costs. Generally, effective limits do exist, and speed is not the key problem. What is critical is that rate filings are elaborate. The basic mechanics of preparing such filings require at least several weeks of effort no matter how many people are assigned to the task. Given commission-staff sizes, another limit is the ability to absorb requests. Thus, we would expect a range of filing practices, with large companies dealing with large commissions filing most often. Available data suggest annual filing is in-creasingly the norm. Some companies find this is too frequent for their own or the regulatory commissions' staffs, but others are thinking of semiannual submission.

As suggested, the fundamental question about regulation is whether it produces serious economic distortions. One proposition for which there is ample evidence is that rate-of-return regulation fails to allow rates to reflect the upward shift in marginal costs in current dollars. The rules of regulation promote underpricing. Instead of charging the cost of a new unit, utilities can only charge the weighted average cost of all plants. Given that the older plants have lower real costs than new plants, the weighted average must be below the marginal cost of new plants. The underpricing is further aggravated by inadequate adjustment of the allowable rates of return to compensate for inflation. However, these pressures can be offset by failing to lower rates to account for economic obsolescence (see chapter 2).

Rate-of-return regulation can use the economic rents from lower costs to subsidize increased output. In the absence of regulation, firms would produce the output at which marginal cost equals marginal revenue and would earn economic rents under present conditions in the electric-utility industry. Regulation requires that output be expanded instead to the level at which average costs are equated to price. The profits that otherwise would have been earned finance the extra capacity that has marginal costs above marginal revenue and price. The definition of *subsidy* is financing something whose marginal cost exceeds price; clearly, profits are subsidizing output expansion. Effectively, each increment of output over the competitive equilibrium level is financed by an implicit tax on the economic rents. By construction, the subsidies equal the rents that would have been earned, so the firm ends up with zero rents, which is economically equivalent to equating price to average cost. (See chapter 2 for a discussion of the similar case of subsidizing expansion on monopoly output by use of income from a franchise bid; see also Gordon 1970, for analysis of the subsidy of output from economic rents.) Briefly, a competitive equilibrium price equals a marginal cost exceeding average cost. The next increment of output, by the definition of competition, earns the going price but because of increasing costs has a marginal cost above price and is unprofitable. The rents provide a possible source of funds for subsidy to induce the extra outputs.

Thus, regulation is a form of price control that does not necessarily create excess demand. However, avoidance of such excess depends critically on the rates of return that suffice to cover costs. If, as the data cited later suggest, rates are below average costs, the effect would lead ultimately to excesses of the quantity demanded over the quantity supplied at the prevailing rates.

Nationwide disputes about access to low-cost power are the clearest evidence that underpricing prevails. A few examples suffice. The most dramatic has been the fight over shares in the low-cost electricity marketed by the Bonneville Power Authority. The disputes were so frenzied that Congress chose to intervene in 1980 to alter the allocations.

The Bonneville controversy about insuring all households access to cheap power involved many issues. Questions were raised about how best to treat the industries that had located in the area because of direct access to Bonneville energy. Concerns were also expressed that the federal government should continue to receive power at low prices.

At least two more basic sources of controversy have arisen: public versus private power, and the Pacific Northwest versus California. The defective logic of providing a preference to public and cooperative power operations over privately owned companies has become clear; all power companies are effectively conduits of electricity to final consumers.

Moreover, the distinction often made between direct household use of power and other uses is faulty. Shifting costs from direct users to others can raise the cost of operations and ultimately raise prices of the goods and services produced with the power. What households appear to gain with lower costs on direct use can be more than offset by losses due to higher costs of electricity using utilities. Indeed, if we start from a position of competitive equilibrium, any transfer of electricity from its most efficient use (such as the shift postulated from industry to direct household use) would increase costs by definition. With underpricing prevailing, favoritism of direct household use aggravates the excess consumption problem in the household sector and lessens it in other uses of electricity.

In any case, it is unlikely that those who benefit from Bonneville power through service by private companies differ greatly from those who get their electricity from publicly owned bodies or cooperatives. The public power and cooperative preference serves only to alter the comparative economics of private power versus the other types. It is often argued that public power and cooperatives already receive too much federal government aid. An illustration of this position is provided by a 1980 DOE Energy Information Administration study of the net effect of U.S. energy policies. Aid to public power and cooperatives was treated as an undesirable subsidy rather than, as a defender would argue, as an offset to market imperfections. Both receive a tax-exempt status and favorable borrowing situations. The public can use the basic credit worthiness of its jurisdiction, and cooperatives can borrow from the U.S. government on favorable terms. Those who believe that stimulating public and cooperative power is inefficient would consider access provisions an additional market imperfection.

One of several interstate disputes over energy arose over Bonneville. Carlifornia regularly argues for a greater allocation of Bonneville power, and California utilities quarrel among themselves about the proper sharing of Bonneville power. (On the first point, see the 1979 Biennial Report of the California Energy Commission.)

Similarly, New England states, notably New Hampshire and Massachusetts, are arguing on the sharing of low-cost power. New Hampshire's regulatory commission has forbidden the export of hydroelectric power. Massachusetts has threatened to retaliate by denying the export of any low-cost power, such as from nuclear plants, that is currently being sold to New Hampshire. Again, what is at issue is the transfer of economic rents between states.

The existence of power plants in the West South Central region with access to underpriced natural gas and lignite has been mentioned (in interviews I conducted) as a barrier to closer interconnections among utilities in the region. Fears exist over transfer of the rents to customers of other companies. New Mexico attempted to react to the existence of lower cost, in-state power plants serving other states by attempting to impose an electricity export tax. This was ruled illegal interference with interstate commerce. A similar tax in West Virginia was the subject of litigation as of 1981.

The question of whether the difficulties are aggravated by inadequate allowable rates of return is much more difficult to resolve. A basic problem concerns settling the perennial issue of the efficiency of capital markets. At one extreme is the view that it is always possible to explain away anything as resulting from market imperfections rather than from defective regulation. At the other extreme, capital markets are considered by far the best available judges of prevailing conditions.

Another key element in the regulatory climate is the variation in the relationships among the private, public, and cooperative sectors of the industry. As noted in chapter 3, major rapproachments have occurred, particularly through the creation of public and cooperative organizations designed specifically to share ownership of plants that are usually designed and operated by a private company. Public companies (with their ability to use the credit ratings of their region and insure that rates will be high enough to prevent defaults) and cooperatives (with their access to U.S. government funds) are better able to finance new investment than private companies. S. David Freeman, until 1981 the head of TVA, has proposed that his agency be made the instrument for avoiding power shortages (Freeman 1980 and 1981).

Nevertheless, review of company reports and discussions with companies indicate frequent cases of filing antitrust suits and intervention with FERC relating to the service levels and rates that private companies offer to municipals and cooperatives. Complaints include assertions that rates unfairly impair the ability of municipals and cooperatives to compete for resale customers and that the private companies are refusing to provide power or to transfer power from other companies. Cases have occurred, for example, in Massachusetts, Connecticut, New York, Delaware, Ohio, Kentucky, Florida, and California.

Access issues have involved such questions as participation in pools (for example, the city of Cleveland versus the Capco companies) and the access to cheap power (for example, California companies that sued over sharing Bonneville Power, and suits over reallocating Power Authority of the State of New York generation from private utilities to municipal or industrial customers).

FERC tends to grant greater rate relief more rapidly than do the states. Thus, wholesale customers such as municipals and cooperatives endure larger, more rapid rate increases than do the direct customers of the private companies. The problems is one of undercharging the direct customers rather than overcharging the cooperatives and municipals.

A company with multistate operations may have problems in simultaneously meeting the requirements of all the state regulatory agencies. Conflicts may arise about proper allocation of costs among units in various states. Another difficulty that can arise is when utilities in the same state have radically different costs. A major example of the problems that can occur is Virginia Electric and Power's (Vepco) North Carolina operations. Vepco had higher costs and rates than the other companies in the state. These costs appear to have been greatly influenced by heavy oil use and mechanical problems with its nuclear plants. Pressures were exerted to have Vepco's North Carolina operations purchased by another company.

The Effects of Regulation

Formidable problems exist in deducing from available capital market data the extent, if any, to which regulation is depressing rates of return. The most basic problems are how to satisfactorily measure the required rates of return and how to determine the true earnings of the industry. The barrier to deducing required rates of return is that the market basically provides only a combined appraisal of all the factors at work, such as growth expectations, the expected rate of inflation, and the required real rate of return that affect the valuation of common stocks. Models designed to deduce the required real rate of return thus involve expedients to isolate other impacts, and no guarantee exists that the approaches taken are fully satisfactory.

The second difficulty is that accounting of rates of return are imperfect measures of whether investments have an adequate net present value (see chapter 2). Accounting conventions can cause values to differ from those appropriate for present-value analysis. Even if the data were normalized, the accounting rate of return still could differ from the true rate of return on a present-value basis.

One indicator of industry problems is the state of its credit ratings. Table 4-3 presents a tabulation of such ratings and associated information for 100 companies. The table was taken from tabulations issued by Merrill Lynch and contains its choices for coverage; the largest companies reported

Table 4-3

Comparison of Security Ratings and Regulatory Climate for 100 Electric Utilities in 1980

Company	States Served	Rating by Moody's	Rating by Standard and Poors	Merrill Lynch Rating of Regulation	Ratio of Market Value to Book Value of Stocks
1. Texas Utilities	TX	Aaa	AAA	5	80(95)
2. Louisville Gas and Electric	KY	Aaa	AA	3	77(72)
3. Houston Industries, Inc.	TX	Aa(A)	AA	5	77(62)
4. Public Service Company of Indiana	IN	Aa	AA	5	81(87)
5. Indianapolis Power and Light	IN	Aa	AA	5	82(87)
6. Southern Indiana Gas and Electric	IN	Aa	AA	5	77(79)
7. Wisconsin Electric Power	WI,MI	Aa	AA	4+	70(82)
8. Wisconsin Public Service	WI,MI	Aa	AA	4+	81(82)
9. Wisconsin Power and Light·	WI,IL	Aa	AA	4+	82(85)
10. Madison Gas and Electric[a]	WI	Aa	AA	4+	76(77)
11. Tampa Electric	FL	Aa	AA	4+	90(102)
12. Southwestern Public Service	TX,NM, OK,KS	Aa	AA	4	113(118)
13. Central and Southwestern Corp.	TX,OK,LA	Aa	AA	4−	78(65)
14. Public Service Company of New Mexico[a]	NM	Aa	AA	4−	85(87)
15. Public Service Electric and Gas	NJ	Aa	AA	3+	68(66)
16. Southern California Edison	CA	Aa	AA	3+	74(83)
17. Northern States Power	MN,WI, ND,SD	Aa	AA	3	81(84)
18. Illinois Power	IL	Aa	AA	3	85(88)
19. Central Illinois Public Service	IL	Aa	AA	3	76(80)
20. Kentucky Utilities	KY,VA,TN	Aa	AA(A+)	3	74(70)
21. Kansas Power and Light	KS	Aa	AA	3−	79(72)
22. Iowa-Illinois Gas and Electric[a]	IA,IL	Aa	AA	2+	74(76)
23. Iowa Public Service[a]	IA,SD,NE	Aa	AA	2	77(75)
24. Northern Indiana Public Service	IN	Aa	AA−	5	61(62)
25. Pacific Gas and Electric	CA	Aa	AA−	3+	68(76)
26. Baltimore Gas and Electric	MD	Aa	AA−	3	70(73)
27. Cleveland Electric Illuminating	OH	Aa(A)	AA−(A)	3	77(76)
28. Cincinnati Gas and Electric	OH,KY,IN	Aa	AA−(A)	3	76(74)
29. Atlantic City Electric	NJ	Aa	A+	3	76(77)
30. Potomac Electric	MD,Dc,VA	Aa	A+	3−	80(84)
31. El Paso Electric	TX,NM	A	AA−(A+)	5−	88(102)
32. Utah Power and Light	UT,ID,WY	A	AA−(A+)	4−	92(95)
33. Florida Power and Light	FL	A	A+	4+	77(86)
34. Florida Power Corp.	FL	A	A+	4+	80(82)
35. Duke Power	NC,SC	A	A+	4−	73(88)
36. Central Illinois Light	IL	A(Aa)	A+	3	69(69)
37. Tucson Electric Power	AZ,NM	A	A+	3	89(103)
38. Pennsylvania Power and Light	PA	Aa	A	3	67(69)
39. New England Electric System	MA,RI, NH,VT	Aa	A	3−	82(83)
40. New England Gas and Electric Association	MA	Aa	A	2	73(67)

Table 4–3 continued

Company	States Served	Rating by Moody's	Rating by Standard and Poors	Merrill Lynch Rating of Regulation	Ratio of Market Value to Book Value of Stocks
41. Oklahoma Gas and Electric	OK,AR	Aa	A	2+	79(76)
42. Iowa Resources	IA	Aa	A	2	73(75)
43. Carolina Power and Light	NC,SC	A	A	4	70(76)
44. Consolidated Edison Co. of New York	NY	A	A(A+)	4−	52(59)
45. Public Service Company of Colorado	CO,WY	A	A	4−	76(83)
46. Hawaiian Electric Co., Inc.	HI	A	A	4−	76(75)
47. Delmarva Power and Light	DE,MD, VA	A	A	3+	75(70)
48. Orange and Rockland Utilities Inc.	NY,NJ	A	A	3+	69(70)
49. Commonwealth Edison	IL,IN	A	A(A−)	3	68(74)
50. Gulf States Utilities	TX,LA	A	A	3	77(74)
51. Duquesne Light	PA	A	A(BBB+)	3	77(73)
52. Minnesota Power and Light	MN,WI	A	A	3	74(78)
53. Sierra Pacific Power[a]	NV,CA	A	A	3	76(73)
54. Allegheny Power System, Inc.	PA,WV, MD,VA, OH	A	A	3−	66(72)
55. Virginia Electric and Power	VA,NC, WV	A	A	3−	58(62)
56. Otter Tail Power	MN,ND, SD	A	A	3−	79(75)
57. Interstate Power	IA,MN,IL	A	A	2+	68(63)
58. Idaho Power	ID,OR,WV	A	A	2+	71(74)
59. South Carolina Electric and Gas	SC	A	A(A−)	2	77(78)
60. Iowa Electric Light and Power	IA,MN, CO,NE	A	A	2	68(76)
61. Kansas City Power and Light	MO,KS	A	A	2	72(69)
62. St. Joseph Light and Power[a]	MO	A	A	2−	72(70)
63. Montana Dakota Utilities[a]	MT,ND, SD,WY	A	A	1+	108(80)
64. Montana Power	MT,WY	A	A	1	99(124)
65. Niagara Mohawk Power Corp	NY	A	A−	4−	70(71)
66. New York State Electric and Gas Corp	NY	A(Baa)	A− (BBB+)	4−	66(68)
67. Rochester Gas and Electric Corp	NY	A	A−	4−	62(61)
68. Arizona Public Service	AZ,NM	A	A−	3	78(77)
69. Washington Water Power	WA,ID,MT	A	A−	2+	72(73)
70. Union Electric Company	MO,IL,LA	A(Baa)	A− (BBB+)	2	73(69)
71. Ohio Edison	OH,PA	A(Baa)	BBB+ (BBB−)	3	82(77)
72. Dayton Power and Light	OH	A	BBB+	3	66(76)
73. Philadelphia Electric	PA,MD	A(Baaa)	BBB+ (BBB)	3	67(73)
74. Central Maine Power	ME	A	BBB+	2	70(70)
75. Consumers Power	MI	A(Baa)	BBB	4−	62(64)

Table 4-3 continued

Company	States Served	Rating by Moody's	Rating by Standard and Poors	Merrill Lynch Rating of Regulation	Ratio of Market Value to Book Value of Stocks
76. Long Island Lighting	NY	A	BBB	4 −	76(76)
77. Central Hudson Gas and Electric Corp	NY	Baa	A −	4 −	65(66)
78. Toledo Edison	OH	Baa	BBB +	3	69(68)
79. Northeast Utilities	CT,MA	Baa	BBB +	3 −	63(65)
80. Middle South Utilities Inc.	LA,AR, MS,MO	Baa	BBB +	2 +	67(72)
81. Detroit Edison	MI	Baa	BBB	4 −	64(63)
82. San Diego Gas and Electric	CA	Baa	BBB	3 +	74(75)
83. Nevada Power	NV	Baa	BBB	3	95(91)
84. Public Service Company of New Hampshire	NH,ME, VT	Baa	BBB	3	68(73)
85. Boston Edison Co.	MA	Baa	BBB	3 −	68(72)
86. Pacific Power and Light	OR,WY, CA,MT,ID	Baa	BBB	3 −	95(94)
87. American Electric Power	Several	Baa	BBB	3 −	79(72)
88. Kansas Gas and Electric	KS	Baa	BBB	3 −	72(71)
89. Fitchburg Gas and Electric[a]	MA	Baa	BBB	3 −	79(69)
90. Southern Company	GA,AL, FL,MS	Baa	BBB	2 +	70(71)
91. Puget Sound Power and Light[a]	WA	Baa	BBB	2 +	67(73)
92. Northwestern Public Service[a]	SD	Baa	BBB	2 −	69(77)
93. Portland General Electric	OR	Baa	BBB −	3	74(75)
94. Savannah Electric and Power[a]	GA	Baa	BBB −	2 +	49(54)
95. United Illuminating	CT	Baa	BB +	3 −	67(65)
96. General Public Utilities Corp.	PA,NJ	Ba	BBB − (BB −)	3 −	21(21)
97. Maine Public Service[a]	ME	NR	BBB	2	55(52)
98. Central Vermont Public Service Corp.[a]	VT,NH	Baa	NR	3	69(n.a.)
99. Missouri Public Service[a]	MO	NR	NR	2 −	73(65)
100. Black Hills Power and Light	SO,WY, MT,NE	NR	NR	1	102(93)

Sources: Company names and places of operation from U.S. Department of Energy, Energy Information Administration, *Statistics of Privately Owned Electric Utilities in the United States—1979 Classes A and B Companies* (Washington, D.C.: U.S. Government Printing Office, 1980), p. 612–613. Wherever possible, these were checked with the company uniform statistical report and the listing of states was ordered by their contribution to sales. Where company data were not available, an [a] appears. States noted by either DOE or the company are included. The abbreviations are those of the U.S. Postal Service. Most corporate names end with "Company," which is usually omitted from the list; alternative designations such as "Corporation" are shown. American Electric Power serves in order of importance: Ohio, Indiana, West Virginia, Virginia, Michigan, and Tennessee.

Securities and regulatory climate ratings and market-to-book-value ratios are from Merrill Lynch, Pierce, Fenner & Smith Inc., *Electric Utilities,* 14 November 1980. (It is a one-page chart of data on 100 companies).

Notes: Companies are ordered here first in order of security quality and within quality group by quality of regulation. Within regulatory quality, an effort is made to group companies by state and present in chapter 3 are all included, and the most important omission is Central Louisiana Light. These ratings clearly indicate that the electric-utility industry is no longer financially strong. Only one company was triple-A rated by both major rating services; one other company rates triple A only from Moody's. Twenty-three companies were rated double A or better. But sixteen companies receive Moody's Baa rating or worse and Standard and Poors BBB or worse. Another six companies are either Moody's Baa or Standard and Poors BBB. Notably, the two largest companies in the industry, American Electric Power and the Southern Company, are among these low-rated companies. Most changes in 1981 were reductions.

Table 4–3 also suggests how the securities ratings correlate with efforts to rate the regulatory climate. It is arranged to show the distribution of regulatory ratings within a given securities-rating group. The underlying ratings are tabulated in table 4–4, together with an alternative set from Goldman Sachs. Table 4–5 presents the distribution of regulatory ratings among the different bond-rating groups.

The tabulations suggest that regulatory ratings tend to be better with higher rated securities. Small size and the existence of special problems, particularly extended problems with completing a nuclear plant, tend to lower the ratings. Large size is usually a source of higher security rating than otherwise would be justified by the regulatory climate, with the major exception of AEP's rating. This might be explained by such special circumstances as the extra difficulties AEP has faced with its regulators. Kentucky has been reluctant to allow AEP to supply the state from plants elsewhere, and FERC, West Virginia, and Ohio have been critical of AEP's fuel procurement practices. More fundamentally, ranking of commissions is quite subjective, and considerable problems are likely to arise in trying to average the ratings of the numerous states served by AEP. It is possible that West Virginia is inadequately weighted in this case. Securities analysts indicated

---

groupings roughly in the order of company size. The Merrill Lynch rating system awards a 5 to the best regulators and the worst rating is 1. The respective top securities ratings are Aaa and AAA. Going down in the alphabet is a reduction. It should be noted that differences in ratings by the two companies can make the overall comparison ambiguous. Thus, two companies are rated Aa and A+ by the services and two others A and AA−; several companies are rated A and A+ and several Aa and A; another such problem is two A and BBB companies versus a Baa and A− company. In every case, the better rating in one pair is roughly offset by the better rating in the other pair. The placement here is somewhat arbitrary.
Figures in parenthesis in last column are 31 July 1981 ratios. Where ratings differ from those of late 1980, the revised one also appears in parenthesis.
New England Gas and Electric Association is now Commonwealth Energy Systems and Tampa Electric is Teco Energy.
NR: not rated.
n.a.: not available.

Table 4–4
Comparison of Merrill Lynch's and Goldman Sachs's Ratings of Utility Commissions in 1980

	Merrill Lynch	Goldman Sachs
1. Indiana	5(4)	1
2. Texas	5	1
3. North Carolina	4 +	2
4. Wisconsin	4 +	2
5. Florida	4 +	1 −
6. Delaware	4	2
7. Colorado	4 − (3 +)	3
8. Hawaii	4 −	2
9. Michigan	4 − (3 +)	4
10. New Mexico	4 −	1
11. New York	4 −	3
12. Utah	4 −	2 +
13. California	3 +	3
14. Alaska	3	n.a.
15. Arizona	3	3 −
16. Arkansas	3	3 −
17. Federal Energy Reg. Comm.	3	n.a.
18. Illinois	3	4 +
19. Kentucky	3(4 −)	2
20. Maryland	3	3 −
21. Minnesota	3(3 −)	3
22. Nevada	3	2
23. New Hampshire	3	3
24. New Jersey	3	3
25. Ohio	3(4 −)	3 −
26. Oregon	3(3 +)	2
27. Pennsylvania	3	4 −
28. Vermont	3	n.a.
29. Wyoming	3(2)	2
30. Connecticut	3 − (3)	4
31. Kansas	3 −	4
32. Massachusetts	3 − (3)	4
33. Virginia	3 −	4
34. District of Columbia	2 +	n.a.
35. Georgia	2 + (3 −)	4
36. Idaho	2 + (3 −)	3
37. Mississippi	2 +	5
38. North Dakota	2 +	n.a.
39. Oklahoma	2 +	3 −
40. Washington	2 + (3 −)	3
41. Alabama	2	5
42. Iowa	2	4
43. Louisiana	2(3 −)	4
44. Nebraska	2(1)	n.a.
45. Rhode Island	2	4

Table 4-4 continued

	Merrill Lynch	Goldman Sachs
46. South Carolina	2(2+)	2
47. Maine	2 – (2)	n.a.
48. Missouri	2 –	5
49. Tennessee	2 –	n.a.
50. West Virginia	2 – (2)	5 +
51. Montana	1(2 –)	5
52. South Dakota	1	5

Sources: Leonard S. Hyman, Glenn R. Pafumi, and Rosemary Avellis, *Utility Research Recent Regulatory Decisions and Trends* (New York: Merrill Lynch, Pierce, Fenner & Smith, 1980); Ernest Liu, *Public Utility Survey* (New York: Goldman Sachs, 1980).

Notes: Under the Merrill Lynch system a higher number is better and 5 is best; the reverse is true for Goldman Sachs; 1 is best.

Figures in parenthesis are May 1981 ratings when different.

n.a.: not available.

Table 4-5
Relationship between Bond Ratings and Rating of Regulatory Climate
(number of companies)

Ratings of Regulatory Climate	Company Rating Groups					
	First 23 Companies	Companies 24–42	Companies 43–64	Companies 65–80	Companies 81–98	Total
5 or 5 –	5	2	0	0	0	7
4+ or 4	6	2	1	0	0	9
4 –	2	2	3	6	1	14
3 +	2	1	2	0	1	6
3	5	7	5	1	6	24
3 –	1	2	3	5	6	17
2	1	1	2	2	2	8
2 or 2 –	1	2	4	2	2	11
1+ or 1	0	0	2	0	0	2
	23	19	22	16	18	98
Chi-squared	18.45	1.97	8.91	10.84	10.84	42.10
Significance level	0.98	0.02	0.65	0.79	0.79	0.89

Source: Taken from table 4-3.

Note: The null hypothesis is that the distribution of regulatory climate is the same whatever the bond rating. Thus, the actual proportions shown in each of the first five columns were compared to the proportions implicit in the last column: the chi-squared value in the last column is a measure of the combined discrepancy of the values in the first five columns from the hypothesized no-effect pattern.

to me, however, that further problems arose from a combination of heavy borrowing and late moves for rate relief.

The regulatory ratings apparently are much more variable than the securities ratings. As a rough check, the distributions in table 4–5 were used to run chi-squared tests of the hypotheses that the regulatory climate differences between each subgroup and the entire population are statistically significant. The chi-squared value for the total discrepancy for the five subgroups was 42, which is significant only at the 90 percent level. The chi-squared value for the highest rated group was 19, which is significant at the 98 percent level. Thus, it appears highly probable that companies with high security ratings have a better than average regulatory climate.

Thus, caution must be taken about inferring strong conclusions about the effect of measured regulatory quality on security ratings. The difficulties of rating, the existence of other impacts including legacies of past regulatory problems (for example, as with Consolidated Edison), and my subjective grouping may distort the results.

Some indication of the impact of subjectivity is provided by the alternative ranking by Goldman Sachs. The rankings are generally quite similar with Merrill Lynch, except that Goldman Sachs gives a much lower rating to Michigan and a much higher rating to South Carolina. As far as the tabulations in table 4–5 are concerned, the Goldman Sachs rating would have major effects mainly on the fourth group. The group contains a particularly high proportion (five out of sixteen) of companies from a single state—New York. Goldman Sachs' lower rating of New York than that of Merrill Lynch, thus, has a greater effect on the fourth group than any other rating difference has on the other groups.

Still another indicator is allowable rates of return and the ability to earn them. Walter French (1980) of Argus Research tabulated averages for fifty companies that his firm regularly follows. Allowable returns on equity averaged 12.5 percent in 1972 and 1973, were at or a bit above 13 percent from 1974 to 1978, 13.5 percent in 1979, and 14.3 percent in 1980. Given that inflation as measured by the implicit deflator for the GNP averaged 7.4 percent per year over the period, even the 14.3 percent rate only allows real returns of 6.4 percent per year. More critically, actual earnings have fallen short of the allowable. The actual rate at 12.3 percent in 1972 was close to the allowable. The widest gap of 2.4 percentage points occurred in 1974 when actual-earnings rates were 10.6 percent. Rates of return then rose somewhat through 1977 when an 11.8 percent level was earned compared to a 13.3 percent allowable rate. French estimates a 1980 return of 11 percent caused a shortfall of 3.3 percentage points. An 11 percent nominal return implies a 3 percent real return with the 7.4 percent inflation rate for the 1972–1980 period but only a 1.8 percent return, given the 9.0 percent inflation rate of 1980.

The Regulation of Siting: From Certification to the One-Stop Solution

Approval of plans to add electric-utility facilities has long been part of public-utility regulation. However, until the rise of environmental concerns, review generally involved routine consideration of the "convenience and necessity" of such construction. Starting in the 1960s, the variety of environmental issues that had to be resolved when siting a power plant produced considerable concern over siting procedures. Reform efforts were instituted in hopes of streamlining decision making, but to date the process has not been noticeably successful. NARUC reports that twenty-six states have enacted siting laws; twenty-two purport to employ a "one-stop" process (NARUC 1980, p. 636). In at least ten states—Arizona, California, Connecticut, Massachusetts, Minnesota, New Hampshire, New York, Ohio, Oregon, and Wyoming—the appraisal is entrusted to a body separate from the public-utility commission (NARUC 1980, p. 637–641). Some of these programs have not been tested because no new major plants have been proposed since the program was established. This is the case in New England.

Under either independent-agency or public-utility commission supervision, there is not the centralization of authority that the one-stop label suggests. The process is one of getting all the relevant agencies to work together more effectively. Thus, Minnesota grants gives an Environmental Quality Board authority to certify major power plants and transmission lines, but "various state agencies" issue permits, and the Minnesota Energy Agency affirms the need (NARUC 1980, p. 639). In practical terms, no matter who has the responsibility for siting, the critical consideration remains the rate-making practices of the state commission. It can undermine the siting approval by refusing to allow rates adequate to make the investment profitable.

Still another limitation to the ability to concentrate decision making is the presence of federal involvement (see chapter 5 for more details). Every nuclear plant must be approved by the Nuclear Regulatory Commission. In western states where the U.S. government is a major landowner, it is virtually impossible to build a power plant that does not involve a major federal action necessitating an environmental impact statement on the plant, its fuel supplier, and the transmission lines.

Thus, institutional reform has left intact the conflicts that delay decision making and has failed to alleviate the problems of resolving siting disputes. Moreover, at least in some highly publicized cases, the agencies involved with siting have made vigorous commitments to the position that electricity demand growth is likely to be low and that conservation and alternative energy sources should be stressed.

Opposition to expansion has taken many forms. California and New

York have gone to considerable lengths to formalize their attitudes in elaborate studies of future energy alternatives (reviewed more fully below and in appendix 4A). Some states have explicitly criticized the desire to expand in siting or certification hearings (Idaho, Maine, Oregon, and Wisconsin). The first two cases involved coal-fired units; the second two, nuclear units. However, construction slowdowns prevail almost everywhere in the United States due to an unknown combination of lower demand growth prospects and a perceived inability to secure adequate rates of return. Just how much of this slowdown is governmentally produced is difficult to determine.

The most obvious difficulties are those of inadequate capacity (see chapter 7). Another possible problem is that regulation prevents economically justified completion of plants in progress and construction of new plants to displace oil and gas.

Regulation and the National Energy Acts

In 1972 President James E. Carter, Jr. proposed in the National Energy Plan (NEP) an elaborate program that led to passage by late 1978 of several laws that altered U.S. energy policies. While all these laws had some effect on electric utilities, two were primarily directed at public utilities. The Public Utility Regulatory Policies Act (PURPA) concerned rate reform to promote, among other things, less consumption and greater electric utility willingness to adopt alternative energy sources. The National Energy Conservation Policy Act (NECPA) was intended to encourage utilities to assist others in reducing energy use and adopting alternative energy sources.

The different components of PURPA combine basic procedures on attaining the objectives of the act, requirements for special studies to assist in the enforcement of the act, and handling a few miscellaneous related problems. Three of the six titles (I, II, and IV) deal entirely with electric-utility issues. Titles III and V deal specifically with gas utilities and oil pipelines. Title VI treats eight different issues. (See appendix 4B for information on how laws are divided into their components.)

Title I establishes rules for a review of electric-utility rate setting. State commissions are required to review their practices and consider the wisdom of numerous actions suggested in the act. Title II orders FERC to establish rules and make studies dealing with coordination within the electric-utility industry and ways to encourage cogeneration and the use of alternative energy sources by electric utilities. Title IV proposes making loans to small hydroelectric projects and requires FERC to establish rules to simplify licensing of such plants.

The miscellaneous requirements in title VI include a mandate that DOE study electric rate-making practices by the states; an authorization for acquisition of rights-of-way for transmission lines in the Dakotas and Nebraska, if DOE judges this will facilitate desirable exchanges of power with Canada; an allowance of DOE grants to a utility-regulation institute; statement of an elaborate program for encouraging shifts of some power plants from natural gas to heavy fuel oil refined in the United States; and authorization of forced conversion in utilities from gas to oil when a gas-supply emergency arises. The title also includes a rider authorizing the establishment of coal-research laboratories at thirteen U.S. universities.

For present purposes, only the first two titles need fuller examination. The rate-review process of title I requires consideration of whether a specific list of rate making and other practices would be an economically efficient way to reduce electricity consumption and requires implementation of other listed procedures. Moreover, the act authorizes the simultaneous existence of these mandatory and voluntary practices with maintenance of the allowable rate of return and introduction of lifeline rates. *Lifeline rates* are various types of lower rates on low levels of consumption. Such rates can be provided universally by charging a lower rate on the first few kilowatt hours every consumer uses and higher rates on additional usage. Alternatively the rates can be given only to selected customers, such as those meeting some need test, for example, eligibility for supplementary social security. Acceptance of such rates was included in President Carter's draft energy bill. Thus, it can be inferred that President Carter and Congress felt that states should be allowed to seek their own resolution of the efficiency equity trade-off.

The other mandatory aspects of title I are requirements that the effects of any provisions for automatic pass-through of costs be regularly reviewed [section 115(e)], that customers be provided information on rate schedules [115(f)], and that termination of service should be restricted to prevent hardships [115(g)]. Each limitation was elaborately defined. For example, reviews must be made at least every four years to determine that the automatic adjustment provision does "provide incentives for efficient use of resources" and at least every two years efforts must be undertaken "to insure the maximum economies" are being produced by the clauses [section 115(e)]. Apparently, the distinction is between the principle and the practice of automatic adjustment.

The law lists approaches that should be considered. These include basing rates on cost of service, banning declining block rates (rates that price additional consumption more cheaply than lower levels of use), encouraging time-of-day rates, proposing seasonal rates, stimulating load-management techniques, and prohibiting use of a single meter in a multiuser building [sections 111(d) and 113(b)(1)]. Elsewhere in the act [section 3(8)] *load management* is defined as actions to affect demand other than by price variation. Evaluations of all measures are supposed to compare benefits to costs.

Title I includes clauses permitting DOE and other groups to intervene in the rate-setting process, requiring the utilities to finance intervenors lacking other funding, allowing DOE to suggest how the act might be implemented, requiring utilities to compile data on the costs of serving different classes of customers, and requiring DOE to finance state programs for studying how best to comply.

Title II requires FERC to undertake a variety of actions to promote improvements in the electric-utility industry. The most radical are those dealing with cogeneration and small-power production (section 210). Under title II, FERC has the triple responsibility of instituting general rules to encourage electric utilities to purchase power from cogeneration and small sources, establishing specific rules insuring that utility buying and reselling rates are "just and fair" to customers and do not discriminate against cogeneration and small producers, and developing procedures to exempt some such facilities from regulation.

The bulk of title II, however, is related to improvement of activities long encouraged by FERC to insure greater coordination among utilities. PURPA requires that FERC work further to promote greater interconnection and access to existing utility lines, study the benefits of greater pooling, and consider regularly the reliability of electric service. FERC is required to explore how its rate-setting practices may be changed to expedite decisions, avoid granting of interim relief, and avoid "anticompetitive" disparities between wholesale and retail rates. This last provision presumably reflects a response to the concerns about how wholesale rates are set. A review of automatic adjustment clauses similar to that at the state level is required, as is setting rules to maintain reliable service to wholesale customers. FERC is required further to establish an office to foster public participation in its hearings.

NEPCA ranges over a broader area than PURPA. The critical part of the act for utilities is part 1 of title II, which encourages utilities to promote conservation without competing (at least too vigorously) with banks and existing suppliers of conservation services. Conservation includes use of solar heating as well as reduced energy consumption.

The critical requirements are that electric and gas utilities and fuel-oil distributors establish programs to inform residential customers about cost-effective opportunities to reduce energy use and direct customers to energy-saving services and financing. The act operates in several ways to circumscribe the scope of action. A list of appropriate conservation measures is provided, and DOE must authorize extension of the list. The allowable actions include heating-system efficiency improvement, caulking and weatherstripping, clock thermostats, insulation, thicker glass, load management, and use of solar and windpower [section 210(11)]. However, a utility that supplies furnace fuel can make suggestions about furnace changes only if it receives written permission from the homeowner [section 215(b)(1)(B).

(One company with a heavy air-conditioning load pointed out to me that these rules prevent it from using its most effective strategy; namely, managing that air-conditioning load.)

The law tries to limit utilities from providing either the actual services or their financing. There is a basic authorization to provide furnace modifications, clock thermostats, and load-modification devices and make loans of $300 or the cost of the services, whichever is greater. Further action can be taken if DOE agrees that charges are "fair and reasonable" and secures the agreement of the Federal Trade Commission (FTC) that the program will not undermine "prevention of unfair methods of competition" [section 216(c)]. Conversely, if DOE and FTC concur that the fairness standards are not met, service provision and loans can be banned. An earlier provision, section 213(b), requires that DOE check utility plans to see that the charge fairness criteria are met. The FTC (section 225) is required to study the effect of utility and fuel-oil supplier actions, including suppliers of the key services.

Congress was clearly following a long-standing practice of limiting the ability of larger companies to compete with smaller ones. However, some groups, such as the California and New York Commissions, argue that utilities should broaden their horizons and promote conservation and alternative energy. This reflects the concept of "marketing myopia" first popularized in 1960 by Theodore Levitt of the Harvard Business School. Levitt suggested that companies concentrated on the specific businesses in which they were engaged, such as electricity generation, and did not consider the broader question of the basic need the business met. Thus, companies were unprepared to adjust to innovations that developed better ways of serving these needs. He noted that railroads should have thought of themselves as transportation suppliers and moved into aviation. He has been criticized for failing to recognize that regulation impeded such shifts. Another criticism is that the firm's skills might better be directed at serving different markets with technologies familiar to the firm. An energy company might consider moving into chemicals or metals as well as into other fuels.

Energy Plans for California and New York: Cases in the Perils of Institutional Reform

The efforts of California and New York to design energy master plans deserve review because these are major efforts by leading states, and the efforts illustrate some problems of institutional reform. A more elaborate treatment is presented in appendix 4A.

Both states are dedicated to preventing extensive construction of new coal- or nuclear-fired power plants. California also is seeking to slow down application of the Powerplant and Industrial Fuel Use Act to California. The basic problem is that this may be a dangerous overreaction to the blind devotion to 7-percent growth that so long prevailed. Faith in reducing the need for new plants may go too far and hinder regulation reform. Few other states are likely to develop the arguments elaborately, but many will adopt policies accepting this antiexpansion approach (California Energy Commission 1979).

The form of the arguments is also bothersome even if it is not clear whether they are taken seriously or merely are used as the best available respectable rationalizations for decisions based on political expediency. Both New York and California are enthusiastic critics of coal and nuclear power and supporters of conservation and new technologies.

While the two state plans are similar in basic goals and underlying rationale, major differences exist. The California proposals for implementing the goals are far more explicit than those in New York. However, the California legislature has already imposed the restrictions that new nuclear plants cannot be built in California until waste storage facilities are available. No comparable action has been taken in New York. Thus, the antinuclear position in the New York report was presented as the view of those preparing the study, while the California report needed only to confirm that the legislative requirements had not been met.

Others (see Landsberg 1979) assert that alternative energy and conservation have been oversold by commentators such as Stobaugh and Yergin (1979), Lovins (1977), and the two state reports. The correctness of viewpoint is far less critical than the use of the ideas to rationalize evasion of regulatory reform. This is further evidence that new institutions do not produce different results unless the new form is based on new substance.

The Northwest Power Act: Congress and the Bonneville Controversy

In late 1980, the U.S. Congress passed the long-debated Northwest Power Act (formally known as the Pacific Northwest Electric Power Planning and Conservation Act). Examining the act and newspaper reports on the subject show that efforts were made to settle simultaneously at least four issues. The first was the debate over allocation of cheap Bonneville power (see the previous discussion). A second issue was the wisdom of Bonneville's involvement in guarantees for new power plants (see chapter 3). The third was fear by other regions that the bill might require them to subsidize the Northwest. Finally, there was concern for fish and other wildlife in the region.

The subsidy issue has at least two aspects. First, Bonneville has been running a deficit. Second, it was feared that the bill would provide cheap financing for expansion of power supplies in the Northwest. The first problem was addressed by section 7, which required that Bonneville set rates at levels that insured cost recovery. However, subsidy avoidance is only one element influencing numerous basic provisions that deal simultaneously with preventing further subvention and finding solutions to the issues of allocating the benefits of cheap power and divising a compromise expansion plan.

These issues are primarily treated in three major sections of the bill: the establishment of a Pacific Northwest Electric Power and Conservation Planning Council (section 4), establishing ground rules for the sale of Bonneville energy within the Northwest (section 5), and defining the terms under which Bonneville can commit to acquire new producing facilities and promote conservation (section 6). Additional key provisions deal with out-of-state sales [section 9(c) and the rules under which entities can remain exempt from regulation, section (9)(h)(1)].

Section 5 deals with the access problem by giving federal agencies second priority behind cooperative and public power, arranging a subsidy for residential customers of private companies, providing for establishment of long-term contracts with all these groups and industrial customers presently being served directly, and setting guidelines for acquiring new power resources. Combined with the rate rules, these provisions involve efforts to recover as much as possible of the cost of new plants from industrial customers, keep down rates to public and cooperative power and federal agencies, and hold down household rates.

The provisions requiring review are those that define the subsidy to residences and the extent to which resources can be acquired. Basically, private utilities will receive and be obligated to transfer to their residential customers a subsidy equal to the difference between their costs, excluding expansion cost, and the costs of Bonneville power. The amount of energy subsidized would start at half the residential load in 1980 and rise in 1985 to equal the entire load [paragraph (c)(1)]. The subsidy is expressed as involving "selling" private power to Bonneville at the private firm's own costs and Bonneville selling back at its (lower) costs. Presumably the transfers will occur only on paper and have the noted subsidy effect. Private company costs are defined to exclude both costs of facilities built to serve load growth within or outside the region and write-offs of canceled investments.

Bonneville acquisition of more energy resources is conditional on meeting regional needs more cost effectively than utility action. The rate provisions of section 7 require that direct industrial customers bear the cost of such acquisition [paragraph (c)(1)(A)]. All rates under the section are subject to FERC review under language requiring "confirmation and approval,'' which could imply a more active FERC role. Conservation and renewables are introduced into the planning process in section 7. The section encourages Bonneville to assist these approaches and might involve procedures similar to those used to underwrite the nuclear plants. The act further states that such obligations are to be considered supported only by Bonneville's resources and not the borrowing power (the full faith and credit) of the U.S. government. Section 3(d) indicates that conservation measures should be considered competitive if their estimated cost does not exceed 110 percent of those of conventional ones. This provision might be considered subsidy, an effort to reflect some externality, or simply a corrective of expected cost estimation biases.

The treatment of out-of-state buyers [section 9(c)] appears quite ungenerous. The out-of-staters still can only obtain power that in-state users do not want. In-state users can lose out if they are unwilling to pay the Bonneville charges. Bonneville electricity that is provided power companies in the region can be taken away if the energy appears to be transmitted out of the region. Section 9(h) exempts from the Public Utility Holding Company Act joint ventures to supply generation to Bonneville if the SEC approves and public bodies and cooperatives are allowed to participate. Apparently, both the Washington Public Power Supply System and the consortiums directed by private companies but having municipal and cooperative participation could be covered.

It was noted that the study of unresolved issues is frequently required in riders to energy and environmental policy laws. Experience suggests that often the studies are modestly financed and long delayed. For example, a study of competition in the coal industry appended to the Powerplant and Industrial Fuel Use Act was due to be completed by late 1979 but only appeared in early 1981.

In contrast, the first substantive section of the Northwest Power Act mandates the creation of a study group called the Planning Council. To resolve the dispute about the proper weighting of the different states in the council, the secretary of energy is directed to select six members from nominating lists provided by each governor. Each state must nominate at least two people and is guaranteed at least one member, suggesting a membership of two people each from Washington and Oregon and one each from Idaho and Montana.

The essence of the council's responsibility is to develop a power plan for the area that will consider conservation, alternative energy sources, and fish and wildlife resources. A considerable part of the mandate of the council is, as the bill states at least nine times, to "protect, mitigate, and enhance fish and wildlife." Apparently a major consideration is the extent to which fish ladders on dams will be improved.

The act also specifies that resource development should select cost-effective measures but sets blanket priority rankings to conservation (first), renewables, use of waste heat or more thermally efficient technologies, and all else.

This ranking is inconsistent with the cost-effectiveness requirement. Options in any broad category all cannot be categorically more cost effective in all alternatives than another category. Criticism of the tendency to ranking can serve to epitomize the present review of regulation. Once again the idea is to encourage greater attention to possibilities that are felt to be unduly neglected by electric utilities. This posture here and elsewhere can be interpreted in a wide variety of fashions. At one extreme, the enthusiasm for conservation and renewables can be seen as offering a questionable substitute for vigorous action to resolve existing problems. At the other extreme, it could be argued that action is needed because utilities do not make sound choices among options.

There is some merit to both views. The program clearly arises from a desire to keep prices below replacement cost. The general criticism raised in chapter 2 that administering such corrective measures clearly attenuates and perhaps more than offsets any benefits of price limitation is applicable to the Northwest Power Act. This defect extends beyond the planning rules to the whole bill. Nevertheless, utilities may be shortsighted and certainly are not encouraged by existing regulations to undertake all cost-effective actions. All the regulatory developments reviewed in this chapter support the hypotheses of chapter 2 that regulation is extremely difficult to conduct in a fashion that pleases anyone and a tendency arises for creating increasingly more complex programs to alleviate problems created by regulation.

Note

1. This discussion simply epitomized the vast literature on tax incidence. Anyone whose business activity is taxed will attempt to adjust behavior to shift some of the burden to customers and suppliers. A tax favor then causes at least partial reversal of the initial reaction and thus reversal of the impacts on others.

Appendix 4A:
The New York and
California Energy
Reports

While most states have taken only tentative steps toward review of their energy programs, California and New York have attempted to produce comprehensive strategies for energy development. Both have issued energy plans that stress the importance of conservation and alternative energy sources, particularly renewable ones. Both are unfavorable to nuclear power. However, the differences between the two states are considerable. Important distinctions can be made about the genesis of the planning process, the participants, the breadth of issues covered, the nature of the evaluation process, the approach to reporting findings, and the actual proposals.

California created an independent Energy Commission in 1974, mandated to study energy problems of the state. A biennial report on key issues was required. The first report appeared in 1977. The second, the focus of this assessment, was issued in early 1980, dated 1979. New York created an energy office in 1976, but an energy study was not required until 1977, also biennially. The California commission's charge is limited to electricity, conservation, and related issues; oil and natural gas are considered only indirectly.

New York must treat all major energy supply and demand issues. Another important difference between the two states is that New York established an Energy Planning Board to develop policy conclusions. The board members included the commissioner of the Energy Office, the chairman of the Public Service Commission, the commissioner of the Department of Environmental Pollution, and one member from each house of the state legislature.

The states' reporting techniques are also different. The California Energy Commission established an extensive program of ongoing research, much of which is conducted by internal staff. Twelve staff-prepared backup reports were generated as supplementary material specifically for the 1979 biennial report (BR II). The commission also established a publications office to facilitate distribution of these reports, the most critical of which are available without charge. The 1979 report was short, nontechnical and makes extensive use of photographs and multicolored tables and figures. It is designed to reach the widest possible audience.

New York employs a smaller staff and relies more heavily than California on outside consultants. The documentation for 1979 was the three-volume *Master Plan* report. This provides a combination of policy proposals, review of energy trends, discussion of existing federal and state policy initiatives, and presentation of energy forecasts. The first volume is an executive summary. The second presents the detailed discussion, beginning with several overview chapters that essentially reiterate the executive summary. A series of chapters follow that rediscuss the proposals in more detail. Each chapter mixes history, forecasts, and policy proposals. The final volume discusses forecasting and also contains the Energy Board's "Order and Opinion." It repeats the conclusions for the third time and presents the fullest discussion of the reasoning behind the proposed program. This is followed by "concurring" statements that, in fact, criticize key aspects of the plan.

Although many aspects of the New York report and California's BR II are similar, it can be argued that the New York report is more antinuclear than California's. The California study stresses the barriers to nuclear power created by federal policy and California legislation prohibiting further nuclear construction until permanent methods of waste disposal are available. The California commission largely avoids taking an independent position on nuclear power.

The New York board chose not to take a similar approach. The statements about nuclear power (for example, see New York 1980, executive summary, p. 1) regularly begin by raising the waste-disposal question. Two of the concurring opinions, those of the head of the Public Service Commission and of a member of the state senate, demur from the nuclear position. Both express fears that the state has gone too far in abandoning the nuclear option. The senator put it more strongly, arguing: "...there is no basis in the record for finding that new nuclear power plants should not be included in the electric supply plan at this time" (New York 1980, appendix p. 161).

In contrast, the substantive proposals in the California report are more radical than those of New York. Similar statements of basic objectives lead to quite different policy proposals. The California strategy is purportedly an effort to lower substantially the level of consumption and alter fuel sources for electricity. The New York strategy is primarily a commitment to insure a flexible response to developing trends.

The New York report lists several very general objectives for state energy policy, presents modest suggestions for implementing the goals, and establishes guidelines for electric power expansion that are specific only in expressing the principle that any new plants must use coal or renewable resources and that numerous coal conversions of electric power plants must occur.

In developing the electric-power plan, the board had available a substantial list of coal, nuclear, and hydro plants in various states of development (see New York 1980, appendix p. 133). The draft energy plan proposed completion of one oil, one coal, and two nuclear units under construction, and the addition of one pumped storage unit and three coal-fired units. The first of these coal units was clearly meant to be the plant the Power Authority of the State of New York (PASNY) has been trying to build in New York City. PASNY is also planning the pumped storage unit. The other two units were termed downstate units (New York 1980, appendix p. 132). On reflection, it was decided that the exact size, number, timing, and siting of the coal plants should be left open so that plans later could be adjusted to market developments. The New York Power Pool responded in its annual report with a plan that included the PASNY projects, one of the two units that had been proposed for a Lake Erie site, and possibly unspecified additional units. A coal-conversion plan was presented in both the state decision and order and in the Power Pool's plan.

More broadly, the plan lists twelve basic propositions (see New York 1980, executive summary, p. 5). Among these are those already mentioned: (1) greater reliance on conservation and renewable resources and (2) not using more nuclear power. The coal-use proposals already noted are the core of a point that (3) coal use should be increased. Other basic goals are: (4) use of natural gas should be encouraged and (5) interconnections should be used to increase electricity availability. More general goals are: (6) increasing the number of available energy alternatives, (7) removing undesirable legal barriers to conservation and supply options, (8) encouraging PASNY and private utilities to become more actively involved in promoting conservation and renewable resources, (9) maintaining a research and development program attuned to the state's needs, (10) insuring that the poor have adequate heat, and (11) considering improvements in transportation oil use. All of these are intended to support a twelfth basic goal of reducing oil consumption.

As suggested, few of the goals lead to concrete action. The transportation discussion notes that the study neglected the problem, and eventually this defect must be corrected. The point about the poor is a review of existing aid programs and suggestions for more of the same. The research proposals suffer from the opposite problem of considering most of the standard areas for energy research to be relevant. Target areas include cleaner burning of coal, extracting synthetic fuels from coal, fuel-cell development, conservation, development of renewables, developing unconventional gas resources, recovering industrial-waste heat, transmitting DC power, managing peak loads, and protecting health and the environment. Obvious questions about the list include whether the state is capable of action on so many fronts. Why fuel cells were singled out from other alternatives is not clear. Similarly, it is not apparent what major research issues are associated with areas such as hydro and DC generation; in the latter case, the specific need apparently is for smaller AC converters for use in urban areas.

The main report does very little to develop the idea that utilities become active in conservation and renewables. A study of potential conservation measures is proposed (New York 1980, p. 62) and suggestions are made that PASNY finance waste recovery, small hydro, and cogeneration (New York 1980, pp. 94–97). Specific suggestions are limited to assorted proposals for tax credits and energy-information programs. Reduced barriers generally prove to involve such unobjectionable actions as altering state mandatory standards for space- and water-heating temperatures. Increasing options, however, can mean tax favors and direct subsidies, many of which may be of questionable merit.

The implementation of the interconnection goal includes proposals to arrange for substantial imports of hydrogenerated electricity from Canada and a general effort to improve connections with regions having coal-fired plants. However, it is also proposed to determine whether out-of-state sales of Niagara Falls power could be reduced.

Another proposal for coal is state and federal actions to permit creation of an Energy Corporation of the Northeast that would provide tax-exempt financing of critical projects; why such a corporation is needed is not indicated. The report also advocates passage of the Carter plan to provide federal loans to aid conversion of power plants to oil.

The gas proposals include a suggestion that pricing not discourage gas use (New York 1980, p. 115). That this implies that prices be kept below marginal costs is confirmed by a later proposal that the incremental pricing provision of the Natural Gas Act of 1978 be repealed (see New York 1980, p. 116). The provision attempts to insure that industrial users pay the marginal cost of gas. While this provision is less satisfactory than moving all prices to marginal costs and can be opposed because of the administrative problem of deciding the marginal cost to any one customer (see appendix 2B), the New York counterproposals lead further away from efficient allocation of resources. The suggestion also conflicts with the statement in the conservation section that prices should reflect replacement cost (New York 1980, p. 60). Other efforts in the gas area include encouraging New York gas utilities to negotiate vigorously for Canadian gas, urging Congress to encourage national deals for Canadian and Mexican gas, and advocating federal subsidies for coal gasification and the Alaskan gas pipeline.

While of limited practical importance, the supporting arguments in the conservation and petroleum sections involve dubious economic reasoning. The conservation chapter begins with the assertion that "Energy conservation is the least expensive, environmentally safest, and most economically beneficial supply option available" (New York 1980, p. 56). Statements of this type, although common, involve defective economics. First, in economic analysis, the three benefits sum to a single measure of social cost. More critically, no broadly defined option (be it conservation, increased oil production, increased coal production, or increased production of anything else) can be categorically characterized as cheaper or safer than all others. Within each option are numerous individual possible actions, which differ considerably in economic attractiveness. It is highly unlikely that every conceivable conservation option is cheaper than every possible expansion option. Indeed, the support for supply development elsewhere in the report is inconsistent with the advocacy for conservation.

The discussion is further marred by the contention that conservation directly creates economic benefits in New York, a clear example of the tendency to ignore the benefits of interstate (and international) trade. Similarly, the report categorically settles the controversy about the need for regulation by asserting that there are unspecified limits to price-induced conservation (New York 1980, p. 59). Economic theory indicates that, in the absence of externalities that the report does not identify, the limit to price-induced action is simply that the steps are too expensive. Conservation, like anything, can be overdone.

Some of the oil proposals—opposition to OPEC, increased stockpiling of oil, and greater leasing of federal oil lands—are supported by many economists. Other suggestions—expressing opposition to OPEC by less favorable tax treatment of U.S. oil company activity in OPEC countries, more favorable tax treatment and subsidies for activity in non-OPEC foreign countries, government-to-government deals with Mexico and Canada, and embarking on an extensive synthetic fuels program—are less acceptable.

In any case, the New York report is more impressive for not proposing much on the basis of its overstatements. Most of the dubious practical proposals are ones for others to implement, and considerable restraint is exercised in making suggestions. The only concrete directives are those about future generation needs, and these seem reasonably flexible, at least in face of the antinuclear pressure.

The California report, in contrast, sets as a goal a radical reduction in electric capacity growth and the implementation of vigorous efforts to insure that a substantial portion of the expansion comes from "alternative sources" (p. 32). The program is designed to insure that in the year 2000, electric generating capacity would be about 9 percent (5,860 Mw) below the 63,750 Mw level consistent with growth of around 2 percent per year and a 31.6 percent reserve margin in 2000. The lower capacity goal would satisfy a 1.7 percent per year growth with a 24 percent reserve margin. More critically, coal-fired capacity, including out-of-state plants partially dedicated to supplying California, would be cut 12,400 Mw below expectations to 5,800 Mw—only 3,300 Mw above 1978 levels. Thus, the 6,550 Mw difference between reduced coal capacity and reduced total capacity is to be replaced by alternative sources. The main sources are rises above the conventional 2 percent growth case of 3,600 Mw of cogeneration; 2,000 Mw of geothermal; and 1,250 Mw of wind. (The 400 Mw excess of increases in alternative sources over the decrease in coal is to offset a net reduction of hydroelectric availability, compared to the conventional case. While the preferred plan increases small hydro, this is more than offset by decreases in large hydro and pumped storage.)

The revised estimate for coal-fired capacity in the year 2000 is difficult to reconcile with the discussion of coal-fired capacity elsewhere in the report. California already had 2,500 Mw out-of-state capacity available to it in 1978 and another 3,750 Mw of out-of-state capacity was planned, a total of 6,250 Mw (California 1979, p. 44) Moreover, a separate treatment of preferred 1991 alternatives indicated that coal-fired capacity available to the state should be 7,800 Mw—2,000 Mw above the year 2000 goal (California 1979, p. 51). This need would be met by allowing coal plants to be built within California. The source of the difference between this 1991 estimate and the goal for 2000 is unclear. Retirements may be one cause. The usual convention is that plants will last at least thirty years. Under that rule, Southern California Edison's 785 Mw share in units 4 and 5 at Four Corners in New Mexico might be lost. Another 1,300 Mw owned by Edison and Los Angeles might be lost at the Mohave plant in Nevada completed in 1971. However, another possibility is that these plants continue to operate, the actual expansion to 1991 is less than estimated, and the year 2000 plan represents a strategy different from that used to develop the preferred numbers for 1991.

Another important element in California policy is an effort to develop a program, supplemented by federal policy changes, to lower the cost of compliance with the Fuel Use Act. The proposals include counting California heavy crudes as an alternative energy source, backing away from the requirements for reducing gas as well as oil use, making synthetic fuels available to displace conventional oil in existing plants, and gaining greater access to Bonneville power.

As did the New York report, the California study cites Stobaugh and Yergin on the virtues of conservation and alternative energy (California 1979, p. 7). However, the commission explicitly argues that Amory Lovins' argument that soft-energy alternatives (simpler, new technologies using smaller facilities that avoid the interconnections associated with electric power) are preferable is overstated and that California must pursue a program that uses both centralized and decentralized approaches to energy supply (California 1979, p. 29). The study further argues that federal policies have not adequately considered interstate differences (p. 1).

To implement this program, the commission indicates California will need to increase use of solar energy and natural gas, develop efficiency standards for appliances, expand local conservation programs, disseminate information about energy prices, review utility research and development plans, develop preferred technologies, improve its assessment capability, and continue to appraise nuclear power. The Public Utility Commission is urged to grant favorable rates to preferred generating alternatives and to encourage utilities to promote customer conservation efforts. The Air Resources Board is urged to consider granting pollution-rule waivers to preferred technologies and treat power plants no more severely than other polluters. The state is urged to undertake research and tax relief measures to stimulate alternative technologies and encourage utilities to provide conservation services. Most of the advice to the federal government relates to securing authorization for the oil displacement strategy outlined above. In addition, the Energy Commission asks that the federal government permit California to institute more stringent efficiency standards than currently required by federal laws, that negotiations be undertaken to secure Canadian and Mexican gas for California, that the then-proposed Federal Energy Mobilization Board not be allowed to override state rules, that an energy rationing law be established, and that nuclear waste and safety issues be studied (California 1979, p. 4–5).

The study compares California to federal goals and questions whether the federal stress on centralized technologies is wise (chapter 1). It then reviews conventional technologies and the implications of relying on them. The discussion is balanced between warnings about the centralized technologies, to justify California's proposals for other approaches, and optimism, to rationalize the specific oil displacement plant. The familiar warnings about oil and gas availability thus are qualified by enthusiasm about heavy crudes in California and an interim period in which gas supplies will be abundantly available. The discussion of synthetic fuels warns of their perils but recognizes their opportunities. The review concludes with the statement that the environmental impacts of a conventionally-fueled future would be intolerable (chapter 2).

The California study involves a vigorous commitment to altering energy-use patterns. The commission provides elaborate instructions to the utilities and their customers. How rigidly this will be implemented remains to be seen. For that matter, the basic direction of utility expansion in California with or without BR II is highly uncertain. Chapter 7 discusses how cautiously the whole U.S. electric-utility industry is moving toward expansion, showing that California utilities are particularly restrained.

The 1981 update of the California report was much longer, more enthusiastic about alternative energy sources, and otherwise similar in substance to the earlier one.

Appendix 4B:
A Note on the
Subdivision of
Federal Legislation

Federal legislation is divided into sections, which are in turn subdivided into unnamed components using a hierarchy different from that in conventional outlines. The first level of disaggregation is denoted by lower case letters, the second by arabic numerals, and the third by capital letters; all are enclosed in parentheses. Thus, we have section 215(b)(1)(A) in NECPA; often, but not always, one or more higher levels of aggregation are adopted. The act may simply be divided into titles; titles may be further broken down into subtitles. When titles or subtitles are established, the section numbering is designed to correspond with the titling. Title II provisions, for example, will begin with the number 201. When subtitles are employed, a similar numbering correspondence prevails. Items in title I, subtitle C would start at 131.

Two complications arise. With a law extensively amending a prior one, a distinction must be made between the sections of the amendments and the sections of the act being amended. For example, section 101(a) of the Clean Air Amendments of 1977 altered section 103(b) of the Clean Air Act. Secondly, the laws are eventually codified in the U.S. Code, which uses a numbering system different from that in the original legislation. Since lawyers use the code, they cite it. However, the original laws are probably more accessible to laymen. Reporting services such as the *Energy Users Report* reproduce the laws, and the original congressional documents can be obtained from congressional offices.

5

Environmental Regulation of Electric Utilities

Environmental regulations have become an increasingly important element in electric-power regulation. As with public-utility regulations, numerous issues are treated by federal, state, and local authorities. Among the critical areas are air pollution, water quality including waste-heat disposal, solid-waste disposal, land use, and nuclear-power problems.

This chapter stresses the air pollution and nuclear aspects of environmental controls. These policies have had the most extensive influence on the electric-power industry. In contrast, land-use disputes have had a limited impact overall (albeit with a few important special cases) and waste-heat disposal does not seem to have caused major problems. Solid-waste disposal remains at most a potential major difficulty.

Air-pollution regulatory practices differ considerably from those for nuclear energy. The former have been greatly influenced by highly specific legislation while the latter have emerged largely from implementation of a broad legislative mandate. Nuclear power has been predominantly the concern of a federal agency with authority to control all nuclear activities. The power was originally given the Atomic Energy Commission (AEC). In 1975, the regulatory powers of AEC were given to the Nuclear Regulatory Commission (NRC). [The research and weapons manufacture roles together with nonnuclear-energy research from other federal agencies were transferred to the Energy Research and Development Agency (ERDA) which in 1977 became a major component of the Department of Energy (DOE).] Nuclear policies consist of the administrative actions of AEC and NRC together with some actions by individual states. In contrast, air-pollution policy has involved constant interaction among the U.S. Congress, the Environmental Protection Agency (EPA), and state and local agencies. The 1977 Clean Air Act Amendments, for example, legislated in five basic areas affecting electric-power plants: new plant rules, general rules for limiting pollution increases in unpolluted areas, specific rules for preserving visibility in critical areas, prevention of harm to local coal industries, and defining tighter rules to apply to areas not meeting air-quality standards.

Given the simultaneous emergence of environmental debates and other problems for the electric-power industry and the variety of environmental policies, neither the general effect of environmental pressures nor the exact

173

influence of a specific policy can be isolated easily. Examples of applications of different policies must be viewed cautiously since the exact influence of the policy is uncertain.

The Scope of Environmental Problems

For present purposes, *environmental problems* are defined as consisting of pollution and the intrusion of industrial facilities in areas into areas believed better not so disturbed. Clearly, broader definitions are possible; everything around us is part of the environment. The side-effect problems discussed in chapter 2, however, consist most clearly of waste-disposal problems and the inappropriate location of facilities.

This proposition, however, is not maintained in the concept of environment used in the annual reports of the Council on Environmental Quality (CEQ) or in environmental impact statements. Typically, the discussion in an environmental impact statement goes well beyond the direct waste-disposal and land-disturbance effects. Attention is given, for example, to the socioeconomic effects, such as the community's provision for additional services. CEQ normally comments, at least in passing, on a variety of natural-resource issues, such as the availability of minerals and the preservation of the quality of agricultural land.

The enforcement of environmental policies is distributed among the different levels of government. Each level, in turn, can organize to deal with the problems in different fashions. Federal policy, for example, is based on numerous laws that spread authority among several agencies.

A distinction prevails between laws directed at a particular cause of problems and those directed at specific effects. Examples of cause-based laws are those dealing with nuclear energy, surface coal-mine reclamation, pesticides, and solid wastes. In the last case, the law stresses impacts of waste disposal on land and water. Impact-based laws include those directed at controlling air and water quality. (It should be noted that discharges to one medium such as the air may ultimately settle in another, and policies to prevent discharge into the air may in large part be directed at the effects of an ultimate transfer elsewhere, particularly on land). Narrower laws have been directed at areas such as endangered species and coastal resources, and preservation of historical sites. As discussed further later, the 1969 National Environmental Policy Act (NEPA) adds a general mandate to examine all impacts when reviewing major federal actions.

The Atomic Energy Commission initially established precedence in this area, and subsequent reorganizations maintained a separate agency to regulate all nuclear issues. Initially, the Department of the Interior (DOI) had responsibility for enforcing water-pollution regulation, and the Department of Health, Education, and Welfare (HEW) was in charge of air-pollution policy. However, in 1970, EPA was created to supervise both an air- and water-pollution policy; subsequently most new waste-disposal problems, such as pesticides and hazardous wastes, have been made the responsibility of EPA. Other new programs have been placed elsewhere; for example, surface-mine reclamation is administered by a newly created group within DOI.

States sometimes have their own unified environmental protection agency and in other cases have separate organizations for different problems, for example, separate air and water quality groups. The power-plant siting agencies discussed in chapter 4 nominally serve as unified environmental appraisers for electric-power plants.

The key environmental impacts of electric power are its use of land for what are generally large facilities and the substantial wastes associated with generation from fossil fuel and nuclear power. By far the greatest hazard potentials come from the wastes from combustion. Nuclear fuel is a hazardous material that generates other hazardous materials when employed to produce energy. The main problem with fossil fuel is its contamination with many other materials, such as sulfur and various metals; in addition, combustion generates nitrogen oxides that are considered a pollutant requiring control. Waste-heat disposal also has been an issue.

NRC control of nuclear power means that the issues largely reduce to the controversial questions of the efficacy of NRC policies. Land disturbance in the East generally proves to be the province of state and local governments; in the West, or at least those substantial parts of it controlled by the U.S. government, NEPA is a key force.

Fossil-fuel waste-disposal issues are treated jointly by EPA and counterpart state and local agencies. The most critical problem is that of preventing discharges into the air. Controls do exist on prevention of undesirable effects on land or water of those wastes that are captured rather than discharged into the atmosphere. However, to date, no major problems have arisen in compliance with these rules. (Pessimists in the electric-utility industry fear that the law governing toxic wastes could be interpreted to make expensive disposal of wastes from coal burning. Cases to date have centered on a chemical used in transformers.)

In contrast, compliance with air-pollution regulations—particularly those relating to sulfur dioxide—have had major effects on electric-utility decision making on fuel use. Fossil-fuel burning produces sulfur dioxides from combustion of sulfur contaminants in the fuel. The remaining contamination consists of whatever discharge occurs of all the other waste material, usually referred to as *particulates*. In addition, nitrogen oxides are produced by heating the nitrogen in the atmosphere, although coal also contains nitrogen. Sulfur dioxide, particulates, and nitrogen oxides are three of five "criteria" pollutants of which federal law specifically requires control. (The other two are carbon monoxide and unburnt hydrocarbons, both of which predominantly come from automobiles and other motor vehicles). However, particulate-control regulation could be satisfied by greater use of the technologies developed in response to the much earlier local programs to eliminate soot discharges from power plants. Regulation of nitrogen oxides has not been severe enough to require major changes in generating practices. (Again, concerns are periodically expressed that this situation eventually will change.)

However, compliance with sulfur-dioxide rules was more difficult to effect. Technically, the available options are selecting fuels naturally low enough in sulfur to comply, treating fuels to reduce sulfur to acceptable levels, or employing devices to prevent the discharge of the sulfur oxides into the atmosphere. The controversy has centered about the wisdom of using such devices, called *stack gas scrubbers*. Perfection of scrubbers proved far more expensive and time consuming than expected. By 1981, considerable improvement in operability had occurred, but the technology is still controversial (see PEDCo).

The waste-heat issue is whether it is desirable to use natural waterways as the initial point of disposal or whether other methods should be used. These include various types of cooling towers that produce direct discharge into the atmosphere or construction of an artificial body of water. Basically, the benefits of not using a natural waterway are prevention of what can be undesirable disturbances in the life systems existing there. The costs include the expenses of the alternative discharge methods and the impacts of the alternative on the environment. At the very least, alternative cooling methods involve a trade-off between returning heated water to the initial source and removing water from that source for use by the tower or pond. Hazards such as fogging also can be created by the direct discharges into the atmosphere.

As suggested in chapter 2, implementation of environmental controls is an area in which a substantial literature has arisen contending that financial incentives to clean up are preferable to the direct regulation actually employed. It is asserted that regulation is an overly expensive, slow moving way to produce results. A few more theoretical studies (for example, the two Baumol and Oates books 1975, 1979 and an article by Weitzman 1974) have suggested that the enthusiasm for financial incentives may have been overdone. More empirical studies are far less tolerant (see, for example, Kneese and Schultze 1975, Mills 1978, Portney 1978, and several articles in Friedlaender 1978). A key distinction here may be the basis of comparison. The theorists may be most concerned with overstatement of the ultimate degree to which financial incentives can replace direct regulation and be concerned that we cannot go as far as enthusiasts would suggest. The empirically oriented can observe that actual use of financial incentives is very limited and far less than desirable.

The National Environmental Policy Act and Its Impact

The critical provision of NEPA was a requirement that an environmental impact statement (EIS) be prepared on every major federal action. Court cases testing the extent of the requirements produced broad definitions. Thus, practically every new spending program or regulation was defined as a major action. In particular, the grant of a license to build or operate a nuclear plant, ceding land for a power plant or transmission line, and lease of coal lands are all deemed major actions. Every nuclear plant anywhere and most power plants in the far West where federal land holdings are extensive require an EIS. The EIS is supposed to have broad coverage. All major environmental impacts, including those subject to specific regulations, must be considered and every conceivable substitute must be considered in determining whether the alternative under consideration is the best possible. Whatever fuel is involved must be compared to all others—for example, coal to nuclear, oil, gas, and solar—and to conservation. The EIS approach has been adopted by various states.

The EIS concept was intended to inspire greater environmental consciousness in policymaking. Questions arise about whether the EIS was the most efficient way to inspire environmental consciousness. It was not the most thorough approach that could have been adopted. An extensive group of fully independent environmental monitors would have provided greater control over environmental impacts than statements issued by the advocates of undertaking a major action. Of course, such extensive control might have been excessive. Power would have passed from advocates of other actions to supporters of preventing environmental damages.

The actual approach, as noted, may have been too heavily reliant on policymakers anxious to proceed and limit the environmental constraints. The sweeping responsibilities that the courts assigned probably have been more than could be handled adequately by the available staffs. As a result, there was considerable resort to *boilerplate:* standard material routinely added to documents to comply with formalities. For example, DOI developed a review of energy alternatives that regularly appeared with modest alterations in every energy-related EIS. Finally, at no point were explicit guidelines given for appropriate decision criteria. The EIS process is subject to the problems of regulation discussed in chapters 2 and 4—large ambitions, small budgets, and vague definition of goals.

The clearest impacts of the EIS requirement on electric power have related to siting fossil-fuel power plants in western states. Impact debates, for example, long delayed approval of the Kaiparowits plant in southern Utah, and its sponsors decided to cancel it shortly before a DOI decision on a second request for approval.

Nuclear Policy: What Was the Effect of Three Mile Island?

The prospects for nuclear power have gyrated considerably since the launching after World War II of a U.S. program to promote civilian uses of atomic energy. It was not until the late 1960s that enough progress emerged to suggest that nuclear power was an economic way to generate electricity. Even then, considerable concern existed that the enthusiasm arose from incorrect perception of the underlying economics—particularly exaggerated concerns over resource exhaustion. However, the early 1970s brought a dramatic reversal of conditions. The rise of oil prices combined with growing environmental restrictions on coal use to advance greatly the relative economic attractiveness of nuclear power. This situation prevails even though nuclear regulation was itself greatly increasing in complexity. This improvement in prospects was reflected in a flurry of reactor orders from 1972 to 1974.

Subsequently, the situation reversed radically; orders virtually ceased, and many of the earlier orders, including most of those placed in 1974 and those ordered subsequently, were canceled (table 5-1). The change was the combined effect of the generally unfavorable climate for electric-utility expansion and the specific problems of nuclear power. The growth slowdown and problems of public-utility regulation discussed already discouraged all types of expansion. As often alleged, to the extent that the regulation is biased against investment, it particularly disfavored nuclear power in which investment is a higher proportion of costs than in other options. Nuclear power faced the special problem of growing regulatory resistance. NRC procedures were becoming increasingly stringent, and states were imposing additional barriers.

Just which of these forces has been most influential is difficult to determine. However, the general disincentives to electric-utility expansion are a major influence. Evidence is mounting that the lack of incentives for building plants was more important than the regulatory climate and the resulting change in the comparative economics of coal and nuclear power in causing cancellation of nuclear plants. A shift in the economics of fuel choice would have led to replacement of the planned nuclear facility with a coal-fired unit. Lack of demand would have meant that no new capacity would be added.

However, until the actual expansion record accumulates, the outcome

Table 5-1
Data on Nuclear-Plant Cancellations: 1970–1981
(number of reactors)

Year of Order	Initial Number	Remaining Number			
		Complete	Licensed for Construction	Unlicensed	Total
To 1964	20	20	0	0	20
1965	7	7	0	0	7
1966	20	19	1	0	20
1967	31	25	5	0	30
1968	14	6	8	0	14
1969	7	1	5	0	6
1970	14	3	10	0	13
1971	21	0	13(11)	0	13(11)
1972	36	0	19	2(1)	21(20)
1973	38	0	17(12)	8(3)	25(15)
1974	32	0	9(6)	2(0)	10(6)
1975	4	0	0	0	0
1976	3	0	0	1(0)	1(0)
1977	4	0	0	2(0)	2(0)
1978	2	0	0	2(0)	2(0)

Source: U.S., Department of Energy, Office of Nuclear Programs, 1981, *U.S. Central Station Nuclear Electric Generating Units Significant Milestones, Status as of April 1, 1981* and issues of this report and predecessor reports from AEC and ERDA.

Notes: Numbers in parenthesis are adjustments of DOE numbers to exclude plants known from other information to be canceled or indefinitely deferred or listed by DOE as having no definite completion date scheduled as follows.

1971: Two units of the Shearon Harris plant of Carolina Power and Light listed as scheduled for the 1990s.

1972: The Clinch River breeder's fate depends on a continuing political battle on financing.

1973: The licensed units with doubtful status include the three indefinitely postponed units of Duke Power's Cherokee Station, Jamesport 1 canceled by Long Island Lighting and New York State Electric and Gas and River Bend 2 indefinitely suspended by Gulf States Utilities. The most imperiled unlicensed units are three at Duke's Perkins Station, which are indefinitely postponed, Unit 1 of Pebbles Springs planned by a consortium headed by Portland General Electric and Skagit No. 1 planned by a consortium headed by Puget Sound Power and Light.

1974: The unlicensed plants are the second units of Pebble Springs and Skagit. The licensed units include two of TVA—Yellow Creek 2 and Phipps Bend 2—for which dates are indefinite. Not deleted but in jeopardy are Units 4 and 5 of the Washington Public Power Supply System and Phipps Bend and Yellow Creek 1.

1976: The Vandalia unit planned by various Iowa companies has no stated completion date.

1977. The two New Haven units of New York State Electric and Gas have been canceled.

1978. The Carroll County units of Commonwealth Edison and its partners are indefinitely deferred.

In addition, the completion of the remaining unlicensed plants—Allens Creek 2 of Houston Lighting and Power, and Black Fox 1 and 2 of Central and Southwest from 1973—remains doubtful. Bailly of Northern Indiana Public Service from 1967 has not been started and was canceled in August 1981. Pilgrim 2 of Boston Edison has also canceled in September 1981.

can only be measured imperfectly. At best, we can obtain indicators of present electric-utility thinking about what to do given the cancellation of nuclear plants. Such indicators are provided by various lists of planned new generating plants. These lists have limitations even as indicators of utility judgments about future trends. In the case of needs in more distant periods, utilities can choose to err in either direction. More or fewer plants than the companies believe are clearly needed may be listed; to complicate matters, the same company may adopt different criteria for inclusion in different lists. A further consideration is that company expectations can be disproved. In fact, utilities have been reducing their expectations and expansion plans. An important result of these revisions is that tentative plans to replace a canceled nuclear plant have been steadily delayed and even canceled.

To the extent that the problems of nuclear power relate to the basic investment climate, reform of nuclear regulation will do little to produce rapidly a major revival of new orders for new nuclear plants. Nevertheless, nuclear policy cannot be ignored in appraising the long-run prospects of electric power. In the shorter term, a substantial amount of nuclear-powered capacity is under construction, and considerable concern exists about the ability of this capacity to secure the regulatory authorization to allow completion. Eventually, resumed growth, or at least the need to replace old plants, will lead to the need to resume planning new plants, and nuclear regulation must be resolved. Unfortunately, the available evidence suggests that prevailing conditions universally are deemed unsatisfactory.

The prior discussion should have suggested that the accident at unit 2 of General Public Utilities' Three Mile Island plant may have done little to affect an already poor climate for nuclear power. However, the accident stimulated a review of NRC that has disclosed widespread discontent with the operation of the commission.

This discontent was vigorously expressed in the report of a Presidential Commission to investigate the Three Mile Island accident (known as the Kemeny Commission after its chairman, who at the time was president of Dartmouth College). The commission assured NRC with "a preoccupation with regulations. . . . Once regulations become as complex and as voluminous as those regulations now in place, they can serve as a negative factor in nuclear safety." The Kemeny Commission added that the NRC commissions did not effectively direct or control the staff. The staff, in turn, was viewed as divided into uncoordinated compartments.

This view expresses the feeling of a wide variety of observers. An ample public record was reenforced by my discussions with electric-utility officials. A view representative of these discussions was presented in a Florida Power and Light report to the Florida Department of Public Affairs. "Florida Power and Light still considers nuclear to be a viable source of energy and the most economical means of producing electricity. However, due to the uncertainties associated with nuclear generation and the resultant excessive financial risks, the Company has been forced to delay its nuclear expansion program'' (Florida Power and Light Company 1980, p. 66). This sentiment follows a discussion noting that both NRC and other agencies keep changing the licensing and technical requirements. Three basic problems were distinguished: frequent changes in nuclear regulations, lack of federal support for nuclear in the overall energy plan, and lack of state recognition of financing needs. Similar views about NRC have also been expressed by critics of nuclear power such as the Union of Concerned Scientists (*Energy Users Report* 26 March 1981, p. 555).

The details of this process are not easily summarized because of their complexity. A broad mandate to supervise nuclear power by licensing plants and monitoring their operation has been implemented by imposing numerous specific regulations. Two licenses are required for a nuclear facility: one to permit the construction and another to allow operations. Under NEPA, specific review of nuclear issues must be supplemented by an EIS meeting the usual rules that all impacts are treated. A further element of the review is antitrust clearance—a legislative requirement designed to facilitate participation of smaller companies in nuclear power. In practice, the growing difficulties of the electric-power industry have encouraged companies to ask others to participate. In particular, private companies have invited their former enemies—the public and cooperative entities—to become partners in nuclear (and fossil) plants. For example, the Georgia Power subsidiary of the Southern Company has two operating units and two units under construction in which shares were sold to cooperatives and municipals (which previously did not own any capacity). Similar ventures have been developed by Pennsylvania Power and Light, Detroit Edison, Duke Power, and the Public Service Company of Indiana. In addition, NRC checks on practices in the construction and operation of plants.

The process involves many procedures. Long reports must be filed by those seeking licenses. Depending on the reaction, it may be necessary to conduct elaborate hearings on the wisdom of granting the licenses. Court appeals can be made to delay further the decision. Three particularly extreme cases illustrate how problems can mount. In November 1966, Pacific Gas and Electric ordered the first unit of its Diablo Canyon plant. While other plants ordered at the same time were completed between 1972 and 1974, Diablo Canyon was only near completion in 1981 (and design flaws were discovered shortly before operations were supposed to start). Similarly, Long Island Lighting's Shoreham plant was ordered in February 1967; several other plants ordered at about the same time were completed by 1973; Shoreham is scheduled for 1983 completion. Northern Indiana Public Service's effort to build a nuclear unit at its Bailly site started in 1967. However, opposition was so intense that by 1981 delay had caused the construction license to lapse with only 1 percent of the work complete. The plans were canceled in 1981.

These cases represent the rare situations in which the regulatory problems were sufficiently intense and protracted that their critical role is obvious. By themselves, the examples only show that regulation can be extremely troublesome. Conclusive measurement of the overall impact of regulation appears infeasible. Administrative policymaking generates massive and difficult-to-acquire records of reports and hearings reposing in company and NRC archives. Moreover, the regulatory development at NRC occurred simultaneously with the other pressures on nuclear power. Available analytic techniques cannot adequately isolate the effects of each of several simultaneously occurring developments. Thus, we must be content to rely on the criticism of numerous people who have direct experience with NRC and have concluded that the agency is not performing satisfactorily. It is being indicted for delaying and making more expensive the development of nuclear power without clearly contributing to increased safety.

Such criticism is similar to that directed at regulation of other environmental issues such as air pollution. It seems natural to ask, as few appear to have done, if the similar complaints imply comparable responses. In particular, it can be asked whether the argument used about pollution—that financial pressures replace detailed regulation—applies to nuclear power.

Clearly, this approach to nuclear power has been given little, if any, serious consideration. The idea that nuclear power is too important to be left unregulated thoroughly dominates the discussion. Reform ideas are most likely to ape the Kemeny Commission in proposing a better NRC or Weinberg in his advocacy of independent operators. Clearly, this implies that nuclear power differs from other sources of environmental side effects in so fundamental a way that the usual arguments about direct regulation versus financial incentives are inapplicable. Presumably, the critical difference is in the effects of a serious nuclear disaster. It is conceivable that substantial loss of life could occur and thus preventing error is much more imperative than preventing sporadic discharges of air pollutants that each are unlikely to cause much harm.

What is unclear is whether this difference in objectives implies that different enforcement procedures are necessary. The case for direct regulations seems to have rested on the proposition that NRC supervision of nuclear power was a superior way to prevent catastrophic error. The past Three Mile Island accident reappraisal has left this proposition badly battered and greatly furthered the development of separate private efforts at insuring safety. Both a Nuclear Safety Analysis Center and an Institute of Nuclear Power Operations were established in 1979 in response to the Three

Mile Island accident. The center was designed to study problems, and the institute, to coordinate training programs and other elements of plant-management practice.

The proderegulation counterargument is that the case for decentralized control by financial pressure is actually stronger than the case for its application to air pollution from fossil fuel. First, the nature of the problem is better defined. While great doubt exists about the critical means and ends of air-pollution regulation, the goal of a nuclear safety is very clear—prevent massive discharge of radiation. Moreover, the strength of the existing system of responsibility for nuclear accidents is that it has already established a mechanism by which the nuclear industry is liable for damages. Given these advantages and the failures of NRC, the traditional case that decentralized actions motivated by profits are more effective than centralized control may be far more applicable to nuclear power than is usually recognized.

Two drawbacks do exist. First, the liability limit of $560 million may be too low. Deregulation may have to be accompanied by some way to raise the limits. Total removal would be the ideal most consistent with minimum regulation. The problem is that in the absence of at least interim limits, removal of the ceilings on liability could lead to state decisions to use high coverage requirements as another indirect way of stifling nuclear energy.

A second problem is that public-utility regulation among other things shifts the risks of investment from stockholders to consumers. Rate-of-return regulation precludes accumulating extra profits on better investment to offset losses on less successful ones. Thus, to prevent bankruptcy, rates must be raised to insure that losses are covered. This may make electric-power companies inadequately concerned about risks. Deregulation of nuclear power may be connected inescapably with deregulation of electric-power rates. Nuclear deregulation may be essential to prevent creation of indirect barriers to profitable operations, and deregulation of rates may be essential to creating a climate that makes financial pressures a preferable alternative to NRC.

Air-Pollution Policy: The Legislative Mandates and Their Implementation

Laws cover many different environmental problems, but air-pollution control is one of the major problem areas for the electric-power industry. Since concerns date back several centuries to the time in the seventeenth century when the introduction of coal burning blackened the skies of Great Britain, a full history of regulation is clearly impractical.

The U.S. Congress passed its first law devoted specifically to air pollution in 1955. In 1963, the Clean Air Act was passed, and subsequent acts were passed in 1965, 1967, 1970, and 1977 that provided for major revisions of the initial act. (See the 1970 report of the Council on Environmental Quality, pp. 73–75, for a summary of the legislation up to that point; the 1971 report, pp. 160–161, on the 1970 amendments; and the 1977 report, pp. 22–27, on the 1977 amendments; Kneese and Schultze 1975, pp. 45–53, and Mills 1978, pp. 89–94, deal with the record from 1955 to 1970.)

The 1955 act simply provided $5 million per year in federal support to state development of air-pollution-control programs. The 1963 act then gave HEW power to impose air-quality rules, but only after the states failed both to adopt regulations voluntarily and respond to a court order to comply. The 1965 amendments were directed specifically at pollution from automobiles but set an important precedent for other policies by specifying that control take the form of emission limits on new cars. Thus, in addition to governing the concentration of pollution in the air—the basic concern—the government was regulating how much a given source could contribute to pollution and thus effectively specifying a major portion of the control tactics. The basic impact of the 1967 amendments was to require that all states set pollution regulations within a prescribed period. HEW was given two years to conduct studies outlining the impacts of critical pollutants. The states were then supposed to declare (within ninety days of the publication of the HEW notices) both that state standards would be set within another six months and that within a year after the HEW report the rules would be implemented.

The 1970 amendments then required that EPA set national standards for air quality that would serve as ceilings for the amount of pollution states could allow. States could set more stringent rules. Initial primary goals preventing health effects were to be supplemented by secondary standards preventing damages to property and other aspects of social welfare. In addition, the concept of control on emissions from a source was generalized so that major new facilities such as fossil-fuel-burning boilers and metals smelters could be subjected to special new source rules. EPA could also identify various materials as sufficiently hazardous that emission limits should be set on new and existing facilities.

The changes made in the 1977 amendments included fundamental alterations of the basis for air quality and source emission standards. The country was divided between nonattainment areas in which inadequate progress had been made toward meeting the air-quality standards and prevention of significant deterioration (PSD) areas in which air quality was better than required.[1] More stringent actions to force compliance were required of nonattainment areas. PSD was to be assured by limiting the allowable *increase* in pollution in clean areas.

New source rules under the 1970 amendments had involved setting limits on emissions. The 1977 amendments went a step further and required that compliance involve use of best available control technology (BACT)—some combination of removing pollutants from the coal and post-combustion cleaning. Among other provisions relevant to electric power was a requirement that existing plants be forced to use local coal to prevent economic damage to local miners and provisions to control pollution impairing visibility at national parks.

Before discussing the details of these provisions, the resulting regulations, their impact, the apparent bases, and the criticisms that have been raised should be noted. A tightening of control would most logically be interpreted as reflecting growing impatience with the efficacy of prior efforts. This impression is confirmed by the reviews in the literature (see Kneese and Schultze 1975, and the various discussions in Friedlaender 1978, especially that of Stewart, pp. 68–137). The efforts through 1970 reflect the combined effect of this concern about inadequate progress and conviction that regulation was the best way to proceed.

The 1977 amendments also were affected by forces other than the concern over air pollution. PSD was produced as a congressional response to a court mandate. In 1972 a circuit court agreed that the preambles to the 1967 and 1970 acts requiring that the government "protect and enhance" air quality meant that significant deterioration must be prevented. This decision was upheld because the Supreme Court was divided four to four on the case (and issued no further decision). EPA efforts at implementing the decision floundered because of the vagueness of the mandate, and Congress was asked to resolve the issue. It chose to impose guidelines on the allowable degree of deterioration.

The shift to BACT has been widely criticized (see, for example, Navarro 1980a, and Landsberg 1979) as resulting from an alliance, often called unholy, of quite disparate interests—protectors of eastern coal mining (particularly of mine workers), opponents of western surface mining, and those who were concerned with tighter air-pollution regulations. Clearly, the local coal provision as written is entirely a measure to protect coal interests without any potential contribution to improved air quality. PSD is similarly criticized as reflecting efforts to protect local industry as well as air quality by reducing the feasibility of shifting location as a compliance strategy.

The general principle of special rules for new sources has been increasingly criticized as particularly unwise given the lagging growth rate of the U.S. economy. The rules are recognized as encouraging retention of old plants to avoid stringent control requirements (see, for example, Crandall 1980).

More broadly, the criticisms are particular examples of the basic case against direct control—that regulators get increasingly involved in details about which they are incompetent to judge. New source rules are an example of the fear that too much burden may be placed on new sources. The views further suggest that one type of complication that frequently arises is that decisions are made on the basis of considerations other than reducing pollution. This last argument is an application of the discussion of the contentions about equity-based policies in appendix 2F. In particular, the critics are concerned that those protected are politically potent groups who are not so obviously needy that their assistance is desirable.

In sum, this air-pollution-control policy involves rules relating both to concentration of pollution in the atmosphere—the air-quality rules—and the discharges from particular facilities—performance standards. The reconciliation of the two occurs through implementation plans that establish rules to insure that the standards are met. Effectively, the result is the promulgation of ideal performance rules to supplement the federally mandated ones.

Since the promulgation of national air-quality standards, implementation has involved interaction among state and local governments, EPA, polluting industries, and environmental groups intervening in the discussion. Ideally, the states would quickly produce rules that EPA could approve and the polluters could then easily comply. In practice, many disputes arose between EPA and the states, among states (involving interstate transmission of pollution), and between the states or EPA with the polluters.

The 1977 amendments simultaneously tightened pressures on those areas not in compliance and established PSD rules. These included requirements for more vigorous implementation programs [section 125(a) adding part D to title I], restricting construction of new facilities [section 108(a) amending section 110(a)], and allowing the worst offenders to be fined amounts equal to their cost savings through noncompliance (section 118 adding section 120).

The PSD rules define how areas are to be classified and what rules apply to each area type. Following principles developed by EPA in its abortive efforts to resolve the issues administratively, three classes of areas were defined. One set of rules then defined allowable increments to each class and another indicated how regions were to be classified. Table 5-2 compares the legislative limits on pollution increases to the corresponding national air quality standards. The class III limits allow increments equal to about half the levels allowed by the national standards. The class II increments in turn are about half those for class III. The class I increments are much smaller.

The law provided for initial classification of regions and possible reclassification. Initially, areas including extant national parks larger than 6,000 acres, international parks, and national wilderness areas and memorial parks larger than 5,000 acres had to be made class I areas and could never be reclassified. All other affected areas would initially be class II. Some of

Table 5-2

**National Ambient Air Standards and Prevention of Significant
Deterioration Increments**

(micrograms per cubic meter)

	Primary Standard	*Secondary Standard*	*Allowable Increment*		
			Class I	*Class II*	*Class III*
Particulates					
Annual	75	60	5	20	37
Twenty four Hour	260	150	10	37	75
Sulfur Dioxide					
Annual	80	n.a.	2	20	40
Twenty four Hour	365	n.a.	5	91	182
Three Hour	n.a.	n.a.	25	512	700

Source: Primary and secondary standards U.S., Council on Environmental Quality, *Annual Report, 1975*, p. 300.

n.a.: not applicable.

these areas—those greater than 10,000 acres with a new national park or any national monument, primitive area, national preserve, recreation area, wild and scenic river, wildlife refuge, lakeshore, or seashore—could be upgraded into class I but could not be made class III. Other regions could be classified III after formal review.

Associated with PSD was a provision that in those class I areas in which visibility was critical, large existing installations would have to adopt the best available retrofit technology to prevent interference with the viability.

The BACT provision requires some use of methods that remove pollutants from the fuel or the stack gas. As discussed later, there proved considerable opportunity for argument about how to implement the requirement. The law suggests and the supporting conference report confirms, moreover, that protective concerns were at work. The law notes that EPA should consider "the mobility and competitive nature of each such category of sources" [section 109(a) adding section 111(f), in which the quoted phrase is in subsection (2)(c)]. The conference report (p. 129) clearly states that one goal is to prevent states with weak controls from competing for new facilities by continuing such controls. The obvious criticism is that as long as ambient air rules are met, it is desirable that the option of moving to less polluted areas be conserved. BACT becomes a concrete example of imposing a higher-cost solution, not to improve air quality but to protect a local interest. A further concern is of the appropriate degree of federal control on ambient air quality. One set of questions relates to the necessity and desirability of the federal government supervising state control of local impacts of local actions. A second set of issues relates to the applicability of the 1960 Coase analysis. Conceivably, litigation among states might be equally or more effective than federal regulation as a means of preventing interstate transmission of pollution.

Finally, the local coal provision indicated that the use of fuels other than local coal could be prohibited in facilities subject to state implementation plans if the fuel shift would create serious unemployment. Governors could request the aid, but federal approval was required.

The developments of air-pollution regulations prior to the 1977 amendments need no further review. Nothing more complex was involved than a desire to develop more effective regulations. However, further comment is needed about the forces inspiring the 1977 amendments and the regulations implementing the amendments and their effects. The critical further point about BACT is that one major stimulus to its adoption was the failure of utilities to accept stack gas scrubbers as a widespread method of pollution control. Instead, utilities, particularly in many North Central states (such as Illinois, Michigan, Minnesota, Wisconsin, Indiana, and Iowa) began substantial use of Wyoming and Montana low-sulfur coal. This occurred at a time that utilities east of the Mississippi were making heavy commitments to nuclear power. Thus, fears of displacement of eastern coal were widespread. Presumably, similar fears were a factor in the support for PSD and local coal provisions.

BACT rules for sulfur dioxides from electric-power plants were the subject of an extensive effort by EPA. It commissioned numerous studies of the subject. For example, ICF Inc., a Washington, D.C. consulting firm, prepared a series of reports estimating the impact on coal production and emissions of different specific BACT rules. The electric utilities used an alternative optimum-fuel-choice model, developed by National Economic Research Associates (NERA), to provide alternative appraisals. EPA found definition of rules required delicate balancing. It was determined not to allow more pollution than would have been produced by compliance with earlier rules. Specifically, it wanted to prevent use of coals so high in sulfur content that even when scrubbing was used, emissions exceeded the 1971 limit of 1.2 pounds of sulfur oxides per million Btu. Simultaneously, it was recognized that discretion existed to give some credit for use of low sulfur coal. Possible interpretations at one extreme imposed such severe limits on high sulfur coal, and such liberal credits for use of low-sulfur coal, that BACT would not greatly aid eastern coal. The other extreme of a flat requirement of scrubbing would have severely penalized western coal. The actual choice gave only modest relief in the form of less severe scrubbing requirements to use of low sulfur coal.

PSD was widely interpreted by utilities in North Central states as negating the effect of BACT on western coal. To meet PSD and BACT rules, heavy scrubbing of low-sulfur coal would be required to stay within the limit of PSD increments. Another potential problem was that in the absence of clear principles for allocating PSD rights, scrambles arose to preempt claims on the increments.

Visibility proved a potentially more thorny issue because the range of possible interpretations was so broad. The number of mandatory class I areas is substantial. *Regulation* magazine's review of visibility (March/April 1981, pp. 12–13) noted that the provision's extent was extended by its breadth combined with the effects of a congressional mania to establish a national park in every congressional district. However, the key lies in the qualifying phrase that visibility must be important in these areas. A broad definition of importance combined with rules providing for particularly stringent protection rules could greatly restrict industrial activity. Most of the West is near enough to class I areas that it all could be affected by stringent rules. A surprisingly large part of the East, including much of the Appalachian coal regions, could also be affected (see Trisko 1980). However, much more limited rules could be adopted and might affect only a few plants, particularly those in Arizona and New Mexico and other scenic areas (see the 1980 ICF report on visibility).

In any case, much of this has become moot, given both the slowdown in electric-power expansion that has greatly limited the construction of plants controlled by BACT, and the Reagan administration's determination to adopt more lenient rules.

In the meantime, we are left with a vast array of air-pollution-related disputes resulting from these policies and fights over how to enforce them. At least in the major coal consuming states, the 10Ks of utilities invariably contain long descriptions of the numerous environmental disputes that prevail. Ohio is probably the area with the greatest problem. The state had great difficulties devising a state implementation plan satisfactory to EPA; enforcement was complicated by pressure to apply the local coal provisions (with local coal narrowly defined to mean Ohio rather than Appalachia), and more eastern states, such as Pennsylvania and New York, objected to eastward transmission of Ohio (and Indiana) pollution. Another set of disputes arose with the reintroduction of coal to the East coast, particularly in the greater New York area. Proposals included reconversion of existing plants from oil to coal and construction of new coal-fired plants. Objections were raised, particularly by New York City officials, to any use of coal. Concerns were expressed by Connecticut and New Jersey about the best way to distribute coal use and the resulting pollution among states. In general, companies are trying to protect the status of plants under construction as being under the 1971 rule rather than BACT. Thus, the 1977 amendments may prove to have minor effects as new plants become rarer and the rules are changed.

Note

1. Three amendments are relevant. Section 103 of the amendments, amending section 107 by adding section (d)(1) defines five possible statuses of attainment of air-quality goals:

1. not meeting a primary standard for pollutants other than sulfur dioxide for particulates.
2. not meeting or not expected to meet without the deadlines the primary standards for sulfur dioxide or particulates.
3. not meeting a secondary standard.
4. not violating a primary or secondary standard for sulfur dioxide or particulates.
5. exceeding the other national primary or secondary standards or not clearly violating them.

Section 129(b) adds section 171 to the act defining as nonattainment areas the first three types defined by amended section 107. Section 127(a) adds part C. section 162 defining as class I PSD regions all international parks, national-wilderness areas and memorial parks exceeding 5000 acres, and existing national parks exceeding 6000 acres. Then section 162(b) adds that areas in the last two categories established in section 107 that are not also class I are initially made class II regions.

6

Regulating Electric-
Power-Fuel Use

The Powerplant and Industrial Fuel Use Act (PIFUA) was passed in 1978. But as of 1981, federal regulation of electric-utility and industrial-fuel use seems to be a policy headed for extinction. The effort suffered from the difficulty that changes in fuel use that were considered worthwhile to compel by regulation were also generally sufficiently profitable that private companies were willing to undertake voluntary conversions. The key barriers were securing both permission to include conversion costs in the rate base and clearance from environmental agencies.

The policy efforts, nevertheless, deserve review because of the regulatory problems that arose. In addition to the difficulties noted of finding things worth doing, issues arose about how best to set rules that would clearly determine when a conversion was appropriate.

Major Fuel Users and National Energy Legislation

The 1977 presidential proposals affecting electric utilities and large industrial users (both of which are described here by the term *major users*) differ markedly from the actual legislation. The key differences are that much less use of the tax system to affect the fuel use of major consumers is authorized than was requested by President Carter and the regulations influencing fuel choice are less stringent than requested. (The Carter proposals included a tax on industrial oil and gas use.)

Before dealing with the evolution from proposals to legislation, some of the technical distinctions established in the act must be discussed. First, both electric-power plants and industrial facilities had to be defined [sections 103(a)(7) to (12)]. The main question about power plants is whether they should include facilities used mainly for supplying power to their owners. The draft bill simply stated that the included power plants were those that produced primarily for sale; the law contains an explicit exclusion for plants that sell less than half their power and also are engaged in producing process heat for their owners (*cogeneration facilities*) [section 103(a)(7)(B)(ii) supplemented by sections 212(c) and 312(c)]. Industrial facilities are those using a boiler, gas turbine, combined cycle (a combustion turbine to which a steam boiler to use the waste heat is coupled), or an internal-combustion engine [section 103(a)(10)(A)]. The legislation explicitly excludes such facilities used in producing oil and gas [section 103(a)(10)(B) (ii)]. A further limitation is that coverage of both power plants and industrial facilities is confined to single units using at least 100 million Btu per hour or plants with combined fuel use in excess of 250 million Btu per hour [section 103(a)(10)(A)(i),(ii)].

The meaning of the coverage rules in the electric-power plant sector is clear. The electric-utility industry operates a readily identified group of plants that are covered by the rules; moreover, as shown later, the number of plants that can convert to coal is quite small. Just how many covered industrial plants exist and what their characteristics are is less apparent. Data on these users are limited to a survey taken by the Federal Energy Administration, about which little has been made public. What can be noted is that the covered facilities could be far smaller than a modern electric-power plant. Such power plants are likely to use upwards of one million tons of coal per year. A covered industrial plant might consume as little as 18,000 tons of coal annually.[1]

A second key distinction is between new and old plants. New plants are subject to tighter restrictions than existing ones, and care had to be taken in delineating the basis of classification. President Carter proposed that a new plant be one that, in the view of the regulatory authorities, had reached a point at which it could no longer reasonably be designed and constructed so as to be capable of using coal without incurring significant financial or operational detriment. In addition, plants already identified as candidates for conversion to coal under the Energy Supply and Environmental Coordination Act of 1974 also were to be considered new plants.

Slightly more detailed versions of both definitions are embodied in the legislation. First, plants clearly instituted after the enactment of the act are new facilities [section 103(a)(8)(A) and 103(a)(11)(A)]. In addition, plants whose "construction or acquisition" began after 20 April 1977 (the date of the president's energy message) are covered unless excessive costs or reliability problems would be caused. The Department of Energy (DOE) is to establish rules defining what constitutes either excessive cost or reliability problems [section 103(a)(8)(B)]. The legislation adds the further provision that sale of an existing plant does not make it a new one [section 103(a) (9)(B)].

At least in the electric-utility sector, the potential for controversy about newness is confined to three units announced before the 1973 oil-price increases but delayed for completion in the early 1980s. The owner of two of the proposed units was engaged in a debate with DOE over whether these should be considered new plants. However, the company, Baltimore Gas and Electric, decided to build the plant with two coal-fired units. The other company, Potomac Electric, actually will complete construction of an oil-fired unit. Because of the lack of knowledge about the industrial sector mentioned, the problems of new plant identification cannot adequately be delineated. Nevertheless, to lessen disputes, DOE has found it necessary to revise the proposed rules for defining new plants.

In any case, the legislation sets roughly the same basic rules for the various classes of facilities as the president had proposed. All new power plants and all new industrial boilers are subject to a ban on oil and natural-gas use [section 201(1), 202(a)]; DOE can prohibit such use in new industrial nonboilers if this is feasible (prohibitions may apply either to classes of facilities or to specific installations) [section 202(b)]. The legislation adds a provision that all new power plants must have the capability of burning coal or some other alternative to oil or natural gas [section 201(2)]. Existing electric-power plants are required to cease natural-gas use by 1 January 1990, may not convert from petroleum to gas, and are prohibited from increasing the proportion of gas used [section 301(a)]. Where feasible, oil and gas use may be prohibited by DOE for such existing power plants [section 301(b)]. Permission must be secured to increase the oil use of plants also burning coal (section 405). Existing industrial facilities are covered only by discretionary conversion requirements; conversions may be required when it is possible to burn other fuels (section 302).

Some additional provisions, however, were added by the Congress. DOE is authorized to ban, when feasible, the use of natural gas in space-heating boilers using more than 300,000 cubic feet of natural gas per day (section 401). Prohibitions have also been placed on decorative use of natural gas lights (section 402). The federal government's own major fuel-burning facilities have been required to limit oil and natural-gas use (section 403).

As proposed by the president and approved by Congress, increases in oil use by existing power plants are restricted, and the president has been given power to allocate coal supplies and restrict oil and gas use in emergencies (sections 404 and 405). A number of assistance programs were added by Congress—loans to aid purchase of pollution equipment by electric utilities converting to coal (section 602), assistance to areas affected by increased coal or uranium mining (section 601), and assistance to railroads in increasing their capacity to transport coal (section 803). Finally, a series of studies on the structure and performance of the coal industry, the effects of the law on small utilities, the socioeconomic impacts of increased coal use, and the use of oil and gas in combustors was authorized (sections 741–747).

The tradition of authorizing studies to assuage concerns that Congress does not wish to face immediately is well known. What may be noted here is that practically every energy bill of the 1970s has had such provisions, and that the work proposed in this statute is in well-trod areas. A prior act—the

Federal Coal Leasing Amendments Act of 1976—established a requirement that the Department of Justice issue an annual report on competition in the coal industry; the first report under that requirement appeared in 1978. Other reports on competition have appeared from the Federal Trade Commission, the General Accounting Office, and the Tennessee Valley Authority. Similarly, numerous studies of regional energy impacts have been sponsored by various government agencies.

The differences between proposals and legislation are most important in the provisions establishing circumstances under which exceptions can be made from the basic rules. The president's proposals allowed for a blanket exemption of peak-load power stations from the controls. New power plants and industrial facilities were to be exempted either permanently or temporarily from the ban on oil use if lack of alternatives, environmental problems, and difficulties in securing reliable coal supplies precluded use of coal or other fuels. Similar exemptions were available for existing power plants and industrial facilities, and a special provision was included allowing a five-year exemption from gas conversion by a power plant if it could be shown that the plant would shift to a synthetic gas from coal or to some other alternative fuel.

Congress expanded on these concepts in various ways. The result was four sets of exceptions: (1) temporary ones for new plants (section 211); (2) permanent ones for new plants (section 212); (3) temporary ones for existing plants (section 311); and (4) permanent ones for existing plants (section 312). Different lists of justifications for exemptions were provided for each type, but the overlap was considerable. The only common basis for all four types was existence of three types of basic conversion problems: the cost of alternative fuels significantly exceeded the cost of oil and gas [sections 211(a)(1), 212(a)(1)(A), 311(a)(1), and 312(a)(1)(A)]; site conditions precluded conversion [sections 211(a)(2), 212(a)(i)(A), 311(a)(1), and 313(a)(1)(A); or environmental restrictions could not be met [sections 211(a)(3), 212(a)(1)(c), 311(a)(3), and 312(a)(1)(c)]. The cost exemption was a congressional addition. The temporary exemption for plants that would convert to synthetic fuels was extended so any facility covered by the act was eligible [sections 211(a) and 311(b)]. As an alternative to eliminating gas use in existing plants, Congress allowed the electric utilities to develop company-wide plans for reducing gas use that could allow continued use of some gas in heavily used (base load) plants for as much as ten years past the 1990 deadline (section 501).

More critically, several new categories of plants eligible in various degrees for permanent exemptions were established. Categories that were applicable to new and old plants included those affected by state or local rules precluding conversion [sections 212(b) and 312(b)], those that could best convert by using a mixture of coal and oil or gas [sections 212(d) and

312(d)], those designed only for use in emergencies [sections 212(e) and
312(e)], those operating as intermediate load plants [sections 212(h) and
312(g)], those used in processes in which fuel substitutions was not feasible
[sections 212(i) and 312(k)], and those designed solely to operate when other
plants were undergoing planned maintenance [sections 312(j) and 312(l)].
The explanation in the conference committee report on the bill indicates
that the state-and-local-rules provision is designed primarily to insure that
consideration is given to problems of plants facing state and local environmental rules stricter than those of the federal government. The report warns
that care must be taken to insure that these regulations were not imposed to
assist evasion of the act. The act defines intermediate load as less than 3,500
hours of operation per year [section 103(a)(18)(B)]. Since there are 8,760
hours in a 365-day year, such plants would operate less than 40 percent of
the time.

A further permanent exemption for new plants can be secured if they
are needed to insure reliability of service [section 212(1)]. Existing plants
can secure only a temporary exemption to insure reliability [section 311(g)].
Existing plants can be exempt if they are base-loaded gas-fired electric-
power plants burning less than 250 million Btu per hour and cannot easily
convert to other fuels [section 312(h)], if they use liquified natural gas for
environmental reasons [section 312(i)], or if they are served by a gas pipeline
from Canada and the termination of gas use would interfere with overall
service on the pipeline or cause substantial financial penalties [section
312(j)]. While new peaking plants could secure a permanent exemption (section 212), existing peaking plants might get permanent or temporary exemptions [sections 311(f) and 312(f)]. New plants could secure an exemption if
financing of the plant were imperiled [section 212(a)(1)(D)].

The details of each exemption differ somewhat from the others. The
key consideration is the stringency of the tests applicable to the exemption.
At one extreme, best represented by the international pipeline provisions, it
is only necessary to establish that the facility is, in fact, one to which the
provisions apply. At the other extreme, the general exemption provision
requires proof that a wide range of direct operating cost, environmental,
or reliability problems makes the conversion infeasible. In the intermediate
cases, the requirements involve consideration of whether the facility falls
into the specified classes and problems of coal use would arise. Presumably,
the purpose of distinguishing these categories is to make them subject to less
stringent tests of whether coal use is infeasible, but the language of the act is
frequently unclear.

A more critical point is that the criteria for exemptions presented in the
act are not much more specific than the summary versions presented here.
Instead, the act invariably calls for DOE development of rules for implementing the law (provisions regarding rulemaking and judicial review

appear in sections 701 and 702). Thus PIFUA, like much economic legislation, delegates an enormous amount of responsibility for determining
exactly how the law will be administered.

The Cost-Exemption Procedure

The most difficult aspect of implementing PIFUA was to define excess of
costs significant enough to justify exemption from forced conversion. The
Economic Regulatory Administration (ERA) of DOE selected the standard
economic criterion that the option with the lower social cost would be
selected. ERA proceeded to provide rules for calculating the social costs.

The basic costing formula required a standard present value calculation, and the difficulties relate primarily to the specific rules imposed on the
calculations. ERA determined what interest rate to assume, the probable
path of fuel-price increases, and the externalities associated with oil use
(and with gas use, on the presumption that large-user gas consumption
deprived someone in another sector of gas and forced increased oil use).

The basic problem with the ERA approach is that satisfactory determination of these figures is difficult, if not nearly impossible. ERA's ability
to document its choices differed considerably. At one extreme, the basis for
estimating interest rate was an extensive study provided by Ernst and Ernst
(now Ernst and Whinney). At the other, no documentation was provided
about how several components of the net externalities were estimated. Similarly, the plausibility of the results could be subjected to considerable chal-
lenge.

Ernst and Ernst developed interest-cost data by straightforward use of
one of the techniques popular in finance—the capital-asset-pricing model.
The model is designed to estimate from market data the risk premium that
should be applied to interest on the securities of different industries. Then
the sum of this premium and the risk-free interest rate is the appropriate
interest rate for the company. (The risk-free rate, in turn, can be expressed
in real or nominal terms, and in either case the assumed inflation factor also
can be specified).

It is easy to present numerous objections to these calculations. The
intrinsic problems of deducing interest rates are sufficiently great that disputes persist about whether the capital-asset-pricing model or any alternative approach produces satisfactory results. These are basic conceptual
issues, and important empirical questions arise about selecting an appropriate measure of long-term expectations about the real risk-free rate of
interest and the rate of inflation.

The externalities associated with imports were composed of the net of
costs from the increase in world oil prices caused by higher U.S. oil con-

sumption, the supply disruption, and the less favorable balance of payments created by higher oil consumption and the benefits of avoided pollution. The three costs of greater imports—higher prices, greater vulnerability to disruption, and greater depreciation of the international value of the U.S. dollar—are intrinsically difficult to quantify, and ERA's work on the issues differed markedly in detail. Several models were developed to treat the impact of higher imports on world oil prices, and the valuation of the import costs was secured by averaging the results. However, the models were in no case based on statistical analyses of the critical functions, and the results were the inevitable outcome of the assumptions of the models. Thus, the most complex of the models is one that indicates how OPEC would work if it were a perfectly functioning cartel. Alternative views, such as Adelman's 1980 assertion that imperfect coordination prevents OPEC from fully maximizing profits, were excluded from review. The reduced vulnerability benefit is more easily quantified. ERA implicitly argued that the cheapest alternative to reduced imports as a means of reducing vulnerability was to increase oil inventories and set the costs of imports at the increase in inventory holding costs.

The remaining two aspects of the costs are problematic because in both cases impacts extraordinarily difficult to measure are involved and very little supporting analysis was provided. The key areas were the balance-of-payments benefits of reduced imports and the environmental costs of producing the import reduction by greater use of coal. In the first case, a vast literature in international trade economics exists dealing with the problem of tracing the impacts of policies on balance of payments and then to economic activity. The theory warns that the effects depend on the response in all the countries involved, and thus quite complex models are needed to deal adequately with the impacts.[2] Such evidence as was available (including my phone conversations with some of those responsible for the estimates) suggests that an informal and inadequately comprehensive analysis was undertaken for ERA. No attention was given to the spending of the dollar receipts by the OPEC countries.

The environmental impact issue is even more difficult to analyze because ERA does not make clear what is being measured. The cost of complying with specific rules apparently would be included in the direct cost of conversion. Thus, additional charges would be appropriate only for neglected impacts. Such neglect in principle could arise in two ways. First, new environmental problems could arise. Second, it might be deemed more cost effective not to regulate some form of pollution damage because the cost of control exceeded the benefit. However, these costs would remain and should be charged to polluting activities. The ERA discussion fails to make clear what environmental damages are actually being included and so makes it difficult to evaluate the impact figure.

The justifications for the costing techniques proved quite difficult for outside analysts to determine. ERA listed a variety of supporting documents in the *Federal Register* presentation of the proposed rules, but the listed documents fell far short of providing a detailed rationale for the conclusions. In fact, estimates of several cost components, including all elements of the net externalities of imported oil use, were unexplained adjustment of data in an earlier memorandum cited by ERA that was provided by the Regulatory Analysis Review Group (RARG). RARG's memorandum simultaneously defined those externalities that might be involved in use of imported oil and tried to suggest plausible estimates of the size of these impacts. The RARG estimates are themselves poorly documented so that the ERA figures are unsupported adjustments of initially unsatisfactory figures.

Finally, ERA failed to provide a clear discussion of the derivation of its estimates of the cumulative impact of price increases for coal and oil on long-run costs. The initial proposed regulations aggravated the difficulties by adopting an inappropriate way of incorporating the external costs and price-escalation impacts into the calculations. Given that the supporting figures were available, it would have been possible to incorporate the externalities and the fuel-price rises into the present-worth calculation. Instead, ERA suggested that costs be calculated assuming stable prices and no externalities. Then a significant cost excess would occur only if the costs of conversion calculated in this fashion exceeded the costs of oil use by 30 percent.

The rationale for this approach is that modeling efforts suggested that use of this ratio produced the same level of conversions as would be produced by direct calculation of actual present worths. The approach puts too much faith in the computer analysis and also ignores that even if the efficient amount of conversion were produced, the wrong group of facilities might be converted. It is doubtful that the models are good enough to determine either what constitutes a socially optimal level of conversions, given ERA's estimate of social costs or what will actually occur. Moreover, the ratio test will overstate the benefits of converting facilities with short remaining lives and understate the benefits of converting new facilities (see chapter 2). The 30-percent difference is essentially an average for all firms over the average remaining life. The actual excess of true social costs compared to costs as estimated by the initial ERA formula would clearly be larger the longer the remaining life of the facility, and the 30-percent test does not adequately compensate for this difference. ERA later retreated from this approach and proposed allowing firms to compute the actual present worths.

In sum, the ERA exercise suggested that extremely difficult forecasting and appraisal issues arise in determining the true social costs of alternative fuel-use patterns and, thus, defining a significant cost excess is a nearly impossible task.

The Economics of Conversion

In the electric-power sector, the critical issue is the extent to which existing power plants could convert to coal. Prior to any regulation, ordering of new oil-fired plants had ceased and all that remained was completion of existing projects. However, prospects existed for converting existing units to coal use, and the critical issue was how much capacity could be converted.

A physical barrier, adequacy of boiler size, to conversion does exist. Unless the boiler is large enough to accommodate coal, conversion is impractical. However, sufficient boiler size is not the only requirement for actual coal use. Facilities are needed to receive the coal, store it, and move it from storage pile to the plant. Moreover, coal is normally ground to a fine powder by pulverizers that are attached to the boiler. Normally, more air-pollution-control equipment is needed with coal burning than with oil or gas burning.

Existing plants differ markedly in the current availability of the equipment needed to burn coal, the extent of the equipment required, the availability of land for these facilities, the age of the units, the size of the units, and the utilization of the units. The conversions to oil during the 1966–1974 period involved different degrees of removal of the coal-burning capabilities. However, many plants removed much of the equipment and some even used the land for new units.

Air-pollution regulations are another major influence. Local authorities may oppose any coal conversion, as has been the case with many New York City politicians reacting to the requests of Consolidated Edison for the authorization to convert some of its units. Alternatively, the utility and environmental regulators may disagree about the appropriate amount of environmental controls. The utilities naturally will seek lesser controls than the environmental agencies prefer.

The fuel-cost saving will necessary be larger at a given plant if the total output of the plant over its remaining life is larger. Total output is the product of annual output and years of remaining life. Given economies of scale in conversion and coal use, larger units may have lower unit costs and higher unit benefits of conversion (see chapter 2).

The public utility regulatory problems discussed already further complicate the conversion process. Public-utility commissions can act to prevent conversions by refusing to put the required investments into the rate base. Critics of such actions suggest that the causes are either a preference for continued reliance on fuel-adjustment clauses to provide rate relief or fears that, at least initially, the conversion will raise rates. A third explanation is fear that the conversion is not profitable.

The arguments have a slightly different basis depending on whether the power companies are actually required to bear the social cost of oil use.

When this requirement arises, states can object, as New York and California have, that they are being forced to assume an unfair share of the national burden. The counterargument is that this is appropriate because these states contribute disproportionately to the social costs. Thus, efficiency does require that oil users bear the true social cost of oil use, but the prior discussion suggests that good reasons exist for suspicion about ERA's estimate of these social costs.

Where only private costs are involved, a profitable conversion by definition can be implemented without ever raising rates. Profitability means lifetime fuel savings sufficient to repay the investment. To prevent rates from rising, the allowed rates simply must never raise capital charges above the level of the fuel saving realized at that moment. For reasons outlined in appendix 2C, actual regulatory rate-setting formulas can produce high early-year repayments that raise rates. Thus, regulatory practice creates an artificially high initial price. The predicted regulatory response is that fear of the effects of such an error leads, not to the choice of a better pricing formula, but to refusal to permit the conversion.

Alternatively, rates may be lower, but the conversion will transfer part of the cost from the fuel-adjustment clause to the rate base. Regulators may find this shift undesirable. Here the problem areas are why an accounting definition should matter and why, if the definition matters, the commissions cannot work out a way of including conversion costs in fuel expenses.

More generally, these arguments about public-utility regulation suggest that it or fuel-shifting regulation have severe defects. If the criticism of public-utility-commission attitudes about fuel shifting is correct, this implies a serious deficiency in the ability to regulate properly. Conversely, if the commissions can overcome these difficulties, the need for federal fuel-shifting policies is decreased.

Fuel Shifting in Practice

Whatever, the conceptual advantages of fuel-shifting regulations, the legislation produced no results. The cumbersome regulatory process proved less able to move than were the electric-power companies. The difficulties involved problems in defining general rules and selecting the most attractive candidates for conversions. An inherent problem with fuel shifting is that the more desirable the shift, the less the need for government pressure. The private cost-savings portion of the benefits to shifting, in the most favorable cases, are likely to suffice to justify conversion even when the external costs are ignored.

The barriers to extensive fuel conversion, moreover, are quite formidable. A major consideration is that a substantial portion of the oil- and gas-

Table 6-1
1979 Deliveries of Fuel Oil to Electric Utilities

	Thousands of Barrels	Percent of Total	Cumulative Percent of Total
Southern California Edison[a]	47,345	9.17	9.17
Florida Power and Light[a]	39,203	7.59	16.76
Pacific Gas and Electric[a]	26,244	5.08	21.84
Virginia Electric and Power	24,476	4.74	26.58
Middle South Utilities[a]	24,197	4.69	31.26
New England Electric	19,540	3.78	35.05
Consolidated Edison	18,867	3.65	38.70
Long Island Lighting	17,003	3.29	41.99
Public Service Electric and Gas	14,265	2.76	44.75
Los Angeles Dept. of Water and Power[a]	14,246	2.76	47.51
Florida Power[a]	14,187	2.75	50.26
Boston Edison	14,165	2.74	53.00
Commonwealth Edison	12,517	2.42	55.43
Northeast Utilities	12,318	2.39	57.81
Central Hudson Gas and Electric	12,027	2.33	60.14
San Diego Electric and Gas[a]	10,685	2.07	62.21
Philadelphia Electric	10,253	1.99	64.19
Pennsylvania Power and Light	10,108	1.96	66.15
Hawaiian Electric[a]	10,106	1.96	68.11
New England Gas and Electric Association	10,205	1.98	70.08
Jacksonville Electric Authority[a]	9,993	1.93	72.02
Niagara Mohawk Power	9,067	1.76	73.77
United Illuminating	8,377	1.62	75.40
Consumers Power	7,844	1.52	76.92
Baltimore Gas and Electric	7,741	1.50	78.42
Potomac Electric	7,563	1.46	79.88
Delmarva Power and Light	7,524	1.46	81.34
Gulf States Utilities[a]	7,472	1.45	81.78
Orange and Rockland Utilities	6,827	1.32	84.10
Detroit Edison	5,916	1.15	85.25

Source: U.S., Department of Energy, Energy Information Administration (1980), *Cost and Quality of Fuels for Electric Utility Plants—1979.* Totals differ from EIA reports because its separate figures for subsidiaries are aggregated here.
[a]All oil used in plants incapable of burning coal.

using capacity is not coal capable in even the broadest sense of having adequately sized boilers. As tables 6-1 and 6-2 show, the large oil and gas users tend to be companies that have never built plants capable of being coal fired.

Examination of the problems of those units that were coal capable suggested to the regulators that most of these were not worth converting. Approximately 350 units at 114 plants were identified by ICF Inc., acting as

Table 6–2
1979 Deliveries of Natural Gas to Electric Utilities

	Million Cubic Feet	Percent of Total	Cumulative Percent of Total
Houston Lighting and Power[a]	469,151	13.14	13.14
Central and Southwest Corporation[a]	398,827	11.17	24.31
Texas Utilities[a]	297,636	8.34	32.65
Middle South Utilities[a]	266,649	7.47	40.12
Pacific Gas and Electric[a]	226,556	6.35	46.46
Gulf States Utilities[s]	221,483	6.20	52.67
Oklahoma Gas and Electric[a]	165,882	4.65	57.31
Southern California Edison[a]	156,635	4.39	61.70
Florida Power and Light[a]	91,248	2.56	64.25
Southwestern Public Service[a]	90,682	2.54	66.79
Central Louisiana Electric[a]	62,819	1.76	68.55
Consolidated Edison	47,868	1.34	69.89
Kansas Gas and Electric	43,973	1.23	71.13
Los Angeles Dept. of Water and Power[a]	30,710	0.86	71.99
Lower Colorado River Authority[a]	28,417	0.80	72.78
San Diego Gas and Electric[a]	28,348	0.79	73.58
Public Service Company of Colorado	27,205	0.76	74.34
Austin City Electric[a]	25,884	0.72	75.06
Detroit Edison	25,703	0.72	75.78
San Antonio City Public Service[a]	24,843	0.70	76.48
El Paso Electric[a]	24,512	0.69	77.17
Western Farmers Electric Coop	23,321	0.65	77.82
Commonwealth Edison	21,991	0.62	78.43
Southern Company	21,494	0.60	79.04
Public Service Electric and Gas	21,414	0.60	79.64
Arizona Public Service	20,649	0.58	80.21

Source: U.S., Department of Energy, Energy Information Administration (1980), *Cost and Quality of Fuels for Electric Utility Plants—1979.*
[a]All gas used in plants incapable of burning coal.

a consultant to the president's Commission on Coal, as possessing fuel-burning capability (Breese and Schweers 1979). DOE conducted several prunings of the list to identify those most worth converting. A rough exclusion criterion that removed plants that were not less than 30 years old or larger than 25 megawatts reduced the list to 181 units at 68 plants. A further screening to identify those plants most deserving of conversion subsidies reduced the list to 107 units at 50 stations. A Senate committee reviewing the legislation authorizing subsidies (never actually enacted) reduced the list to 80 units at 38 stations (See U.S., General Accounting Office 1980).

Even this last reduction may not have been sufficient to eliminate all the dubious candidates for conversion aid. The lists include the two units

Baltimore Gas and Electric is building at Brandon Shores, although the company has indicated that these will be coal-burning plants. The remaining units on the list are predominantly plants of eastern utilities, specifically mostly in New England, the Middle Atlantic states, and the northern part of the South Atlantic region.

Examination of the lists shows the most interesting conversion candidates are those whose owners are seeking to make conversions. Conversely, many of the units which the utilities are not seeking to convert are ones in which the barriers are formidable.

Through mid-1981, the most important conversion efforts in the United States were by Virginia Electric and Power and Florida Power. Each had made major shifts to oil in the early seventies; Florida Power, in fact, ceased to use coal. Florida Power had used coal at only one plant, and both the shift to oil and the return were simple. Virginia Electric and Power has several coal-using plants and thus reconversion was more time-consuming and had not been completed by the end of 1980. Both New England Electric and Northeast Utilities have major coal reconversions under way. The next most important area for potential conversions is the New York City area. At least two companies in the area—Consolidated Edison of New York City and Public Service Electric and Gas, which serves most of New Jersey— wish to convert back to coal. Nearby utilities in New York and Connecticut have units included on the Senate conversion list. These companies differ considerably in their enthusiasm for conversion, but the environmental barriers are formidable. A major difficulty is the vigor of local opposition to coal use.

Four of the units listed by the Senate for conversion are in the East North Central region. Two are units of Detroit Edison that apparently are already using substantial proportions of coal. Another two are units that Commonwealth Edison, the Chicago area utility, built as oil units convertible to coal. Commonwealth apparently is avoiding coal conversion because is believes that oil will be a low-cost option for plants that have rates of utilization that while low, exceed those possible with a combustion turbine.

Notes

1. Assuming a capacity factor of 50 percent, that is, 4380 hours of operation per year, and a coal content of 24 million Btu per ton, Btu consumption is 438 billion, and 18,250 tons of coal are used.

2. The literature is vast with the standard texts including those by Kindleberger and Lindert (1978) and Caves and Jones (1973). The most rigorous and difficult treatment available is Takayama's book (1972).

7 Measuring the Impacts of Regulation

This chapter provides estimates of the impacts of regulation on electric-power costs and output. Given the conceptual problems discussed in chapter 2 and the empirical problems noted later, the measurement is necessarily imprecise. Nevertheless, the evidence suggests that underpricing clearly prevails for all but one or two electric utilities in the United States. However, power shortages are not the most probable result of regulatory problems.

Problems of Analysis

All the specific critical questions discussed here are variants of the basic general inquiry proposed in chapter 2: How much economic inefficiency will prevailing policies produce? Power shortages play a role in this debate similar to gaps in the oil and gas markets; that is, a sufficiently high price will eliminate any excess demand, and only public policy will prevent the attainment of that price. The level of the price and particularly whether it is higher than the marginal cost of efficiently supplying the market depends on the prevailing investment climate.

A critical consideration is that the longer an unsatisfactory investment climate persists, the more likely is an inefficiently low level of investment. Therefore, the deficiency of supply steadily will rise, and so will the price needed to ration the available supply. The perceived inequity of allowing the price increase in turn will make intervention to prevent price rises more likely. Excess demand rationed by fiat is one possible outcome.

Another possibility is that fears of shortage will cause overreaction and extensive, heavily subsidized efforts to expand capacity. The engineering lead times are far shorter than the ten-year period needed to complete the combined legal and engineering requirements for a new power plant. Thus, with sufficient panic, any desired capacity could be available by 1990.

In any case, if utilities either miscalculate demand growth or complete rather than abandon plants under construction, then capacity could be built that could easily serve demand at prevailing prices. Inefficiency need not mean a power shortage. The key indicator of inefficiency is the gap between marginal cost and price. Other inefficiencies may arise from overly or underly vigorous environmental policies and ill-conceived fuel-shifting policies. No basis exists for quantification of these costs.

Chapter 2 suggested that the structure of an efficient set of prices and output limitation policies for the electric-power industry would be very complex. Stress was put on the problems of designing pricing procedures that will respond optimally to demand variation in a given power system. Left implicit was the further complication that these rates should reflect the economics specific to operation in a particular region and the characteristics of individual customers. The earlier discussion emphasized that fuel costs differ among regions. Other important differences arise with construction costs and from differences in customer density.

It is recognized that the average costs of service are higher for small customers than for larger ones. Very large customers can be served without use of transformers to lower the voltages at which the power is received. Certain basic cost such as installation of service-power lines, billing, and repairs are likely to be lower on a per kWh basis for larger users than for small ones.

The optimal structure must distinguish differences among major customers and charge them appropriately. Since more flexible prices are more expensive to administer, they are most likely to be efficient when used by large consumers. For each customer, the choice of a pricing scheme must be made from the possibilities available: prices that never change between meter readings, prices that do change but on a schedule announced well in advance, and the prices that change as often as every five minutes in response to developments that occurred a few minutes earlier. Further choices arise with possible extension of the right to interrupt service. All this must be attuned to the basic regional economics of the companies.

Thus, the efficient world will be a very complex one, and even providing crude measures of some key indicators is a formidable task. The analysis in chapter 2, however, suggests a principle of the economics that can be used to simplify the problem: no investments would be undertaken if they were not profitable. This requires that revenues at least equal the weighted average cost of an optimal expansion. Estimated weighted average costs, therefore, serve as an easier-to-calculate yardstick than the optimum-price pattern.

While this simplification greatly eases estimation problems, they remain formidable. Chapter 2 stressed the basic theoretical difficulties of properly determining a utility's revenue requirements in any one year. The optimum mix of investments and fuels, given future prices, may differ markedly from the mix prevailing in the past, and data on historical patterns are incomplete. Recovery of capital investment may not take place in equal annual real installments. Taxes complicate the relationship between customer payments and net income to companies. The interaction of inflation with taxes further confuses the relationship between before- and after-tax income.

These problems are handled here by considering a range of assumptions about the critical variables. Calculations proceed as if capital were recovered in equal annual real installments with an annual adjustment for the inflation actually incurred in that year. The generation mix is assumed to involve a smaller proportion of peaking-plant output than has occurred in the past, and capacity utilization factors are set higher than those that prevailed in the 1970s. The resulting estimates predictably encompass a wide range of values, although the minimum figure exceeds rates in most companies.

The magnitude of the underpricing is so great in some areas that even the most conservative estimates of the price elasticity of electric-power demand would imply radical reductions in power use. These effects could more than eliminate the demand-stimulating effects of economic growth. A conceivable situation for much of the country is that with efficient prices little or no capacity additions would be needed. However, charging prices equal only to the running costs of existing plants might lead to excess demand. Thus, to ration output, it would be necessary to price at a higher level. Higher prices would serve to prevent, rather than finance, capacity expansion. If efficient prices cause electric-power output to remain below 1980 levels for many years, policymakers may be particularly reluctant to use prices to allocate supply.

Data Availability

Before reviewing the estimates, the problems of data availability need further examination. The basic difficulties are standard ones. The dollar-volume figures are in historical cost terms and so ignore the impacts of inflation. Many cost determinants are imperfectly reported. This is particularly true of the nongenerating activities of the industry. Its analysis is limited and usually primitive. Finally, we are dealing with forecasting, which is always difficult, especially when the usual assumption of continuation of past trends clearly is invalid.

Nongeneration costs consist of those for transmission, distribution, customer service, and general administration. In estimating these costs, generally simple regressions are run on data in FPC and trade press reports. With the critical exception of Baughman and Bottaro (1975), most of these estimates fail to consider either regional differences or major differences among customer classes.

The difficulties are aggravated because so much of nongeneration cost involves substantial capital investment, particularly capital investment in distribution. All published asset figures are economically unacceptable, and the problems are particularly severe for the long lead-time investments that electric-utilities undertake (see appendix 7A).

The only satisfactory measures that could be devised would be figures on additions to stocks that incorporated a correct charge for interest paid during construction. In fact, the interest charges are too low because they fail to compensate for the heavy rates of inflation during the 1970s. Individual firm data are available on additions with the reported interest during construction, but aggregated numbers have only been reported since the Energy Information Administration (EIA) assumed control over Federal Power Commission (FPC) reports. Someone attempting an adequate appraisal of nongenerating capital costs would be best advised to attempt a pooled time-series cross-section on individual firms' analysis using these data and appropriate adjustment factors. (Such work has been done, but the results are not publicly available.)

The other available alternative measures of outlays and the stock of assets have major problems. *Asset figures* are the summation of initially imperfect estimates of a plant's cost at the time of entry into service of all surviving assets; further, they fail to adjust for inflation from the earlier periods. *Outlays* show net spending for projects whose completion is spread over many future years. This distribution of expenditures could differ in complicated ways from the distribution of costs of capacity completed in any one year. For example, the expenditures exclude the interest charges that are part of the final costs. To the considerable extent that the ratio of costs, including interest to costs excluding interest, differs among types of investment, the shares in total costs could vary considerably from the share in costs before interest payments.

All this suggests that any analyses based only on published data of non-generating costs are suspect, and the existing studies to date have been less elaborate than would be ideal. However, for present objectives, the estimates are satisfactory and insure that my calculations of underpricing do not overstate any cost component.

Given the multiplicity of relevant rates and the discontinuation of U.S. government publication of rate schedules, further difficulties arise in relating optimal prices to actual ones. Universal problems occur regarding where and on what rate schedule a particular customer will be at any moment. There can be different rate schedules depending on the type of electricity use as well as on the type of customers. Industrial rates generally incorporate a factor for capacity utilization as well as for electricity consumption; the same consumption over a shorter period of time involves use of more capacity and leads to higher charges. Increasingly, seasonal rate variations are being introduced and range from a small penalty for very large residential users to differences that more than double the charges.

Each rate schedule, moreover, sets incremental charges for different blocks of service and the rate at any moment depends on which is the marginal block.

An extremely important consideration is marked interutility differences in average historical costs, and, therefore, in rates. Many examples can be provided of large disparities in rates within the same state because of radically different generation mixes. While most states tend to have uniform rates for each company throughout its service territory, some do not. However, these variations tend to be smaller than intercompany or interstate.

Thus, considerable problems can arise in selecting the proper actual rate for comparison to the optimal one when measuring the extent of underpricing.

A major difficulty in interpreting existing prices is that their structure may have little relationship to cost variations among customer type and time of use. The failure to reflect costs adequately is often and unfortunately called *cross-subsidization.* Actually, two different types of price distortions can occur. Economic theory long has stressed the role of price discrimination in establishing price differentials. A monopolist that can control the flow of products would set a lesser excess of price over marginal cost for its more price-sensitive customers than for its less price-sensitive ones. Electric utilities, for example, would have lower price/marginal-cost ratios for manufacturing firms that are mobile and selfgenerate without inordinate cost penalties than for immobile households. However, subsidy in the sense of prices below cost would never prevail; everyone would pay a price at or above marginal costs. The differences are less subsidies than lesser exploitation by monopolists.

In the context of regulation, subsidies can arise. Monopoly profits or economic rents from diseconomies of scale can be used by regulators to hold down rates. However, the concept of cross-subsidy in the sense of transfers among customer classes may not be appropriate. One form of underpricing would be to charge prices at or above marginal costs for some types of services while pricing below costs on other services. Another possibility is that everyone is charged less than marginal costs, and what is involved is differences in the share of the underpricing. More generally, appropriation of rents due to increasing costs is essentially a transfer from producers to consumers rather than among consumers. The only case of inappropriate pricing that involves something that sensibly could be called cross-subsidization is when a firm is allowed by regulators to charge prices above marginal costs to some customers on the condition that some of the extra revenue be used to subsidize below-cost sales to other customers. One possible form of distorted price patterns curiously has lent its name to broader problems. This certainly is not for lack of a better term. The problem is simply one of inefficient price structures.

Another area in which an excess of unsatisfactory data exist is in the projection of consumption growth and capacity expansion. At least two major public forecasting efforts are available annually: the estimates in the Energy Information Administration's annual report to Congress and the figures produced by the industry itself. The latter are supported by lists of the specific capacity additions planned to meet the forecast. The Department of Energy, moreover, and the National Electric Reliability Council have begun publishing these details.

A special problem is that the evidence is clear that these expansion plans are subject to considerable change. Even plants well along in construction can be delayed. Many plants, in fact, are in much less advanced states of development. There are cases in which the company has not yet decided where the plant will be located. Reported siting may be tentative, and a plant that has not been started is easy to cancel or delay. Thus, the projections compare questionable consumption estimates to dubious capacity-projections.

Treatment of capacity/load relationships, however, is more straightforward than the other issues. The load growth-rate possibilities are bounded between 0 and 5 to 7 percent. Declining loads would have implications similar to that of no growth. The principal analytic task would be to examine the implications of assertions that oil prices are so high that it pays to replace existing oil-fired plants with new coal- or nuclear-fired ones. We would only have to examine the extent to which these claims are valid. (Declining loads or flattening the load-duration curve would effect the optimal amount of response.)

The highest growth that seems even remotely imaginable is the 7 percent the industry historically considered normal. Some combinations of accelerated economic growth and substitution of electricity for other fuels might lead to such rapid growth, but the likelihood is small.

Given the long lead times on capacity additions, the upper limits through the late 1980s can be determined from the reports of the reliability councils on planned additions. Adjustments can be made by use of ample data indicating the status of various major projects and thus possible departures from plan as projects fail to begin, are canceled while under way, or are delayed.

Estimating the Weighted Average Cost of Power

Given the problems noted, estimates of the minimum revenue required to justify electric-utility investments are subject to considerable uncertainty. Nevertheless, available data suggest that these requirements cannot be less than 60 mills per kilowatt hour sold, that the cost may be closer to 80 mills, and that the uncertainty largely concerns capital costs. The details of a sensitivity analysis undertaken to develop these estimates appear as appendix 7C. Only two electric utilities in the United States had average 1979 revenues in excess of 60 mills; only one had in excess of 80 mills (see table 7–1). (Both also operated under conditions, noted later, that make their costs higher than average for their region and thus their true costs also may exceed their rates.) Therefore, raising prices to meet marginal costs will greatly increase electric-power costs, and little, if any, of the country will be immune to the effects.

Table 7–1
Average Revenues by Customer Types of U.S. Electric Utilities in 1979
(cents per kWh)

	Overall	*Residential*	*Commercial*	*Industrial*
Consolidated Edison	8.895	10.536	8.942	8.708
Long Island Lighting	6.415	7.161	6.750	6.186
United Illuminating	5.868	6.230	6.030	5.131
Orange & Rockland Utilities	5.859	8.524	7.870	5.280
PS E&G (New Jersey)	5.704	7.008	6.052	4.335
San Diego G&E	5.519	5.304	6.454	5.436
New England Electric	5.343	6.021	5.506	4.711
Boston Edison	5.311	6.388	6.124	5.299
Atlantic City Electric	5.241	5.605	5.621	3.791
Jersey Central P&L[a]	5.155	6.050	5.243	3.842
Central Illinois Light	4.942	5.723	6.351	3.827
Iowa EL&P	4.896	5.348	4.652	4.138
Delmarva P&L	4.872	5.862	5.743	3.735
Iowa PS	4.785	5.300	5.434	3.714
PS New Mexico	4.783	6.206	5.545	4.713
Potomac Electric	4.761	5.020	5.263	4.098
Central Hudson G&E	4.727	6.010	5.629	4.261
Philadelphia Electric	4.689	5.811	6.486	4.740
Florida Power	4.679	5.148	5.317	3.723
El Paso Elec.	4.632	5.640	4.923	3.870
Savannah E&P	4.629	5.070	5.178	3.822
Toledo Edison	4.612	5.867	5.762	3.623
PS New Hampshire	4.607	5.783	6.440	4.029
Northeast Utilities	4.594	5.202	4.881	3.800
Columbus and So. Ohio Electric[g]	4.572	5.336	6.029	3.990
Florida P&L	4.572	4.660	4.847	3.855
Duquesne Light	4.546	6.230	4.800	3.550
Arizona PS	4.504	5.581	5.138	3.666
Kansas City P&L	4.414	5.405	4.636	3.198
New England G&E Association	4.390	6.299	5.810	4.395
Detroit Edison	4.386	5.106	5.528	3.605
New York State E&G	4.365	4.978	4.533	3.307
Tampa Electric	4.354	5.173	4.903	3.369
Virginia E&P	4.335	5.142	4.707	3.418
Tucson Electric Power	4.328	5.854	6.048	3.836

Table 7–1 continued

	Overall	Residential	Commercial	Industrial
Pennsylvania Electric[a]	4.306	5.264	4.782	3.566
Los Angeles	4.297	5.085	4.243	3.681
Southern California Edison	4.290	4.722	4.765	3.387
Cleveland Elec. Illum.	4.245	5.459	4.823	3.484
Baltimore G&E	4.230	4.986	5.460	3.198
Commonwealth Edison	4.227	5.142	4.743	3.173
Ohio Edison	4.219	5.418	5.124	3.207
Consumers Power	4.190	4.686	4.663	3.582
New Orleans PS[e]	4.185	4.678	4.916	3.627
Central Maine Power	4.139	4.614	4.852	2.920
Central Illinois PS	4.121	5.186	5.366	3.350
Metropolitan Edison[a]	4.071	4.914	4.318	3.378
Interstate Power	4.055	5.420	4.524	3.159
Iowa P&L	4.053	4.746	4.571	2.850
Central P&L[b]	4.039	4.987	4.691	3.338
Gulf Power[c]	4.003	4.334	4.737	3.181
Northern Indiana PS	3.987	5.450	6.562	3.595
Salt River Project	3.968	5.073	4.685	2.403
Iowa-Illinois G&E	3.936	5.554	4.460	2.867
Madison G&E	3.860	4.617	4.265	3.581
Dayton P&L	3.858	4.548	3.976	3.220
Rochester G&E	3.837	4.569	4.492	3.441
San Antonio	3.747	4.425	3.252	3.553
Pennsylvania P&L	3.746	4.235	4.183	2.992
Central Louisiana Elec.	3.734	4.455	3.815	3.108
Wisconsin Electric	3.733	4.395	4.522	2.909
Wisconsin P&L	3.732	4.742	4.460	3.130
Wisconsin PS	3.721	4.784	4.402	2.927
Alabama Power[c]	3.708	4.438	4.659	3.023
Dallas P&L[d]	3.693	4.119	3.663	3.176
Kansas P&L	3.624	4.394	4.412	2.964
Mississippi Power[c]	3.611	3.992	3.836	3.063
Pacific G&E	3.597	3.537	4.152	3.218
S. Carolina E&G	3.576	4.678	3.923	2.779
Indianapolis P&L	3.567	4.123	4.205	3.027
Niagara Mohawk Power	3.561	4.346	4.252	2.524
Mississippi P&L[e]	3.545	4.314	4.560	3.654
Cincinnati G&E	3.507	3.854	4.318	3.101
Georgia Power[c]	3.482	4.009	4.421	3.008
Southwestern PS	3.472	4.988	4.295	3.134
PS Colorado	3.440	4.239	3.840	2.546
Union Electric	3.424	4.370	3.696	2.768
PS Indiana	3.414	4.391	4.000	2.802
Utah P&L	3.389	4.899	4.051	3.137
Illinois Power	3.346	4.291	4.371	2.587
West Texas Utilities[b]	3.334	4.325	4.051	3.137
Arkansas P&L[e]	3.235	4.152	4.135	2.543
Texas P&L[d]	3.232	4.002	4.172	2.480
Northern States Power	3.232	4.225	4.016	2.962
Kansas G&E	3.217	3.967	4.002	2.892

Table 7-1 continued

	Overall	Residential	Commercial	Industrial
Houston Lighting and Power	3.208	4.092	3.971	2.698
Carolina P&L	3.202	4.080	3.741	2.782
Kentucky Utilities	3.196	3.883	3.910	2.851
Nevada Power	3.178	3.170	3.478	3.101
Minnesota P&L	3.169	4.514	4.308	3.028
West Penn Power[f]	3.092	3.990	3.470	2.504
Southern Indiana G&E	3.069	4.281	3.160	2.610
Louisville G&E	3.045	3.659	3.562	2.320
Appalachian Power[g]	3.019	3.782	3.723	2.729
Potomac Edison[f]	2.997	4.126	3.977	2.266
Indiana and Michigan Electric[g]	2.993	3.942	4.038	2.918
PS Oklahoma[b]	2.987	4.063	2.990	2.610
Monongahela Power[f]	2.966	3.887	3.654	2.343
Duke Power	2.950	3.840	3.410	2.420
Oklahoma G&E	2.880	3.596	3.503	2.458
Kentucky Power[g]	2.802	3.315	3.743	2.433
Gulf States Utilities	2.795	3.941	3.564	2.242
Texas Elec. Serv.[d]	2.755	3.659	3.183	2.172
Ohio Power[g]	2.596	3.964	4.235	2.122
SW Elec. Power[b]	2.577	3.318	2.959	2.229
Portland General Electric	2.526	2.777	2.599	2.032
Louisiana P&L[e]	2.377	3.008	3.159	1.869
S. Carolina PS Authority	2.256	3.442	3.344	1.976
Pacific P&L	2.106	2.552	2.327	1.706
Montana Power	2.044	2.821	2.586	1.267
Idaho Power	1.784	2.294	2.139	1.135
Washington Water Power	1.546	1.595	1.801	1.004
Seattle	1.156	1.117	1.295	0.702
Benton County	1.142	1.367	1.268	0.729
Tacoma	1.002	1.328	0.962	0.679

Sources: Holding Companies and Ohio Edison from Uniform Statistical Reports. Other private companies: U.S., Department of Energy, *Statistics of Privately Owned Electric Utilities in the United States—1979* (Washington, D.C.: U.S., Government Printing Office, 1980).
Public companies: U.S., Department of Energy, *Statistics of Publicly Owned Electric Utilities in the United States—1970* (Washington, D.C.: U.S., Government Printing Office, 1980).

[a]General Public Utilities
[b]Central and Southwest
[c]Southern Company
[d]Texas Utilities
[e]Middle South Utilities
[f]Allegheny Power System
[g]American Electric Power

Before discussing these effects, some notes are needed about the basis of the figures and the problems using them. The basic inputs are from the DOE and others on generation costs. The numbers shown in appendix 7C were the most comprehensive of those reviewed, and other sources cite similar figures. An estimate for nongenerating costs was developed from the Baughman-Bottaro study (1975). If anything, it seems to be conservative figures on costs, since the numbers are at or below those based on historical relationships shown in appendix 7A.

My estimates are dominated by capital costs, and these are very sensitive to assumptions about the cost of each generation type, the utilization rates, the mix, and the capital charge rate. An effort was made to stress patterns that involve high overall utilization and significant reduction in reliance on peaking units. The impacts of most other uncertainties are much smaller than those of the uncertainty about capital costs.

However, it remains true that it will cost significantly more to serve residential and commercial customers than industrial ones. The minimum estimates are that nongenerating costs are about 25 mills for residential and commercial customers and 10 mills for industrial. Thus, the 60-mill estimate for average required revenues amounts to required revenues of about 65 mills for residential and commercial customers and 40 mills for industrial. The corresponding figures with 80 mills are about 85 and 60 mills. If the lower estimates of required prices in separate sectors are used instead of the company average, far more companies charge rates above the minimum estimate of costs and might be charging sufficient amounts. (However, high residential rates are more germane. Industrial rates in excess of 40 mills tend to occur with those companies whose industrial customers are more expensive to serve.)

The impact of charging higher prices will be substantial. In 1979, average revenues for the electric-power industry were 3.74 cents. Thus, a rise to 60 mills is a 60 percent increase, and a rise to 80 mills, a 114 percent increase. Given the 4.33-cent average charge to residential customers, they face increases on the average of 50 to 96 percent; the 2.99-cent charge to large light and power users implies 40 to 114 percent increases. Given the imprecision of the figures, this should be interpreted as indicating that all customer types face a 50 to 100 percent average rate increase.

As has already been suggested, the regional differences in impacts will be great. Table 7–1 confirms the points already discussed that oil-using utilities tend to be high cost and public power in the Pacific Northwest is the cheapest power source by far. Another critical influence is that, as would be expected, urban companies tend to have higher rates than companies with more dispersed territories. The key influences are the lower role of large customers and the need for underground distribution. (This difference is illustrated by the higher industrial rates of largely urban companies, such as Boston Edison, that do not have many very large customers, such as the refineries served by Public Service Electric and Gas; see appendix 7A.) Greater distance from coal fields also raises costs and rates.

Rates one step above those in the Pacific Northwest are in the 2- to 3-

cent range. A combination of companies with largely rural service areas close to coal fields and companies still using significant amounts of under-priced natural gas charge such rates. Other companies with below-average rates also tend to be coal or gas using. The impact of raising rates to better reflect marginal costs could range from reductions in a few cases to eight-fold increases in others.

The critical impacts could be expected to come in those areas where substitution possibilities are the greatest, particularly space heating, general heat use by industry, and industrial processes that rely heavily on electric power. The problems with the last area are quite different from those with the other two. The effect on electricity-using technologies (such as reduction of aluminum to metal and electric arc-furnace manufacture of steel and ferroalloys) is likely to be major changes in the location of industry and in the processes used. Where electricity is simply an alternative fuel, the impact of higher prices is to reduce consumption and encourage interfuel substitution.

Historically, processes that used large amounts of electricity often were located at sites where great amounts of power were available with low real as well as apparent marginal costs. For many years, the Pacific Northwest had more hydroelectric power than could economically be used locally or sent out of state. It appeared economically efficient to encourage use of the power at low rates for aluminum reduction. This view may have been erroneous when it was adopted, but the critical problem is that whatever over-abundance once existed has been absorbed by growing demand.

Process- and space-heat users will respond, as noted, both by curtailing use and considering alternatives, principally coal and natural gas for pro-cess-steam and natural gas for space heating. Thus, appraisal is complicated by difficulties in estimating where natural-gas prices will head under the phased deregulation instituted in 1978, where gas prices will go under imme-diate total deregulation, and the comparative economics of fuel use.

With space heating, the main considerations are what premium should be paid for electricity over gas because of higher thermal efficiency, and where both electricity and gas prices would end up with more efficient pricing. The debates of the early 1970s about electric heat suggested con-siderable uncertainty about the economics using the prevalent technique of resistance electric heating. Subsequently, improvements in heat pumps have made them increasingly usable for electric heating with higher thermal efficiency than resistance electric heat.

Similar considerations arise with process heat, although a further com-plication is the need for accurate estimates of the economics of coal use for producing process heat while meeting environmental regulations. It is known that these costs vary with the stringency of environmental regula-tions, the size of the facility (due to scale economies), and, as usual, with fuel cost. Uncertainties are great about the situation since the relevant rules under the 1977 Clean Air Act Amendments had not been issued as of November 1981, the costs to firms of different sizes of complying with any set of rules are poorly known, and the data on the size distribution of users are unsatisfactory.

It is conceivable that substantial pockets of energy with low marginal costs still exist around the world, for instance, hydroelectric facilities in less-developed countries and natural gas in oil-exporting countries with low populations. Therefore, one possible response to high electricity costs in the United States and all other industrialized nations would be to move industries that use large amounts of energy to regions having cheap immobile energy. Whether this is a satisfactory expedient remains unclear. There must be sufficient amounts of cheap power in these areas so a relocation of industry will not exhaust these local surpluses and raise the marginal cost to the levels prevailing in industrialized countries. The distinct possibility exists that what will happen ultimately is there will be a shift of resources away from industries that are large users of electricity. Aluminum may lose much of the ground to steel; electric-furnace steel making may lose ground to fossil-fuel-based processes.

It may be noted parenthetically that these developments suggest the great difficulty in assessing who benefits from keeping energy prices below marginal costs. The low prices promote the use of products in which energy is a major cost element. This produces lower prices and higher consumption of the final product, and higher prices and consumption of raw materials, such as the bauxite ore imported for aluminum manufacture. Therefore, some substantial gains may go overseas—a haphazard way to provide foreign aid.

The Adequacy of Power Supply in the 1980s

The relationships between actual price structures and the probable efficient structure, as noted above, are such that imposing efficient prices could eliminate growth for a considerable period. Whatever growth that did occur could easily be financed if a favorable regulatory climate were to develop. The only critical question about capacity is whether a less vigorous response to underpricing will produce strains on the industry.

Industry planning has involved conceiving but not fully implementing plans to insure meeting peak-load growth that would exceed 4 percent per year in the summer. As growth prospects and the financial climate have deteriorated, expansion plans have been scaled back. The industry annually expresses these expectations in the NERC report. This report summarizes more detailed material produced by the regional councils. It indicates the expected demand and capacity levels for each of the next twenty years, starting with the year in which the report is prepared. Backup material includes data on all the changes in generating capacity expected during the first ten years covered. These backup data are released in a report by DOE. (The 1981 NERC report also contains this material.)

The estimates indicate that plans are designed to insure that the expected demands will be covered. Any dangers arise from either a major underestimate of growth or failure to implement the plans sufficiently. The plans clearly are subject to great uncertainty. A sizeable amount of the capacity scheduled for the late 1980s consists of plans to institute construction at an as yet unspecified site. Discussion with companies about their plans indicate considerable hesitation about actually undertaking the expansion.

Moreover, the lags in reporting are substantial. The reliability councils submitted their estimates in the spring, the summary report was issued by the national council in late summer, and DOE did not issue a compilation of specific expansion plans until December 1980. By that time, many changes were made in the plans (as can be seen from a compilation in the January 1981 issue of *Electrical World*). Therefore, the plans reported by DOE were obsolete before they were issued. Major changes have occurred since the *Electrical World* survey appeared, and much of the capacity scheduled for completion by 1989 is so tentative that it could easily be canceled.

The minimum adjustment needed with the data is to account for the actual cancellations and deferrals past 1990. Further changes can be made for plants that have a high probability of cancellation or deferral. Almost any plant that has not been started or has already been delayed until the late 1980s is not likely to be available before 1990. Such adjustments almost totally eliminate these plants on the schedules for 1987, 1988, and 1989 and most of the plants scheduled for 1986. Among the special problems of note are the nuclear plants that are awaiting construction permits or that have very little construction complete, the numerous coal-fired units that have not been started, plants particularly in New York and California that use such alternative energy sources as waste and cogeneration, and pumped storage plants facing environmental opposition. Except for the alternative energy plants in California, most of these were deleted.

Table 7-2 summarizes the NERC forecasts. Table 7-3 tabulates the possible growth given different initial reserve margins and an ultimate goal of either 10 or 20 percent reserves. Table 7-4 presents data on capacity. The NERC figures are contrasted to figures that eliminate known cancellations, all plants scheduled for 1987 and 1989 except for the Intermountain Project in Utah, and all plants scheduled for 1985 and 1986 that have not yet been started. These calculations have the predictable implication that areas without high reserves in 1979 and with high expected growth would be short of

Table 7-2
Data on Electric-Power Load Growth: 1979-1989
(peak and resources in Mw: reserves in percent)

1979-1980 Load-Capacity Relations

	Summer 1979			Winter 1979-1980		
	Peak	*Resources*	*Reserves*	*Peak*	*Resources*	*Reserves*
NPCC	34,673	52,156	50.42	34,552	53,121	53.74
New England	14,271	21,039	47.42	15,241	21,681	42.25
New York	20,402	31,117	52.52	19,311	31,440	62.81
MAAC	31,780	44,851	41.13	27,858	48,685	74.76
ECAR	61,716	85,307	38.23	59,560	92,574	55.43
SERC	83,209	113,161	36.00	82,612	121,094	46.58
Florida	16,762	22,841	36.27	18,549	24,392	31.50
Southern	20,163	27,411	35.95	16,722	28,122	68.17
TVA	18,759	26,848	43.12	20,745	29,647	42.91
VACAR	27,409	36,061	31.18	26,596	38,933	46.39
MAIN	33,751	44,851	32.89	27,449	46,177	68.23
MARCA	18,132	26,315	45.13	17,269	27,138	57.15
SWPP	37,607	51,757	37.63	28,289	51,231	81.10
ERCOT	27,828	42,141	51.43	21,444	40,598	89.32
WSCC	69,728	96,385	38.23	69,893	98,842	41.42
NWPP	21,827	35,488	62.59	32,102	37,287	16.15
RMPA	4,824	6,766	40.14	4,828	7,160	48.30
Arizona-New Mexico	7,937	11,112	40.00	5,625	11,568	105.65
California-Nevada	35,982	43,530	20.98	27,973	42,325	51.31
U.S. total	398,424	556,957	39.79	396,812	579,460	46.03

1989-1990 Load-Capacity Relations

	Summer 1989			Winter 1989-1990		
	Peak	*Resources*	*Reserves*	*Peak*	*Resources*	*Reserves*
NPCC	41,960	61,936	47.61	44,300	63,561	43.48
New England	16,660	25,577	53.52	20,040	26,914	34.30
New York	25,300	36,359	43.71	24,200	36,647	51.06
MAAC	42,370	55,841	31.79	39,620	58,393	47.20
ECAR	91,421	120,505	31.81	95,050	124,494	30.98
SERC	128,452	164,032	27.70	131,137	169,682	29.35
Florida	26,459	33,585	26.93	29,166	35,404	21.39
Southern	30,418	37,933	24.71	26,911	37,589	39.68
TVA	28,292	40,758	44.06	31,752	44,310	39.55
VACAR	43,283	51,756	19.58	43,308	52,325	20.82
MAIN	50,691	59,586	17.53	43,856	60,562	38.09
MARCA	30,614	35,341	15.44	28,292	35,318	24.83

Table 7-2 continued

1989–1990 Load-Capacity Relations (continued)

	Summer 1989			Winter 1989–1990		
	Peak	*Resources*	*Reserves*	*Peak*	*Resources*	*Reserves*
SWPP	64,866	72,275	11.42	48,107	77,263	60.61
ERCOT	49,032	59,942	22.25	36,416	58,362	60.26
WSCC	108,568	142,734	31.47	106,977	145,533	36.04
NWPP	36,099	51,935	43.87	46,378	55,035	18.67
RMPA	8,771	11,783	34.34	8,571	12,380	44.44
Arizona-New Mexico	13,654	18,348	34.39	9,819	18,242	85.78
California-Nevada	50,542	61,601	21.88	42,065	60,702	44.31
U.S. total	607,974	772,192	27.01	573,805	793,114	38.22

Expected Average Annual Percent Increases in Load 1979–1989

	Summer	Winter
NPCC	1.93	2.52
New England	1.52	2.78
New York	2.18	2.31
MPCC	2.92	3.60
ECAR	4.01	4.79
SERC	4.44	4.73
Florida	4.67	4.63
Southern	4.20	4.87
TVA	4.17	4.35
VACAR	4.64	5.00
MAIN	4.15	4.80
MARCA	5.38	5.06
SWPP	5.60	5.45
ERCOT	5.83	5.44
WSCC	4.53	4.35
NWPP	5.16	3.75
RMPA	6.16	5.91
Arizona-New Mexico	5.57	5.73
California-Nevada	3.46	4.16
United States	4.32	3.76

Source: National Electric Reliability Council, *1980 Summary of Projected Peak Demand, Generating Capability, and Fossil Fuel Requirements for the Regional Reliability Councils of NERC* (Princeton: 1980).

Note: Pools are as defined in chapter 3. The portions of WSCC are the Northwest (NWPP), Rocky Mountains (RMPA), and California-Nevada (CA-NV) and Arizona-New Mexico (AZ-NM). VACAR is Virginia and the Carolinas.

Table 7–3
Growth Possible with Initial Reserve Margin
(percent per year)

| | | | | Initial Reserve Margin Ratio | | | | |
	120	*125*	*130*	*135*	*140*	*145*	*150*	*155*
Reserve: 1.1	1.0909	1.136	1.182	1.227	1.273	1.318	1.364	1.409
Years of Growth								
1	9.09	13.64	18.18	22.73	27.27	31.82	36.36	40.91
2	4.45	6.60	8.71	10.78	12.82	14.81	16.77	18.71
3	2.94	4.32	5.73	7.06	8.37	9.65	10.89	12.11
4	2.22	3.25	4.25	5.22	6.15	7.15	8.06	8.95
5	1.78	2.62	3.42	4.20	4.94	5.66	6.36	7.03
6	1.49	2.19	2.86	3.51	4.14	4.74	5.32	5.89
7	1.29	1.89	2.47	3.03	3.56	4.08	4.58	5.07
10	0.87	1.29	1.68	2.07	2.44	2.80	3.15	3.49
20	0.44	0.64	0.84	1.03	1.21	1.39	1.56	1.73
Reserve: 1.2	1.00	1.042	1.083	1.125	1.167	1.288	1.25	1.29
Years of Growth								
1	0.00	4.17	8.33	12.50	16.67	20.83	25.00	29.17
2	0.00	2.06	4.08	6.07	8.01	9.92	11.80	13.65
3	0.00	1.38	2.71	3.98	5.21	6.51	7.72	8.91
4	0.00	1.05	2.04	3.00	3.93	4.83	5.69	6.53
5	0.00	0.84	1.64	2.41	3.11	3.88	4.57	5.25
6	0.00	0.70	1.37	2.02	2.64	3.25	3.83	4.39
7	0.00	0.60	1.18	1.74	2.28	2.80	3.30	3.78
10	0.00	0.41	0.80	1.18	1.55	1.91	2.26	2.59
20	0.00	0.20	0.40	0.59	0.77	0.95	1.12	1.29

Table 7–4
Actual and Adjusted NERC Figures on Capacity Expansion: 1980–1989
(Mw)

| | Forecast Net Change in Capacity | | | | |
	Additions	Retirements	Up-Ratings	Down Ratings	Net Increase
New England	5,898.5	183.3	44.4	63.3	5,696.3
New York	6,753.0	437.0	66.0	170.0	6,212.0
NPC total	12,651.5	620.3	110.4	233.3	11,908.3
MAAC	13,848.5	2,086.9	196.0	1,075.3	10,882.3
Allegheny	3,516.0	0.0	46.0	10.0	3,552.0
AEP	6,680.0	0.0	140.0	0.0	6,820.0
CAPCO	3,947.0	0.0	146.0	627.0	3,466.0
Other Ohio	4,427.0	129.0	0.0	5.0	4,293.0
Kentucky	5,840.0	0.0	0.0	613.0	5,271.0
Indiana	8,717.0	121.0	0.0	255.0	8,341.0
Michigan	4,712.0	2.0	832.0	635.0	4,907.0
ECAR total	37,883.0	252.0	1,164.0	2,145.0	36,650.0

Table 7–4 continued

Forecast Net Change in Capacity (continued)

	Additions	Retirements	Up-Ratings	Down Ratings	Net Increase
Florida	11,925.0	264.0	179.0	128.0	11,712.0
Southern Co.	10,665.0	640.0	74.0	0.0	10,099.0
TVA	15,811.0	0.0	0.0	0.0	15,811.0
VACAR	18,566.0	511.0	105.0	0.0	18,160.0
SERC total	56,967.0	1,415.0	358.0	128.0	55,782.0
Commonwealth Edison	8,166.0	0.0	0.0	0.0	8,166.0
Illinois-Missouri	5,289.0	294.5	336.0	26.0	5,304.5
Wisconsin	2,326.0	327.0	13.0	0.0	2,012.0
MAIN total	15,781.0	621.5	349.0	26.0	15,482.5
Middle South	10,862.0	886.0	0.0	0.0	9,976.0
Gulf State	8,410.0	0.0	0.0	50.0	8,360.0
Missouri-Kansas	6,701.3	452.2	85.0	264.0	6,069.8
Oklahoma-Texas	10,255.0	1,483.2	0.0	0.0	8,771.8
SWPP total	36,228.0	2,821.4	85.0	315.0	33,177.6
ERCOT	21,762.0	2,969.0	30.0	30.0	18,793.0
MARCA	10,627.0	243.0	130.0	5.0	10,509.6
Rocky Mountains	6,545.0	21.0	100.0	0.0	6,624.0
Northwest	12,965.0	857.0	119.0	72.0	12,151.5
Arizona-New Mexico	7,807.0	140.0	0.0	42.0	7,625.0
S. California-Nevada	12,303.0	379.0	111.0	66.0	11,969.0
N. California-Nevada	11,112.0	796.0	15.0	59.0	10,272.0
Idaho-Utah	3,013.0	0.0	43.0	0.0	3,056.0
WSCC total	53,741.5	2,193.0	388.0	239.0	51,697.5
U.S. total	259,490.1	13,222.1	2,810.4	4,195.6	244,882.8

Initial Estimates of Additions

	Total	Fossil	Nuclear	Other
New England	5,898.5	764	4,600	534.5
New York	6,753.0	3,647	1,900	1,206.0
NPCC total	12,651.5	4,411	6,500	1,740.5
MAAC	13,848.5	5,050	8,577	231.5
Allegheny	3,561.0	2,516	0	1,000.0
AEP	6,680.0	6,500	0	180.0
CAPCO	3,947.0	769	3,178	0.0
Other Ohio	4,427.0	3,375	792	260.0
Kentucky	5,884.0	5,819	0	65.0
Indiana	8,717.0	5,223	2,904	590.0
Michigan	4,712.0	2,319	2,381	12.0
ECAR total	37,883.0	26,521	9,255	2,107.0

Table 7–4 continued

Initial Estimates of Additions (continued)

	Total	Fossil	Nuclear	Other
Florida	11,925.0	10,612	795	518.0
Southern Co.	10,665.0	6,085	3,107	1,473.0
TVA	15,811.0	0	15,811	0.0
VACAR	18,566.0	5,070	10,962	2,534.0
SERC total	56,967.0	21,767	30,675	4,525.0
Commonwealth Edison	8,166.0	1,650	6,516	0.0
Illinois-Missouri	5,289.0	1,325	3,248	716.0
Wisconsin	2,326.0	2,300	0	26.0
MAIN total	15,781.0	5,275	9,764	742.0
Middle South	10,862.0	5,960	4,522	380.0
Gulf State	8,410.0	7,290	940	180.0
Missouri-Kansas	6,701.0	5,168	1,150	383.0
Oklahoma	10,255.0	8,889	1,150	216.0
SWPP total	36,228.0	27,307	7,762	1,159.0
ERCOT	21,762.0	15,832	5,930	0.0
MARCA	10,627.6	10,494	0	133.6
Rocky Mountians	6,545.0	5,770	0	775.0
Northwest	12,961.5	3,302	6,080	3,579.5
Arizona-New Mexico	7,807.0	3,228	3,810	769.0
S. California-Nevada	12,303.0	7,300	2,200	2,803.0
N. California-Nevada	11,112.0	4,454	2,190	4,468.0
Idaho-Utah	3,013.0	1,700	0	1,313.0
WSCC total	53,741.5	25,754	14,280	13,707.5
U.S. total	259,490.1	142,401	93,743	24,346.1

Revised Estimates of Additions

	Total	Fossil	Nuclear	Other	Reduction
New England	4,162.5	178	3,450	534.5	1.736
New York	2,106.0	0	1,900	206.0	4,647
NPCC total	6,268.5	178	5,350	740.5	6,383
MAAC	7,187.5	1,620	5,336	231.5	6,661
Allegheny	626.0	626	0	0.0	2,890
AEP	4,080.0	3,900	0	180.0	2,600
CAPCO	2,768.0	769	1,999	0.0	1,179
Other Ohio	2,252.0	1,200	792	260.0	2,175
Kentucky	3,749.0	3,684	0	65.0	2,135
Indiana	4,293.0	3,073	1,130	90.0	4,424
Michigan	4,512.0	2,119	2,381	12.0	200
ECAR total	22,280.0	15,371	6,302	607.0	15,603

Table 7–4 continued

Revised Estimates of Additions (continued)

	Total	Fossil	Nuclear	Other	Reduction
Florida	5,412.0	4,099	795	518.0	6,513
Southern Co.	5,884.0	3,129	1,957	798.0	4,781
TVA	7,076.0	0	7,076	0.0	8,735
VACAR	13,512.0	2,450	8,528	2,534.0	5,054
SERC total	31,884.0	9,678	18,356	3,850.0	25,083
Commonwealth Edison	6,516.0	0	6,516	0.0	1,650
Illinois-Missouri	2,941.0	575	2,100	266.0	2,348
Wisconsin	1,886.0	1,860	0	26.0	440
MAIN total	11,343.0	2,435	8,616	292.0	4,438
Middle South	7,482.0	2,960	4,522	0.0	3,380
Gulf State	4,350.0	3,230	940	180.0	4,060
Missouri-Kansas	4,488.0	3,153	1,500	383.0	2,013
Oklahoma	4,464.0	4,248	0	216.0	5,791
SWPP total	20,984.0	13,593	6,612	779.0	15,244
ERCOT	10,265.0	5,465	4,800	0.0	11,497
MARCA	5,782.6	5,649	0	133.6	4,845
Rocky Mountains	3,245.0	2,470	0	775.0	3,300
Northwest	11,631.5	1,972	6,080	3,579.5	1,330
Arizona-New Mexico	6,577.0	1,998	3,810	769.0	1,230
S. California-Nevada	6,837.0	1,835	2,200	2,802.0	5,466
N. California-Nevada	7,640.0	4,004	2,168	4,468.0	3,472
Idaho-Utah	2,513.0	1,200	0	1,313.0	500
WSCC total	38,443.5	10,479	14,258	13,706.5	15,298
U.S. total	154,483.1	64,468	69,630	20,340.1	103,820

Relationship of Revised Capacity Estimates to Demand

	Peak	NERC Capacity	Adjust-ment	Net Capacity	Reserve Ratio
New England	20,040[a]	26,714	1,736	25,178	25.6
New York	24,260[a]	36,647	4,647	32,000	31.9
NPCC total	44,300[a]	63,561	6,383	57,178	29.1
MAAC	42,370	58,393	6,661	51,732	22.1
ECAR	95,050	124,494	15,603	108,891	14.6
Florida	29,116[a]	35,404	6,513	28,889	(0.9)
Southern Co.	30,418	37,589	4,781	32,808	7.9
TVA	31,752[a]	44,310	8,735	35,575	12.0
VACAR	43,308[a]	52,325	5,054	47,271	9.2
SERC total	131,137[a]	169,628	28,083	141,545	7.9

Table 7–4 continued

Relationship of Revised Capacity Estimates to Demand (continued)

	Peak	NERC Capacity	Adjust-ment	Net Capacity	Reserve Ratio
MAIN	50,691	60,562	4,338	56,224	10.9
MARCA	30,614	35,318	4,845	30,473	(0.5)
SPP	64,866	77,263	15,244	62,019	(4.4)
ERCOT	49,032	58,362	11,497	46,865	(4.4)
Northwest	46,378[a]	55,035	1,330	53,705	15.8
Rocky Mountains	8,771	12,380	3,800	8,580	(2.2)
Arizona-New Mexico	13,654	18,242	1,230	17,012	14.6
California-Nevada	50,542	60,702	8,938	51,764	2.4
WSCC total	108,568	145,533	15,298	130,235	20.0
U.S. total	643,563	793,114	103,800	689,314	7.11

Relationship of Revised Capacity Estimates to Demand

	Percent Reserve	Projected Percent Growth	Percent Growth to Maintain Reserve Margin of		
			10%	15%	20%
ECAR	14.6	4.79	4.84	4.37	3.93
Florida	(0.9)	4.73	3.54	3.08	2.64
Southern Co.	7.9	4.20	3.99	3.53	3.09
TVA	12.0	4.35	4.54	4.08	3.63
VACAR	9.2	5.10	4.57	4.11	3.66
SERC total	7.9	4.44	4.46	3.99	3.55
MAIN	10.9	4.15	4.24	3.78	3.33
MARCA	(0.5)	5.38	4.33	3.87	3.43
SPP	(4.4)	5.60	4.13	3.67	3.23
ERCOT	(4.4)	5.83	4.35	3.89	3.45
Northwest	15.8	3.75	4.28	3.82	3.38
Rocky Mountains	(2.2)	6.16	4.92	4.46	4.01
Arizona-New Mexico	24.6	5.57	6.90	6.42	5.97
California-Nevada	2.4	3.46	2.72	2.26	1.83
California-Arizona	7.1	3.87	3.60	3.14	2.70
WSCC total	20.0	4.53	5.44	4.97	4.52

Source: Capacity Additions: U.S. Department of Energy, *Proposed Changes to Generation Capacity 1980-1989 for the Contiguous United States* (Springfield, Va.: National Technical Information Service, 1980).

Forecasts: National Electric Reliability Council, *1980 Summary of Projected Peak Demand, Generating Capability, and Fossil Fuel Requirements for the Regional Reliability Councils of NERC* (Princeton, 1980).

[a]Winter peaks are denoted by [a]. The peaks were higher summer 1989 or winter 1980–1990. Totals do not add due to this mixing.

[b]NERC capability deals with winter 1989–1990, since table 7-3 is deducted from this figure.
[c]The adjustment figures are derived from table 7-3.

capacity if growth proceeded as forecast, but capacity expansion was lower than planned. It is surprising that the problem is not particularly acute in the Northwest, which is the region most concerned about power availability. The critical consideration is that the Northwest is forecasting growth that is sufficiently slow to insure a 16-percent reserve margin even with an adjustment for slippage. The areas that might face capacity problems are SWPP, ERCOT, the Rocky Mountain area, MARCA, and Florida. The forecasts could be wrong. Estimates have been scaled down as the effects of higher prices become more apparent. It is possible that the reductions will be overdone as prevailing pressures encourage stress on planning only for slow growth. Where regulations have not explicitly encouraged companies to expect limited expansion, the disincentive of low profits has had the same effect.

The adjustments made here have proved sufficient to anticipate further revisions of the NERC estimates. The report issued in 1981 scaled back summer peak-load growth to 3.5 percent per year, recorded slippages of construction similar to that anticipated here, but indicated reserves would be even more ample than the 1980 report indicated. The calculations again proceed as if the slippages will not continue.

Appendix 7A:
Data on Critical
Characteristics of the
Electric-Power Industry

Before a sensible discussion of the relationship between actual and efficient prices for electricity can be developed, it is critical that some indicators of the composition of sales and the costs of serving them be devised. Ideally, a substantial cross-section of companies should be observed over long periods of time. However, the compilation efforts involved would be formidable and produce material not easily incorporated in this book. Therefore, the review here stresses private-sector aggregates that are readily computed from available U.S. government and Edison Electric Institute reports.

A primary concern is how to delineate the breakdown of sales by basic end use. Table 7A–1 provides summary data on this area. Average revenues and percent of gross sales figures are presented for the three categories distinguished in FPC-EIA data. Examination of supporting data from the companies and the Edison Electric Institute yearbook suggests that "commercial" and "industrial" do not have precisely the meanings used in most U.S. government data. Electric utilities are encouraged to follow general usage and try to do so. However, some merely distinguish between larger and smaller nonresidential users of electricity. (The last, moreover, may include large apartment houses.) Other sales predominantly (15 of the 18 percent in 1979) consist of gross resales to others, which may or may not be other private companies. The remainder consists of four miscellaneous categories with the majority being in the class of sales to public authorities.

Company uniform statistical reports were used to delineate further the nature of sales. Table 7A–2 lists for those companies for which I possess data figures on sales to different customer types. In addition to data on broad areas, percents were calculated for sales to primary metals and the chemical industry and the sector other than those two to which the company made its greatest sales.

As expected, the relative proportions of end users in sales reflects the nature of the economy in the service area. The lowest dependence on large industrial users occurs for companies predominantly in those urban and suburban areas in which little heavy industry is located, such as Boston, New York, and Florida. Conversely, the highest dependence on industry occurs in less-populated areas that have important industries. the extreme case is Minnesota Power and Light, which sells the majority of its power to

Table 7A-1
Composition of Revenues and Sales Volume of Private Electric Utilities: 1959-1979

	Average Rate in Cents per kWh			Percent of Sales in kWh			
	Resi-dential	Commer-cial	Indus-trial	Resi-dential	Commer-cial	Indus-trial	Other
1959	2.64	a	1.48	22.5	a	57.9a	19.6
1960	2.62	a	1.49a	22.7	a	57.2a	20.1
1961	2.60	2.43	1.08	24.2	17.9	40.3	17.6
1962	2.56	2.38	1.05	24.1	18.7	39.3	17.9
1963	2.51	2.34	1.04	24.2	18.7	39.3	17.8
1964	2.45	2.26	1.02	24.3	19.0	39.1	17.6
1965	2.39	2.18	1.00	24.2	19.7	38.2	17.9
1966	2.34	2.13	0.98	24.0	19.6	37.9	18.5
1967	2.31	2.11	0.98	24.3	19.7	37.2	18.8
1968	2.25	2.07	0.97	24.6	19.7	36.7	19.0
1969	2.21	2.06	0.98	25.0	19.4	36.0	19.6
1970	2.22	2.08	1.02	25.9	19.9	35.0	19.2
1971	2.32	2.20	1.10	26.3	20.3	34.7	18.7
1972	2.42	2.29	1.16	26.4	20.4	34.9	18.3
1973	2.54	2.41	1.25	26.4	20.5	35.0	18.1
1974	3.10	3.04	1.69	26.4	20.4	34.8	18.4
1975	3.51	3.46	2.08	27.2	21.1	32.4	19.3
1976	3.77	3.73	2.25	26.1	20.6	33.2	20.1
1977	4.06	4.02	2.54	26.7	21.3	33.1	18.9
1978	4.31	4.37	2.79	26.8	20.6	33.5	19.1
1979	4.64	4.68	3.04	26.7	20.9	34.3	18.1

Source: U.S., Federal Power Commission and U.S., Department of Energy, Energy Information Administration, *Statistics of Privately Owned Electric Utilities in the United States* (Washington, D.C.: U.S. Government Printing Office, various years).

aCommercial included in industrial.

iron-ore mining and processing operations. Examination of the data shows that some differences arise from the differences in definition noted above.

As tables 7A-2 and 7A-3 show, many different patterns of purchase and resale of power prevail. Many companies that are net sellers seem to be taking advantage of the existence of capacity that is excess but cheaper to operate than those of nearby companies. For example, American Electric Power is known by industry analysts for its long-standing policy of building large plants and making power available to its neighbors. Boston Edison's heavy gross resales reflect the advantages of making its nuclear generation available to others when the opportunity arises. Another source of resale is cooperatives and municipals that neither own generating capacity nor have access to substantial amounts of state or federal power. Conversely, where substantial amounts of state of federal power exist (such as on the West Coast or in New York State), private companies tend to be net buyers.

Table 7A–2
Percent Distribution of 1979 Electric-Power Quantities of Selected Private Companies

	Residential	Commercial	Industrial	Re-Sale	Primary Metals	Chemicals	Other Major	Name of Other Major Customer
1. American Electric Power	18.89	10.27	38.75	31.11	16.70	4.00	4.33	Coal mining
2. Southern Company	26.33	19.10	40.59	13.45	4.65	6.56	5.71	Textiles
3. Commonwealth Edison	27.71	29.47	31.79	1.88	7.88	2.59	2.82	Petroleum refining
4. Southern California Edison	27.20	28.77	33.13	8.37	2.83	2.96	3.84	Petroleum
5. Texas Utilities	32.14	24.51	31.92	8.35	8.04	1.96	5.65	Oil production
6. Houston Lighting and Power	21.16	16.83	55.98	5.83	4.06	27.47	5.54	Petroleum refining
7. Duke Power	25.50	17.44	40.26	16.10	0.75	4.58	20.65	Textiles
8. Pacific Gas and Electric	32.78	35.67	25.50	4.69	0.86	1.11	4.20	Petroleum refining
9. Central and Southwest	23.76	18.83	31.37	23.30	3.44	8.03	4.10	Oil production
10. Florida Power and Light	50.18	34.25	7.50	6.11	0.72	0.60	1.02	Electrical
11. Middle South Utilities	27.59	16.53	42.17	10.33	1.62	13.64	4.07	Petroleum refining
12. Detroit Edison	27.85	16.94	48.68	4.24	9.66	2.19	16.96	Transportation
13. Allegheny Power System	24.98	13.19	48.95	12.61	13.77	5.07	13.77	Fabricated metals
14. Pennsylvania Power and Light	35.76	24.62	36.06	2.60	10.05	2.48	3.33	Glass
15. Virginia Electric and Power	32.99	24.38	17.19	12.83	0.45	4.53	1.90	Paper
16. Carolina Power and Light	25.10	16.01	33.52	22.17	1.20	6.32	12.96	Textiles
17. Union Electric (Consolidated)	31.86	27.27	33.17	5.66	6.81	5.36	3.41	Transportation
18. General Public Utilities	33.61	23.00	37.43	4.79	5.76	3.43	3.96	Paper
19. Northern States Power	26.93	12.82	38.47	19.69	2.01	0.34	3.41	Food
20. Public Service Electric and Gas	26.29	34.94	37.41	0.39	2.52	8.58	3.10	Petroleum refining
21. Gulf State Utilities	17.93	13.09	52.27	8.47	2.09	34.31	3.18	Paper
22. Public Service Co. of Indiana	26.14	18.08	34.52	20.80	6.39	4.82	3.40	Glass
23. Consolidated Edison	26.26	57.62	5.47	9.07	0.31	0.41	0.97	Food
24. Ohio Edison	28.96	20.44	42.81	7.07	19.73	2.01	4.03	Fabricated metal
25. Consumers Power	29.75	23.01	43.03	3.20	7.51	5.68	3.20	Transportation

Table 7A–2 continued

	Residential	Commercial	Industrial	Re-Sale	Primary Metals	Chemicals	Other Major	Name of Other Major Customer
26. Niagara Mohawk Power	24.82	27.85	37.43	9.07	7.69	7.37	3.67	Paper
27. Oklahoma Gas and Electric	25.09	15.55	23.38	29.43	0.61	1.26	5.71	Oil production
28. Philadelphia Electric	28.87	10.61	55.90	0.40	7.34	3.42	4.62	Petroleum refining
29. Baltimore Gas and Electric	32.67	17.39	47.80	0.00	13.05	2.26	1.05	Machinery
30. Cleveland Electric Illuminating	22.87	21.24	48.70	5.09	18.76	6.35	6.45	Transportation
31. Florida Power	39.43	20.75	18.30	17.33	0.04	1.85	10.29	Nonmetal mining
32. Illinois Power	26.27	16.93	47.37	7.44	3.79	3.20	5.20	Food
33. Northeast Utilities	36.30	27.96	26.00	8.82	2.35	1.52	3.01	Paper
34. Wisconsin Electric Power	29.65	24.55	35.65	8.27	5.16	0.79	5.79	Machinery
35. Utah Power and Light	19.81	14.22	34.39	28.56	4.92	10.26	4.17	Metal mining
36. Cincinnati Gas and Electric	34.23	22.59	33.77	1.22	9.83	5.64	4.32	Transportation
37. New England Electric System	35.88	30.04	24.29	8.57	2.01	2.21	3.14	Electrical
38. Boston Edison	21.37	37.34	14.46	25.43	0.15	0.35	2.68	Electrical
39. South Carolina Electric and Gas	30.04	22.95	35.60	8.59	1.59	6.65	7.50	Textiles
40. Arizona Public Service	29.55	30.16	23.73	15.51	0.68	0.31	8.86	Metal mining
41. Long Island Lighting	42.03	5.14	42.09	6.54	0.08	0.30	1.18	Electrical
42. Idaho Power	27.56	29.98	25.69	16.55	0.00	15.31	4.34	Food
43. Columbus and So. Ohio Electric	35.67	30.35	23.58	6.50	1.50	1.74	3.06	Electrical
44. Indianapolis Power and Light	29.31	19.87	45.01	5.07	2.13	3.75	9.45	Transportation
45. New York State Electric and Gas	40.13	22.75	26.35	0.09	2.12	0.95	3.99	Glass
46. Dayton Power and Light	35.52	19.42	30.42	5.20	1.59	1.12	5.14	Electrical
47. Central Illinois Public Service	25.02	10.34	40.42	22.55	0.44	3.91	6.07	Coal mining
48. Northern Indiana Public Service	15.81	3.47	73.56	5.97	39.34	12.53	1.75	Petroleum refining
49. Delmarva Power and Light	26.27	21.33	35.03	16.57	2.94	14.16	5.55	Food
50. Montana Power	22.42	19.01	34.80	21.78	0.00	0.00	14.07	Metal mining

51. Kentucky Utilities	29.46	16.95	27.52	18.58	1.56	1.48	8.30	Coal mining
52. Kansas Gas and Electric	24.70	18.47	36.68	19.31	0.60	8.62	7.42	Petroleum refining
53. Kansas City Power and Light	27.44	38.74	29.00	3.99	11.66	2.42	4.64	Transportation
54. Kansas Power and Light	27.93	30.33	26.13	12.68	0.44	3.61	4.62	Food
55. Toledo Edison	25.09	16.29	46.17	7.25	10.99	0.88	10.83	Petroleum
56. Wisconsin Public Service	26.53	22.44	31.87	16.46	3.91	0.13	19.57	Paper
57. Central Louisiana Electric	20.77	8.34	19.28	47.69	0.00	3.24	9.31	Paper
58. Tucson Electric Power	18.83	15.80	28.15	33.53	0.00	0.00	18.42	Metal mining
59. Public Service of New Hampshire	29.16	10.32	33.96	25.63	0.00	3.08	5.84	Paper
60. Atlantic City Electric	45.43	29.77	23.65	0.00	0.68	4.82	8.57	Glass
61. New England Gas and Electric Assoc.	20.63	15.62	12.59	45.90	0.27	0.45	1.64	Rubber
62. United Illuminating	35.09	32.74	30.71	0.00	6.64	1.39	4.43	Transportation
63. Washington Water Power	36.34	18.41	21.77	23.07	0.00	0.00	9.52	Metal mining
64. Central Illinois Light	31.29	20.13	46.40	1.23	19.18	0.97	15.59	Machinery
65. Minnesota Power and Light	8.65	7.32	73.02	10.28	0.00	0.00	57.43	Iron ore
66. El Paso Electric	27.39	27.73	19.92	4.78	6.36	0.00	3.12	Petroleum refining
67. Southern Indiana General Electric	22.16	16.60	31.56	29.03	0.51	12.35	5.60	Coal mining
68. Central Hudson Gas and Electric	25.40	16.11	25.15	27.92	0.85	0.29	11.96	Machinery
69. Iowa Electric Light and Power	36.03	26.00	29.23	7.45	1.07	0.51	14.97	Food
70. Iowa Power and Light	38.74	24.31	34.49	0.37	0.91	0.00	4.40	Rubber
80. Interstate Power	22.97	26.74	39.35	9.33	0.44	16.17	8.39	Food
81. Central Maine Power	39.18	19.52	38.27	2.18	0.33	0.79	18.47	Paper
All Power Companies	26.72	20.85	34.30	15.50	n.a.	n.a.	n.a.	n.a.

Source: Company Uniform Statistical Reports.

Note: Percents omit minor categories of sales, primarily to public authorities. Other major is the company's largest buying sector besides the two shown explicitly. Industry names are shorthands for full title of Standard Industrial Classification two-digit industries; all are mining or manufacturing. Thus, transportation here invariably means transportation equipment and glass stands for stone, clay, and glass; the other shorthands are close enough to the full title to require no specific explanation.

n.a.: not available.

Table 7A-3
Power Interchanges for Selected Companies in 1979
(thousand kWh)

	Purchases					
	Private	*Public*	*Cooperative*	*Industrial*	*Net Foreign*	*Total Purchase*
Central Maine Power	4,175,998	2,099	0	57,801	135	4,236,033
Boston Edison	341,941	6,208	0	0	0	348,149
New England Electric System	4,496,119	26,392	0	15,001	0	4,537,512
New England Gas and Elec. Assoc.	824,603	0	0	0	0	824,603
Consolidated Edison	3,870,790	1,792,579	0	0	4,061,767	9,666,692
Long Island Lighting	2,697,382	790,678	0	0	0	3,488,060
Niagara Mohawk Power	4,571,313	8,999,005	0	34,487	0	13,604,805
Public Service Electric and Gas	7,275,175	0	0	0	0	7,275,175
Pennsylvania Power and Light	(8,964,325)	0	0	0	0	(8,964,325)
General Public Utilities	7,774,478	36,034	0	0	171,001	7,981,513
Philadelphia Elec.	9,180,443	0	0	0	0	9,180,443
American Electric Power	3,474,045	38,632	0	0	0	3,512,677
Allegheny Power System	1,718,296	0	0	21,132	0	1,739,428
Public Service Co. of Indiana	(4,026,469)	15,565	0	0	0	(4,010,904)
Northern Indiana Public Service	5,524,453	0	0	738	0	5,525,191
Kentucky Utilities	(1,171,285)	3,254,402	729,593	0	0	2,812,710
Detroit Edison	915,978	(247,820)	0	(77,350)	3,654,264	4,245,072
Consumers Power	7,222,849	(9,758)	0	1,782	0	7,214,873
Virginia Electric	3,125,876	4,523,939	0	0	0	7,649,815
Duke Power	(676,174)	163,439	0	0	0	(512,735)
Carolina Power and Light	(195,810)	192,867	0	588	0	(2,355)
Southern Company	(4,443,922)	1,797,256	2,739,259	17,099	0	571,830
Florida Power and Light	(114,925)	697,519	0	0	0	582,594
Florida Power	1,547,471	262,408	0	0	0	1,809,879
Commonwealth Edison	5,824,157	0	0	0	0	5,824,157

Company	Resales: Private	Cooperative	Municipal	Federal and State		Total
Illinois Power	(1,748,310)	105,537	(24,116)	0	0	(1,666,889)
Central Illinois Public Service	(785,918)	8,942	31,442	0	0	(745,534)
Central Louisiana Electric	(1,034,881)	(223,209)		0	0	(1,250,090)
Gulf State Utilities	4,114,534	1,221,638	531,192	1,667	0	5,869,031
Central and Southwest	358,583	337,180	301,809	0	0	997,572
Oklahoma Gas and Electric	69,865	0	0	0	0	69,865
Southwestern Public Service	21,686	0	0	0	0	21,686
Houston Lighting and Power	377,387	0	0	0	0	377,387
Texas Utilities	9,718	60,810	5,167	0	0	75,695
Northern States Power	(685,027)	2,688,939	(198,234)	50,115	0	1,855,793
Minnesota Power and Light	648,548	578,220	2,865,580	17,674	840,424	4,950,446
Utah Power and Light	1,149,567	260,471	48	3,072	0	1,413,158
Pacific Power and Light	370,932	4,432,389	0	446,468	0	5,269,789
Portland General Electric	1,347,605	5,974,586	0	57,220	374,610	7,754,021
Washington Water Power	699,484	3,022,411	0	0	0	3,721,895
Southern California Edison	2,349,569	4,334,160	59,240	52,700	22,559	6,818,227
Pacific Gas and Electric	1,862,792	9,512,104	0	161,802	0	11,536,778

Company	Private	Cooperative	Municipal	Federal and State		Total
			Resales			
Central Maine Power	60,382	5,221	65,239	0	0	130,842
Boston Edison	2,101,980	0	989,689	0	0	3,091,669
New England Electric System	108,597	0	1,254,636	39,229	0	1,402,462
New England Gas and Electric Assoc.	2,492,058	0	94,896	0	0	2,586,954
Consolidated Edison	1,726,961	0	0	934,331	0	2,661,192
Long Island Lighting	847,753	0	19,310	4,357	0	871,420
Niagara Mohawk Power	2,877,620	0	184	144,419	0	3,022,223
Public Service Elec. and Gas	0	0	116,057	0	0	116,057
Pennsylvania Power and Light	152,195	0	435,168	0	0	586,381
General Public Utilities	364,428	804,720	362,481	0	0	1,531,629

Table 7A-3 continued

		Resales			
	Private	*Cooperative*	*Municipal*	*Federal and State*	*Total*
Philadelphia Elec.	106	0	110,961	0	111,067
American Electric Power	25,552,498	903,705	3,012,706	263,733	29,715,674
Allegheny Power System	3,564,266	180,211	529,123	0	4,273,600
Public Service Co. of Indiana	0	2,228,034	1,502,209	0	3,790,243
Northern Indiana Public Service	0	669,962	135,895	0	835,857
Kentucky Utilities	393,480	404,552	832,474	249,919	1,880,425
Detroit Edison	1,166,325	334,772	62,696	0	1,563,787
Consumers Power	342,504	22,574	495,281	0	857,830
Virginia Electric and Power	0	2,974,678	1,834,539	0	4,819,818
Duke Power	886,320	3,057,052	4,160,080	0	8,103,552
Carolina Power and Light	48,876	2,481,085	3,826,621	0	6,356,672
Southern Company	196,906	7,083,688	4,284,715	0	11,567,509
Florida Power and Light	0	2,116,961	445,823		2,562,784
Florida Power	0	1,812,266	1,226,805	5,707	3,044,778
Commonwealth Edison	306,806	0	899,510	0	1,206,316
Illinois Power	1,874	885,035	172,078	0	1,058,987
Central Illinois Public Service	141,215	1,460,129	357,859	0	1,959,203
Central Louisiana Electric	2,690,206	816,101	0	0	3,506,307
Gulf State Utility	0	1,650,054	780,423	0	2,430,477
Central and Southwest	3,150,492	3,616,870	757,410	2,502,458	10,027,238
Oklahoma Gas and Electric	4,676,570	279,590	835,570	91,985	5,883,715
Southwestern Public Service	468,483	1,913,664	38,609	0	2,420,756
Houston Lighting and Power	3,051,583	0	0	0	3,051,593
Texas Utilities	2,240,196	2,070,182	70,645	139,994	4,521,017
Northern States Power	3,583,934	421,241	1,028,928	6,818	5,040,921
Minnesota Power and Light	425,527	35,835	393,749	3,885	858,996
Utah Power and Light	3,417,957	660,727	232,217	21,484	4,332,385
Pacific Power and Light	3,767,909	0	458,643	156,860	4,377,412
Portland General Electric	513,158	0	0	0	513,158
Washington Water Power	1,262,156	161,780	161,817	357,865	1,943,618
Southern California Edison	627,396	16,224	4,340,970	0	4,984,590
Pacific Gas and Electric	556,775	0	2,250,474	0	2,807,249

Table 7A–4 provides indicators of the composition of generating costs and their relationship to sales. The basic pattern is one of operating costs (the money outlays immediately chargeable to sales) shrinking in proportion to revenues and on a per kilowatt hour basis during the 1960s, then radically reversing in the 1970s. Not surprisingly, the rise has been predominantly in generation cost, particularly in fuel expense. What is surprising is that the decline in the 1960s was greater outside of generation than within it.

The faster declines of nongenerating operating costs in the 1960s and slower rises in the 1970s had the expected effect of making generating costs a growing fraction of total operating costs and absorbing a growing fraction of sales revenue. In fact, the nongenerating share in cost went from 45 percent to 19 percent, so its influence greatly diminished. When nongenerating expenses are related to each other, it can be seen that the mix has altered considerably over the twenty-year period covered. The share of transmission has risen a bit, but that of distribution has fallen sharply. Sales and service outlays are a markedly lower part of the total, while administrative expenses are a higher proportion. Given the tendency of regulators to discourage sales promotion, some of the drop in the role of sales and service and the rise in administrative expense may involve redefinition. However, the sharp rise in administration is so much greater than the drop for sales and service that other forces must have been at work.

Finally, a view is taken of capital stocks and investment outlays. Data on gross value of private electric-utility plants show that the majority of these assets have been for nongenerating facilities and that the share of generating facilities fell in the 1960s and rose in the 1970s (table 7A–5). The component that had the most marked increase in share during the 1960s and early 1970s was transmission. The increase in share by generation during the 1970s reduced the role of distribution and, starting in the middle 1970s, the share of transmission. When ratios are calculated for nongenerating capital, the pattern among these types is for transmission to increase in importance relative to distribution.

As additional information, the table relates construction in progress to plants in operation. As would be expected because of rising nominal costs and increasing lead times, construction in progress has become an increasing burden. Where incomplete assets in the early 1960s were 5 percent of the value of operating plants, the rate had reached 30 percent by 1979.

Asset values are a weighted average of values of plants added over many years, and these plants in turn were constructed over long periods. Thus, asset values lag behind current outlay patterns by many years. To suggest the implications of this, Table 7A–6 examines investment outlay data. These show that generation has increased in importance to investment to a much greater extent than it has increased in importance to gross assets. Even so, 30 percent of investment in the late 1970s was for nongenerating facilities. Therefore, $0.40–0.45 ($30 \div 70 = 0.43$) are invested in nongen-

Table 7A–4
Data on Costs of Electricity for Private Companies: 1969–1979

	Fuel	Total Production	Transmission	Distribution	Customer Acct.	Sales and Service	Admin. and General	Total Non-production	Total
Mills/kWh									
1959		4.3	0.3	1.3	0.5	0.3	1.1	3.4	7.7
1960		4.2	0.3	1.3	0.5	0.3	1.1	3.4	7.6
1961		4.2	0.2	1.2	0.5	0.3	1.1	3.3	7.5
1962		4.1	0.2	1.1	0.5	0.2	1.1	3.2	7.3
1963		4.1	0.2	1.1	0.5	0.3	1.0	3.1	7.2
1964		4.0	0.2	1.1	0.5	0.3	1.0	3.0	7.0
1965		4.0	0.2	1.1	0.4	0.3	1.0	2.9	6.9
1966		4.0	0.2	1.0	0.4	0.3	0.9	2.8	6.8
1967		4.0	0.2	1.0	0.4	0.3	0.9	2.8	6.8
1968	2.4	4.1	0.2	0.9	0.4	0.3	0.9	2.7	6.8
1969	2.4	4.2	0.2	0.9	0.4	0.3	0.9	2.7	6.9
1970	2.9	4.8	0.2	1.0	0.4	0.2	0.9	2.7	7.5
1971	3.5	5.5	0.2	1.0	0.4	0.2	1.0	2.8	8.3
1972	3.8	6.0	0.3	1.0	0.4	0.2	1.0	2.9	8.9
1973	4.3	6.7	0.3	1.0	0.4	0.1	1.1	2.9	9.6
1974	7.7	10.7	0.3	1.1	0.5	0.1	1.2	3.2	13.9
1975	9.0	12.7	0.3	1.1	0.6	0.1	1.4	3.5	16.5
1976	9.8	13.7	0.3	1.1	0.6	0.1	1.5	3.6	17.3
1977	11.2	15.9	0.4	1.2	0.6	0.1	1.6	3.9	19.8
1978	12.0	17.3	0.4	1.3	0.7	0.2	1.8	4.4	21.7
1979	13.9	19.7	0.4	1.4	0.7	0.1	2.0	4.6	24.3
As Percent of revenues									
1959		25.1	1.5	7.6	3.0	1.7	6.3	20.1	45.2
1960		24.8	1.5	7.5	3.0	1.7	6.3	20.0	44.8
1961		25.0	1.4	7.0	2.9	1.6	6.4	19.3	44.3
1962		24.8	1.4	6.8	2.8	1.7	6.4	19.1	43.9
1963		24.8	1.4	6.7	2.8	1.7	6.3	18.9	43.7

Year									
1964		25.0	1.4	6.8	2.8	1.8	6.3	19.0	44.0
1965		25.4	1.4	6.7	2.7	1.8	6.2	18.8	44.2
1966		26.3	1.4	6.5	2.6	1.8	6.0	18.4	44.7
1967		26.6	1.4	6.5	2.6	1.8	5.9	18.2	44.8
1968	16.2	27.3	1.4	6.3	2.5	1.7	5.7	17.8	45.1
1969	16.7	28.4	1.5	6.3	2.5	1.7	5.7	17.7	46.1
1970	20.0	31.0	1.5	6.3	2.5	1.6	5.9	17.8	48.8
1971	20.8	33.4	1.5	5.9	2.5	1.3	5.8	17.0	50.4
1972	21.6	34.5	1.5	5.6	2.4	1.1	5.9	16.4	50.9
1973	23.2	36.3	1.4	5.4	2.4	0.7	5.8	15.7	52.0
1974	32.3	45.3	1.2	4.4	2.2	0.4	5.2	13.5	58.8
1975	32.6	46.0	1.1	3.9	2.2	0.3	5.0	12.5	58.5
1976	32.9	46.4	1.1	3.8	2.1	0.4	5.0	12.4	58.8
1977	34.5	48.5	1.1	3.6	1.9	0.4	4.9	11.9	60.4
1978	34.4	49.4	1.1	3.6	1.9	0.4	5.1	12.0	61.4
1979	36.3	51.3	1.0	3.6	1.9	0.4	5.2	12.2	63.5

As Percent of Operating Costs

Year								
1959		55.5	3.3	16.8	6.6	3.8	13.9	100.0
1960		54.4	3.3	16.7	6.7	3.8	14.1	100.0
1961		56.4	3.2	15.8	6.5	3.6	14.4	100.0
1962		56.5	3.2	15.5	6.4	3.9	14.6	100.0
1963		56.8	3.2	15.3	6.4	3.9	14.4	100.0
1964		56.8	3.2	15.5	6.4	4.1	14.3	100.0
1965		57.5	3.2	15.2	6.1	4.1	14.0	100.0
1966		58.8	3.1	14.5	5.8	4.0	13.4	100.0
1967		59.4	3.1	14.5	5.8	4.0	13.2	100.0
1968	35.8	60.7	3.2	14.0	5.5	3.9	12.7	100.0
1969	36.1	61.6	3.2	13.7	5.4	3.7	12.4	100.0
1970	38.8	63.6	3.0	13.0	5.2	3.2	12.0	100.0
1971	41.4	66.3	2.9	11.7	4.9	2.6	11.6	100.0
1972	42.5	67.7	2.9	11.0	4.7	2.1	11.6	100.0
1973	44.5	69.9	2.7	10.3	4.6	1.4	11.1	100.0
1974	54.9	77.0	2.1	7.6	3.4	0.7	8.8	100.0
1975	55.7	78.6	1.9	6.7	3.7	0.6	8.5	100.0
1976	56.0	79.0	2.0	6.4	3.6	0.7	8.4	100.0
1977	57.2	80.4	1.8	5.9	3.2	0.6	8.2	100.0
1978	55.9	80.4	1.7	5.6	3.1	0.6	8.3	100.0
1979	57.3	80.9	1.7	5.6	3.0	0.6	8.2	100.0

Table 7A–4 continued

Nongenerating Cost Components as Percent of Total Nongenerating Costs

1959	7.5	37.8	14.9	8.5	31.3	100.0
1960	7.5	37.5	15.0	8.5	31.5	100.0
1961	7.3	35.6	14.7	8.9	33.5	100.0
1962	7.3	35.6	14.7	8.9	33.5	100.0
1963	7.4	35.4	14.8	9.0	33.3	100.0
1964	7.4	35.8	14.7	9.5	33.2	100.0
1965	7.4	35.6	14.4	9.6	33.0	100.0
1966	7.6	35.3	14.1	9.8	32.6	100.0
1967	7.7	35.7	14.3	9.9	32.4	100.0
1968	7.9	35.4	14.0	9.6	32.0	100.0
1969	8.5	35.6	14.1	9.6	32.2	100.0
1970	8.2	35.7	14.3	8.8	33.0	100.0
1971	8.6	34.7	14.5	7.7	34.4	100.0
1972	9.0	34.1	14.6	6.5	35.9	100.0
1973	9.0	34.2	15.3	4.7	36.9	100.0
1974	9.1	32.9	16.5	3.1	38.4	100.0
1975	8.9	31.3	17.3	2.8	39.7	100.0
1976	9.2	30.5	16.9	3.0	40.4	100.0
1977	9.2	30.0	16.2	3.0	41.7	100.0
1978	8.8	29.7	15.9	3.0	42.5	100.0
1979	8.7	29.5	15.9	3.0	43.0	100.0

Source: U.S., Federal Power Commission and U.S., Department of Energy, Energy Information Administration, *Statistics of Privately Owned Electric Utilities in the United States* (Washington, D.C.: U.S. Government Printing Office, various years).

Note: The calculations are those presented by the source or easily calculable from it. Raw data exist on fuel cost but calculation of averages was not undertaken by the source.

[a] Does not add because of error introduced by computing from rounded numbers.

Table 7A-5
Private Electric-Utility Plant and Equipment: 1959-1979

Year	Intan-gible Plant	Produc-tion Plant	Trans-mission Plant	Distri-bution Plant	General Plant	Other	Total Service
Gross Value in Millions of Dollars							
1959	23	16,934	6,315	15,466	1,195	5	39,938
1960	23	18,401	6,777	16,715	1,279	3	43,197
1961	23	19,560	7,181	17,692	1,332	34	45,822
1962	23	20,673	7,739	18,781	1,415	9	48,640
1963	24	21,545	8,296	19,952	1,503	1	51,321
1964	24	22,457	8,767	21,120	1,586	1	53,955
1965	23	23,476	9,438	22,396	1,686	7	57,025
1966	22	24,310	10,255	23,838	1,771	60	60,257
1967	22	26,118	11,479	25,437	1,894	4	64,953
1968	21	27,938	12,617	27,229	2,054	5	69,864
1969	20	30,317	13,937	29,155	2,222	14	75,665
1970	20	33,035	15,444	31,329	2,370	10	82,208
1971	19	36,084	17,226	33,650	2,570	9	89,558
1972	20	40,660	18,802	38,244	2,770	15	100,512
1973	20	46,204	20,380	37,222	3,004	78	106,909
1974	21	53,581	22,217	41,877	3,297	18	121,012
1975	22	60,051	23,452	44,557	3,574	44	131,700
1976	23	66,054	25,236	47,159	3,733	54	142,259
1977	24	74,646	26,682	50,083	4,332	34	155,800
1978	28	83,449	28,485	53,341	4,473	59	169,836
1979	32	89,382	30,085	57,041	4,867	27	181,433
Percent Distribution of Plant							
1959	0.06	42.20	15.81	38.73	2.99	0.01	100.00
1960	0.05	42.60	15.69	38.69	2.96	0.01	100.00
1961	0.05	42.69	15.67	38.61	2.91	0.07	100.00
1962	0.05	42.50	15.91	38.61	2.91	0.02	100.00
1963	0.05	41.98	16.16	38.88	2.93	0.00	100.00
1964	0.04	41.62	16.26	39.14	2.94	0.00	100.00
1965	0.04	41.17	16.55	39.27	2.96	0.01	100.00
1966	0.04	40.34	17.02	39.56	2.94	0.10	100.00
1967	0.03	40.21	17.67	39.16	2.92	0.01	100.00
1968	0.03	39.99	18.06	38.98	2.94	0.01	100.00
1969	0.03	40.07	18.42	38.53	2.94	0.02	100.00
1970	0.02	40.18	18.79	38.11	2.88	0.01	100.00
1971	0.02	40.29	19.23	37.57	2.87	0.01	100.00
1972	0.02	40.45	18.71	38.05	2.76	0.02	100.00
1973	0.02	43.22	19.06	34.82	2.81	0.07	100.00
1974	0.02	44.28	18.36	34.61	2.72	0.02	100.00
1975	0.02	45.60	17.81	33.83	2.71	0.03	100.00
1976	0.02	46.43	17.74	33.15	2.62	0.04	100.00
1977	0.02	47.91	17.13	32.15	2.78	0.02	100.00
1978	0.02	49.14	16.77	31.41	2.63	0.03	100.00
1979	0.02	49.26	16.58	31.44	2.68	0.01	100.00

Table 7A-5 continued

Year	$ Million	As Percent of Value of Plant in Service
1959	2,189	5.48
1960	2,089	4.84
1961	2,088	4.56
1962	1,873	3.85
1963	1,960	3.82
1964	2,146	3.98
1965	2,438	4.27
1966	3,569	5.95
1967	4,418	6.80
1968	5,896	8.44
1969	7,731	10.22
1970	10,330	12.57
1971	13,531	15.11
1972	16,623	16.54
1973	20,246	18.94
1974	22,846	18.88
1975	26,319	19.98
1976	36,717	22.30
1977	36,484	23.42
1978	42,476	25.07
1979	53,991	29.76

Source: U.S., Federal Power Commission and U.S., Department of Energy, Energy Information Administration, *Statistics of Privately Owned Electric Utilities in the United States* (Washington, D.C.: U.S. Government Printing Office, various years).

Table 7A-6
Construction Expenditures by Private Utilities in the Contiguous Forty-eight States: 1959-1979

	Millions of Dollars				
	Production	Transmission	Distribution	Other	Total
1959	1,519	554	1,163	147	3,383
1960	1,342	537	1,300	152	3,331
1961	1,267	579	1,265	145	3,256
1962	1,078	609	1,305	162	3,154
1963	1,165	644	1,323	187	3,319
1964	1,114	824	1,424	189	3,551
1965	1,300	940	1,585	202	4,027
1966	1,789	1,137	1,769	237	4,932
1967	2,553	1,323	1,977	267	6,120
1968	3,189	1,503	2,135	313	7,140
1969	3,992	1,554	2,421	327	8,294
1970	5,429	1,680	2,614	422	10,145
1971	6,702	1,806	2,774	612	11,894

Table 7A-6 continued

| | Millions of Dollars | | | | |
	Production	Transmission	Distribution	Other	Total
1972	7,931	1,748	3,073	633	13,385
1973	8,775	2,047	3,371	714	14,907
1974	10,145	2,060	3,360	785	16,350
1975	9,828	1,734	2,817	711	15,090
1976	11,512	1,758	2,844	865	16,979
1977	13,875	1,854	3,254	775	19,758
1978	15,938	1,933	3,614	908	22,393
1979	16,908	2,209	4,076	1,185	24,378

| | Percent of Totals | | | | | | |
| | All Investment | | | | Nongenerating Investment | | |
	Genera-tion	Trans-mission	Distri-bution	Other	Trans-mission	Distri-bution	Other
1959	44.90	16.38	34.38	4.35	29.72	62.39	7.89
1960	40.29	16.12	39.03	4.56	27.00	65.36	7.64
1961	38.91	17.78	38.85	4.45	29.11	63.60	7.29
1962	34.18	19.31	41.38	5.14	29.34	62.86	7.80
1963	35.10	19.40	39.86	5.63	29.90	61.42	8.68
1964	31.37	23.20	40.10	5.32	33.81	58.43	7.77
1965	32.28	23.34	39.36	5.02	34.47	58.12	7.41
1966	36.27	23.05	35.87	4.81	36.18	56.28	7.54
1967	41.72	21.62	32.50	4.36	37.09	55.42	7.49
1968	44.66	21.05	29.90	4.38	38.04	54.04	7.92
1969	48.13	18.74	29.19	3.94	36.12	56.28	7.60
1970	53.51	16.56	25.77	4.16	35.62	55.43	8.95
1971	56.35	15.18	23.32	5.15	34.78	53.43	11.79
1972	59.25	13.06	22.96	4.73	32.05	56.34	11.61
1973	58.86	13.73	22.61	4.79	33.38	54.97	11.64
1974	62.05	12.60	20.55	4.80	33.20	54.15	12.65
1975	65.13	11.49	18.67	4.71	32.95	53.53	13.51
1976	67.80	10.35	16.75	5.09	32.16	52.02	15.82
1977	70.22	9.38	16.47	3.92	31.51	55.31	13.17
1978	71.17	8.63	16.14	4.05	29.95	55.99	14.07
1979	69.36	9.06	16.72	4.86	29.57	54.56	15.86

Source: Edison Electric Institute, *Statistical Yearbook of the Electric Utility Industry, 1979* (Washington, D.C.: 1980), p. 56.

erating facilities for every $1.00 invested in generation. When nongenerating outlays are related to each other, the share of transmission proves to have risen in the 1960s and fallen in the 1970s back to where it started. The role of distribution seems to be declining while other expenses have greatly increased in importance.

Appendix 7B:
The Structure of
Electric-Power Rates

To determine the nature of prevailing rates, those reported in the EIA report *Typical Electric Bills, 1 January 1980* were examined. The report presents the charges for different amounts of electricity in different communities in the United States. Three sets of schedules are shown: residential, commercial, and industrial. Residential rates are reported for all communities with populations greater than 2,500, and the other rates are given for communities with 50,000 or more people. This creates a considerable loss of data, with the most extreme case being the Allegheny Power System, which does not serve any community with a population greater than 50,000.

Residential rates are reported for five different levels of consumption. The rates from higher levels are associated with use of electricity in more applications. The rates for 250 and 500 kWh per month apply to lighting, appliance, refrigeration, and cooking customers; 750 and 1,000 kWh additionally use water heat; users of 2,500 kWh also use electric space heating.

The commercial and industrial rates are reported for combinations of capacity use and kilowatt hours consumed. The commercial rates associate a higher kilowatt hour consumption with higher capacity use; for example, 6 kW and 750 kWh, and 12 kW and 1,500 kWh are the first two combinations reported. The industrial rates are more complex. Rates for two consumption levels are reported for each of five capacity-use levels.

The choices are as follows:

Capacity (kW)	kWh	Implicit Utilization Rate (%))
150	30,000	2.28
150	60,000	4.57
300	60,000	2.28
300	120,000	4.57
500	100,000	2.28
500	200,000	4.57
1000	200,000	2.28
1000	400,000	4.57
5000	1,200,000	3.42
5000	2,500,000	5.71

(*Utilization rate* is the kWh figure divided by the maximum supply possible from the capacity).

243

Thus, in two cases the same kWh consumption is shown for two capacity-utilization levels, and in one case a lower kWh figure is shown for a higher kW figure (500 kW). The capacities are far greater than needed to supply the kWh on a continual basis. In addition to the seasonal and underground–delivery charges similar to the residential ones, companies may have several different rates reflecting such factors as the voltage at which power is supplied, whether a transformer is provided, and other characteristics, many of which EIA does not explain.

Examination of these rates suggests that the nature of the generation capacity of the supplying company, the distribution facilities required, customer characteristics, and the regulatory climate all are major influences. Further, the rates provide evidence that most regulatory agencies set the same rates for every community served by a specific company. Major exceptions occur in Illinois, New York, Minnesota, Missouri, Arizona, Utah, and Washington. Rates tend to be higher in more densely populated areas, where distribution is likely to be more expensive. Consolidated Edison charges its highest rates in New York City; Commonwealth Edison, in Chicago.

A tabulation providing only selected figures is included in table 7B–1, which shows the top and bottom rates reported for each of the three user types. The data show clearly that rates in the Pacific Northwest are by far the lowest in the States. Private company rates in that area greatly exceed those for public power but are still well below rates elsewhere in the United States. Generally, a group of utilities close to coal fields plus the companies (notably Gulf States Utilities, Oklahoma Gas and Electric, and Louisiana Power and Light) with access to large amounts of underpriced gas (under $2.00 per million Btu compared to prices of $2.25 and up for other companies) are the lowest cost operations outside the Northwest. Oil-dependent companies have high rates with Consolidated Edison's being the highest by far. These rates reflect fuel cost, an expensive underground distribution network, and a tax burden equal to 17 percent of revenues (about triple the average proportion).

Some interesting anomalies emerge. Central Main Power's access to Maine Yankee and Sacramento's nuclear plant yield rates well below the regional average. Potomac Electric generally receives markedly lower rates from the District of Columbia than from Maryland or Virginia, particularly in the residential sector. Residential rates of TVA's distributors are notably lower than those of nearby companies as are those to smaller commercial users. Rates to large users are more comparable.

Table 7B-1
Summary of Bills
(dollars)

	Residential		Commercial		Industrial	
	250 kWh	*2500 kWh*	*6kW 750kWh*	*100kW 30,000kWh*	*150kW 30,000kWh*	*5,000kW 2.5m kWh*
Central Maine Power	15.60	104.63	52.93	1,318.64	1,432	74,624
Public Service Co. of N.H.	19.74	134.60	71.27	1,569.70	1,759	103,325
Boston Edison[a]	19.06	150.53	84.91	2,239.35	2,094	135,858
Mass. Electric	18.70	135.33	63.15	2,234.63	1,812	117,469
Conn. Light and Power	19.91	128.77	70.86	1,604.19	1,771	103,719
Hartford Electric Light	20.33	128.94	79.56	1,629.56	1,872	106,967
United Illum.	20.21	164.44	73.93	2,079.70	2,058	141,233
Consolidated Edison[a]	31.70	264.28	101.26	3,080.20	3,641	198,078
Long Island Lighting[a](RC)	21.93	189.10	62.66	2,032.14	2,260	138,086
Central Hudson G&E[a]	21.42	156.24	n.a.	n.a.	n.a.	n.a.
Orange and Rockland[a]	26.48	215.95	n.a.	n.a.	n.a.	n.a.
Niagara Mohawk	13.47	89.89	47.18	1,500.33	1,530	80,048
N.Y. State E&G	15.42	106.59	54.25	1,314.14	1,562	76,917
Rochester G&E	12.72	87.07	57.38	1,215.17	1,524	56,732
PSE&G (NJ)[a]	20.62	164.25	79.72	2,080.49	2,036	98,380
Philadelphia Electric (NC)[a]	18.68	181.13	85.34	2,333.15	2,027	123,968
Penn. P&L	14.18	87.93	51.05	1,171.89	1,340	67,463
Penn. Electric (R)[a]	16.62	119.01	51.19	1,534.69	1,791	84,997
Metropolitan Edison (R)[a]	16.62	121.88	56.53	1,351.95	1,499	91,330
Baltimore G&E[a]	16.06	124.43	64.71	1,478.05	1,716	63,597
Delmarva P&L (DE)[a]	22.54	161.67	87.55	2,117.58	2,150	122,214
Potomac Electric DC[a]	11.01	114.39	57.10	1,819.94	2,025	99,330
Potomac Electric (VA)[a]	15.46	131.10	54.87	1,895.65	2,144	111,153
Potomac Electric (MD)[a]	17.05	126.92	57.89	1,833.05	1,992	108,108
Duquesne Light (R)[a]	18.61	142.72	72.96	1,703.97	2,104	94,005

Table 7B-1 continued

	Residential		Commercial		Industrial	
	250 kWh	2500 kWh	6kW 750kWh	100kW 30,000kWh	150kW 30,000kWh	5,000kW 2.5m kWh
Appalachian Power (VA)	14.12	93.89	41.81	1,261.48	1,522	74,334
Appalachian Power (WV)	13.18	87.41	42.88	1,265.41	1,275	68,319
Ohio Power	13.50	85.87	47.84	1,258.58	1,346	68,839
Indiana and Michigan (IN)	15.99	89.43	51.77	1,374.72	1,229	78,627
Columbus and S. Ohio[a]	15.56	137.74	53.04	1,708.75	1,838	91,951
Ohio Edison	17.72	121.36	62.43	1,740.11	1,803	84,406
Cleveland Elect. Illum[a]	17.94	151.92	51.16	1,831.36	2,028	106,182
Dayton P&L	16.93	99.78	52.25	1,302.24	1,501	79,825
Cincinnati G&E	13.43	82.75	50.72	1,284.91	1,452	76,689
Toledo Edison[a]	19.87	159.00	73.26	2,133.34	2,179	104,413
Public Service Co. of Ind.	17.20	84.85	51.51	1,211.90	1,251	69,304
No. Ind. P.S.	17.73	108.29	63.97	1,734.23	1,753	95,998
So. Ind. G&E	14.73	102.91	50.87	1,162.40	1,229	72,003
Indianapolis P&L	12.89	74.28	44.58	1,171.51	1,172	79,523
Kentucky Utilities	12.55	78.16	41.68	1,017.40	1,093	62,755
Louisville G&E[a]	11.93	101.28	37.61	1,235.30	1,126	65,239
Consumers Power	15.76	143.39	59.63	1,846.20	1,984	116,575
Detroit Edison	13.71	105.82	44.62	1,572.26	1,572	85,743
Virginia E&P[a]	20.06	169.84	62.13	1,860.22	2,122	111,866
Duke Power NC (R)[a]	12.91	95.72	46.11	1,090.55	1,191	64,004
Carolina P&L NC (R)[a]	15.09	95.65	42.90	968.15	1,152	63,710
South Carolina E&G	17.15	123.24	41.37	1,334.80	1,135	75,400
Georgia Power (R)[a]	12.49	119.38	58.40	1,360.10	1,705	69,482
Alabama Power	14.98	99.76	51.77	1,552.59	1,770	77,815
Gulf Power (R)[a]	15.49	109.80	57.93	1,378.88	1,554	88,859

Mississippi Power[a]	14.26	113.33	56.95	1,446.46	1,590	85,600
Memphis	8.50	76.68	32.71	1,044.70	1,321	67,316
Florida P&L	12.94	109.12	58.70	1,481.76	1,618	82,361
Florida Power	13.68	108.99	54.32	1,478.40	1,524	85,244
Tampa Electric	16.40	127.16	51.39	1,543.20	1,706	94,880
Jacksonville	18.88	161.35	56.85	2,003.50	2,001	13,370
Mississippi P&L	17.79	107.41	56.52	1,479.62	1,585	93,596
Arkansas P&L (R)[a]	16.43	104.19	49.85	1,270.86	1,273	71,904
LA P&L Other LA (R)[a]	11.58	81.88	43.42	1,020,63	1,042	63,045
LA P&L New Orleans (R)[a]	10.13	67.32	39.05	846.02	872	48,495
New Orleans PS (R)[a]	11.11	87.56	54.99	1,296.70	1,437	76,518
Gulf States Util. (LA)	12.79	82.58	45.49	1,071.33	1,158	71,904
Gulf States Util. (TX)[a]	15.79	128.13	47.31	1,413.21	1,506	95,961
PS Oklahoma[a]	13.08	78.10	42.02	1,402.65	1,278	68,152
SW Elec. Power (TX) (R)[a]	11.32	80.62	39.01	863.20	1,791	51,239
W Texas Utilities (R)[a]	13.51	98.86	42.57	1,203.61	1,273	72,893
Central P&L	15.04	97.66	47.91	1,380.84	1,631	88,053
Oklahoma G&E[a]	12.61	97.12	47.00	1,422.66	1,317	67,227
Dallas P&L (R)[a]	15.32	114.47	45.74	1,259.85	1,412	74,261
Texas P&L (R)[a]	14.46	104.47	56.52	1,294.38	1,494	69,302
Texas Elec. Service (R)[a]	14.62	99.02	43.02	1,005.50	1,271	56,202
Houston L&P[a]	16.17	113.13	50.85	1,250.45	1,409	78,728
SWPS (TX) (R)	16.73	126.78	55.39	1,420.46	1,641	90,038
Commonwealth Edison[a]	17.17	143.40	58.03	1,736.00	1,917	90,584
Illinois Power[a]	14.88	123.47	50.34	1,465.89	1,729	73,556
Central Illinois PS[a]	20.11	171.62	n.a.	n.a.	n.a.	n.a.
Central Illinois Light[a]	18.62	154.77	65.89	2,009.39	2,183	105,550
Union Electric (R)[a]	13.68	111.28	60.51	1,296.81	1,297	73,473
Wisconsin Elec. Power[a]	15.63	137.25	54.75	1,905.00	1,967	82,245
Wisconsin P&L	13.89	108.86	35.62	1,314.00	1,281	70,320
Wisconsin PS[a]	14.17	108.86	41.92	1,414.67	1,410	78,128
No. States Power (MN)[a]	13.65	120.56	39.49	1,221.99	1,446	74,362
So. Cal. Edison	11.93	135.41	56.05	1,589.90	1,795	112,325
Pacific G&E (RI)[a]	9.75	106.76	38.91	1,261.60	1,361	93,741
Los Angeles (R)[a]	15.20	151.95	43.79	1,514.40	1,527	145,717

Table 7B-1 continued

	Residential		Commercial		Industrial	
	250 kWh	*2500 kWh*	*6kW 750kWh*	*100kW 30,000kWh*	*150kW 30,000kWh*	*5,000kW 2.5m kWh*
San Diego G&E[a]	13.54	165.94	56.75	1,976.39	2,026	140,782
Sacramento[a]	8.19	53.06	23.50	638.75	754	33,858
Pacific P&L (OR)[b]	9.68	69.75	27.81	704.05	785	51,584
Pacific P&L (WY)	8.04	65.55	29.94	719.95	786	33,708
Portland Gen. Elec.[b]	10.39	76.85	32.92	1,061.81	1,206	76,735
Utah P&L	19.09	96.36	73.70	1,500.90	1,390	70,028
Idaho Power	9.43	56.43	33.72	766.20	907	34,354
Montana Power	8.45	64.26	34.50	644.17	725	35,285
Seattle[b]	3.65	31.76	15.38	407.25	434	16,258
Washington Water Power	6.58	42.95	20.09	624.49	686	33,509
Arizona PC (RC)[b]	19.92	142.36	59.30	1,722.85	1,942	98,675
Salt River Project[b]	20.33	135.96	55.12	1,687.25	1,933	91,365
PS of Colorado[b]	14.11	96.58	42.73	1,315.88	1,403	70,396
Nevada Power	11.62	98.20	35.07	1,373.53	1,524	103,196
PS of NM (R)[b]	18.01	149.22	59.57	1,757.78	1,950	124,835
El Paso Elec. (TX)(R)[b]	18.45	143.70	61.94	1,660.23	2,036	109,350

[a]Summer rate.
[b]Winter rate.
(R) Residential seasonal rate only.
(RC) Residential commercial seasonal rates.
(RI) Residential and industrial rates.
n.a. not available.
Except for Long Island Lighting, for which the most prevalent rate is shown, rates for multirate companies are for largest city served.

Appendix 7C:
Estimating the Costs
of Electric Power

The literature on electric-power costs is predominantly concerned with generation, and the subissue of optimum choices of base-load plants has been the principal concern. This tendency was produced by the continuing debate over the social economics of nuclear power. Extension of the work has been inspired by the rise of large-scale energy market models. Such models require as inputs estimates of many elements of electric-power costs and are designed to determine fuel prices implied by the assumptions made about market conditions.

The most publicly available work of this type is the "medium-term" energy-market modeling of the U.S. government. This work began in 1974 with the Project Independence Evaluation System (PIES) developed by the Federal Energy Administration (FEA). When DOE was established in 1977, Congress required that DOE's EIA incorporate energy forecasts in its annual report to Congress. PIES was transformed into the Midrange Energy Forecasting System (MEFS) to provide projections for 1985, 1990, and 1995. The model uses linear programming to determine the socially efficient pattern of energy consumption, given demand-and-supply functions for energy. The annual reports to Congress have differed considerably in the amount of detail provided about inputs and outputs; the 1981 data used here cover capital costs and nonfuel operating costs (see table 7C-1).

Table 7C-1
1981 DOE Estimates of Electric-Power Costs in the United States

Fuel	Costs of Major Options (1979 dollars) Capital Charges ($ per kilowatt per year)	Operating and Management (mills per kWh)
Coal	107.9	2.5
Lignite	99.8	2.5
Residual fuel Oil	76.6	0.9
Natural gas	76.6	0.5
Distillate fuel oil	57.2	2.8
Nuclear	117.0	7.3

Table 7C-1 continued

	Fossil-Fuel Capital Cost (1979 dollars per installed kW)
Fuel	*Cost*
Low-sulfur bituminous	930
Medium-sulfur bituminous	940
High-sulfur bituminous	1000
Low-sulfur subbituminous	1015
Medium-sulfur subbituminous	1025
Low-sulfur lignite	1010
Medium-sulfur lignite	1050
Combined cycle	405
Gas turbine	175
Oil-fired steam turbine	600

	Nuclear Plant Costs by Region (dollars per kW)		
DOE Region	*Low*	*Medium*	*High*
1. New England	1,155	1,285	1,505
2. New York and New Jersey	1,055	n.a.	n.a.
4. East South Central, NC, SC, GA, FL	970	1,085	1,340
5. East North Central, MN	1,205	1,340	1,620
6. West South Central, NM	1,010	1,120	1,390
7. KS, MO, NB,	1,265	1,400	n.a.
9. CA, NV, AZ	990	1,100	1,290
10. WA, OR, ID	1,525	n.a.	n.a.
United States	1,085	1,205	1,450

Source: U.S. Department of Energy, Energy Information Administration, 1981, *1980 Annual Report to Congress,* vol. 3, Forecasts, pp. 262, 273, 274, respectively.

Notes: Nuclear costs are not provided for regions 3 and 8 because nuclear is presumed uncompetitive for new units.

The n.a.'s for the regions relate to cases in which nuclear is deemed uncompetitive.

More detailed data are collected by ICF, Inc., for use in its coal and electric utilities model, originally developed for FEA and currently used by ICF in work for various government and private clients. These data are periodically compiled into an ICF summary of the model, and the data as of mid-1980 were made available to me. These data combine basic cost estimates developed during work for the Electric Power Research Institute with detailed work on pollution control costs developed during work by the Environmental Protection Agency.

ICF adds considerable detail. While EIA shows regional cost differences only for nuclear plants, ICF provides such regional distinctions for many other variables. ICF divides nonenvironmental operating costs into a component that is fixed per kilowatt of capacity and a component that varies with generation. The analysis of sulfur-dioxide pollution-control costs estimates the effect of differences in sulfur content on costs. Table 2C-1 summarizes the key EIA data, and table 7C-2 lists ICF's figures.

On the basis of these data, tables 7C-3 and 7C-4 present a range of estimates on nuclear and coal costs. Table 7C-5 shows data on oil-fired generation. The first half of the table indicates the cost per kilowatt hour implied by various oil prices and the heat rates for oil plants reported in table 7C-2. These costs so greatly exceed the costs of coal or nuclear generation that oil is likely to be competitive only at low levels of capacity utilization. Total cost figures are presented only for 5 and 10 percent operating rates. Not surprisingly, the data suggest that the choice between coal or nuclear power is not clear-cut. Two steps are needed to convert these data into the estimates of weighted average expansion costs. First, some method is needed to determine weights for generation types. Then nongenerating costs must be estimated and added.

The weighting is developed by using other data available from ICF. ICF divides generation into four types: base load, intermediate load, seasonal peak, and daily peak. Data are provided on the utilization rates and contribution of each plant type. These data are consistent with many different load-duration curves and so cannot be used to deduce optimal prices. However, weighted average costs can be computed. Table 7C-6 takes a range of utilization rates and shares in generation and deduces the implied shares in capacity. An effort is made to suggest the impact of variable prices and load management in flattening-load curves. Table 7C-7 uses the weights from table 7C-6 and capital costs from prior tables to estimate weighted average costs per kilowatt of efficient expansion. Table 7C-8 parts 1 and 3 then shows the annual and levelized capital costs associated with various capital costs, capital-charge factors, and utilization rates. The charge rates range from 20 to 24 percent. This provides a rough adjustment of the constant dollar factors shown for the 8 percent inflation rate of 1979. The capacity factors range from 45 to 55 percent. In table 7C-8 part 2, estimates are made of weighted average fuel and other operating costs. The ranges in tables 7C-8 part 1 and 7C-8 part 2 are combined in table 7C-8 part 3 to provide ranges of generating costs.

Table 7C–2
ICF, Inc., Estimates of Nonfuel Cost of Electric-Power Generation

	North-east	South-east	East Central	West Central	South Central	Pacific and Mountain
Coal-Fired Plants Capital Costs in $/kWh						
Capital cost of bituminous coal plant under 1971 regulations	756	622	716	689	627	720
Capital cost with 1979 regulations						
Coal with less than 0.83 lb. S/MM Btu	819	685	779	752	690	783
Coal with 0.84 to 1.67 lb. S/MM Btu	880	746	840	813	751	907
Coal with 1.68 to 2.50 lb. S/MM Btu	890	756	850	823	761	917
Coal with more than 2.50 lb. S/MM Btu	892	558	852	825	763	919
Cost increase if subbituminous burned	75	57	71	63	58	67
Cost increase if lignite burned	77	211	117	140	208	115
Coal-Fired Plant Fixed Operating Costs in $/kW/year						
Bituminous	10.17	8.45	9.02	9.02	8.88	9.31
Subbituminous	11.03	9.31	9.88	9.88	9.74	10.17
Lignite	10.17	10.17	10.17	10.17	9.88	9.88
Coal-Fired Plant Variable Operating Costs in Mills/kWh						
Basic Costs	0.14	0.28	0.56	0.42	0.42	0.42
Bituminous	0.07	0.14	0.28	0.28	0.28	0.28
Subbituminous	0.28	0.28	0.28	0.28	0.28	0.28
Scrubber Operating Costs						
Coal with less than 0.83 lb. S/MM Btu	1.69	1.69	1.69	1.69	1.69	1.69
Coal with 0.84 to 1.67 lb. S/MM Btu	2.04	2.04	2.04	2.04	2.04	2.04
Coal with 1.68 to 2.50 lb. S/MM Btu	2.36	2.36	2.36	2.36	2.36	2.36
Coal with more than 2.5 lb. S/MM Btu	2.65	2.65	2.65	2.65	2.65	2.65
Heat Rates for Coal Options (Btu/kWh)						
Base-load bituminous						
Under 1971 rules	9592	9643	9693	9967	9920	9722
0.5% penalty	9640	9691	9741	10017	9970	9771
3.75% penalty	9952	10005	10056	10341	10292	10087
3.80% penalty	9956	10009	10061	10346	10297	10091
Intermediate-load bituminous						
Under 1971 rules	9922	9975	10028	10311	10262	10109
0.5% penalty	9972	10015	10078	10363	10313	10160
3.75% penalty	10294	10349	10404	10698	10647	10488
3.80% penalty	10299	10354	10409	10703	10052	10493
Seasonal peak-load bituminous						
Under 1971 rules	10584	10640	10696	10999	10946	10783
0.5% penalty	10673	10693	10749	11054	11001	10837
3.75% penalty	10981	11039	11097	11411	11356	11187
3.80% penalty	10986	11044	11102	11417	11362	11193

Table 7C–2 continued

	North-east	South-east	East Central	West Central	South Central	Pacific and Mountain
Base-load subbituminous						
Under 1971 rules	*9863*	*9915*	*9967*	*10049*	*10200*	*10049*
0.5% penalty	9912	9965	10017	10099	10251	10099
3.75% penalty	10233	10287	10341	10426	10583	10426
3.80% penalty	10238	10292	10346	10431	10588	10431
Intermediate-load subbituminous						
Under 1971 rules	10203	10257	10311	10395	10552	10396
0.5% penalty	10254	10398	10363	10447	10575	10448
3.75% penalty	10586	10642	10698	10785	10917	10786
3.80% penalty	10591	10647	10703	10790	10992	10791
Seasonal peak-load subbituminous						
Under 1971 rules	10884	10941	10999	11088	11255	11089
0.5% penalty	10983	10996	11054	11143	11311	11144
3.75% penalty	11291	11381	11411	11503	11677	11505
3.80% penalty	11298	10357	11417	11509	11683	11510
Base-load lignite						
Under 1971 rules	n.a.	n.a.	n.a.	10695	10559	n.a.
0.5% penalty	n.a.	n.a.	n.a.	10748	10612	n.a.
3.75% penalty	n.a.	n.a.	n.a.	11096	10955	n.a.
3.80% penalty	n.a.	n.a.	n.a.	11101	10960	n.a.
Intermediate-load lignite						
Under 1971 rules	n.a.	n.a.	n.a.	11064	10923	n.a.
0.5% penalty	n.a.	n.a.	n.a.	11119	10987	n.a.
3.75% penalty	n.a.	n.a.	n.a.	11479	11333	n.a.
3.80% penalty	n.a.	n.a.	n.a.	·11484	11338	n.a.
Seasonal peak-load lignite						
Under 1971 rules	n.a.	n.a.	n.a.	11802	11657	n.a.
0.5% penalty	n.a.	n.a.	n.a.	11861	11709	n.a.
3.75% penalty	n.a.	n.a.	n.a.	12245	12088	n.a.
3.80% penalty	n.a.	n.a.	n.a.	12250	12094	n.a.
Capital Costs for Other Options (dollars/kW)						
Gas turbine	203	196	203	203	196	203
Combined cycle	378	378	378	378	378	378
Nuclear	1140	960	1061	1014	987	1054
Fixed Operating Costs for Other Options (dollars/kW/year)						
Gas turbine	3.44	3.01	3.29	3.15	2.86	3.15
Combined cycle	4.30	4.15	4.30	4.30	4.30	4.30
Nuclear	4.07	3.49	3.87	3.72	3.58	3.87
Variable Operating Cost for Nuclear Plants (mills/kWh)						
Nuclear	0.07	0.14	0.42	0.28	0.28	0.28

Table 7C-2 continued

Heat Rates for Noncoal Options
(Btu/kWh)

	National
Nuclear	10400
Base-combined cycle	8600
Intermediate load-combined cycle	8600
Seasonal peak-combined cycle	10000
Daily peak combined cycle	15000
Intermediate-load gas turbine	12500
Seasonal peak-gas turbine	13000
Daily peak-gas turbine	15000

Source: ICF, Inc., *Coal and Electric Utilities Model Documentation* (Washington, D.C., 1980). Reprinted with permission.

n.a: not available.

Table 7C-3
Cost Estimates for Nuclear Power

	Low	*Medium*	*High*
Capital cost ($/kW)	1000	1500	2000
Annual charge (percent)	12	12	14
Annual charge (dollars)	120	180	280
Levelized cost/kWh (mills)			
at 75 %	18.3	27.4	42.6
70%	19.6	29.4	45.7
65%	21.1	31.6	49.2
60%	22.8	34.2	53.3
55%	24.9	37.4	58.1
50%	27.4	41.1	63.9
45%	30.4	45.7	71.0
40%	34.2	51.4	79.9
Operating costs (mills kWh)	0.1	0.3	0.3
Fuel (mills/kWh)	4.0	5.0	8.0
Total costs (mills/kWh)(rounded)			
75%	22	33	51
70%	24	35	54
65%	25	37	58
60%	27	40	62
55%	29	43	66
50%	32	46	72
45%	34	51	79
40%	38	57	88

Table 7C–4
Cost Estimates for Coal-Fired Plants

	Low	Medium	High
Capital cost ($/kW)	600	800	1000
Annual charge (percent)	12	12	14
Annual charge (dollars)	72	96	140
Levelized cost/kWh (mills)			
at 75 %	11.0	14.6	21.3
70%	11.7	15.7	22.8
65%	12.6	16.9	24.6
60%	13.7	18.4	26.6
55%	14.9	19.9	29.1
50%	16.4	21.9	32.0
45%	18.3	24.4	35.5
40%	20.5	27.4	40.0
30%	27.4	36.5	53.3
20%	41.1	54.8	79.9
10%	82.2	109.6	159.8
Operating costs (mills kWh)	2.0	2.5	3.0
Fuel (mills/kWh)	10.0	15.0	20.0
Total costs (mills/kWh)(rounded)			
75%	23	32	44
70%	24	33	46
65%	25	34	48
60%	26	36	50
55%	27	37	52
50%	28	39	55
45%	30	42	59
40%	33	45	63
30%	39	54	76
20%	53	72	103
10%	94	127	183

Table 7C–5
Oil-Generation Costs

Oil Price per Million Btu	Oil Cost per kWh for Selected Heat Rates and Oil Prices (mills)				
	Heat Rate				
	8,600	10,000	12,500	13,000	15,000
5.00	43.0	50.0	62.5	65.0	75.0
5.50	47.3	55.0	68.8	71.5	82.5
6.00	51.6	60.0	75.0	78.0	90.0
6.50	55.9	65.0	81.3	84.5	97.5
7.00	60.2	70.0	87.5	91.0	105.0
7.50	64.5	75.0	93.8	97.7	112.5
8.00	68.8	80.0	100.0	104.0	120.0

Table 7C–5 continued

	Total Costs			
	10% Utilization		*5% Utilization*	
Capital cost ($/kW)	175	200	175	2000
Capital charge rate per year	.12	.14	.12	.14
Hours per year	876	876	438	438
Cost (mills/kWh)	24	32	48	64
DOE estimate of operating costs		3		3
ICF's $3/year divided by hours of operation	1		1	
Fuel cost in mills/kWh	50	100	50	100
Total cost in mills/kWh	75	135	99	157

Table 7C–6
The Effect of Capacity Factors and Generation Shares on Plant Mix

		Total	Base	Inter-mediate	Seasonal Peak	Daily Peak
Case 1						
1	Percent of output	100	70	20	6	4
2	Utilization rate	.377	.60	.45	.25	.05
3	Hours (2 × 8760)	3304	5256	3942	2190	438
4	Capacity per kWh (1–3)	.000303	.000133	.000051	.000027	.000091
5	Percent of total capacity	100.00	44.01	16.76	9.05	30.18
Case 2						
1	Percent of output	100	70	20	8	4
2	Utilization rate	.390	.65	.45	.25	.05
3	Hours (2 × 8760)	3420	5694	3942	2190	438
4	Capacity per kWh (1–3)	.000292	.000123	.000051	.000027	.000091
5	Percent of total capacity	100.00	42.04	17.35	9.37	31.23
Case 3						
1	Percent of output	100	75	18	5	2
2	Utilization rate	.444	.60	.45	.25	.05
3	Hours (2 × 8760)	3893	5256	3942	2190	438
4	Capacity per kWh (1–3)	.000257	.000143	.000046	.000023	.000046
5	Percent of total capacity	100.00	55.55	17.78	8.89	17.79
Case 4						
1	Percent of output	100	80	14	4	2
2	Utilization rate	.454	.60	.45	.25	.05
3	Hours (2 × 8760)	3974	5256	3942	2190	438
4	Capacity per kWh (1–3)	.000252	.000152	.000036	.000018	.000046
5	Percent of total capacity	100.00	60.48	14.11	7.26	18.15

Table 7C-6 continued

	Total	Base	Inter-mediate	Seasonal Peak	Daily Peak
Case 5					
1 Percent of output	100	80	14	4	2
2 Utilization rate	.499	.60	.45	.25	.10
3 Hours (2 × 8760)	4370	5256	3942	2190	876
4 Capacity per kWh (1–3)	.000229	.000152	.000036	.000018	.000023
5 Percent of total capacity	100.00	66.52	15.52	7.98	9.98

Notes: The overall utilization rate shown in the first column of line 2 is calculated as 1 divided by 8760 times the total capacity per kilowatt hour.

Note that the total capacity on line 4 is the sum of the capacity for the individual plant types.

Table 7C-7
Estimated Average Cost per Kilowatt of Generation Capacity
(dollars)

Cases with Coal in Base, Intermediate, and Seasonal Peak, Oil in Daily Peak			
	Coal	*Oil*	*Weighted Average*
Weight in total	80	20	100
cost	600	200	n.a.
weighted cost	480	40	520
cost	700	200	n.a.
weighted cost	560	40	600
cost	800	200	n.a.
weighted cost	640	40	680
cost	900	200	n.a.
weighted cost	720	40	760
cost	1000	200	n.a.
weighted cost	800	40	840
Weight in total	90	10	
cost	600	200	n.a.
weighted cost	540	20	560
cost	700	200	n.a.
weighted cost	630	20	650
cost	800	200	
weighted cost	720	20	740
cost	900	200	n.a.
weighted cost	810	20	830
cost	1000	200	n.a.
weighted cost	900	20	920

Table 7C–7 continued

	Base	Intermediate		Seasonal Peak		Daily Peak
					Combined	
		Nuclear	Coal	Coal	Cycle	Turbine
	(1)	(2)	(3)	(4)	(5)	(6)
Weight	40	20	20	10	10	30
Case 1						
Cost	1000	1000	600	600	400	200
Weighted Cost	400	200	120	60	40	60
Case 2						
Cost	1000	1000	700	700	400	200
Weighted cost	400	200	140	70	40	60
Case 3						
Cost	1000	1000	800	800	400	200
Weighted cost	400	200	160	80	40	60
Case 4						
Cost	1000	1000	900	900	400	200
Weighted cost	400	200	180	90	40	60
Case 5						
Cost	1200	1200	600	600	400	200
Weighted cost	480	240	120	60	40	60
Case 6						
Cost	1200	1200	900	900	400	200
Weighted cost	480	240	180	90	40	60
Case 7						
Weight	65	15	15	10	10	10
Cost	1000	1000	600	600	400	200
Weighted cost	650	150	90	60	40	20
Case 8						
Cost	1200	1200	600	600	400	200
Weighted cost	780	180	90	60	40	20
Case 9						
Cost	1500	1500	600	600	400	200
Weighted cost	975	225	90	60	40	20
Case 10						
Cost	1500	1500	900	900	400	200
Weighted cost	975	225	135	90	40	20

The header spanning row "Cases with Nuclear and Combined Cycle" covers the Base, Intermediate, and Seasonal Peak columns.

Table 7C-7 continued

Case	High Nuclear Low Coal (1 + 2 + 4 + 6)	Weighted Average Costs Low Nuclear High Coal (1 + 3 + 4 + 6)	Low Nuclear Low Coal Combined Cycle (1 + 3 + 5 + 6)
1	720	640	620
2	730	670	640
3	740	700	660
4	750	730	680
5	840	720	700
6	870	810	760
7	880	820	800
8	1040	950	930
9	1280	1145	1125
10	1310	1220	1170

n.a.: not applicable.

Table 7C-8
Levelized Costs of Generation

Charge	Annual Charge (dollars/kW) 500	600	700	800	900	1000	1100	1200	1300
20	100	120	140	160	180	200	220	240	260
22	110	132	154	176	198	220	242	264	286
24	120	144	168	192	216	240	264	288	312

Annual Charge	Levelized Cost (mills/kWh) Utilization Rate 55%	50%	45%
100	20.76	22.83	26.37
125	25.94	28.54	31.71
150	31.13	34.25	38.05
175	36.32	39.95	44.39
200	41.51	45.50	50.74
225	46.70	51.37	57.08
250	51.89	57.08	63.42
300	62.27	68.49	76.10
325	67.46	74.20	82.45
350	72.64	79.91	88.79
375	77.83	85.62	95.13
400	83.02	91.32	101.47

Table 7C-8 continued

	Coal	Oil	Total Fuel	Nonfuel	Total Operating
Weight	98	2			
Cost	10	90			
Weighted cost	9.8	1.8	11.6	2.0	13.6
Cost	15	90			
Weighted cost	14.7	1.8	16.5	2.5	19.0
Cost	20	90			
Weighted cost	19.6	1.8	21.4	3.0	24.4

	Nuclear	Coal	Oil	Total Fuel	Nonfuel	Total Operating
Weight	70	28	2			
Cost	4	10	90			
Weighted cost	2.8	2.8	1.8	7.4	0.60	8.00
Cost	5	15	90			
Weighted cost	3.5	4.2	1.8	9.5	0.75	10.25
Cost	6	20	90			
Weighted cost	4.2	5.6	1.8	11.60	0.90	12.50
Weight	80	18	2			
Cost	4.	10	90			
Weighted cost	3.2	1.8	1.8	6.8	0.40	7.20
Cost	5	15	90			
Weighted cost	4.0	2.7	1.8	8.5	0.50	9.00
Cost	6	20	90			
Weighted cost	4.8	3.6	1.8	10.20	0.60	10.80

The ranges are deliberately broad. The most optimistic figures in the tables call for 21 mills of capital costs and 14 mills operating costs for a predominantly coal system for a total of 35 mills. However, a 35-mill capital cost representing $800 in system investment per kW at 22 percent and a 50 percent utilization factor is a more appropriate, realistic minimum as is a 19-mill operating cost for a 54-mill total. The low for a nuclear system would be about 25 mills in capital costs (from levelizing $700 at 55 percent utilization and a 20 percent charge). Adding 7 mills of operating costs yields a total of 32 mills. With an $800 cost levelized at 22 percent and 50 percent operations, the capital cost is 40 mills and the operating cost about 10 mills, for a 50-mill total. Thus, the minimum cost is 30–35 mills, and the more likely level is at least 50–55 mills because the minimum involves overly optimistic assumptions.

The handling of nongenerating costs is hindered by the absence of data and the complex indirect relationship between these costs and generation levels. The costs support delivery of electricity. As has been suggested, delivery costs will differ among customer types. At one extreme, the transmission component of nongenerating costs involves a substantial component that links new capacity with its users. However, the creation of transmission lines for diversity and emergency interchange can occur independently of capacity growth. Transmission can be increased to allow location nearer fuel source or simply away from urban congestion. Distribution involves a customer-number related component, a portion attributable to the special expenses of serving those who need to have voltages reduced before delivery, and some costs that are proportional to capacity delivered to a given type of customer. It would be expected that such other costs as customer service and administration would differ with customer type but would vary within each type more with the number of customer than with the amount of consumption.

Most formal studies of electric power involve extremely simple models of generating costs. The only systematic discussion in the public literature is that done for the 1979 Baughman-Joskow-Kamat model of electric power; nongenerating costs were more fully discussed in a separate paper by Baughman and Bottaro (1975). They undertook regression analysis of the determinants of nongenerating costs. A pooled time-series cross-section approach was used, covering forty-seven regions for the years 1965–1971; the regions were the coterminous forty-eight states with the District of Columbia combined with Maryland. Nebraska was omitted because of the absence of privately-owned companies. Regressions were calculated for six types of equipment: miles of transmission lines, transmission-substation capacity, miles of distribution poles, distribution-substation capacity, line-transformer capacity, and number of meters. Separate regressions were calculated for cash cost of transmission, distribution, and other costs. The independent variables considered in the investment cases included total sales in kilowatt hours, the residential-commercial portion of sales, the industrial portion, the number of customers in each of the two customer groups, the size of the region, and the kilowatt hours sold per square mile (load density). The cash expenses were related to the number of customers and sales volume in the residential-commercial and industrial sectors. Different combinations of these variables proved significantly to influence different components. The miles of transmission lines were a function of total sales, size, and load density, and transmission substations were a function of sales to the two customer types. Meter numbers depended on customer numbers (one to a residential or commercial customer and fourteen to an industrial).

To determine the capital-related costs per kilowatt hour of sales to each of the two customer types, estimates of costs of specific equipment were combined with estimates of the required amounts to produce the investment figure. These costs were then converted to the annual required receipts and allocated between customer groups. A per-kilowatt-hour figure was produced by dividing costs by kilowatt-hour.

A Case Study

National Economic Research Associates (NERA) made available testimony (Ambrose 1980) prepared for an Arizona Public Service Company rate hearing. This report presents estimates of nongenerating costs. Load-related transmission capital costs per kilowatt were estimated by dividing expected expenditures from 1980 to 1989 by the expected increase in load over the same period. The resulting cost is $94.13 per kW. Load-related distribution capital costs are calculated by deducting from the total costs incurred by adding customers and dividing the remainder by the load increase. A distinction is made between the primary and secondary systems. The latter differs from the former because of the need to add transformers and other additional facilities. The calculations begin with estimated outlays, and customer-related costs are deducted. The remainder is divided by load growth to yield an estimated cost of $185.73 per kW. Then the cost of load-related secondary distribution is computed, again by starting with total investment. The consumer costs are deducted. The remainder is divided by 78 percent of load growth, the portion of load served by the secondary system, representing a $35 per kW cost. Operating and maintenance costs for transmission are estimated by dividing cost by peak demand for 1974 to 1979. These were then inflated to 1980 dollars. This implies a cost of $1.53 per KW. Distribution operating and maintenance costs are deemed to be 60 percent customer related and 40 percent demand related. By dividing allocated costs by customer numbers and load, and adjusting to 1980 dollars, costs of $21.64 per customer and $2.44 per kW are estimated.

Customer-account costs are argued to vary with customer mumber and type. The average effect of larger customers on costs is equivalent to increasing numbers by 16 percent. The basic cost is estimated at $17.28 per customer and is argued to be the actual cost for residential customers. Small general-service customers would cost twice as much ($34.56) to serve. A medium-generation service customer would be served at quadruple the residential cost: $62.12. Finally, a fifteenfold cost rise to $759.20 occurs for large general-service and industrial customers (Ambrose 1980).

Cost Recapitulation

Table 7C–9 summarizes the Baughman-Bottaro national average figures. Their capital costs are inflated to 1979 dollars, and then weighted averages are computed for a range of weights based on table 7A–1. The resulting figures are divided by the capital-charge factor used by Baughman and Bottaro and multiplied by the 1972 average hours of utilization implicit in DOE data on private utilities. This indicates a capital-cost range of $400–$450

($1979) per kW—a range reasonably consistent with the NERA estimate. The assumption that nongenerating capital costs are 55–100 percent of generating capital costs would make $400 a minimum estimate. The inflation and weighting of operating costs gives a 4.5–5.5 mill range reasonably consistent with the national average for 1979. Levelizing the capital costs suggests 20–25 mills in costs. Therefore, total nongenerating costs average approximately 25–30 mills.

Table 7C–9
Nongenerating Costs Estimated from Baughman-Bottaro Estimates

	Calculation of Implicit Capital Investment			
	Residential and Commercial	Industrial	Weighted Average (mills/kWh)	Capital Cost ($/kW) 13.5% Annual Charge 50% Use
Cost inflated to 1979$ (mills/kWh)	16.8	8.0		
Weight	50%	50%		
Weighted costs (mills/kWh)	8.4	4.0	12.4	402
Weight	55%	45%		
Weighted costs (mills/kWh)	9.2	3.6	12.8	417
Weight	60%	40%		
Weighted costs (mills/kWh)	10.1	3.2	13.3	431
Weight	65%	35%		
Weighted costs (mills/kWh)	10.9	2.8	13.7	445

	Annual Costs (dollars/kWh)		
	Total Investment		
Charge Rate	400	425	450
20%	80	85.0	90
22%	88	93.5	99
24%	96	102.0	108

	Levelized Capital Costs (mills/kWh)		
	Utilization Rates		
Annual Cost ($)	55%	50%	45%
80	16.6	18.3	20.3
90	18.7	20.5	22.8
100	20.8	22.8	25.4
110	22.8	25.1	27.9

Table 7C–9 continued

	Operating Costs		
	Residential Commercial	*Industrial*	*Weighted Average*
Baughman-Bottaro Estimates (mills/kWh))1979$)	*8.1*	*1.3*	
Weights	50%	50%	
Weighted costs (mills/kWh)	4.1	0.7	4.7
Weights	55%	45%	
Weighted costs (mills/kWh)	4.5	0.6	5.1
Weights	50%	40%	
Weighted costs (mills/kWh)	4.9	0.5	5.4
Weights	65%	35%	
Weighted costs (mills/kWh)	5.3	0.5	5.7

Total costs, then, would be in the 70–85 mills range—a substantial excess over average rates prevailing in 1979. The minimum possible figure would probably still exceed 60 mills. Calculations of the weighted average revenue for 1979 indicate that only Consolidated Edison with 8.9-cent power and Long Island Lighting with 6.4 percent power have rates above my cost estimates. Given the high distribution costs of these companies, their heavier-than-average proportion of more expensive-to-serve customers, and the fact that my estimate is of the minimum level of marginal costs, even these two New York companies may be underpricing.

The only efforts that have been encountered to provide similar estimates of weighted average costs are those of a group of the Pacific Northwest Laboratory (Nieves et al. 1980). Their procedure is quite different from that used here. They estimate costs by regressions on historical data. Real costs are used instead of nominal ones. They treat the costs of baseload generation instead of those of the whole system. Their estimate (about 6 mills) of nongenerating costs is much lower than that presented here. Their full range of 1980 costs includes those for plants that were built under pre-1977 rules that permit use of low-sulfur coal without scrubbers.

When the cost range for generation in areas in which coal-burning units without scrubbers are not an option is considered, their estimates are in the 4.0–4.7 cent range. A minimum adjustment to convert their figures to nominal costs of the whole system would raise the range to 4.5–5.5 cents. (They estimate that capital costs are 36 percent of the total or about 1.5–1.7 cents. Their assumed utilization rate is about 18–30 percent higher than an appropriate rate for a system, and another 8–10 percent increase is needed to convert from real to nominal capital costs. Thus, capital costs would be

28–43 percent higher or 0.4–0.7 cents higher; an upward rounding gives the 4.5–5.5 cent estimate.)

Use of a higher figure of 1–2 cents for nongenerating costs would then cause their numbers to lie in a range of 5.5–7.5 cents. This is close enough to the 6–8 cent estimate to lie well within the margin of error.

8

Summary and Conclusions on Reforming the Regulation of Electric Utilities

Throughout the 1970s, difficulties encountered by the electric-power industry created fears that the industry might not survive the 1980s in its present form. The basic problems are increasing complexity and rigidity of regulations. Radical reform, possibly including abolition of regulatory agencies, is essential. This chapter reviews the roots of these difficulties, the implications of prevailing trends for the future of the industry, and the potential impacts of various reforms.

The main difficulty is endemic to energy. Energy shifted during the 1970s from an area in which supply-and-demand changes were small and reasonably predictable to one in which a high degree of uncertainty prevailed. Public policy responded by limiting the ability of the industry to react freely to these and other forces.

A primary uncertainty concerns the Organization of Petroleum Exporting Countries' (OPEC) impact on world oil prices. Other uncertainties include inflation, rising real construction costs, and growing concern about the environmental impacts, including those associated with nuclear power, of energy production and use.

Problems have arisen both with policies developed in response to these uncertainties and with the traditional reluctance of public-utility regulators to permit the electric-power industry to pass on cost increases. To complicate matters further, regulatory processes have become so intertwined that jurisdictions have become confused. For example, environmental agencies may encroach on the responsibilities of public-utility regulators and vice versa. The resulting confusion threatens to paralyze electric-power-industry decision making.

Public-Utility Regulation

Public-utility regulation requires that public-utility commissions determine whether cost increases can be passed on to consumers. Thus, the effect of market forces and other regulations on the industry depends on what actions these commissions take.

267

Public-utility regulation abounds with difficulties, particularly the inherent problem of balancing conflicting objectives. Its basic goal is to prevent excess profits without bankrupting the regulated industries. Regulators have erred in either direction. They can be *captured*—become so conscious of the need for utilities to remain profitable that they permit excess profits—or they can be *populists*—become so concerned about preventing excess profits that they imperil industry survival.

The intricacy of regulation generates other uncertainties. Responsibility is shared by the Federal Energy Regulatory Commission (FERC), state commissions, and, in some instances, municipal governments. Any level of government can directly control some aspect of the industry through ownership or indirectly through regulation. Each agency undertakes elaborate procedures to limit profits, such that the prices of electric energy, accounting methods, and even investment decisions all are supervised by regulators. The resulting structure seems unmanageably complex.

Environmental Policy

Excess complexity prevails with environmental regulation. Here federal control over the states is more clear-cut, although federal control is fragmented. For example, federal policies separately cover most air, water, and land-use problems, but a separate program treats all impacts of nuclear energy. Similarly, each policy is quite convoluted. Three different concepts govern air-pollution control: air quality, including prevention of significant deterioration (PSD), visibility concerns, and new source performance standards. The first relates to the concentration of air pollutants in the atmosphere with PSD restricting allowable *increases* in pollution in areas deemed to have high-quality air; the second requires special action to preserve visibility around national parks and wilderness areas that Congress considered to be of aesthetic importance; the third limits pollution from large new facilities.

A basic criticism of existing environmental regulations is that rigid, overly detailed rules are used to control pollution instead of financial incentives. Financial incentives would produce desired ends more rapidly and more cheaply than regulations, whose enforcement tends to be delayed and overly expensive. Moreover, the financial approach—for instance, a tax on emissions—would decentralize the choice of abatement measures, so individual plants could choose the most efficient measures pertinent to their locale, size, and industry. A tax would inspire abatement measures to reduce the tax burden. Some reduction in emissions would occur because a tax discourages production. In addition, a tax higher than the cost of using an efficient abatement technology insures the use of such a technology.

A tax would allow firms to select the mix of output reductions and pollu-tion-control technologies that would most efficiently minimize the cost of abatement.

There are also concerns about the accuracy and reliability of the data on which control goals are based. It is widely agreed that estimates of the impact of various emissions on human health and environmental integrity are poor. More important, a growing number of studies have suggested that the earlier work on which the federal sulfur-dioxide standards were based may have greatly overestimated or misidentified the harm caused by pollu-tion.

Another widespread criticism is that regulations have been used to further irrelevant private interests, particularly those of the eastern coal industry and its laborers. The Clean Air Act Amendments of 1977 are the most frequently mentioned examples. The amendments required use in new sources of the best available control technology (BACT) to clean fuels or capture pollutants before emission. Previous to BACT, it was possible to comply with new source rules for sulfur-dioxide-pollution control by using low-sulfur western coals. BACT's requirement that clean-up technologies, mostly scrubbing devices, be used even with low-sulfur coal was intended to remove or greatly reduce reliance on low-sulfur coal and encourage use of high-sulfur eastern coals.

The amendments also furthered the PSD concept which was intended, among other things, to prevent the flight of industry to presently unpolluted areas. The actual effect of PSD may be quite different. Where it is necessary to meet the revised new source performance standards and the PSD rules *simultaneously*, the only feasible compliance strategy may be to use low-sulfur coal *and* scrubbers. Furthermore, the areas to which PSD rules apply are so broadly defined that many power plants find it more economical to burn low-sulfur western coal. Thus, the efforts to protect local industries may have combined to produce effects opposite to those intended.

Nuclear Regulation

Although nuclear regulation is primarily the responsibility of the U.S. Nuclear Regulatory Commission (NRC), many states have imposed a variety of additional controls. These may involve explicit restrictions on new construction, such as in California, which forbids authorization of new nuclear-plant construction until the state Energy Commission certifies that there is a satisfactory method of nuclear waste disposal. The restrictions on nuclear power may be more subtle; the authority of public-utility commis-sions to forbid construction because a need does not exist could be used effectively to ban nuclear energy for political motives. California's Energy

Commission and New York's Siting Board have used this method to halt nuclear power-plant construction.

Orders for new nuclear units have come to a halt in the United States. Critics contend that nuclear power has become less economic than coal; supporters generally accept that contention but insist that unsound regulation is responsible for artificially higher costs. In particular, nuclear-advocates argue that if NRC acted rapidly to license both the construction and operation of nuclear plants, they would be cheaper to build. The excess costs come from regulatory delays in licensing and frequent imposition of shutdowns on operating plants. The unfavorable investment climate faced by the industry is another, probably more critical influence.

Whatever the contributions of different influences to the problems of nuclear power, it is widely recognized that the NRC is malfunctioning. The commission that investigated the Three Mile Island accident, headed by John G. Kemeny, vigorously presented this view. It noted "a preoccupation with regulations. . . . Once regulations become as complex and as voluminous as those regulations now in place, they can serve as a negative factor in nuclear safety" (President's Commission p. 9). The Kemeny Commission argued that the NRC commissioners do not lead the agency effectively and that the NRC's various divisions are poorly coordinated.

The Kemeny Commission indicated that it was unable to determine what functions the NRC commissioners served and contended that the commissioners themselves did not know. It was further stated that NRC commissioners placed too much stress on their "adjudicative impartiality" and did not supervise the staff sufficiently. The staff, in turn, was characterized as "highly compartmentalized with insufficient communications among the major offices." The Kemeny Commission proposed that the problem be resolved by replacing the five NRC commissioners with a single chairman having undivided responsibility. President Carter chose instead to propose that a strong chairman be appointed while retaining the five commissioners. The implementation of that proposal was greatly delayed by election-year politics, then by delay of the Reagan administration in selecting a chairman. An appointment was not made until May 1981, and no further reforms were made.

By themselves, regulation of air pollution and nuclear power would increase costs for the electric-power industry. If regulatory controls are excessive or deficient, resources will be wasted, and these inefficiencies are of serious concern to society as a whole. However, were public-utility regulation sufficiently responsive, these costs could be passed on to customers without affecting the health of the electric-power industry.

However, the same cannot be said about environmental regulatory *procedures*. Delays in decisions about whether proposed actions comply with regulations present major financial problems for the industry. Furthermore, numerous tiers of control may be added, greatly reducing the ability of the industry to act. The most obvious example is with nuclear power. The inability to secure NRC decisions about licensés for construction and operation greatly increases financial risks. Some companies have invested in such pre-construction activities as site preparation and equipment procurement, only to have construction permits delayed for years; others have spent billions on plants licensed for construction, only to find that operating licenses take years to obtain.

Reform of Public-Utility Regulation

Other problems may prove insignificant compared to the grosser failures of public-utility rate regulation. There is little question that the electric-power industry is seriously ailing. Many companies have curtailed investment because profit prospects are unsatisfactory, and the leading financial-rating services give their highest rating to only a few electric-power companies. Allowed rates of return are too low in face of inflation, and most companies fail to earn even the allowed rate.

The difficulty lies with the reluctance of public-utility commissions to grant proper rate relief. The ratemaking process is ill designed to respond quickly to difficult-to-forecast changes in market conditions. Regulators require lengthy, complex, formal requests for rate relief on the basis of available information, and regulators in many states are not required to consider forecasts of future developments. Rapid response to cost increases is allowed only in the most pressing cases, mainly those of rising fuel costs. Thus, regulation is most responsive to moderate changes that occur infrequently and predictably. The difficulties have been aggravated by the tendency of many regulators to respond slowly and modestly to formal requests for rate relief. It has become necessary in many cases to sue for further relief.

An additional, more technical problem involves the efficiency of rate-of-return regulation. The critical concern is the relationship of rates and *marginal costs*—the costs of efficiently expanding output. These costs are the measure of the cost to society of expanding output. The price of the output, in turn, is the value to society. It is inefficient to expand output unless the increased value is at least as great as the cost increase. Output should be expanded only if marginal costs are less than or equal to the price.

The relationship between average and marginal values is analogous to the average record of an athlete versus his record during a winning streak. The marginal cost of a high-cost-expansion situation, like the performance record during a streak, is much higher than the average. An athlete with 45 wins in his first 100 games who then wins 9 out of his next 10 games has a marginal performance level of .900, an initial average of .450, and an average at the end of 110 games of .491.

The available evidence suggests that basing electric-power rates on average historical costs produces rates that are *below* marginal costs. The historical average includes older plants built when real construction costs were lower and subject to less stringent environmental regulations. The resulting higher costs of new plants compared to existing ones is a major reason why marginal costs exceed average costs.

Land availability problems make units built to provide additional capacity even more expensive than those built to replace existing plants. Electric-power stations need sites with such special characteristics as access to water for cooling waste heat, and siting is greatly influenced by environmental regulations. Therefore, expansion requires use of ever more expensive locations. The cost increase is due less to direct payment for the land than to the increased costs of transmitting electricity over a longer distance; it is often possible to buy land more cheaply in distant locations than near the area being supplied.

Another pressure arises from the impact on fuel and particularly coal costs of expanding electric-power use. Two-thirds of U.S. coal production is used to generate electricity, and substantial expansion in coal use by these utilities could produce higher coal prices. This, in turn, would increase the cost of raising electric-power output.

Efficient Pricing

Marginal costs exceeding average costs implies that rates are too low and regulation may be unnecessary for those sectors of the electric-power industry in which these conditions prevail. Regulation is most frequently justified by the *natural-monopoly argument,* which states that some industries naturally have marginal costs below average costs. A price equal to marginal cost, therefore, will result in losses. It is argued that regulation should be used to prevent losses without unduly enriching firms.

The source of marginal costs below average costs can be illustrated by reversing the prior argument. Where below-average costs are associated with expansion, average costs fall. Continuing the sports analogy, the performance during a slump is below average and lowers the average. Below-average marginal costs, in turn, arise from the advantages, if any, of operating on a larger scale.

The generation of electricity is more likely to encounter marginal costs in excess of average costs. Moreover, because there are many separate generating units, it has become popular to argue that generation is not a natural monopoly and should not be regulated. The same argument can be applied to transmission at least in the numerous regions in which separate lines exist; transmission too is subject to cost-increasing pressures.

Distribution within a community is the only part of the industry in which a natural monopoly exists. However, indirect competition is provided by interfuel competition and by competition among power companies in different regions for electric-power business. These competitive restraints could contribute as much as does regulation to limiting inefficiency in electric-power production and pricing. This argument recognizes that the absence of regulation may produce limited inefficiencies and the presence of regulation may cause even more serious inefficiencies.

The Lights that Will Not Fail

While there will be unpleasant results from the continuation of existing regulatory policies, the outcome may not be the massive power failures envisioned by some. Fear of such outages is heavily influenced by the spectacular (but short and localized) outages of the 1960s. There are many safeguards against such outages. A few areas of the country, notably the Northeast, have so much existing capacity and such limited growth prospects that capacity will not be a problem through the 1980s. Other areas could encounter trouble, but enough units are already under construction to insure sufficient capacity through the mid-1980s. If policies or conditions change, new plants could be built later in the decade to meet demand.

Although regulation could conceivably prevent this capacity from coming-on-line, a more likely reaction would be in the opposite direction, with government actions facilitating expansion. This could involve precipitous retreat from environmental restrictions and provision of financial relief. The financial aid could take at least two forms: rate relief or government financing of capacity expansion. The second route is emerging as an important influence. For example, the Power Authority of the State of New York stepped in to purchase two units from Consolidated Edison during its financial crisis and is seeking to provide expansion capacity for the New York City area. A consortium of newly created cooperatives and municipal utilities purchases shares in plants of Georgia Power. Similar actions were taken with plants under construction elsewhere. Public-power organizations around the United States have moved to expand when private companies have retrenched.

However, the actual pattern of response to capacity issues is difficult to predict. At least until the end of the 1970s, the electric-power industry felt obligated to meet whatever demands emerged. Capacity expansion planning was designed to insure low probabilities of power cutoffs. Only slowly did it become apparent that a new system of rewards and penalties was emerging; the prevailing policies of public-utility commissions encouraged a shift to limited expansion. Commissions now seek to restrict rate increases and may impose the heaviest penalty of all—bankruptcy—on firms undertaking investments that appear excessive after the fact. Incentives increasingly are encouraging conservative expansion programs.

As part of this changed climate, companies are more willing to purchase power from others or promote measures that reduce load growth. Forecasts have been reduced, and some companies are deliberately planning to reduce their margin of reserve capacity.

Advocates of these policies argue that they represent a belated response to previously neglected opportunities. However, given the prevailing anti-expansion regulatory climate, the true situation is not so clear-cut. Shifting from high-growth expectations and from building large, self-owned plants has become essential regardless of the merits of alternative approaches. Therefore, the validity of the alternative view cannot be accurately assessed because the new regulatory bias favors these alternative approaches anyway.

It will take several years for these new responses to work their way into the system. By then or possibly sooner, the basic problems might have been recognized and corrected. Therefore, it is probable that blackouts or other undesirable effects of present trends will be avoided. What the consequences will be if we fail is much less apparent. However, as suggested, overreaction and a massive government bailout are at least as likely as power failures.

Letting Go

Given this climate, the desirability of regulation, particularly of the public-utility type, is becoming increasingly doubtful. One alternative is to deregulate all or part of the industry. Two other basic alternatives have been proposed: reforming the regulatory system, and expanding government financing of electric power. Given the relationship between public-utility regulations and environmental rule making, changes in public-utility regulations may have to be accompanied by reform of environmental policies.

The reform-deregulation distinction is a prevalent issue in the debate over the future of the electric-utility industry. Increased government ownership occupies an anomalous, ironic position in the discussion. Executives of privately owned electric-power companies have begun to see government involvement, once so bitterly opposed as an intrusion on the private sector, as the only possible bailout. Public-power organizations seem to agree. For example, S. David Freeman earlier criticized public-power agencies for behaving like other power companies, but as head of TVA, he became an advocate of continuing to expand capacity to meet both its own needs and those of neighboring, privately-owned power firms (Freeman 1980 and 1981). However, outside observers are not enthusiastic about increased government involvement. For example, the 1980 Pacific Northwest Electric Power Planning and Conservation Act imposed, among other things, limits on the extent to which the Bonneville Power Administration could continue to expand and sell output at a loss.

The critical point of the prevailing debate is whether reform or partial deregulation is preferable. Deregulation is advocated for generation and, in a few cases, for transmission. It is usually presumed that distribution will remain regulated, on the assumption that regulation of distribution is necessary and unlikely to cause major harm. The standard counterargument is that regulation is so entrenched and competition so uncertain that regulatory reform is the preferable alternative.

A special version of the reform argument is that the federal government should increase its role in electric-power regulation. FERC already regulates power sales between companies (with subsidiaries of the same parent considered as separate companies for regulatory purposes). Several New England holding companies have found it desirable to concentrate generation in one subsidiary and have other subsidiaries conduct the distribution. FERC then controls the rates of the generating company and has been more responsive than New England regulators.

FERC authority could be increased to cover most of the industry, although there obviously would be much political opposition to this. State regulators would object. In fact, they already complain that FERC has too much power. So would companies who believe that FERC is less responsive than local commissions (some large utilities in Texas feel so strongly about this issue that they go to elaborate lengths to avoid FERC control, including self-imposition of severe limits on the interstate exchange of power). A real danger of federal control is the usual one of excess concentration of political power. Poor appointments to a FERC that regulated all of U.S. electric power obviously will cause more wide-ranging damages than the defective decisions of any one state.

An additional set of reform arguments, which are related to the management of nuclear power, advocates moves in a different direction. Alvin Weinberg of the Institute for Energy Analysis contends that the public cannot be assured of nuclear safety unless plants are operated by highly skilled organizations dedicated to safety rather than production; he also recommends that nuclear plants be concentrated in as few sites as possible (see Firebaugh and Ohanian 1980). Clearly the wisdom of these views can be challenged. However, accepting Weinberg's views does not preclude deregulation. He implies that the nuclear power-plant owners, who market the power, would be separate from the operators. The owners effectively would buy operating services from one or more giant operating organizations.

There are variations of the Weinberg argument that have quite different implications. It could be concluded that large organizations are needed to run nuclear plants, but they are best integrated with ownership. Therefore, large companies would be preferable. The benefits of integrating generation, transmission, and distribution and building larger facilities also might justify maintaining larger power companies.

Whether large companies are necessary to effect integration is unclear. Numerous alternatives exist and have been used widely. Anecdotal evidence suggests that cooperation among separate but well-established organizations can work at least as well as creating new organizations. Company size, organization, and experience with nuclear power may not have clear-cut effects on performance. For instance, General Public Utilities was a large company with considerable nuclear experience (albeit in a different subsidiary) and still had the Three Mile Island accident. On the other hand, the joint ventures to run nuclear plants in New England have performed well despite the small size of the participants and the assignment of the management of two such plants to very small companies.

In any case, the argument for reorganizing the electric-power industry to deregulate generation, transmission, or both has at least three pitfalls. First, there could be losses in coordination that could extend far beyond the efficient operation of nuclear plants. Regularly constructing plants creates skills that reduce costs, and these benefits might be lost if independent firms ordered single plants. Alternatively, independent engineering firms might perform as well as engineering departments within operating companies. Similarly, coordination among generation, transmission, and distribution might be more cheaply conducted by maintaining the current pattern of integrated utilities or by power pooling. Second, there could be substantial costs associated with restructuring an existing, complex industry.

Third, and most critical, the industry is governed by an elaborate and inflexible regulatory apparatus, and partial deregulation may prove infeasible. Public-utility commissions may refuse to abandon their powers over generation and transmission. Nominal deregulation must be legislated, and public utility commissions would certainly lobby to maintain their powers. So long as distribution is regulated, commission approval will be required of transactions to secure power and its transmission. These regulations will probably have the same effect as direct controls on generation and transmission companies. The danger of commissions refusing to grant adequate rates before or after a plant was completed could prove to be a serious barrier to the construction of independently owned generating plants or to the purchase of such plants by independent companies.

The relations between FERC and state regulators graphically illustrate these perils of partial deregulation. States have attempted to prevent companies from paying FERC-established rates on purchased power. These efforts failed because of federal precedence, but unregulated generating companies would lack such protection.

The problem is further demonstrated by utilities that venture into un-regulated businesses, primarily fuel production. Some companies are subject to rules requiring that total company earnings be reduced to levels allowed the regulated portion of the business. Thus, above-average return on unregulated activities must be lowered by the below-average returns of the regulated activities. This constitutes a subsidy of the regulated activities by the unregulated ones. At least one company (Montana Power), which is not subject to an explicit limit on overall returns, complains that such limits are imposed in practice. The company enjoys profits on coal sales that yield a rate of return much higher than that usually allowed electric-power companies. Regulators have reacted by setting low allowable returns on the utility side of the business so that the overall average is similar to those of undiversified utilities. Another company, Central Louisiana Energy, which diversified from its electric-utility business into oil and gas production, has now spun off the utility business and distributed its shares to the stockholders.

An obvious problem with decontrol is that it would create windfall profits equal to the difference between current and historical costs and cause the usual political reactions to such profits. The public-utility literature proposes use of franchise bidding to alleviate this problem. Such bidding would involve competition among potential suppliers for the right to serve an area, a device used to award cable-television franchises. More encouragingly, the lease of oil- and gas-bearing lands by competitive bidding has been shown to be an effective way to transfer to the public the windfall profits from access to low-cost resources. An alternative approach would be simply to impose a windfall profits tax on utilities.

Both approaches have drawbacks. The primary problem with the franchise-bidding concept is that it is difficult to imagine what would constitute effective competition for the existing utilities. Additionally, local governments, like European governments leasing North Sea oil, have chosen to trade promises to perform in some special fashion for financial compensation. It is doubtful that these sacrifices have been cost effective. The basic problem with profits taxes is that they can be set at punitive levels.

The alternatives all have unattractive features. The status quo is leading to massive inefficiency. Radical reform may create windfalls unless supplementary measures are imposed. Such measures, however, might vitiate the efficiency of reform.

A further problem lies in the legacy of the Public Utility Holding Company Act of 1935. This act was designed to undo the complex public-utility reorganizations popular in the 1920s. The fear was that these reorganizations, originally intended to make the industry more efficient, had degenerated into exercises in questionable financial manipulation. Given this legacy, there is concern that the act as currently administered by the SEC constitutes an overreaction to the dangers of financial manipulation or monopoly. The SEC may be overly hostile to reorganizations. At least two groups of companies (one in New England and the other, Capco, in western Pennsylvania and northern Ohio) that were cooperating closely were discouraged from moving to a merger that might have changed their relations only slightly.

The act stresses form over substance. Presently integrated companies can persist even if they possess monopoly power, but it is difficult to create new organizations whatever the market effect.

The Public Utility Holding Company Act should be replaced by application of regular antitrust laws to the electric-power industry structure. The Holding Company Act, as noted, does not base decisions on a rigorous concern with the vigor of competition. Moreover, the SEC lacks the expertise of the Department of Justice in appraising competition. The SEC is primarily concerned with the quite different question of securities fraud; it secured its power over holding companies because of this concern in the 1930s. This is not the current problem. (A compromise approach would be to transfer jurisdiction to the Department of Justice or FERC). Similarly, state limits on reorganizations should be removed.

Antitrust could also be used to monitor the anticompetitive effects of deregulation. The necessity of such antitrust action and its efficacy remain unclear. Possible outcomes include the absence of monopoly problems, monopolization through collusive price fixing, monopoly power through merger, and monopoly power only in sales to residential and commercial customers. In the first case, antitrust action would be unnecessary. Collusive price fixing can be effectively controlled by antitrust. However, considerable doubt prevails about the ability of antitrust enforcers to handle mergers and monopolization restricted to a portion of the customers. The price discrimination provisions of the Clayton Act (as amended by the Robinson-Patman Act) are directed at the last problem. Enforcement has been cumbersome, with almost impossible-to-meet requirements for proving that price differences reflect cost differences. Given the demonstrably higher costs of serving residential and commercial rather than large industrial customers, these excessive proof requirements could make applying the Clayton Act to electric-power pricing disastrous. The role of antitrust policy in electric power remains to be determined but deserves study. Concerns exist that limits on mergers are too stringent, but application of the monopoly test of the Clayton Act seems preferable to the guidelines of the Public Utility Holding Company Act.

Partial deregulation has the drawbacks of serious costs of implementation because of possible inefficiencies in generation, transmission, and their integration plus the possibility that continued regulation of distribution would not contribute to efficient distribution. To make matters worse, regulatory reform may not suffice to cure electric-power-industry problems. Concurrent reform of environmental regulations, particularly those related to nuclear power, may also be essential. Whatever the wisdom of heavy commitment to nuclear power, the utilities were responding to prior federal government policy postures that created the impression that nuclear power was a favored alternative.

A New Look for Nuclear Power

The vigor of prior government support for nuclear power implies that others in society besides investors in the electric-power-industry ought to share the burdens of changes in nuclear policy. No one gains from the prevailing policy of decision by indecision. The implicit policy posture currently is that nuclear power is treated with considerable but unspecified reservation.

No one can tell whether this reservation means that action should proceed slowly or whether nuclear power should be curtailed drastically. In either case, more precise definitions are needed. There are infinite interpretations of both slower development and retreat. In short, the fate of large amounts of money invested in existing and incomplete nuclear plants must be considered when developing a satisfactory resolution of electric-power-industry problems. NRC and state nuclear regulations could supersede public-utility commissions as the key barrier if commissions were reformed but nuclear policy was not.

However, reforming the NRC may not be enough. As with any established approach that has gone astray, radical changes in the NRC ought to be considered. At the least, discussion of possible radical alternatives exposes problems that narrower inquiries may conceal.

Criticism of regulation in other areas has led to suggestions of deregulation, and it is desirable to ask whether such an approach is appropriate for nuclear power. To be sure, nuclear accidents affect a large scattered group that may not be able to protect itself without government aid, and only the federal government may be able to insure that electric utilities are made accountable for the damages. However, reliance on financial incentives rather than regulation may be a more effective approach.

In fact, use of financial incentives to control nuclear-related problems may be easier to effect than similar applications to fossil-fuel-related problems. First, the drawbacks of existing regulation are particularly evident in the nuclear case, as the Kemeny Commission made apparent. Second, the objectives and the available methods to attain them are far clearer with nuclear power than with fossil-fuel air pollution. The goal is to prevent discharge of dangerously large amounts of radiation. Many techniques are available to further this goal. Third and most critically, we are much further down the road in terms of placing major responsibility for nuclear accidents on the electric-power industry. The industry has acted to develop cooperative programs to deal with nuclear problems by sharing information on safety problems and establishing a program to develop training programs and other operating practices.

A major element of nuclear power is the program for insuring plants under the Price-Anderson Act. The act has been properly criticized for limiting liability to $560 million per accident. The difficulty could be overcome by removing or raising the ceiling on damage payments. In the absence of other regulatory pressures, it would be preferable that the industry select a level of insurance on the basis of its experience and that no ceilings be set politically. However, antinuclear regulators then might set coverage requirements much higher than warranted as a means to prevent nuclear power. As a transition measure, ceilings might be set on how much insurance could be required. Still another alternative would be to set limits on how much state or local government agencies could restrict the nuclear-power industry.

Finding Sites

Whether state policies governing fossil-fuel-powered generation will prove as restrictive as nuclear regulation remains to be seen. There are several cases in which different mixtures of environmental and public-utility regulatory considerations relating to "need" have delayed construction of fossil-fuel-fired plants. There is a considerable danger that such intervention will increase if deregulation occurs. This would be another reason to replace to the greatest degree possible direct regulation of environmental problems with environmental damage taxes. This would lessen the ability of environmental agencies to become overly involved in details.

The principal problem with such an approach relates to the aesthetics of power-plant location. Any tangible damages, such as air and water pollution, can be handled by taxes on emissions. However, a simple tax system to control aesthetic impacts would be difficult to devise. To make matters worse, local land-use regulation is an area with a strong potential for misuse. The system is biased toward protecting the interests of existing landowners—particularly homeowners—and this protection may be excessive.

The resolution of siting problems will not be simple. However, the decentralization of controls to the local level combined with air and water pollution taxes seems the alternative best able to achieve a balance between environmental goals and healthy development of electric power.

The details of these reorganizations and their implementation are far less important than recognizing that severe problems exist and acting vigorously to overcome them. Defenders of regulation are correct when they assert that, in principle, reform can simply mean better regulation. Critics of regulation are also correct that the practice of regulation inspires doubts that the potential can be realized. This second concern raises considerable skepticism about the efficacy of seeking to improve regulation, but it does not settle the argument. However, it is clear that a critical American industry is being enervated by slow regulatory agency reactions and reform is critical. Policymakers to date have ignored these realities.

The actions required are unattractive and more likely to produce setbacks than rewards to political leaders. However, the problem cannot be avoided. The history of U.S. energy policy includes many unwise reactions to crisis. Most recently, the United States managed to create price controls that badly interfered with the efficient gasoline distribution process that we previously and subsequently enjoyed. We can hope that for once the error will be avoided in electric power, but we must recognize that thus far the traditional reluctance to act boldly has prevailed, imposing substantial costs on our society. Even those talking about how important reform is have been overly timid. Easy answers do not exist. The suggestions made here are designed not as definitive answers, but as illustrations of the more daring actions that should be considered. The actions will certainly not restore the era of rapid growth and cannot guarantee the return of technical progress or resolve the uncertainties about the best investment decisions. However, reform is essential if the industry is to break out of the paralysis that prevents realization of its maximum potential for increased efficiency.

Bibliography

Ackerman, Bruce A., Susan Rose-Ackerman, James W. Sawyer, Jr., and Dale W. Henderson. 1974. *The Uncertain Search for Environmental Quality*. New York: Free Press.

Adelman, M.A. 1972. *The World Petroleum Market*. Baltimore, Md.: Johns Hopkins University Press, for Resources for the Future.

———. 1979. Untitled transcript in *Seminar on Energy Policy: The Carter Proposals*. Edited by Edward J. Mitchell, Washington, D.C.: American Enterprise Institute for Public Policy Research..

———. 1980. "The Clumsy Cartel." *The Energy Journal* 1:43–53.

Abramson, Barry M., and Leonard S. Hyman. 1980. *A Cross Section of the Electric Utility Industry*. New York: Merrill Lynch, Pierce, Fenner & Smith.

Allen, R.D. 1938. *Mathematical Analysis for Economists*. London: Macmillan and Co.

Ambrose, Bruce J. 1980. *Arizona Public Service Company Phase II Direct Testimony*. New York: National Economic Research Associates.

Anderson, Frederick R. 1973. *NEPA in the Courts: A Legal Analysis of the National Environmental Policy Act*. Baltimore, Md.: Johns Hopkins University Press, for Resources for the Future.

Anderson, Frederick R., Allen V. Kneese, Phillip D. Reed, Serge Taylor, and Russell B. Stevenson. 1977. *Environmental Improvement Through Economic Incentives*. Baltimore, Md.: Johns Hopkins University Press, for Resources for the Future.

Areeda, Phillip. 1980. *Antitrust Analysis, Problems, Texts, Cases*. 3d ed. Boston: Little, Brown.

Averch, Harvey, and Leland L. Johnson. 1962. "Behavior of the Firm under Regulatory Constraint." *American Economic Review* 52:1053–1069.

Bailey, Elizabeth E. 1973. *Economic Theory of Regulatory Constraint*. Lexington, Mass.: Lexington Books, D.C. Heath.

Baughman, Martin L., and Drew W. Bottaro. 1975. "Electric Power Transmission and Distribution System's Costs and Their Allocation." IEEE Power Engineering Society, Preprint for Winter Meeting.

Baughman, Martin L., Paul L. Joskow, and Dilip P. Kamat. 1979. *Electric Power in the United States: Models and Policy Analysis*. Cambridge, Mass: The MIT Press.

Baumol, William J., and Alvin K. Klevorick. 1970. "Input Choices on Rate-of-Return Regulation: An Overview of the Discussion." *Bell Journal of Economics and Management Science* 1:162–190.

Baumol, William J., and Wallace E. Oates. 1975. *The Theory of Environ-*

mental Policy: Externalities, Public Outlays, and the Quality of Life.
Englewood Cliffs, N.J.: Prentice-Hall.

———. 1979. *Economics, Environmental Policy, and the Quality of Life.*
Englewood Cliffs, N.J.: Prentice-Hall.

Baxter, William F. 1974. *People or Penguins: The Case for Optimal Pollution.* New York: Columbia University Press.

Benderly, Z.I. 1980. *Testimony* (Montaup Electric Company Rate Hearing). New York: National Economic Research Associates.

Berle, Adolph A., and Gardiner C. Means. 1968. *The Modern Corporation and Private Property.* Rev. ed., (original 1932). New York: Harcourt Brace and World.

Berlin, Edward, Charles J. Cicchetti, and William J. Gillen. 1974. *Perspective on Power,* Cambridge, Mass.: Ballinger Publishing Company.

Bierman, Harold, Jr., and Seymour Smidt. 1975. *The Capital Budgeting Decision: Economic Analysis and Financing of Investment Projects.* 4th ed. New York: Macmillan Publishing Company.

Blair, John M. 1972. *Economic Concentration: Structure, Behavior and Public Policy.* New York: Harcourt Brace Jovanovich.

———. 1976. *The Control of Oil.* New York: Pantheon Books.

Bohn, Roger. 1981. "A Theoretical Analysis of Customer Response to Rapidly Changing Electricity Prices." MIT Energy Laboratory Working Paper, MIT-EL 81-001WP.

Bohn, Roger E., Michael C. Caramanis, Fred C. Schweppe. 1981. "Optimal Spot Pricing of Electricity Theory." MIT Energy Laboratory Working Paper, MIT-EL 81-008WP.

Bork, Robert H. 1978. *The Antitrust Paradox, a Policy at War with Itself.* New York: Basic Books.

Breese, Jack, and Ken Schweers. 1979. *Preliminary List of Plants Which Could Convert to Coal.* Washington, D.C.: ICF, Inc.

Breyer, Stephen G., and Paul W. MacAvoy. 1974. *Energy Regulation by the Federal Power Commission.* Washington, D.C.: Brookings Institution.

Breyer, Stephen G., and Richard B. Stewart. 1979. *Administrative Law and Regulatory Policy.* Boston, Mass.: Little, Brown.

California Energy Commission. 1979a. *1979 Biennial Report.* Sacramento, Calif.

———. 1979b. *Technical Assessment Manual,* vol. 2, Management and Technologies.

———. 1979c. *Towards an Alternative Energy Path for California, A Preliminary Action Agenda.*

———. 1980a. *Commercial Availability of Generation and Nongeneration Technologies.*

————. 1980b. *Electricity Tomorrow: 1980 Preliminary Report.*

————. 1981. *Energy Tomorrow Challenges and Opportunities for California.* Sacramento, Calif.

Caves, Richard E., and Ronald W. Jones. 1973. *World Trade and Payments: An Introduction.* Boston, Mass.: Little, Brown.

Cicchetti, Charles J., and John L. Jurewitz, eds. 1975. *Studies in Electric Utility Regulation.* Cambridge, Mass.: Ballinger Publishing Company.

Clark, Charles E., Richard B. Fancher, David M. Nesbitt, and Stephan G. Regulinski. 1980. *Calculating the Cost of Producing Energy for Regulated and Nonregulated Industry.* Palo Alto, Calif.: Decision Focus, Inc.

Coase, Ronald H. 1937. "The Nature of the Firm." *Economica,* New series 4:386–405. Reprinted in Kenneth E. Boulding, and George J. Stigler, eds. *Readings in Price Theory,* pp. 331–351. Homewood, Ill.: Richard D. Irwin, 1952.

————. 1960. "The Problem of Social Costs." *Journal of Law and Economics* 3:1–44.

Corden, W.M. 1974. *Trade Policy and Economic Welfare.* Oxford: Oxford University Press.

Corey, Gordon R. 1971. "The Averch and Johnson Proposition: A Critical Analysis." *Bell Journal of Economics and Management Science* 2:358–373.

Corey, Gordon R., Charles Benore, Thomas L. Chrystie, Raymond J. O'Connor, Irwin M. Stelzer, and Joseph C. Swidler. 1980. "Recommendations for the Restoration of Financial Health to the U.S. Electric Power Industry." Report of an Informal Task Force to the Energy Transition Team.

Courville, Leon. 1974. "Regulation and Efficiency in the Electric Utility Industry." *Bell Journal of Economics and Management Science* 5: 53–74.

Cowing, Thomas G., and Kerry Smith. 1978. *A Survey of Econometric Models of the Supply and Cost Structure of Electricity.* Palo Alto, Calif.: Electric Power Research Institute.

Crandall, Robert W. 1980. "Regulation and Productivity Growth." In *The Decline in Productivity Growth,* Proceedings of Conference, pp.93–111. Boston: Federal Reserve Bank of Boston.

Crocker, Thomas D., and A.J. Rogers, III. 1971. *Environmental Economics.* Hinsdale, Ill.: Dryden Press.

Dasgupta, P.S., and G.M. Heal. 1979. *Economic Theory and Exhaustible Resources,* Cambridge, England: Cambridge University Press.

Deese, David A., and Joseph S. Nye, eds. 1981. *Energy and Security.* Cambridge, Mass.: Ballinger Publishing Company.

Dolbear, F. Trenery, Jr., 1967. "On the Theory of Optimal Externality." *American Economic Review* 57:90–103.

Dorfman, Robert, and Nancy E. Dorfman, eds. 1977. *Economics of the Environment.* 2d ed. New York: W.W. Norton & Company.

Downs, Anthony. 1957. *An Economic Theory of Democracy.* New York: Harper and Row.

Edison Electric Institute. annual. *Statistical Yearbook of the Electric Utility Industry.* Washington, D.C.: Edison Electric Institute.

———. 1974. *Historical Statistics of the Electric Utility Industry through 1970.* New York: Edison Electric Institute.

———. 1980. *1980 Annual Electric Power Survey.* Washington, D.C.: Edison Electric Institute.

———. 1981. "Comments for Federal Regulatory Commission Public Conference on the Financial Condition of the Electric Utility Industry in the United States."

Energy and Environmental Analysis, Inc. 1977. *Methodology: Replacing Oil and Gas with Coal in the Industrial Sector.*

Ernst and Ernst. 1979. *Costs of Capital and Rates of Return for Industrial Firms and Class A & B Electric Utility Firms.* Washington, D.C.

Firebaugh, M.W., and M.J. Ohanian, eds. 1980. *Gatlinburg II, An Acceptable Future Nuclear Energy System, Condensed Workshop Proceedings.* Oak Ridge: Institute for Energy Analysis, Oak Ridge Associated Universities.

Fisher, Irving. 1930. *The Theory of Interest.* New York: Macmillan Publishing Co.

Florida Power and Light Company. 1980. *Florida Power and Light Company Ten Year Power Plant Site Plan 1980–1989,* submitted to the State of Florida Department of Community Affairs, Miami.

Freeman, A. Myrick, III, Robert H. Haveman, and Allen V. Kneese. 1973. *The Economics of Environmental Policy.* New York: John Wiley & Sons.

Freeman, A. Myrick, III. 1979a. *The Benefits of Air and Water Pollution Control: A Review and Synthesis of Recent Estimates.* Washington, D.C.: U.S. Council on Environmental Quality.

———. 1979b. *The Benefits of Environmental Improvement: Theory and Practice.* Baltimore, Md.: Johns Hopkins University Press, for Resources for the Future.

Freeman, S. David. 1974. *Energy: The New Era.* New York: Random House.

———. 1980. "Testimony Before the Senate Subcommittee on Energy and Water Development of the Committee on Appropriations."

———. 1981. "Remarks Before the Financial Women's Association."

French, Walter G. 1980. "Presentation at Workshop on Rate of Return/ Earnings Regulation."

Friedlaender, Ann F., ed. 1978. *Approaches to Controlling Air Pollution,* Cambridge, Mass.: The MIT Press.

Gordian Associates. 1977. *Structural Reform in the Electric Power Industry.* Springfield, Va.: National Technical Information Service.

Gordon, Richard L. 1966. "Conservation and the Theory of Exhaustible Resources." *Canadian Journal of Economics and Political Science* 32:319–326.

————. 1967. "A Reinterpretation of the Pure Theory of Exhaustion." *Journal of Political Economy* 75:274–286.

————. 1970. *The Evolution of Energy Policy in Western Europe: The Reluctant Retreat from Coal.* New York: Praeger Publishers.

————. 1974. "The Optimization of Input Supply Patterns in the Case of Fuels for Electric Power Generation." *Journal of Industrial Economics* 22:19–37.

————. 1975. *U.S. Coal and the Electric Power Industry.* Baltimore, MD.: Johns Hopkins University Press, for Resources for the Future.

————. 1978a. *Coal in the U.S. Energy Market: History and Prospects.* Lexington, Mass.: Lexington Books, D.C. Heath.

————. 1978b. "The Hobbling of Coal: Policy and Regulatory Uncertainties." *Science* 200(14 April):153–158.

————. 1978c. "Hobbling Coal—Or How to Serve Two Masters Poorly." *Regulation* vol. 2, no. 4, pp. 36–45.

————. 1979a. *Economic Analysis of Coal Supply: An Assessment of Existing Studies,* Final Report, Vol. 3. Palo Alto, Calif.: Electric Power Research Institute; Springfield, Va.: National Technical Information Service.

————. 1979b. "The Powerplant and Industrial Fuel Use Act of 1978—An Economic Analysis." *Natural Resources Journal* 19:871–884.

————. 1980. "Coal Policy and Energy Economics." *The Energy Journal* 1:77–86.

————. 1981. *An Economic Analysis of World Energy Problems.* Cambridge, Mass.: The MIT Press.

Gray, Lewis C. 1914. "Rent under the Assumption of Exhaustibility." *Quarterly Journal of Economics* 28:466–489. Reprinted in Mason Gaffney, ed. *Extractive Resources and Taxation,* pp. 423–446. Madison, Wisc.: University of Wisconsin Press, 1967.

Handler, Milton, assisted by Joshua F. Greenburg. 1967. *Cases and Materials on Trade Regulation.* 4th. ed. Brooklyn, N.Y.: Foundation Press.

Henderson, James, and Richard E. Quandt. 1971. *Microeconomic Theory: A Mathematical Approach.* 2d ed. New York: McGraw-Hill Book Company.

Herfindahl, Orris C. 1974. *Resource Economics: Selected Works.* Edited by David B. Brooks. Baltimore, Md.: Johns Hopkins University Press, for Resources for the Future.

Hicks, J.R. 1946. *Value and Capital.* 2d ed. Oxford University Press.

Hirshleifer, J. 1970. *Investment, Interest, and Capital.* Englewood Cliffs, N.J.: Prentice-Hall.

Hotelling, Harold. 1931. "The Economics of Exhaustible Resources." *Journal of Political Economy* 39:137–175.

Hughes, William R., and Richard L. Gordon, project directors. 1979. *Economic Analysis of Proposed Regulations Under the Fuel Use Act.* Boston: Charles River Associates.

Hyman, Leonard S. 1978. *The Merrill Lynch Electric Utility Report, What It Is, How to Use It and Why.* New York: Merrill Lynch, Pierce, Feener & Smith.

————. 1979. *The Merrill Lynch Handbook of Public Utility Regulation, An Outline of the Development, Proceedings, and Economics of Public Utility Regulation.* New York: Merrill Lynch, Pierce, Fenner & Smith.

————. 1980. *The Development and Structure of the Electric Utility Industry.* New York: Merrill Lynch, Pierce, Fenner & Smith.

————. 1981. *Electric Utility Industry Financial Structure,* New York: Merrill Lynch, Pierce, Fenner & Smith.

Hyman, Leonard D., and Rosemary Avellis. 1980. *Utility Research, A Statistical Analysis of Regulatory Trends.* New York: Merrill Lynch, Pierce, Fenner & Smith.

————. 1980 and 1981. *Utility Research, Recent Regulatory Decisions and Trends.* New York: Merrill Lynch, Pierce, Fenner & Smith.

ICF, Inc. 1977. *Coal and Electric Utilities Model Documentation.* Washington, D.C.: Amended version of *The National Coal Model: Description and Documentation.* Springfield, Va.: National Technical Information Service, 1976.

————. 1978a. *Effects of Alternative New Source Performance Standards for Coal-Fired Electric Utility Boilers on the Coal Market and on Utility Capacity Expansion Plans.* Washington, D.C.: ICF.

————. 1978b. *Further Analysis of Alternative New Source Performance Standards for New Coal-Fired Power Plants.* Washington, D.C.: ICF.

————. 1979a. *The Final Set of Analyses of Alternative New Source Performance Standards for New Coal-Fired Powerplants.* Washington, D.C.: ICF.

————. 1979b. *Still Further Analyses of Alternative New Source Performance Standards for New Coal-Fired Powerplants.* Washington, D.C.: ICF.

————. 1980a. *Coal and Electric Utilities Model Documentation* (update). Washington, D.C.: ICF.

————. 1980b. *Economic and Environmental Impacts of the President's Commission on Coal's Program to Restore Oil and Gas in Utility Boilers.* Washington, D.C.: ICF.

———. 1980c. *Preliminary Assessment of Economic Impact of Visibility Regulations.* Washington, D.C.: ICF.

———. 1980d. *Reducing Oil and Gas Consumption in the Utility Sector: A Background Paper Discussing the President's Program.* Washington, D.C. ICF.

———. 1980e. *Utility Financial and Rate Impacts of Adding Coal Capacity to Replace Oil Generation: The Case of Florida Power and Light Company.* Washington, D.C.: ICF.

———. 1980f. *Utility Financial and Rate Impacts of Reconverting Coal Capacity to Replace Oil Generation: The Case of Northeast Utilities.* Washington, D.C.: ICF.

Jones, Douglas, N. 1980. "A Defense of Rate Regulation in the Classic Style." *Public Utilities Fortnightly,* (19 June):3–4.

Joskow, Paul L. 1975. "Applying Economic Principles to Public Utility Rate Structures: The Case of Electricity." In *Studies in Electric Utility Regulation,* edited by Charles J. Cicchetti and John Jurewitz, pp. 17–72. Cambridge, Mass,: Ballinger Publishing Company.

Kahn, Alfred E. 1970. *The Economics of Regulation.* 2 vols. New York: John Wiley & Sons.

Katzmann, Robert A. 1980. *Regulatory Bureaucracy, the Federal Trade Commission and Antitrust Policy.* Cambridge, Mass.: The MIT Press.

Keeny, Spurgeon M.Jr., (chairman, Nuclear Energy Policy Study Group). 1977. *Nuclear Power Issues and Choices.* Cambridge, Mass.: Ballinger Publishing Company.

Kelley, Doris A. 1981. *Nuclear Power-Plants—The Outlook for the 80's.* New York: Merrill Lynch, Pierce, Fenner & Smith.

Keystone Coal Industry Manual. 1980. *U.S. Coal Production by Company 1979,* New York: McGraw-Hill.

Kindleberger, Charles P., and Peter H. Lindert. 1978. *International Economics.* 6th ed. Homewood: Richard D. Irwin.

Kneese, Allen V., and Charles L. Schultze. 1975. *Pollution, Prices and Public Policy.* Washington, D.C.: Brookings Institution.

Landsberg, Hans H., Chariman. 1979. *Energy the Next Twenty Years,* report by a study group sponsored by the Ford Foundation and administered by Resources for the Future. Cambridge, Mass.: Ballinger Publishing Company.

———. ed. 1980. *Selected Studies on Energy, Background Papers for Energy: The Next Twenty Years.* Cambridge, Mass.: Ballinger Publishing Company.

Lange, Oscar. 1936–1937. "On the Economic Theory of Socialism." *Review of Economic Studies* 4:53–71 and 123–142. (Frequently reprinted, first in B. Lippincott, ed., *On the Economic Theory of Socialism.* Minneapolis: University of Minnesota Press, 1938. See e.g., Harry

Townsend, ed. *Price Theory,* pp. 32–35, Harmondsworth: Penguin Books, 1971, and Alec Nove and D.M. Nuti, eds., *Socialist Economies,* pp. 92–112, Harmondsworth: Penguin Books, 1972.

Lave, Lester B., and Eugene P. Seskin. 1977. *Air Pollution and Human Health.* Baltimore, Md.: Johns Hopkins University Press, for Resources for the Future.

Levitt, Theodore. 1980. "Marketing Myopia," *Harvard Business Review.* vol. 38, No. 1, pp. 45–56.

Levy, Yvonne. 1980. "Pricing Federal Power in the Pacific Northwest: An Efficiency Approach." *Federal Reserve of San Francisco Economic Review.* Winter, pp. 40–61.

Liu, Ernest. 1980. *Public Utility Survey.* New York: Goldman Sachs Company.

Lovins, Amory B. 1977. *Soft Energy Paths: Toward a Durable Peace.* Cambridge, Mass.: Ballinger Publishing Company.

McDonald, Forrest. 1962. *Insull.* Chicago: University of Chicago Press.

Massachusetts Institute of Technology, Homostatic Control Working Group. 1980. "Homostatic Control: A Research Plan."

Meade, J.E. 1955. *Trade and Welfare, The Theory of International Economic Policy,* vol. 2. London: Oxford University Press.

Merrett, A.J., and Allen Sykes. 1973. *The Finance and Analysis of Capital Projects.* 2d ed. New York: John Wiley & Sons.

Merrill Lynch, Pierce, Fenner & Smith, Utility Research Group. 1980 and 1981. "Electric Utilities."

Messing, Marc H., Paul Friesema, and David Morell. 1979. *Centralized Power, The Politics of Scale in Electricity Generation.* Cambridge: Oelgeschlager, Gunn & Hain.

Mills, Edwin S. 1978. *The Economics of Environmental Quality.* New York: W.W. Norton & Company.

Mishan, E.J. 1976. *Cost-Benefit Analysis.* New York: Praeger Publishers.

Mitchell, Edward J., ed. 1979. *Seminar on Energy Policy: The Carter Proposals.* Washington, D.C.: American Enterprise Institute for Public Policy Research.

Moody's Public Utilities. annual. New York: Moody's Investors Service.

Musgrave, Richard A. 1959. *The Theory of Public Finance.* New York: McGraw-Hill Publishing Company.

———. 1969. "Provision for Social Goods." In *Public Economics,* edited by J. Margolis, and H. Guitton, pp. 124–144. New York: St. Martins Press.

Musgrave, Richard A., and Peggy B. Musgrave. 1976. *Public Finance in Theory and Practice.* 2d. ed. New York: McGraw-Hill Publishing Company.

Myers, Stewart, C. 1979. "Verified Statement: Williams Pipeline Company FERC Docket No. OR79-1."

Myers, Stewart C., A. Lawrence Kolbe, and William B. Tye. 1981. "Inflation and Rate of Return Regulation." Draft Manuscript.

National Association of Regulatory Utility Commissioners. 1980. *1979 Annual Report on Utility and Carrier Regulation.* Washington, D.C.: National Association of Regulatory Commissioners.

National Coal Association. annual. *Steam Electric Plant Factors.* Washington, D.C. National Coal Association.

———. 1960. *Trends in Electric Utility Industry Experience 1946-1958.* Washington, D.C.: National Coal Association.

National Economic Research Associates. 1979. *The Impact of Alternative Policy Reaction to Three Mile Island.* 2 vols. New York: National Economic Research Associates.

National Economic Research Associates and Kidder Peabody and Company. 1979. *Utility Planning and Management in an Era of Increasing Constraints.* New York: National Economic Research Associates.

National Economic Research Associates. 1980. *The Empirical Analysis of Energy Gains from Conservation Policy: A Critical Review.* New York: National Economic Research Associates.

National Electric Reliability Council. 1980. *1980 Summary of Projected Peak Demand Generating Capability and Fossil Fuel Requirements for the Regional Reliability Councils of NERC.* Princeton: National Electric Reliability Council.

———. 1981. *Electric Power Supply and Demand, 1981-1990.* Princeton: National Electric Reliability Council.

National Research Council. 1977a. *Perspectives on Technical Information for Environmental Protection.* Washington, D.C.: National Academy of Science.

———. 1977b. *Decision Making in the Environmental Protection Agency.* Washington, D.C.: National Academy of Science.

———. 1977c. *Implication of Environmental Regulations for Energy Production and Consumption.* Washington, D.C.: National Academy of Science.

Navarro, Peter. 1980a. "The Politics of Air Pollution." *The Public Interest.* 59:36-44.

———. 1980b. "Public Utility Commission Regulation: Performance, Determinants, and Energy Policy Impacts." Energy and Environmental Policy Center, John F. Kennedy School of Government, Harvard University Discussion Paper E80-08.

———. 1981a. "The 1977 Clear Air Act Amendments. Energy, Environmental, Economic and Distributional Impact." Energy and Environmental Policy Center, John F. Kennedy School of Government, Harvard University Discussion Paper E81–03.

———. 1981b. "Electric Utility Regulation and National Energy Policy," *Regulation* vol. 6. no. 1, pp. 20–27.

Newlon, Daniel H., and Norman V. Breckner. 1975. *The Oil Security System: An Import Strategy for Achieving Oil Security and Reducing Oil Prices.* Lexington, Mass.: Lexington Books, D.C. Heath.

New York State Energy Office. 1980. *New York State Energy Master Plan and Long-Range Electric and Gas Report.* 3 vols. Albany: New York State.

New York State Power Pool. 1980. *Report of Member Electric Systems of the New York State Power Pool and the Empire State Electric Energy Research Corporation.*

———. 1981. *Report of Member Electric Systems of the New York Power Pool and the Empire State Electric Energy Research Corporation.*

Nikodem, Zderek D., Andrew W. Reynolds, and R. Gene Clark. 1980. *Nuclear Power Regulation.* U.S. Department of Energy, Energy Policy Study no. 10, Washington, D.C.: U.S. Government Printing Office.

Nieves, L.A., W.P. Patton, B.J. Harrer, and J.E. Emery. 1980. *The Marginal Cost of Electricity 1980–1995: An Approximation Based on the Cost of New Coal and Nuclear Generating Plants.* Springfield: Virginia: National Technical Information Service.

Nordhaus, William D. 1980. "The Energy Crisis and Macroeconomic Policy." *The Energy Journal* 1:11–19.

Nozick, Robert. 1974. *Anarchy, State, and Utopia.* New York: Basic Books.

Ohanian, M.J., ed. 1977. *An Acceptable Future Nuclear Energy System.* Oak Ridge, Tenn.: Institute for Energy Analysis, Oak Ridge Associated Universities.

"On a Clear Day You Could Pay Forever." 1981. *Regulation.* vol. 5, no. 2, pp. 12–13.

Ostergren, C.N. 1975. "Is the Averch-Johnson Thesis Tenable." *Public Utilities Fortnightly,* 30 January, pp. 28–32.

PEDCo Environmental, Inc. quarterly, formerly bimonthly. *Summary Report Flue Gas Desulfurization Systems.* Cincinnati, Ohio: PEDCo Environmental.

Pennsylvania, Commonwealth of, Governor's Energy Council. 1980. "Staff Draft Pennsylvania Energy Choices and Energy Policy Plan for Pennsylvania."

Portney, Paul R., ed. 1978. *Current Issues in U.S. Environmental Policy.* Baltimore, Md.: John Hopkins University Press, for Resources for the Future.

Posner, Richard A. 1974. "Theories of Economic Regulation." *Bell Journal of Economics and Management Science* 5:335–338.

Posner, Richard A., and Frank H. Easterbrook. 1981. *Antitrust: Cases, Economic Notes, and Other Materials.* 2d ed. St. Paul: West Publishing Company.

Ramsay, William. 1979. *Unpaid Costs of Electric Energy: Health and Environmental Impacts from Coal and Nuclear Power.* Baltimore, Md.: Johns Hopkins University Press, for Resources for the Future.

Rawls, John. 1971. *A Theory of Justice.* Cambridge, Mass: Harvard University Press.

Robinson, Joan. 1933. *The Economics of Imperfect Competition.* London: Macmillan & Co.

Roseman, Herman G. n.d. *Testimony in Support of the Petition of Rochester Gas and Electric Corporation et al for a Determination of Accounting Treatment and Ratemaking Principles—Sterling Power Project Nuclear Unit No. 1.* New York: National Economic Research Associates.

———. 1980. *Testimony in the Matter of Proceedings on Motion of the (New York State Public Service) Commission to Investigate the Financing Plans for Major New York Combination Electric and Gas Companies.* New York: National Economic Research Associates.

———. 1981. *The Ability of Electric Utilities to Finance Projected Construction in the 1980s.* New York: National Economic Research Associates.

Samuelson, Paul A. 1947. *Foundations of Economic Analysis.* Cambridge, Mass.: Harvard University Press.

———. 1966. *The Collected Scientific Papers of Paul A. Samuelson,* edited by Joseph E. Stiglitz, 2 vols. Cambridge, Mass.: The MIT Press.

———. 1969. "Pure Theory of Public Expenditures and Taxation." In J. Margolis, and H. Guitton, eds., *Public Economics.* New York: St. Martins Press, pp. 98–123. Reprinted in *Collected Scientific Papers of Paul A. Samuelson,* edited by Robert C. Merton, vol. 3, pp. 492–517. Cambridge, Mass.: The MIT Press, 1972.

———. 1976. *Economics.* 10th ed. New York: McGraw-Hill.

Schmalensee, Richard. 1979. *The Control of Natural Monopolies.* Lexington, Mass.: Lexington Books, D.C. Heath.

Schultze, Charles L. 1977. *The Public Use of Private Interest.* Washington, D.C.: Brookings Institution.

Schumpeter, Joseph A. 1950. *Capitalism, Socialism, and Democracy.* 3d ed. New York: Harper & Brothers.

Schurr, Sam H., Joel Darmstadter, Harry Perry, William Ramsay, and Milton Russell. 1979. *Energy in America's Future, the Choice Before Us.* Baltimore, Md.: Johns Hopkins University Press, for Resources for the Future.

Schweppe, Fred C., Richard D. Tabors, James L. Kirtley, Jr., Hugh R. Buthrel, Fredrick H. Pickel, and Alan J. Cox. 1980. "Homeostatic

Utility Control." *IEEE Transactions on Power Apparatus and Systems.* V. PAS-99:151-163.

Spann, Robert M. 1974. "Rate of Return Regulating and Efficiency in Production: An Empirical Test of the Averch-Johnson Thesis." *Bell Journal of Economics and Management Science* 5:38-52.

Stauffer, C. Hoff. 1979. *Additional Documentation of List of Plants Capable of Reconverting to Coal.* Washington, D.C.: ICF.

Stelzer, Irwin M., and Roseman, Herman, G. 1974. *Testimony Before the Senate Committee on Interior and Insular Affairs.* New York: National Economic Research Associates.

Stelzer, Irwin M. 1980. *A Policy Guide for Utility Executives: Know When to Hold 'Em; Know When to Fold 'Em.* New York: National Economic Research Associates.

Stigler, George J. 1971. "The Theory of Economic Regulation." *Bell Journal of Economics and Management Science* 2:3-21.

Stobaugh, Robert, and Daniel Yergin, eds. 1979. *Energy Future, Report of of the Energy Project at the Harvard Business School.* New York: Random House.

Takayama, Akira, 1972. *International Trade.* New York: Holt, Rinehart and Winston.

Taschdjian, Martin. 1979. *The Effect of Legislative and Regulatory Actions on Competition in Petroleum Markets,* Energy Policy Study vol. 2 Washington, D.C.: U.S. Department of Energy, Energy Information Administration.

Taschdjian, Martin, and James Hewett. 1980. *State Regulation of Electric and Gas Utilities,* Energy Policy Study vol. 4. Washington, D.C.: U.S. Department of Energy, Energy Information Administration.

Telson, Michael L. 1975. "The Economics of Alternative Levels of Reliability for Electric Power Generation Systems," *The Bell Journal of Economics* 6:679-694.

Trisko, Eugene M. 1980. *Prevention of Significant Deterioration and Visibility Protection Critical Constraints to Domestic Energy Development.*

Turvey, Ralph. 1968. *Optimal Pricing and Investment in Electricity Supply.* Cambridge, Mass.: The MIT Press.

U.S. Congress, Congressional Budget Office. 1978. *Replacing Oil and Natural Gas with Coal: Prospects in the Manufacturing Industries.* Washington, D.C.: U.S. Government Printing Office.

U.S. Congress, House. 1977. *National Energy Act, Communication from the President of the United States Transmitting a Draft Proposed Legislation to Establish a Comprehensive National Energy Policy.* House Document 95-138, 95th Cong., 1st sess.

————. 1977. *Clean Air Act Amendments of 1977,* Conference Report, Report No. 95-564. Washington, D.C.: U.S. Government Printing Office.

————. 1978. *National Energy Conservation Policy Act of 1978,* (PL 95-619) 95th Cong., 2nd Sess.

————. 1978. *Natural Gas Policy Act of 1978,* (PL 95-621), 95th Cong., 2nd Sess.

————. 1978. *Public Utility Regulatory Policies Act of 1978,* (PL 95-617), 95 Cong., 2nd Sess.

————. 1978. *Power Plant and Industrial Fuel Use Act,* (PL 95-260), 95th Cong. 2nd. Sess.

————. 1980. *Pacific Northwest Electric Power Planning and Conservation Act,* (PL-501), 96th Cong., 2nd Sess.

U.S. Congress, House, Library of Congress Congressional Research Service. 1980. *Will the Lights Go On in 1990.* Study for the Subcommittee on Energy and Power, Committee on Interstate and Foreign Commerce, 96th Cong., 2nd Sess. Washington, D.C.: U.S. Government Printing Office.

U.S. Congress, Senate Subcommittee on Energy Regulations of the Committee on Energy and Natural Resources. 1980. *Powerplant Fuels Conversion Act of 1980.* 96th Cong., 2nd Sess. Washington, D.C.: U.S. Government Printing Office.

U.S. Council on Environmental Quality. annual. *Environmental Quality,* The annual report of the Council on Enviromental Quality. Washington, D.C.: U.S. Government Printing Office.

U.S. Department of Energy, prepared by David E. Mead, Frederic H. Murphy, and W. David Montgomery. 1978. *Analysis of Proposed U.S. Department of Energy Regulations Implementing the Powerplant and Industrial Fuel Use Act.* Washington, D.C.

————. 1981. *Coal Competition: Prospects for the 1980s, Draft Report.*

————. Economic Regulatory Administration. 1979. "Powerplant and Industrial Fuel Use Act Criteria for Petition for Exemption from Prohibitions." *Federal Register* 17 May:28950-29019.

————. Economic Regulatory Administration, Office of Utility Systems. 1979-1980. *National Power Grid Study.* 2 vols. Washington, D.C.: U.S. Government Printing Office.

————. Economic Regulatory Commission. 1980. *Proposed Changes to Generating Capacity 1980-1981 for the Contiguous United States as Projected by the Regional Electric Reliability Council in Their April 1, 1980 Long-Range Coordinated Planning Report to the Department of Energy.*

U.S. Department of Energy, Energy Information Administration. annual.

Annual Report to Congress. Washington, D.C.: U.S. Government Printing Office. (1978 report in 5 vols.: 1, report; 2, data; 3, forecasts; and 4 and 5, data on forecasts.)

———. annual. *Gas Turbine Electric Plant Construction Cost and Annual Production Expenses* (former FPC report). Washington, D.C.: U.S. Government Printing Office.

———. annual. *Hydroelectric Plant Construction Cost and Annual Production Expenses* (former FPC report). Washington, D.C.: U.S. Government Printing Office.

———. annual. *Inventory of Power Plants in the United States* (former FEA report). Washington, D.C.: U.S. Government Printing Office.

———. annual. *Steam-Electric Plant Construction Cost and Annual Production Expenses* (former FPC report). Washington, D.C.: U.S. Government Printing Office.

———. annual. *Statistics of Privately Owned Electric Utilities in the United States—Class A and B Companies* (former FPC report). Washington, D.C.: U.S. Government Printing Office.

———. annual. *Statistics of Publicly Owned Electric Utilities in the United States* (former FPC report). Washington, D.C.: U.S. Government Printing Office.

———. annual *Typical Electric Bill—January 1* (former FPC report). Washington, D.C.: U.S. Government Printing Office.

———. monthly. *Electric Power Monthly.* Washington, D.C.: U.S. Government Printing Office. (Established July 1980 to replace several old FPC reports).

———. monthly. *Monthly Energy Review* (former FEA report). Washington, D.C.: U.S. Government Printing Office.

———. Energy Information Administration. monthly with annual supplements. *Cost and Quality of Fuels for Electric Utility Plants* (former FPC report). Springfield, Va.: National Technical Information Service.

———. quarterly. *U.S. Central Station Nuclear Electric Generating Units: Significant Milestones.* Springfield, Va.: National Technical Information Service. (Successor to similarly named report instituted by the U.S. Atomic Energy Commission and continued by U.S. Energy Research and Development Administration).

———. 1980a. *Energy Programs/Energy Markets Overview.* Washington, D.C.: U.S. Government Printing Office.

———. 1980b. *Power Production, Fuel Consumption and Installed Capacity for 1979 (Final).* Washington, D.C.: U.S. Government Printing Office. (Consolidated of former FPC releases).

———. 1981. *Power Production, Fuel Consumption, and Installed Capac-

ity Data, 1980 Annual. Washington, D.C.: U.S. Government Printing Office.

———. Office of Economic Analysis, Financial and Industry Studies Division Energy Information Administration. 1981. *Federal Support for Nuclear Power: Reactor Design and the Fuel Cycle.* Washington, D.C.: U.S. Government Printing Office.

———. Office of Electrical Systems, Policy and Evaluation. 1980. *Staff Analysis of the Energy and Economic Impacts of the President's Program for Reducing Oil and Gas Consumption in the Utility Sector.*

U.S. Environmental Protection Agency. 1971. *Air Quality Criteria for Nitrogen Oxides.* Washington, D.C.

———. 1977. *National Air Quality and Emission Trends Report, 1976.* Research Triangle, N.C.

U.S. Executive Office of the President, Energy Policy and Planning. 1977a. *The National Energy Plan.* Washington, D.C.: U.S. Government Printing Office.

———. 1977b. *Replacing Oil and Gas with Coal and Other Fuels in the Industrial and Utility Sectors.* Washington, D.C.

U.S. Federal Power Commission. 1971. *The 1970 National Power Survey.* 4 vols. Washington, D.C.: U.S. Government Printing Office.

———. 1977a. *Annual Summary of Cost and Quality of Electric Utility Plant Fuels, 1976.* Washington, D.C.

———. 1977b. *The Status of the Flue Gas Desulfurization Applications in the United States: A Technological Assessment.* 2 vols. Washington, D.C.

U.S. Federal Trade Commission, Bureau of Economics. 1977. *Report to the Federal Trade Commission on the Use of Automatic Fuel Adjustment Clauses and the Fuel Procurement Practices of Investor-owned Electric Utilities.* Washington, D.C.: U.S. Government Printing Office.

U.S. General Accounting Office. 1977a. *An Evaluation of the National Energy Plan.* Washington, D.C.

———. 1977b. *Reducing Nuclear Powerplant Leadtimes: Many Obstacles Remain.* Washington, D.C.

———. 1980. *Financial and Regulatory Aspects of Converting Oil-Fired Boilers to Coal.* Washington, D.C.: U.S. Government Printing Office.

U.S. National Air Pollution Control Administration. 1969a. *Air Quality Criteria for Particulate Matter.* Washington, D.C.: U.S. Government Printing Office.

———. 1969b. *Air Quality Criteria for Sulfur Dioxides.* Washington, D.C.: U.S. Government Printing Office.

———. 1969c. *Control Techniques for Particulate Air Pollutants.* Washington, D.C.: U.S. Government Printing Office.

————. 1969d. *Control Techniques for Sulfur Oxide Air Pollutants.* Washington, D.C. U.S. Government Printing Office.

————. 1970a. Air Quality Criteria for Carbon Monoxide. Washington, D.C.: U.S. Government Printing Office.

————. 1970b. *Air Quality Criteria for Hydrocarbons.* Washington, D.C.: U.S. Government Printing Office.

————. 1970c. *Air Quality Criteria for Photochemical Oxidants.* Washington, D.C.: U.S. Government Printing Office.

————. 1970d. *Control Techniques for Carbon Monoxide, Nitrogen Oxide, and Hydrocarbon Emissions from Mobil Sources.* Washington, D.C.: U.S. Government Printing Office.

————. 1970e. *Control Techniques for Nitrogen Oxide Emissions from Stationary Sources.* Washington, D.C.: U.S. Government Printing Office.

U.S. Nuclear Regulatory Commission. 1975. *Reactor Safety Study: An Assessment of Accident Risks in U.S. Commercial Nuclear Power Plants.* 8 vols. Springfield, Va.: National Technical Information Service.

U.S. President's Commission on the Accident on Three Mile Island. 1979. *Report of the President's Commission on the Accident at Three Mile Island, The Need for Change. The Legacy of TMI.* Washington, D.C.: U.S. Government Printing Office.

U.S. Rural Electrification Administration. annual. *Annual Statistical Report Rural Electrification Borrowers.* Washington, D.C.: U.S. Government Printing Office.

Uri, Noel D. 1975. *Towards and Efficient Allocation of Electrical Energy.* Lexington, Mass.: Lexington Books, D.C. Heath.

Vardi, Joseph, and Benjamin Avi-Itzhak. 1981. *Electric Energy Generation, Economics, Reliability and Rates.* Cambridge, Mass.: The MIT Press.

Viner, Jacob. 1931. "Cost Curves and Supply Curves," *Zeitschrift für Nationalökonomie,* vol. 3:23–46. Reprinted with supplemental note in George J. Stigler and Kenneth E. Boulding, eds., *Readings in Price Theory,* pp. 198–232. Homewood, Ill.: Richard D. Irwin, 1952.

Walsh, Annmarie Hauck. 1978. *The Public's Business: The Politics and Practices of Government Corporations.* Cambridge, Mass.: The MIT Press.

Weaver, Suzanne. 1977. *Decision To Prosecute: Organization and Public Policy in the Antitrust Division.* Cambridge, Mass.: The MIT Press.

Weiss, Leonard W. 1975. "Antitrust in the Electric Power Industry." In *Promoting Competition in Regulated Markets,* edited by Almarin Phillips, pp. 138–173. Washington, D.C.: The Brookings Institution.

Weitzman, Martin L. 1974. "Prices vs. Quantities." *Review of Economic Studies* 41:477–491.

Whittle, Charles E., Edward L. Allen, Chester L. Cooper, Frances A. Edmonds, James A. Edmonds, Herbert G. MacPherson, Doan L. Phung, Alan D. Poole, William G. Pollard, David B. Reister, Ralph M. Rotty, Ned L. Treat, Alvin M. Weinberg, and Leon W. Zelby. 1979. *Economic and Environmental Impacts of a U.S. Nuclear Moratorium 1985–2010.* Cambridge, Mass.: The MIT Press.

Wildavesky, Aaron. 1962. *Dixon-Yates: A Study in Power Politics.* New Haven: Yale University Press.

Williamson, Oliver E. 1975. *Markets and Hierarchies: Analysis and Antitrust Implications. New York: Free Press.*

Willrich, Mason, and Theodore B. Taylor. 1974. *Nuclear Theft: Risks and Safeguards.* Cambridge, Mass.: Ballinger Publishing Company.

Wilson, Richard, Steven D. Colame, John D. Spengler, and David Gordon Wilson. 1980. *Health Effects of Fossil Fuel Burning, Assessment and Mitigation.* Cambridge, Mass.: Ballinger Publishing Company.

Index

About the Author

Richard L. Gordon is professor of mineral economics in the Department of Mineral Economics at the College of Earth and Mineral Sciences of The Pennsylvania State University. He is engaged in the department's broad program of teaching and research on the economic analysis of mineral-industries problems. His primary interest has been in coal economics on which he has written extensively. His work on coal includes *Evolution of Energy Policy in Western Europe* (1970), *U.S. Coal and the Electric Power Industry* (1975), *Coal in the U.S. Energy Market: History and Prospects* (1978), and *An Economic Analysis of World Energy Problems* (1981). He is a member of several professional societies, was chairman of the Council of Economics of the American Institute of Mining, Metallurgical, and Petroleum Engineers in 1973, and won the institute's Mineral Economics Award in 1981. He has been consultant to numerous government agencies, consulting firms, and industrial corporations.